NEW PLAYWRIGHTS
The Best Plays of 2004

SMITH AND KRAUS PUBLISHERS
Contemporary Playwrights / Full-Length Play Anthologies

Humana Festival: 20 One-Act Plays 1976–1996
Humana Festival 1993: The Complete Plays
Humana Festival 1994: The Complete Plays
Humana Festival 1995: The Complete Plays
Humana Festival 1996: The Complete Plays
Humana Festival 1997: The Complete Plays
Humana Festival 1998: The Complete Plays
Humana Festival 1999: The Complete Plays
Humana Festival 2000: The Complete Plays
Humana Festival 2001: The Complete Plays
Humana Festival 2002: The Complete Plays
Humana Festival 2003: The Complete Plays

New Playwrights: The Best Plays of 1998
New Playwrights: The Best Plays of 1999
New Playwrights: The Best Plays of 2000
New Playwrights: The Best Plays of 2001
New Playwrights: The Best Plays of 2002

Women Playwrights: The Best Plays of 1992
Women Playwrights: The Best Plays of 1993
Women Playwrights: The Best Plays of 1994
Women Playwrights: The Best Plays of 1995
Women Playwrights: The Best Plays of 1996
Women Playwrights: The Best Plays of 1997
Women Playwrights: The Best Plays of 1998
Women Playwrights: The Best Plays of 1999
Women Playwrights: The Best Plays of 2000
Women Playwrights: The Best Plays of 2001
Women Playwrights: The Best Plays of 2002
Women Playwrights: The Best Plays of 2003

If you would like information about forthcoming Smith and Kraus books, you may receive our annual catalogue, free of charge, by sending your name and address to *Smith and Kraus Catalogue, PO Box 127, Lyme, NH 03768.* Or call us at (888) 282-2881, fax (603) 643-1831. www.SmithandKraus.com.

NEW PLAYWRIGHTS

The Best Plays
of 2004

CONTEMPORARY PLAYWRIGHTS
SERIES

SK
A Smith and Kraus Book

A Smith and Kraus Book
Published by Smith and Kraus, Inc.
177 Lyme Road, Hanover, NH 03755
www.SmithKraus.com

Manufactured in the United States of America
Cover and text design by Julia Gignoux, Freedom Hill Design, Reading, Vermont

First Edition: December 2005
10 9 8 7 6 5 4 3 2 1

The Library of Congress Cataloging-In-Publication Data

New Playwrights: the best plays of 2004. —1st ed.
p. cm. — (Contemporary playwrights series)

ISBN 1-57525-424-7
1. American drama—20th century. I. Series.
PS634.N416 2000
812'.5408—dc21   00-029707

CONTENTS

FOREWORD

As you may have noticed, most of the shining faces on the cover of this book belong to women. I always make an effort in editing this series to find plays by women playwrights to include therein, to do my bit to counteract the heretofore grievous underrepresentation of work by women playwrights in our national dramatic repertory. In the 2003–2004 theatrical season, this effort was easy, because there were so many plays by women produced; and so many of them were so strong. I'm not the only one who's dubbed 2003–2004 the "Year of the Woman Playwright." Look at the 2004 Humana Festival. Five of the six full-length plays presented there were by — you guessed it — women.

So, here we have seven terrific new plays. I just realized, after reading the above paragraph, that Thomas Gibbons might feel rather slighted, like he's the token male in this book. So, to compensate, let me start, in my brief words of description of these plays, with *Bee-luther-hatchee,* which I saw at the Blue Heron Arts Center in New York City in what I was told was its twenty-fifth production, the previous ones being amateur and professional productions around the country. It's about a high-powered, black, female, book editor who finds, to her chagrin, that her recent best seller, a memoir by a mysterious black female housekeeper, is actually written by a white male. Does this make the book a fraud? Or, a great work of the imagination?

Race as an issue is also dealt with imaginatively in Lynn Nottage's *Intimate Apparel,* which focuses on a black seamstress for rich white people in early twentieth-century New York; with Lisa Loomer's *Living Out,* about an "illegal alien" nanny from South America, trying to please her harried employer as she tries to maintain some semblance of a home life; and Tracey Scott Wilson's *The Story,* which is about a female black reporter with a fabricated past who may also have fabricated a story about female black gang members. Although these plays had productions outside New York originally, I saw them in New

York City, at the Roundabout *(Intimate Apparel),* Second Stage *(Living Out)* and the Public Theater *(The Story).*

I also saw *The Beard of Avon* off Broadway in New York — at the New York Theatre Workshop. This play is an inventive, theatrically charged comedy about the "Shakespearean Authorship Controversy," which it comes at in a way you may not have ever considered. What if Shakespeare *was* a front for the Earl of Oxford, but gradually became "Shakespeare" over the course of time? I'll say no more. Read it — it's great.

Also very theatrically-inventive: Carson Kreitzer's *The Love Song of J. Robert Oppenheimer,* an award-winning play still unproduced in New York that deals with the controversial "Father of the Atom Bomb."

Finally, I ventured far afield (for me) up to the wilds of northern New England, to see a summer stock production of a comedy by Marisa Smith. Since this was Ms. Smith's first play and its premier production, I was wary. To my surprise, delight, and relief, her play, *Book Group,* turned out to be a hilarious, well-constructed comedy.

— D. L. Lepidus

INTRODUCTION

I'd like to salute the seven playwrights included in this 2004 Smith and Kraus *New Playwrights* book. I had been seeing my plays produced in New Orleans, New York, Paris, London, and elsewhere for twelve years and had been the founding artistic director of an equity company for fifteen years, when I got a call from my agent that Smith and Kraus was publishing my play, *Degas in New Orleans* in its *Women Playwrights: The Best Plays of 2002* anthology. What a thrilling day that was. To have one of my eleven plays immortalized in print. To see *Degas in New Orleans* go from being a closet manuscript, xeroxed for friends, to one available to the world. Finally: legitimacy! When I taught on a Fulbright Award in Germany, my students would have access to my work and that of the other American playwrights. A handful of we lucky ones were IN PRINT.

Even produced plays remain stillborn if not published. All plays have limited runs. Some great plays (e.g., *Night of the Iguana*) are greeted with bad reviews, which *hit* most unknown playwrights like the guillotine. I shudder to think how many great plays have been trashed before or after their author's deaths.

Theater is the most temporary art. "An actor is an artist who carves in snow," Lord Byron said, and the impermanence of theater is magnified by the permanence of film. With the media seducing so many of our best writers, to remain in the precarious profession of playwright requires daring, determination, and brilliance. My father once compared my being a playwright during the age of film and television to my being like a candle maker when electricity came in, or a wagon maker when the car was introduced. "You like candles," he said, "but you use electricity." Apparently one of my ancestors, in the wagon and carriage business, when the automobile was invented went bankrupt because he couldn't believe wagons would become obsolete.

Playwrights are something more than candle and wagon makers; they are the soul makers of the written word. They imagine the spirit of actors inside words, and the kinetic world embracing the actor. Across America, universities continue to award degrees in playwriting because stripped to the bone, the word and the actor root performance. And when a play can fly into the souls of audiences and transform them, a playwright functions like a magician, invisibly pulling the strings behind the performance.

The playwright is the soul carrier of his or her time. While other writers can be discovered posthumously, the playwright must sing to a live audience. Tennessee Williams said he wrote his plays to make the world a kinder place, and there is not doubt great playwrights change the culture, by the issues they explore and present. These issues may make audiences uncomfortable but ultimately they pack a wallop and spectators come away uplifted, inspired, for "God" has entered the theater.

Thank goodness for our playwrights. Please join me in celebrating their valor, tenacity, and the shimmering beauty of their words.

Rosary O'Neill, Ph.D.
New York City

Dr. O'Neill founded New Orleans' only professional theater company, Southern Repertory Theatre, which she ran for several years while teaching at Tulane and Loyola Universities. She has published a book on acting, one on directing, and many articles on the theater in general. Her plays have been produced at Southern Rep, in London and in Paris, and one, Degas in New Orleans, *has been published by Smith and Kraus in* Women Playwrights: The Best Plays of 2002.

THE BEARD OF AVON

Amy Freed

To Peter Franklin

PLAYWRIGHT'S BIOGRAPHY

Amy Freed's most recent play, *The Beard of Avon*, premiered at the South Coast Rep and has been produced by the Goodman Theatre, ACT, Seattle Rep and other theaters throughout the country. Her play *Freedomland* was a Pulitzer finalist in 1998, with productions at South Coast Rep, Woolly Mammoth, and Playwrights Horizons. *The Psychic Life of Savages* was the 1995 recipient of the Joseph Kesselring Award, a national award presented each year by the New York Arts Club to an outstanding new play. *Psychic Life* was also named the winner of the prestigious Charles McArthur Award for an Outstanding New Play at the annual Helen Hayes awards in Washington, D.C. The play had an extended run after a successful premiere at the Woolly Mammoth Theatre. An earlier version of the play was first developed and performed in San Francisco under the title *Poetomachia* where it was recognized by the Bay Area Critic's Circle and awarded an Outstanding Achievement Award for an Original Script. In its earlier version, it was also a finalist for the Susan Smith Blackburn Prize in 1994.

A native New Yorker and former actress, Freed lives in San Francisco. She has worked as an acting teacher and director for the various training programs of the American Conservatory Theatre, VITA Shakespeare Festival, and California Shakespeare Festival, as well as conducting playwriting workshops for A.C.T. and S. F. State University. She has a B.F.A. from Southern Methodist University, and a M.F.A. from American Conservatory Theatre. She is currently Artist-in-Residence in the Drama Department of Stanford University.

CHARACTERS

WILLIAM SHAKSPERE: A lad of Stratford. In his early thirties, mostly. Simple, honest, very appealing fellow. Possessor of hidden gifts.

EDWARD DE VERE: Seventeenth Earl of Oxford. In his forties. Wicked, charming, sexy, brilliant. A closet writer.

ELIZABETH: Queen of England. Between forty and sixty. A sacred monster. Wants a boyfriend.

ANNE HATHAWAY: Shakspere's wife. Lively, illiterate, promiscuous.

*HENRY WRIOTHESLEY: Twenties. Young and beautiful. Third Earl of Southampton. Edward De Vere's lover. (*See pronunciation note.*)

*OLD COLIN: an ancient shepherd, and Shakspere's friend.

*JOHN HEMINGE: manager of an acting company

*HENRY CONDEL: his partner

*GEOFFREY DUNDERBREAD: a boy player

*RICHARD BURBAGE: a leading man

(*Actors in these parts also double or triple in the following roles:)

Members of Elizabeth's court:

    FRANCIS BACON

    LADY LETTICE

    FRANCIS WALSINGHAM

    LORD BURLEIGH

    EARL OF DERBY

    WALTER FITCH: A playwright

Others:

    A MINSTREL WITH BEAUTIFUL VOICE

PRONUNCIATION NOTE

For the pronunciation of Wriothesley's name, I used Kokeritz's pronouncing dictionary *Shakespeare's Names,* as my authority which gave us "ROT-sley." I preferred this over the other variant suggestions I unearthed. A. L. Rowse in his biography of the Earl argues for RIS-ley, which I found less pleasing.

A NOTE REGARDING CAST SIZE

The play has been performed with casts of ten and eleven or more. However, it's possible to perform it with an ensemble of nine (2 female, 7 male) in the following manner:

JOHN HEMINGE also plays LORD BURLEIGH.

HENRY CONDEL also plays FRANCIS BACON and playwright WALTER FITCH (may play small roles in *Taming of the Shrew* sequence, such as Baptista).

HENRY WRIOTHESLEY also plays EARL OF DERBY.

OLD COLIN also plays FRANCIS WALSINGHAM and RICHARD BURBAGE (in the roles of Alexandrio, Marcus, Marc Antony, and Petruchio. Also may appear in small roles in *Taming of the Shrew* such as Baptista and Grumio.

GEOFFREY DUNDERBREAD (who acts the roles of Ludibundus, Cleopatra, Lavinia and Kate) also plays MINSTREL WITH BEAUTIFUL VOICE and LADY LETTICE.

ANNE HATHAWAY may also play Lucentio with Player's company.

WILL, DE VERE, and ELIZABETH play only themselves.

THE BEARD OF AVON

ACT I

SCENE ONE

Pouring rain. An old barn in Stratford. William Shakspere is sitting in a hay bale with Colin, an aged farmhand. Shakspere has a quick face, full of sensitivity, but his hair is beginning to go. He looks like a young version of the famous Droeshout portrait.

WILL: Oh, this rain, this rain, this RAIN! Eh, Colin?

COLIN: Eh, Will.

WILL: Look at it — pouring. Well, nothing to do about it. We can't very well DO anything with it all muck like this.

COLIN: No. You have to make hay when the sun shines.

WILL: Aye. There's wisdom in what you say. Mark it.
   (Pause.)

COLIN: Aye.
   (Pause. Anne calls, offstage.)

ANNE: WILLIAM!

WILL: *(Gloomily taking in the dripping eaves.)* Like to a mouse drowning in a jughead, which all about it sees its watry fate — so every task conspires to damp my spark without escape!

ANNE: WILLIAM!

WILL: Oh, what wouldn't I give to find me this very minute aboard a wide-bottomed frigate sailing the bounding main!

COLIN: A wide-bottomed frigate! Ooh, you're a witty man, Will Shakspere! Make no mistake! Oo hoo hoo hoo!

ANNE: *(Offstage.)* WILLIAM!!

COLIN: . . . what would I not give for a wide-bottomed — HEE HEE HEE HEE.
   (A rat runs across the stage, a loud snap of the rattrap. Will pulls dead rat in trap up from behind bale. Contemplates it darkly.)

WILL: Oh Rat! who longed for frolic
   In his wild and hairy youth —
   Who lunged to seize the fatal cheese
   But met the bitter truth —
   But no! Yet stay!

A blessed day, that ended his young life —
Oh happy snap! that freed him from
The crueler jaws of his —
(Anne Hathaway enters, she is a handsome woman older than her husband.)
ANNE: *(To audience.)* Is here I find him? Playing at epitaphs again? Whilst I do
labour all alone in care and tending — of our weedy garden!
COLIN: *(To Will.)* (— ooh, NOW thou hast caught it!)
ANNE: *(To Colin.)* — Shut UP! *(To Will.)* — to ME the tanning of those stink-
ing hides that lend us small but CRUCIAL profit!
WILL: *(Overlapping.)* No one's asked you to —
ANNE: *(Overlapping.)* — must I, a WOMAN, frail and — *(Swiping at Colin,
as he attempts to crawl out.)* DELICATE! —
COLIN: Aargh!
ANNE: — daily mend those fences that keep the PIG at home? And leave me
stranded with all burden of your CHILD — *(Beginning to break.)* —
whose reckless violence of disposition yields not to reason or the STRAP!
WILL: My child, I would say, but for a fretful whisper that haunteth my
soul — and makes me to wonder wherefore her HAIR came to be RED!
COLIN: Hee hee hee!
ANNE: Shut up, filthy old man.
WILL: He's a good man and true as a hunk of honest bread.
COLIN: HOO HOO HOO!
ANNE: Get out, the both of you — before I swear to GOD I'll break your
thinning pate across —
(Pause. Colin's hands fly to his mouth. Will is stricken.)
WILL: Oh Cruelty, will you say it? 'tis true what I would fain deny — that I
do lack some deal of hair. Get you gone and leave me to my friend!
ANNE: Beshrew my tongue. No sooner had my wayward words escaped the
halter of my lips then I did wish me to recall them.
WILL: Have I not on sound advice spread sulfur, salts and putrid DUNG upon
my ball-ed front in desperate hopes of HAIR — only to be reviled anew
and called SHIT-head? The butt and jest of maids?
ANNE: Good Colin, give us leave awhile t'untie those thorny elf-knots that
matrimony does delight to weave. . .
COLIN: I go, I go. Marry, I do but go. Aye and for a ha'penny biscuit and will
I not go —
ANNE: LEAVE US!
(Colin exits.)
WILL: You understand me not!

ANNE: — I care not! The ROOF doth ROT!

WILL: I have great . . . thought-like "things" within my head —

ANNE: You don't care to fix the roof, then why don't YOU cook?

WILL: *(Overlapping.)* Oh — great Fortune — I see thou art a JESTER — who raises us in youth to \ dream —

ANNE: *(Overlapping.)* — thou sayest thou "Cannot" Cook. I say 'tis only thy stubborn WILL and nothing of \infirmity —

WILL: *(Overlapping.)* — then wracks us on those \dreams!

ANNE: *(Overlapping.)* — thy stubborn WILL\ I say!

WILL: *(Overlapping.)* Dash me to pieces, GODS, at once. I cannot bear slow death by railing!

ANNE: My lord WON'T tend the cattle, because he can't abide the smell, well, BULLSHIT cry I — WHY! thinkst thou that I enjoy it?

(Starting to cry.)

WILL: Don't —

ANNE: Thou hast plucked me to the last inch of my penultimate nerve! Oh I'm so unhappy!

WILL: GOD! I'm so unhappy —

ANNE: I didn't know —

WILL: *(Overlapping.)* I didn't know —

BOTH TOGETHER: It would be like this —

(A miserable silence.)

ANNE: Was it always so dreadful? Didn't we have some good times, once, you and me?

WILL: — You was supposed to look after me for my mum — not what you did. I was only a kid with you coming after me — dragging your spicery traps all over me, and me confused by the dangly hair, and the popping out whatnots coming at me when I'm all a'fire with God knows what. What do I know, a bubbling idiot and head of steam! Next thing I know I'm the head of an 'oushold! What shall I do? Shall I be put out as if I'd never lived?

(He puts his head in her lap.)

ANNE: Thou makst me to hear mine own tongue as sharp in mine own ears as the haggard's shriek. Good husband, be thy spirits lifted. There's Players at the Guild hall.

WILL: I'm not in the mood.

ANNE: I hear 'tis a very low comedy.

WILL: Low comedy. Well, we might go at that.

SCENE TWO

Sound of tabor and drum. the Stratford Guild Hall — The Players are in town. Everyone has come to see the play The Conquest of Alexandrio. *Burbage plays Alexandrio, a warrior, Geoffrey plays Ludibundus, a maiden. Ludibundus has a little bird on her finger. Two players are playing stringed instruments.*

LUDIBUNDUS: Happy be this day, as our two kingdoms join —
  And may our union elevate the common flock —
  With those lofty arts, that with VIRTUE do conspire —
  for Virtue is the use of Right Desire.
  (She modestly shields her crotch. Audience applauds politely.)
ALEXANDRIO: I shall forwith hold as dear, my Dear,
  Only those delights, that do as well, instruct —
  For 'tis Learning, from a woman wise as thee —
  That brought my soul to sweet Philosophy.
  (Musicians strum. Audience is becoming restive. Burbage senses this.)
ALEXANDRIO: But SILENCE awhile, Sweet Music —
  (Suggestive, to audience.)
  And let me WOO my love. . .
  (Urbanely, to Ludibundus.)
  But soft, Ludibundus — come and say — can'st guess what pretty lover's trinket have I brought for thee from fair Carthage?
LUDIBUNDUS: Oh, I beg thee — do not tease but tell!
ALEXANDRIO: It's a SAUSAGE!
  (Reveals an enormous stuffed codpiece.)
LUDIBUNDUS: *(In horror, trying to make it go away.)* Nay, by heaven, it is a cat's TURD! Fye it STYNCKS!
ALEXANDRIO: Nay, it is my PRICK! By the rood thou will KISS it!
  (Approval from all.)
LUDIBUNDUS: Nay and is that all that thou cans't say to Agrippina's Daughter?
ALEXANDRIO: None but this! And also THIS!
BOTH: *(Sing rousingly.)* I stuffe my skyn so full within
  Of jolly good ale and olde.
  Though Back and side go bare go bare
  And foote and hande go colde!
  (Applause and cheers.)
LUDIBUNDUS: *(Over.)* Good folk, Our candle is at an ende, let us leave all in quiet —

And come another tyme, when we have more ly-ett!

(Crowd clears, happy. Will walks the empty stage, entranced. Anne trots along behind him.)

ANNE: There. Now wasn't that something! I was moved to TEARS as well as LAUGHTER! One word — WONDERFUL! One should RUN, never walk, to see it, whilst one still haveth the CHANCE!

WILL: *(Turns on her.)* Shut UP!! WILL you!

ANNE: William!

WILL: Oh, it makes me MAD to hear you go on! Oh, these were ARTISTS — so full in fire and fearfulness that I could scarce draw mine own breath! I could give my life to live with MEN like THESE! Instead I sit in a cow-shed watching my insect's life posting to its death!

(Ludibundus is working the remaining crowd.)

LUDIBUNDUS: Some beer, some beer! You, there, you whoreson with the proverb book! Is that an egge pie in your pouch — ?

WILL: Excuse me? Here? Over here? If the young lady would please to dine? We'd be really pleased. Tickled! All of you! Really!

LUDIBUNDUS: Right!

(He goes to fetch others.)

ANNE: Art MAD! dine on WHAT!

WILL: Shhhh! Wilt shame me! Come up with something!

ANNE: Out of nothing!

WILL: Embarrass me before my fellows?

ANNE: These strangers?

WILL: You kill all that gives me pleasure!

ANNE: You provide nothing and blame me for it!

WILL: — You take from me all heart. And do deprive me of my necessary space!

ANNE: Oh JUNO great goddess of domestic JUSTICE strike him dead!

(Players have gathered to watch with interest.)

WILL: Trouble yourself not! You have killed my soul already!

ANNE: Invite them to our house to eat? Eat what! Porridge and small beer!

ACTORS: Huzzah! We're there! Good enough for us! Let's go!

ANNE: What hast thou done.

WILL: — There is a great spirit in me that thou seekest to subdue — it will rebel.

(He heads off, players after, singing.)

ANNE: Where goest thou? Walkst away from me! I shall not serve them din-ner, I tell you I shall not! I shall die first!

(Scene transforms around her. Someone puts a porridge pot in her hands. They are now at home. The Players are at table — eating, drinking.)

PLAYERS: *(Singing.)* Fifty-nine bottles of ale on the wall

Fifty-nine bottles of ale —

Ye take one down ye pass it around

Fifty-eight bottles of —

PLAYER ONE: Excellent porridge — doth any more remain?

ANNE: Thou hast eaten everything.

PLAYER TWO: More ale, more ale!

PLAYERS: FIFTY-six bottles of —

WILL: Here's ale for you, gentle friends!

ALL: Huzzah!

(A player-musician begins a simple old ballad. The lights dim around them as Will crosses down to where Geoffrey, who had played Ludibundus, is eating quietly by himself. Will is shy, but fascinated. The others are forgotten. Except for the occasional ripple of music, they are effectively alone.)

WILL: Upon my life — a woman's face as if by nature drawn! What is thy name, fair youth?

GEOFFREY: *(Mouth full.)* Geoff Dunderbread.

WILL: All the softness and lineaments of the other sex — oh most perfect illusion!

GEOFFREY: So all do say. Well, what gets the shit beat out of you one day, makes you a star the next. Any more porridge?

WILL: Here, finish mine.

GEOFFREY: Thanks. Good man. I was SO stinking hungry. I could have eaten your stinking cat. I've never been so stinking hungry.

WILL: Thine sweet accents remind me of a girl I once loved.

That girl I loved became my wife. I haven't seen her since.

(In the background, a burst of song.)

PLAYER: "Cupid ease a lovesick maid —

And bring a shepherd to her aid —

ALL: But what of that, but what of that!"

ANNE: *(Impressed.)* Oooh, that's TERRIBLE! HOW does it —

(They play and hum softly for her . . .)

WILL: *(Fixated on Geoffrey.)* — Forgive my staring looks. But thou appear'st to be the prettiest maid I ever saw. But for thy one little thing —

GEOFFREY: Meanst thou my PRICK whoreson!

WILL: Ay thy Prick, Sirrah!

GEOFFREY: Nay 'tis not little! I'd show thee but it would affright thee!

WILL: Then I should show thee one wouldst affright thee more!

WILL\GEOFFREY: HA HA HA! HA HA HA!

WILL: Oh, manly soul wrapped in a pretty hide! Oh goodly unaccustomed laughter! Yes, I had many a good lad's revel before my WIFE drove all my friends away —

ANNE: I'm going up to bed. I said! I'm going up to bed —

(In the background, players serenade her to the stairs and begin to disperse. Will takes no notice of her or others.)

WILL: How came you to this actor's life, young Master-Best-of-Both-Worlds?

GEOFFREY: My father whipped me every day to bend me to his stupid trade. 'Twas found out by accident I could sing. They put me in a boy's choir — and then I played before the Queen —

WILL: The Queen?

GEOFFREY: — who did note me well and call me Master Dunderbread. And said excellently well done.

WILL: What a life you've led! for one so young!

GEOFFREY: Had I stayed at home, I'd be a stupid ass, shit-heel retarded tinker like my stupid ass shit-heel retarded brother.

WILL: *(Searchingly.)* "— My wife is warm and up the stairs.
"Ludibundus" is only a . . . "seeming" —
How comes it that I HATE my life, and only live —
For dreaming?

GEOFFREY: *(Mildly impressed.)* Thou hast a gift for rhyme — Farmer Will!

WILL: No, Geoffrey. I, TOO, am an actor. But one condemned forever to play in a most tragical comedy.

GEOFFREY: Nay, thou cans't not couple comedy with tragedy.

WILL: But nature mixes both with one blind hand.

GEOFFREY: Well, it looks as if the lads are leaving —

WILL: — 'Tis not the sum total of my efforts —

GEOFFREY: Look us up in London!

WILL: I've other thoughts — for poems, for plays for —

ALL: Farewell, Good-bye, Godspeed! Bless you for your provender (BURBAGE:) GOOD-BYE!!

WILL: Good-bye, boys — good-bye, good-bye!

ACTOR: Give us a song, Geoffrey —

(As he sings, others pause with their belongings —)

GEOFFREY: *(A quick and bawdy ballad.)* I asked a maid to marry me
But she said — nothing —
(A ripple of laughter and applause.)

I said I burn for love of thee
And — she said nothing —
I put my hand upon her . . . knee
(More laughter, other men may join.)
Why she said nothing —
And then I took my liberty
And she said nothing — !

(Geoffrey runs back up to the stair-landing to where he's left his bundle. He turns. Something inexplicably magical happens. Suddenly we can see him as if he was playing to the best at court — . Whether it's the night, the attention of the players, or the flattering fascination of Will, or some other energy in the air, Geoffrey chooses to display another, different song — probably from his boy-choir days. He's like a bird, or a spirit. The song he sings now is old, austere, haunting, utterly unnatural. Will stands alone, beneath, receiving it.)

GEOFFREY: *(Sings.)* Ere "anything" was, creation was not.
And from "nothing at all," "ALL" was straight begot
And so in the mind of man, below as so above
Everything from nothing comes —
To those who love —
(Geoffrey is gone. Will slowly picks up a bundle and a jacket and leaves his home.)

SCENE THREE

London. Backstage at the Theater. Chaos reigns. Lurid and colorful banners advertise such plays as Lusty Monks, The Bawdy Alewife, The Miller's Poxy Daughter, The Ur-Hamlet. *Actors rush on and off with costume pieces, weapons, bloody severed heads or limbs in various stages of manufacture. At the center of it all, judging, approving, stitching, gluing, dismissing, or consoling are John Heminge and Henry Condel, the theater managers. Heminge is fatherly and dyspeptic, Condel is ascerbic. Will enters.*

WILL: Excuse me — Be you Mister John Heminge? And you Mister Henry Condel?

CONDEL: Ay. What's thy business?

HEMINGE: His hopeful looks declare it as well as the Town Crier might.

WILL: I want — to be — an "Actor."

HEMINGE: What arts dost thou possess?

WILL: Arts?

HEMINGE: That fitteth thee. For traffick on the stage.

WILL: I follow not your meaning.

CONDEL: No dancing, musick, song?

WILL: No! But I will learn me!

HEMINGE: Can you read?

WILL: Such question makes the very GODS to laugh. Can I read. I tell thee. HA HA HA HA HA. Can I not READ!

HEMINGE: *(Throws him a script.)* Here. Have a go at Galatea.

WILL: Pray, gentle Masters. Give me leave to study it awhile. Then, tomorrow — at this very houre, when Phaeton's chariot impales itself upon the sign of the Three Balls —

CONDEL: The present moment serves us.

WILL: — then will I show you a Galatea. A Galatea such as will set all sides to splitting! Cheeks shall CRACK with laughter, and mirth shall rise like a gaseous nymph from the bed of Jove — bowlegged with her own audacity!

CONDEL: He can't read.

WILL: Nay, I can! But slowly. I have a most pernicious deficit of my attention's ordering —

HEMINGE: What makes you think you're fitted for the stage? You aren't very quick. You haven't any skills or training. And you haven't much in the way of hair.

(Tiny pause.)

WILL: What you say, Mr. Heminge, only confirms my deep assurance that theater is my home.

HEMINGE: I'm sorry.

CONDEL: Listen, my friend. What do you think there IS. To BEING. An — "Actor."

WILL: Well. I don't really know.

CONDEL: It is the highest of all high callings! That which leads us to represent the spirit of Man to Men. And also to well impersonate a WOMAN in a way that FOOLS a man.

HEMINGE: At close quarters. *(Thoughtful.)* Sometimes VERY close.

CONDEL: — To illuminate the very highest and the lowest of this angelic BEAST we are. THAT is our craft.

HEMINGE: — and it is A CRAFT — !

CONDEL: Not accident that makes a Burbage a Burbage or a Kemp a Kemp, or a Heminge a Heminge. My boy, to be an Actor is:
To know just how to saw the air with your hand, thus —.

HEMINGE: Ay. And how to contort one's features of a piece with the sawing.

CONDEL: — how to simulate, manipulate and never fear to grandly FEIGN a passion —

HEMINGE: — 'Tis the very art of — fine "indication."

CONDEL: — it is — to sink thy voice to a thrilling whisper and then all unexpectedly to SPEW! SHOUT! THUNDER!

HEMINGE: — 'tis to cover the groundlings with the spray and filth and spit of a most violent energy!

CONDEL: When Heminge here, did play the King of Goths he worked himself so into a frenzy that he forgot himself in the hot passion of his playing and ate the very properties!

WILL: *(Beside himself.)* Oh GOD! That I might have seen such playing!

HEMINGE: Ah, well, I was younger then, and full of vinegar.

CONDEL: We'll none of us ever forget it, John.

HEMINGE: Or Henry, full of invention, never out of his part — even when he goes stone dry —

CONDEL: I dry? I never dried in my life.

HEMINGE: Oh, Ay? St. Stephen's day before the QUEEN?

CONDEL: *(Winces.)* Oh, that!

WILL: Before the Queen?

HEMINGE: 'Twas during the rending of Cassandra —

CONDEL: I was playing Agamemnon —

WILL: Agamemnon!

CONDEL: Ay, and they didn't think I could do it. Nobody thought I was right — I had to LOBBY for it. I —

HEMINGE: Well, Henry's mind did of a sudden FLEE his body. There he stood struck dumb —

CONDEL: — as to a wooden block! a POST!

HEMINGE: — a paralytic thing bereft of wit —

CONDEL: Beyond all HOPE of rescue — all before my face went white! Went WHITE! I say.

HEMINGE: But then did "Sweet Deliverance" descend —

CONDEL: Some convenient God did with golden pliers loose my tongue —

HEMINGE: — And forth from Henry issued such a Speech, so fitted to the circumstance of Agamemnon's time and hour —

CONDEL: (— 'twas fear — pure FEAR did fodder the swift cannons of my invention —)

HEMINGE: — And in perfect rhyming do-DE-ca-trains he brought the act to the close with a roar of such approbation from the court as we haven't heard before or since, and the playwright told us keep it in!

CONDEL: Well he told us we could shove it up our arse, anyway!

ALL THREE: HAHAHAHAH!

WILL: Oh, Please. Mr. Heminge, Dear Mr. Condel, can't you find me anything at all?

(Pause.)

CONDEL: *(To Heminge.)* Well. We did just lose a — "Spear-Shaker . . ."

WILL: What did he play? Had he a big part?

CONDEL: Dear Boy. In the THEATER, there are no small parts.

WILL: There aren't?

HEMINGE\CONDEL: No. Oh, no. (H:) The professionals know it. (C:) There are no small parts.

WILL: What's a Spear-Shaker?

HEMINGE: During the battle scenes, they come on with spears. And they — "shake" — them. Why, we don't let just anyone do it, though.

WILL: *(Scarcely daring to ask.)* Could I BE one?

CONDEL: I don't know. You wouldn't get paid, you know.

WILL: Oh, I don't care about THAT!

(The men exchange a quick glance.)

HEMINGE: Can you pick up that broom and brandish it like it was a pike and a head on it —

WILL: A head! A head on a PIKE!

CONDEL: Well, don't get ahead of yourself. We'd have to see how you do, first.

WILL: *(Picks up broom, excited —)* Oh, "Staff," "Pick," "Stave," oh. . .

(Suddenly he really looks at it — almost surprised. It's as if the object itself has a charged life that is trying to reach out to him. This may have happened to him before, but not quite like this. It's as if both violence and the memory of beauty are imprinted in the atoms of the wood. He feels it. The lyric rise of the words are almost a form of channeling —. It's eerie and wonderful.)

— bare, stripped, thing —

Weep thou still — for a dappled glade —

Where once thy leafing vault didst used to shade

The tender fledgling from the Summer's heat,

There thy wanton boughs did often meet

And toy with the delicate spinner's feet

Who's silken skein with dewdrops hung

Would catch the careless bounty of the Sun —

(Pause — no one quite knows what happened. Shakspere slightly embarrassed —)

CONDEL: *(To Heminge.)* A good extempore, doggerel man. . .

HEMINGE: I think we can find something for you.

WILL: Really? Really? Oh do you mean it? Am I a PLAYER?

(The men clap him on the back.)

ALL: AHAHAHAHAH — AHAHAHAHAHAH — AHAHHAHAHAH!!

SCENE FOUR

An ancient manor. Sound of a lute. A large stone window ledge. A Minstrel sits in it, along with a rook. The sky outside is bleak. We are very high up. This is the bed chamber of Edward De Vere, who is reclining on a wretched-looking divan. His boyfriend, Henry Wriothesley is sitting D.S., loosely wrapped in a bedsheet. He is putting the finishing touches to his long curly hair by means of a primitive curling iron, which he heats over a taper. There's also a table, covered with books, and manuscripts, some of them spilling from an old trunk beneath the desk. There's a gyroscope, a skull, a thumbscrew, crystals, specimens, and other evidences of the Earl's varied and unwholesome interests.

MINSTREL: *(Singing mournfully.)* For all doth blossom but to die —

The ripest fruit doth fall —

Soon thy day of birth draws nigh —

And darkness covers all —

Happy day of birth to you. . .

Happy day of birth to you . . .

Lullay lullay lullay

. . . mmm. . . mmm. . . mmm . . .

(He hums, plays lute softly — silence.)

OXFORD: How empty 'tis to be myself, today.

WRIOTHESLEY: To be Edward De Vere — Seventeenth Earl of Oxford? 'Tis a name most mighty and famously depraved.

OXFORD: Thinkst thou I glory in it? As you glory to be Henry Wriothesley? The beautiful and effeminate Third Earl of Southampton?

WRIOTHESLEY: 'Tis true, I am he. I am that girlish Earl.

OXFORD: *(Rising. He's in a restless and dangerous mood.)* Alas, Ay me, ah. . . welladay. This painful exposition shows — I am not what I was. There was a time I should have, rather, died.

MINSTREL: *(Singing.)* — Lullay, lullay, loo —

(Oxford pushes him casually out of the window. Crosses to Wriothesley, who continues to do his hair.)

WRIOTHESLEY: Cheer up. Thy great estate is the envy of all men.

OXFORD: Call you this my Estate? This rotting castle-keep where Rooks, o'er-bold with feeding on dead De Veres — perch the very rails of our bed and o'erwatch our foul love nest? Skeletons line my filthy halls — rotting pissy rushes abound on freezing floors — the stench of ancient merriments even now assault the nose — ghastly reminder that no SERVANTS can be found who'll stay the course! *(Pause.)* And yet YOU stay, Henry. Who have much kinder circumstance at your disposal.

WRIOTHESLEY: *(Turning to him.)* I've thrown away my lot with yours. For your dark eccentricities alone on earth arouse me. 'Tis the fetid and brilliant turnings of your mind, like to the moldy veins of some rich cheese — hath lured me to this point of no return.

OXFORD: Blame not me for your outcast state! Your mother begged me use my words to woo you to a wife — not for myself. You mis-read my poetry.

WRIOTHESLEY: "Beautiful boy, my love, my dear —"

OXFORD: I spake only in the metaphoric terms of Platonic love.

WRIOTHESLEY: — thou dost abuse the natures both of metaphor and Plato, De Vere, Dear —

OXFORD: *(Throwing himself on divan.)* Oh God oh God! How weary stale flat and unprofitable seem to me all the uses of this world. Were it not for my astonishingly PROLIFIC pen — and my secret trunk of follies, my unperform-ed DRAMAS! I should be down-and-out indeed, Henry. Except for them and thee, my young, young, friend.

WRIOTHESLEY: *(Crossing to him, sits.)* Methinks this unaccustomed melancholy gains sway because thy birthday doth approach.

OXFORD: Forty summers! Well, though my face be chopped and rough, at least I've kept my hair. Ironic, isn't it. At the end, all that's left to the heir of the De Veres may well be the Hair of the De Veres.

WRIOTHESLEY: Ah, Youth — 'tis but a phantom.

OXFORD: I can no deny.

WRIOTHESLEY: Yet, though rough of chap and rucked and seamed — thy visage still attracts.

OXFORD: Think you so, think you so?

WRIOTHESLEY: And a BETTER man you are than he who in thy greener years did with his sword taste so reckless the blood of thy lessers —

OXFORD: Oh joyful boy! (— 'twas me —)

WRIOTHESLEY: A WISER man than when thou didst desert thy wife — and left thy bastards wards unto the court —

OXFORD: O mad lad — I was.

WRIOTHESLEY: — a more TEMPERATE man than he who — with sodomies, and buggeries, and rapes and divers pederastic flings —

OXFORD: O silly, fond, young person — GOD! THOSE WERE THE DAYS!

WRIOTHESLEY: — Did o'ersmirch the grimy name of ROME herself — with the profligation of thy weekend parties.

OXFORD: Speak ON! and twist the cords of time's tightening RACK! It's been a rich life. And Death, ever Envious — longs to sack my frail citadel.

WRIOTHESLEY: Nay, 'tis but the crisis of thine middle years.

OXFORD: My sadness doth increase.

WRIOTHESLEY: Then write thy melancholy out. It's worked before.

OXFORD: 'Tis not enough to pen my works and lock them in a TRUNK! WHY must I not see my poems printed, my plays performed? Shall Genius be bottled in a jug and forever tossed into oblivion's bottomless well?

WRIOTHESLEY: — Nay, all at court do know thine wit precocious, learning rare and gift for phrase most nonpareil.

OXFORD: 'Tis true, 'tis true. But Henry. I must speak the thing I fear.

WRIOTHESLEY: Say on.

OXFORD: At times I fear me that my work lacks — warmth. To coin a word . . . "Hu-man-i-ty."

WRIOTHESLEY: Say not SO !! Oh, never SO!

OXFORD: I had a secretary said it, once. I stabbed him for his impertinence, and left him in a swamp. — I am haunted still.

WRIOTHESLEY: By his angry spirit?

OXFORD: Nay. He was but a clerk. But his accusation. Lack I tenderness of feeling? I know I soar the lonely heights. But have I Breadth? Henry? Depth?

WRIOTHESLEY: These be damp and killing humours bred of moldering playscripts locked too long in drawers. Expose them to the joyful sun of public revels and those attendant thrills which critickal appraisal doth provide!

OXFORD: No!

WRIOTHESLEY: Withhold not thy gift from its destination. The public sewer, where it tendeth, as a river to the sea.

OXFORD: Shall I withdraw me from the lofty requirements of my station (— hawking, whoring, dogging, and slaughter —) to scribble Plays! DRAMAS! PAGEANTS for the unwashed? It tempts me —

WRIOTHESLEY: — give the work to The Players, and let them do it without at-
tribution.

OXFORD: — my soul quickens — my heart lifts — ! Oh, I couldn't!

WRIOTHESLEY: How much is left to go of this *Titus Andronicus?*

OXFORD: Just the third, fourth, and fifth acts. A day's work, maybe two.

WRIOTHESLEY: The power of your persuasive art will sway the world a hundred lives from now.

OXFORD: Think so?

WRIOTHESLEY: I know.

OXFORD: Enough. I am engaged.

BOTH: *(Embracing.)* HAHAHAHAH!!

SCENE FIVE

*Sound of tabor and fife. A rehearsal at The Theater. Full company, Shakspere
is there, dressed as a Spear Carrier. The play is* Cleopatra, Queen of Nilus,
*by Walter Fitch. Onstage are Burbage, as Mark Antony, and Geoffrey, as
Cleopatra. Two Players are serving as slaves. Heminge is directing.*

CLEOPATRA: But soft — Mark Antony stay — stay awhile
Beside the gilded Serpent of the Nilus —
And say what gift hast for me — what rare love token bringst from
Balmy Italy!

ANTONY: It's a sausage!

CLEOPATRA: Nay, but it is a hyena's shite! Fye it styncks!

ANTONY: Nay, but it is my PRICK!

CLEOPATRA: Have you this to say to the Sphinxes' own CHILD!

ANTONY: By Great Anubis himself you will KISS it!

HEMINGE: And then that's you, Shakspere. You're on.

WILL: *(Comes forward with his spear.)* "Good people may see in the second part
what Cleopatra doth reply.
In the mean time you shall avaunt yourselves to buy oranges
and meat-pie —"

HEMINGE: I am encouraged by this, our run-through. 'Tis not full blown but
yet it flowers, our play. It hath been more subtle on occasion, but all will
right itself by Tuesday next, I have no misgiving. *(Brightening.)* Oh, boys,
we got the playwright here.
(Pause.)

ANTONY: The who?

HEMINGE: The playwright? The — author.

(Company looks blank. Heminge turns to a wretched, huddled figure in the corner.)

HEMINGE: Mr. — I'm sorry, what is it — FITCH! Anything to say to us, Mr. Fitch —

FITCH: *(Raising a trembling finger.)* Well, yes, actually, I —

HEMINGE: *(Distracted.)* All right! Everyone — don't stray, this is a short break, this isn't a real break!

(Heminge goes off. Shakspere goes to Fitch.)

WILL: You're the "author"?

FITCH: Author. Author. — I suppose that in some manner of SPEAKING. I mean, I had a play, once. It was a great DREAM of a play. A play where two great enemies met, and learned again to LOVE — who had been bred in the stony arms of war.

WILL: Oh, it sounds most profound — a thousand times BRILLIANT! You must write it, Mr. Fitch — you must WRITE this play!

FITCH: *(Turns on him.)* Idiot! I DID! I DID! WRITE this play. And the best thing that ever I wrote. But I perceive it hath been improved upon!

(His voice cracking.)

"By ANUBIS you will KISS IT??"

WILL: — oh, we can hardly bear to keep the laughter in — it's my favorite line in the play.

FITCH: It's not IN the PLAY. I didn't write it.

WILL: — you should have heard the laughs during the run-through —

FITCH: It was meant to be a tragedy! Good day.

(Exits, bumping into Oxford, who is concealed by a hood, and Wriothesley, as they enter.)

OXFORD: I feel better already. The roar of the amphitheater is in my blood! You, with the spear — have you seen John Heminge?

WILL: He'll be back in a half a shake of a lamb's tail, Sir. We're on break.

WRIOTHESLEY: A country boy, by thy sweet accents. Can you fetch him hither for us? There's a shilling for you.

WILL: See how God provides for the actors! I haven't had twopenny for a bun all week —.

OXFORD: One of John's apprentices, eh? All starvation for the distant promise of someday a tiny part?

WILL: *(Shocked.)* There ARE no tiny parts.

WRIOTHESLEY: Of course not. Well said. There's another shilling for you.

WILL: I'll get John Heminge for you. Whom shall I say wants him?

WRIOTHESLEY: Edward de —

OXFORD: O.

WILL: Mister Doe, your servant.

(He exits.)

WRIOTHESLEY: Thou art over-fretful of thine secrecy.

OXFORD: My guardian would cut me off. The Queen would refuse to receive me —. The ghost of my raping, murdering, polygamous Father would bolt from all his friends in Hell and walk the earth in shame!

WRIOTHESLEY: Why?

OXFORD: Well, to fraternize with ACTORS — is to debase oneself.

WRIOTHESLEY: Ah.

(Heminge and company return, eating and talking — a babble of voices. Geoffrey Dunderbread goes off to the side still dressed as Cleopatra. He has a string sausages around his neck, which serve as Cleopatra's Asps and his lunch. He practices applying them to his breast from time to time and occasionally takes a bite of one.)

HEMINGE: Company — !

OXFORD: I say, Heminge —

HEMINGE: Oh, hello, your Lordship!

OXFORD: I have some little business to discuss with you —

HEMINGE: Company — work the Dance, will you? Quietly, please. Tony, take them through it. What can we do for you, Sir Edward? Box seats? Taken care of. Have you met our new Leading Lady? Our Geoffrey? He's over there on the barge.

OXFORD: I didn't come for —

WRIOTHESLEY: Geoffrey you say? No. It is a miracle. It cannot be. Say you rather Mary, Lily, Jane, but never Geoffrey.

HEMINGE: Yes. That's young Geoff Dunderbread of Christchurch Boy's Choir.

WRIOTHESLEY: I'd swear to it that he were of the other sex — the one to which I'm indifferent. How strange a thing 'tis that merely knowing in the mind transforms the eye. That where, before, I was unmoved by a smooth rounding of a feminine cheek, the graceful undulation of a wig — languid crook of a manipulating finger — just that little word of Geoffrey works some strange magic on my senses. I think that I shall wander there.

(Crosses to Cleopatra-Geoffrey.)

OXFORD: John, I have a play.

HEMINGE: YOU!

OXFORD: SHHH. I shall want you to put it on. It's very good.

HEMINGE: But when? We're fully booked —

OXFORD: What's next?

HEMINGE: Why, *Scurvy Wives*, and then we're giving a new thing by —

ACTOR: Hey LOOK where Old FITCH has HANGED himself!

ALL: HAHAHAHAH!

WILL: Wherefore do you LAUGH! Is it a great thing to see a man driven to distraction by the misuse of his work!!!

(All hang their heads.)

ALL: *(Quickly.)* He's right. What a shame. Poor Fitch.

HEMINGE: We may have a slot. What's it called.

OXFORD: *Titus Andronicus.* A most Bloody and Beastly Tragedy! It has wicked prevarications, heinous decapitations, multiple mutilations, lawless fornications —

HEMINGE: Ah. But where's the LOVE, your Lordship! Where's the LOVE?

OXFORD: Love there is! Between a wicked Queen and a wicked Moor.

HEMINGE: OH!! I like it. I quite LIKE it. Let's see —. How could it go. There's the Queen. And she says — Nay, what is that bulges there, under your Moorish CLOAK — have you brought me a good flagon of Algerian wine? And HE says —

OXFORD: NO!! John. Never. Not like that! If I give it you, it shall be performed as it was set down. Not a thing changed, not a jot, not a tittle, not a scrap.

HEMINGE: RE-ally? Oh.

OXFORD: Look at the SHIT you do.

HEMINGE: The HITS I do —

OXFORD: The DRIVEL you perform.

HEMINGE: It suits the temper of the time —

OXFORD: Offer better fare and they will eat it —

HEMINGE: Better fare?

OXFORD: Do you dare greatness?

HEMINGE: Greatness. Oh. GREATness.

OXFORD: John. FORSWEAR the merely vulgar, bawdy, bloody, and crude.

HEMINGE: Here's my penknife, here's my chest.

OXFORD: NAY! I offer you the vulgar, bawdy, bloody, crude, but Excellent as WELL! — EARTHSHAKING, ROUSING and ETERNAL!

HEMINGE: Well, it's quite an honor. Have you thought if we're quite worthy enough?

WILL: Excuse me your Lordship. I heard what you were saying, and I just want to be in it.

OXFORD: And you shall be, hale fellow. Plain, good, gentle fellow. What's your name?

WILL: Oh, they call me honest Will Shakspere —

OXFORD: *(Aside to Heminge.)* Heminge, I need a Mask. A Beard. To lend me his name. A front man who can be trusted.

WILL: Discreet Will Shakspere.

OXFORD: *(Aside to Heminge.)* If anyone breathes that I am connected to this filthy disgusting theater of yours, I will have them garroted. Understand me?

HEMINGE: What's not to understand?

WILL: Trustworthy-to-the-grave-Will Shakspere.

OXFORD: How about him.

HEMINGE: HIM?

WILL: Most-Damnably-without-Hair- Will SHAKSPERE.

OXFORD: Will, wilt thou lend me thy Will for some great Will of mine?

WILL: What? I'm rather simple. True, but simple.

OXFORD: — And in doing MY will, Be MY will, for this brief sum of Time?

WILL: Come again?

OXFORD: And in MY WILL I will reward thee for thy WILL's use to ME.

WILL: By GOD I will do it! Whatever it shall be.

OXFORD: Only this. Be thou the Stepfather of Mine Invention's Heir.

WILL: How do you mean?

OXFORD: I will WRITE. You will sign your name.

WILL: That — could be difficult. I can DO it you know, its just this old trouble with my hand —

OXFORD: Only give me your hand on it, and we will fix the trouble.

HEMINGE: Shakspere is an most odoriferous name.

WILL: Oh, thank you! It's quite old, you know. It's a derivative of Sheep's Pee, we think. My ancestors had many a sheepscote.

HEMINGE: Why doth he not be signed Shakes-speare, is that not how he is listed on the roles?

WILL: A STAGE NAME! Fancy ME with a STAGE NAME —

OXFORD: And a nom-de-plume, to boot.

WILL: A what?

OXFORD: But — never a word gentle Will — must thou spill.

WILL: Not I.

OXFORD: Heminge, the author hath the right to attend all rehearsals —

HEMINGE: Of course I'd welcome the input.

OXFORD: Casting — design and director approval —

HEMINGE: — an honour to be sure —

OXFORD: Where the hell is Wriothesley — *(Sees Wriothesley with boy, off.)* Oh. A designated number of house seats —

HEMINGE: Well, how many are we talking about?

(They exit.)

WILL: Wonderful wonderful, and most wonderful — and after this more wonderful still! To lend my name to such an enterprise! — to be made use of in such a fashion! Oh, Great Fate! Fortune has raised me in her ranks from foul footstool to first-class footman! There is no fathoming her means with her favorites!

SCENE SIX

The Court: Earl of Derby, Sir Francis Bacon, Lady Lettice, Lord Burleigh, Francis Walsingham. Sound: A spinet. Everyone is intently reading a manuscript. They are wearing glasses.

LETTICE: *(Inflamed.)* This "Venus and Adonis!"

(Pause.)

BACON: I liked it —

LETTICE: And so did I —

ALL TOGETHER: (BURLEIGH: And I! DERBY: And I WALSINGHAM: I too! BACON: The best I ever read!)

DERBY: Thrice oe'r I read it without stopping!

LETTICE: I too! I confess it!

BURLEIGH: It seemed the pages turned all of themselves!

BACON: — and when the lascivious Goddess says "— Graze on my lips and if those hills be dry —"

ALL: "Stray LOWER!"

LETTICE: *(An outburst.)* Oh WANTON Goddess, wayward LINE and wonderful wicked writer! WHO IS — this — "Will-ee-yam Shak-es-Speare!"

ALL: Yes. Yes. Yes. (LETTICE: Who is he?)

BACON: Is he . . . well, he MUST be . . .from Cambridge?

DERBY: *(Thoughtfully.)* Do you know what, all, this poem. It's strange, but, it doth — remind me of something —

ALL: LETTICE: What? BACON: What? BURLEIGH\WALSINGHAM: What — what?

DERBY: Well, call me of wit distempered, but this TALE, you know, of this fleeing MAN, and the older, LOVE-crazed Goddess in pursuit . . .

ALL: *(Thoughtfully.)* Hmmm. Ahh. *(Pause.)* OH!

LETTICE: *(Lowering her voice.)* Why doth it not savor of my Lord of Oxford and —

> *(Fanfare. Queen Elizabeth enters. She is dressed magnificently and stiffly. She has a large collar that may somewhat restrict her peripheral vision. She carries a riding crop, which she occasionally cracks on something or someone, for emphasis. General genuflection.)*

ALL: *(Overlapping.)* WALSINGHAM: The QUEEN! DERBY: Elizabeth! LETTICE: Regina! BACON: Regia Virginia! BURLEIGH: Magnificatus Verissimus, TOGETHER: Our QUEEN our QUEEN our QUEEN!!

ELIZABETH: At ease, Good Friends, do not let me keep you from those sweet diversions by which you do beguile the time and tempt it from its course that leads all men and women to the grave.

> *(Applause.)*

ALL: BURLEIGH: Oh WELL said. WALSINGHAM: Well said. BACON\ DERBY\ LETTICE: Brava, Majesty.

ELIZABETH: But where is my Lord of Oxford?

> *(Courtiers exchange glances.)*

What? De — "Vere"? . . . not — "here"?

> *(Indulgent chuckles.)*

ELIZABETH: I had thought to see him. Burleigh? Where's your wayward ward?

BURLEIGH: I have not seen him this fortnight.

ELIZABETH: Lord Walsingham?

WALSINGHAM: *(Darkly.)* His movements be unknown.

ELIZABETH: But doth he HIDE himself? One would think he doth avoid his queen!

ALL: Hahahahah!

ELIZABETH: Well then. Gentle friends all! How ist doth amuse thyself this day? What no hawking, or hounding, nor gaming nor gossiping? How ist doth pass the time 'twixt now and then?

BACON: We've started a reading group, actually.

ALL: He did. He did. He did.

LETTICE: *(Quickly.)* Bacon. It was his idea.

> *(Pause.)*

ELIZABETH: A reading group? What Jollity the name doth promise. What good elevation of the common wit. Why, my Lord of Oxford should know of this. It would delight him, and please his hours. SEND to him, Burleigh —

BURLEIGH: I know not to which whorehouse to send, Your Majesty.

(Elizabeth circles to the back of a chair, which may or may not contain a courtier — she may occasionally whack it in frustrated passion.)

ELIZABETH: I do sicken without my Edward, for he doth so amuse me, that when he is not nigh, I feel the world a dull — *(Whack.)* STALE — *(Whack.)* TIRED — ! *(Whack.)* place. Is that not strange?
(Court is very alarmed.)

ELIZABETH: Perhaps I do . . . "love" . . . him. *(Pause. She remembers herself.)* I do JEST, all.

ALL: HAHAHAHA!

ELIZABETH: *(Elegant, recovered.)* So tell us more of this "Reading Society."

LETTICE: Just a place to come, and we read out loud, the best of the time, the worst of the time —. We all read the same thing so we can discuss it, and —

ELIZABETH: Sir Francis? Why dost thou pale and what is it hath so sudden put away?

BACON: 'Tis nothing, good my Queen.

ELIZABETH: Then let me see this nothing —

BACON: It is — we are reading an most astonishing poem. Your Majesty. 'Tis called "Venus and Adonis."

ALL: *(Overlap.)* BACON: 'Tis good, LETTICE: 'Tis good. WALSINGHAM ET AL.: 'Tis really, really GOOD!

ELIZABETH: And what is the matter of it?
(Pause.)

BACON: 'Tis a ballad of the Queen of LOVE Herself. Great VENUS, as the title doth suggest.

ELIZABETH: Why — in this our day — this era, if I might be so bold, our "Elizabethan" era, that can only be myself!

ALL: Oh, no no! WALSINGHAM: I shouldn't think so!

LETTICE: Oh, not SO your Majesty —

ELIZABETH: Who ELSE, Minion, should INSPIRE such a work but I the great descendant of they that wrote the Magna Carta, Elizabeth Tudor, Virginia Suprema — REGINA DENTATA!! *(To all, quivering with pride and pleasure.)* What of this Great "Venus," and her — "Adonis"? — oh, my Edward if you ask me — for I detect HIS very hand in this — *(Silence.)* Hath the cat got all your tongues? Well say! Is there a "Lady" it be dedicated to?

ALL: WRIOTHESLEY! WRIOTHESLEY! YOUNG WRIOTHESLEY!

LETTICE: — the Effeminate Earl of SouthHAMPTON.
(Pause.)

ELIZABETH: *(Absorbing this great blow, somewhere deep within her metal bosom.)* Well. Well. That way goes the game.

BACON: Oh. It sayeth — the author is one "William Shake-speare."

ALL: HaHaHaHaha!

ELIZABETH: *(Stoic.)* Lord Burleigh, tell your ungracious ward he may return to court. I will "hear" this poem of Master "Shakes-peare" although I find I . . . fear it.

(At a look from the Queen, Lettice rises with the manuscript.)

LETTICE: "Even as the sun, with purple colored face —"

BACON: Purple Colored face . . . that's GOOD . . .

(Lights fade and we pick up Oxford, Will in tow, en route to Oxford's rooms. Oxford is reciting from his same poem — uncontrollably and happily full of himself)

OXFORD: *(Reading from a new copy.)* — has ta'en his last leave of the weeping morn —

Rosecheek'd Adonis hied him to the chase;

Hunting he loved, but love he laughed to scorn —

Sick-thoughted Venus —

Makes amain unto him

And likes a bold-fac'd suitor 'gins to woo him —"

SCENE SEVEN

New scene completes building as Will and Oxford enter Oxford's rooms. Oxford is in high good humor. They are carrying short stacks of the newly printed "Venus and Adonis."

OXFORD: *(Beaming.)* The Booksellers can't keep' em in the stalls. EVERYONE who is NO one is reading me. Oooh. It's really disgusting.

WRIOTHESLEY: *(Entering, fastening his doublet.)* Thou lookst thirty-SEVEN again. Doth he not, Will?

WILL: Oh, ay.

OXFORD: Will. I've got another. Read it over, sign and take it to the printer tomorrow — he'll be expecting you.

WILL: *(Awestruck.)* Already? Why thou art as the gilded pike whose belly swells with countless bursting eggs —

WRIOTHESLEY: Ugh!

OXFORD: *(Struck.)* Nay — NAY! a pithy image — alive with horror of the breeding world . . . are you sure that you're not one of us?

WILL: Pardon?

OXFORD: *(Handing Will a manuscript.)* Never mind. Here it is — your latest.

WILL: "The Rape of Lucrece." What is the subject?

(A pause. Wriothesley exaggeratedly mouths "The. Rape. of. Lucrece.")

WILL: I — I'm sorry. I meant — the "Theme."

OXFORD: — innocence defiled, lust triumphant — rape, despair and death —. A playful little nothing, really.

WRIOTHESLEY: Oh, now, you've horrified him.

OXFORD: Oh, no. I think I've aroused him.

WRIOTHESLEY: *(Picks up hourglass.)* Oh, Edward, look at the time! We're LATE!

WILL: *(Reading.)* "Let him have time to tear his curled hair

Let him have time against himself to rave. . .

Let him have time . . ."

What in the WORLD is that repeating thing?

WRIOTHESLEY: What — fellow — wert born in a BARN! *(Catches himself.)* — sorry.

OXFORD: Why 'tis a poetic figure. It's called "Anaphora."

WRIOTHESLEY: Everyone knows that . . .

WILL: Of course. . .

OXFORD: *(Selecting a book.)* And you might read this. You'd better know SOMETHING, if you're to be in the game.

WILL: Forgive me, Lordship, for a clodpate and a fool.

OXFORD: Why, never ask pardon for thine inquiry. 'Tis a marvelous thing — when a man's hunger grows greater than his shame. *(He smiles at Wriothesley — touches him lightly. They start out.)* Oh, lower the Gate when you leave, will you?

(They exit. Will sits down tentatively at Oxford's desk, opens book — probably Puttenhams' The Art of English Poesy or something like it.)

SCENE EIGHT

The barn in Stratford. Anne enters, a folded packet in her hand.

ANNE: He hath left my heart in PIECES! Lies not WITH me, lies TO me — then gone from me! — GONE without a word these many months! And now this morning comes another packet — *(Unseals packet — impressed.)* Ten shillings! I've never even SEEN ten — Ooooh! Oooh! Once he loved me. I know it by all of woman's surety. Oh, damned be my woman's pride! Desperate measures for a desperate time! I'll follow him and charm him back anew!

(Colin enters with a bowl of milk.)

COLIN: Has't seen my pussy? *(Goes behind hay bale.)* Here puss puss puss!

ANNE: A plan informs me! 'Tis desperate — ill, yet well! This night I'll steal away clad in Old Colin's vile rags — for then who on all the vasty stretch of highway wouldst dare to lay finger to such a loathsome bundle! Colin!

COLIN: Harrgh?

ANNE: Sweet Colin, good Colin, gentle Colin — give me thy disgusting other outfit. The one that thou art wont to wear to church — and I will give thee a silver shilling for it.

COLIN: Hoohoohoo. I will for a shilling, No marry I will. For one such a shilling I will —

ANNE: Curb thy TONGUE!

COLIN: I go, I go.

ANNE: And thus disguised, to London I will stray
And there my husband may discover —
That meat again as sweet — that once was cast away!

SCENE NINE

Sound of tabor and drum. The Theater. A frustrating rehearsal of Titus Andronicus. Geoffrey, as Lavinia, bleeding stumps for arms. Burbage is Marcus, and Will holds a spear and hunting horn. Oxford sits, somewhat traumatized, to the side while a player or two enthusiastically show him severed heads, buckets of blood, etc. Others sit on sidelines, sewing, reading, stretching.

HEMINGE: All right, Richard. Once more from "speak gentle niece," and I think . . . *(Confidentially.)* We might be MISSING something here. A different . . . color, perhaps.

(Oxford looks up in horror.)

HEMINGE: This Lavinia IS his FAVORITE niece, of course, and this dreadful THING hath happened — her hands have been hacked OFF of course — her tongue hath been ripped OUT of course — but Uncle Marcus isn't a man without HUMOR. There's a bit of a glimmer to the man, don't you think?

(Burbage radiates good cheer.)

HEMINGE: A TWINKLE in him? Find the warmth. *(Heminge looks reflexively to Oxford for approval, Oxford gestures a "no.")* Forget what I said. Once more, then.

MARCUS: Speak, gentle niece!

Why dost not speak to me?

(Lavinia spits out an enormous bloody tongue.)

Alas! a crimson river of warm blood,

Like to a bubbling fountain stirred with wind,

Doth rise and fall between thy ros-ed lips —

(Beats his breast — a rising shout of anguish.)

aaaaaaaAAAAAHHH!

WILL: *(As Huntsman, sobbing.)* Gahh! GAHH GAHH!

BURBAGE: WHAT! Though upstart piece of Stage Dressing! Maks't sound upon my LINE — Hayseed! MOVE while Burbage SPEAKS! KNAVE! I KILL thee! *(Flies at him.)*

HEMINGE: PEACE! Richard — RICHARD! Let's break. Huntsman?

WILL: Yes?

HEMINGE: Don't pull focus. Just stand there!

WILL: Could any Huntsman look on such a spectacle unmoved?

HEMINGE: Yes, I think so.

WILL: Nay, I'll not believe it! Nor will I so betray my art to show NOT the passion of the Huntsman's heart! HOW shall I keep it IN if I so feel it!

HEMINGE: He would not MOVE!

WILL: Give me one REASON! I crave but a REASON that he may in good conscience stand stock-still as you would have me!

OXFORD: *(Looking up from his manuscript.)* The Huntsman — is — bewitched. Some strange spell rooteth him, soundless, to the ground.

HEMINGE: That's it.

WILL: Marvelous! Most Marvelous! I can PLAY that.

(Heminge leaves in disgust. Burbage starts for Shakspere in a fury.)

BURBAGE: Play THIS you butchering fumbler! Nitwit! FEEL THIS you snotterweeded — halfbaked jack'o'leg!!

OXFORD: Hullo, Dick. I hear 'tis good to sit cross-legged and say your prayers backward.

(Burbage stops.)

BURBAGE: What say you?

OXFORD: *(Provokingly.)* What say you? How? — so far from thy good kidney?

BURBAGE: Am I a lion that I shall roar, or do you put me in mind of the asses' poxy fable —

OXFORD: An ass? Who's an Ass!

BURBAGE: Why, asses are everywhere, lookst well upon thy boot-top!

OXFORD: Nay, I cannot for my Leg is too high and will not Bend!

BOTH: HAHAHAHAH!

BURBAGE: *(Fondly.)* A plague upon your Lordship, I am out!

BOTH: HAHAHAHAH!

(They exchange a hearty embrace, and Burbage exits.)

WILL: What was that!

OXFORD: Extemporaneous mother wit. I believe he would have killed you had I not so deftly diverted him.

(Oxford is making notes. Will approaches him timidly.)

WILL: — Well, my Lord, 'tis a part to DIE for.

OXFORD: What's that?

WILL: The Huntsman.

OXFORD: Really.

WILL: Behold, my hands. They shake with wonder and terror and pity.

OXFORD: Really?

WILL: "A crimson river of warm blood
Like to a bubbling fountain stirred with wind"
How can'st thou think of such a thing, where I might just have said —
(Searchingly.)
"Howl. Howl. Howl."

OXFORD: Ah. Hmm.

WILL: 'Tis wonderful.

OXFORD: Yes, my boy, 'tis the extra and unnecessary artifice that is the spark and superfluity of our art.

WILL: I wonder, well. It's just a little thing —

OXFORD: What is it? Speak freely if th'art not afraid to die —
(Grabs him by the lapels.)

WILL: Nay — it's just this. How came'st thou so to dip thy pen in light — and write in words so bright that e'en the surpris-ed sun doth dim when Oxford doth appear?

OXFORD: *(Pleased. a little surprised.)* Oh! Well said! Thou art a witty fellow. *(Releasing him.)* You know, it's true. Never has the thrill and surge of my mighty language carried me so high aloft and yet so dizzyingly deep. This *Titus Andronicus* shall make — thy — name, Shakespeare.
(They laugh.)

WILL: On what anvil turn thee thy mighty lines? How comes such GENIUS to pass!

OXFORD: Why, let me think. Oh, well, there's my many years of fine, fine, education and enforced culture at the hands of my Hated Guardian, of course . . .

WILL: Ah.

OXFORD: Yes, I had all the best Masters, all great poets in their own rights.

WILL: How I regret me that I did not stick in school.

OXFORD: *(Overlapping him.)* — brave Pliny and Good Lucas, Sweet Ovid, Plato, yes I had to become utterly familiar with them all.

WILL: *(Despairing.)* I have but small Latin and less Greek!

OXFORD: Why Will! 'tis no matter for an actor.

WILL: Doth think thy marvelous art derives from thy course of study?

OXFORD: Oh, nay, nay. Art — loveth not a pedant. One must write what one hast lived, of course.

WILL: Of course!

OXFORD: My painful life hath gi'n me most expensive opportunities to taste of tragedy.

WILL: Mine TOO!

OXFORD: The murder of my Lordly Father, the treachery of my beautiful and gifted mother. Then the long exile I endured to the continent while my lover languished in the tower.

WILL: I have seen a girl of fifteen drowned in a duck pond —

OXFORD: Ay, and thou shall speak to me of it, anon. I was captured by Pirates, you know, did I tell you?

WILL: No, but this girl, she — was floating face up and she had flowers in her hair —

OXFORD: *(Overriding him.)* What else — what else, hath seasoned the deep roots of mine invention? Oh! I've fought, you know, at the front lines —

WILL: GOD!

OXFORD: — thrown myself in the thundering cannon's path for Rank doth have its Obligations.

WILL: Now, I've poached, of course. And run me like hell from those as who would have done me deep injury. 'Twas reckless, but I was a youth, tasting of adventure.

OXFORD: What more, what more. I've loved both men and women, Whores of either sex, Royalty and those of royal blood.

WILL: I was trapped into marriage by the first woman I lay with.

OXFORD: *(Throwing a thoughtful arm around Will.)* — yes, I've waded deep in every kind of fornication that the waste of my estate could yield. And now, like to the ancient eagle, whose beak hath, unexpected, broke with plucking on the young rabbits — dream only of some peaceful aerie where I might with only one young lamb (or maybe two at most) feed more restfully and rake the countryside no more.

WILL: I stand amazed.

OXFORD: And from all this, my friend, this tattered, checkered and wild expanse of my life — have I welded my great Art!!
(Pause.)

WILL: My Lord? I have a question burns me, kills me, leaves me no peace till it be answered.

OXFORD: What?

WILL: Do you think that I have. . . "talent"?

OXFORD: Why Will! You're serious!

WILL: From the bottom of my heart.

OXFORD: Well, thou art indeed honest, and of an open and free nature. Thou art a regular Philomel. Artless and sweet.

WILL: My heart sinks.

OXFORD: Thou hast an excellent fancy, brave notions, and gentle expressions. Thou art a truehearted and goodly fellow.

WILL: Worse and worse!

OXFORD: Beware, Will Shakspere. Fly not near the flame of ART. If thou are not made of strong enough mettle she will snap thee in half —

WILL: I'm game —

OXFORD: — cut thy balls off —

WILL: I am not afraid!

OXFORD: — and throw thee back to the world with all the world spoilt for thee —

WILL: Then let it COME — ! though I be charred, blasted, shamed, wrecked for it — a twitching idiot who looked into the sun — a broken man who dared to love a Goddess — too burned to fly, too sad to crawl — a sot-wit tavern dreamer — a mumbling prophet surrounded by halfwits, judged by fools, ABANDONED BY THOSE BRIGHT ANGELS THAT HE ONCE HARNESSED TO HIS WILL —

OXFORD: *(Surprised.)* That's not bad . . .

WILL: It's — what — I — want!

END OF ACT I

ACT II

SCENE ONE

London. Upstage is Will's room. It's furnished simply, an unmade bed, a table, and some books. Downstage, Anne alone. She talks to us.

ANNE: Ooooh, LONDON! Well, life is certainly strange. 'Twould never be believed in a FICTION that my own husband might not penetrate my disguise —. Oooh, what adventures have I had! Once arrived in Colin's rags, I went to see my cousin Lucy, a bawd about town.

(A man dressed as Lucy enters, with an assistant and an armful of clothes and a hairpiece.)

ANNE: She took me in and thrilling to my device, outfitted me in her own sluttish fashion.

(Fast, festive Music. Through the following, Lucy disrobes Anne of Colin's rags, snaps her into pieces of costume appropriate for a woman of lively morals, including a corset, a hairpiece, choker, and gloves)

ANNE: Such THINGS she has! That push you IN where you go OUT, and puff you OUT where you — don't, actually. Paints as white as poison and rouge as red as roses! Cheek patches, corsets, chokers, and gloves . . . shoes that make you taller than your own dumpy self — for once in my life I'm slender! *(Her transformation is now complete.)* No wonder why my husband loves the theater! I never want to go home again — and just look at this hair!

(Lucy and assistant exit with rags. Anne looks at herself enthralled. She tears up.)

ANNE: Had I only been a man, I might have been an . . . actress. *(Pause.)* Well. Thus trimmed and decked I sought out my own love — *(Crosses to Will's room.)* and contrived to meet him just after the matinee. (*Titus Andronicus* — now THAT be entertainment!) Well. He knew me not as his wife, but thought me a wicked whore. He took me to his rooms, and we've scarcely been apart for a week. I've been just AWFUL to him. Its been WONDERFUL. Well, he himself hath taught me cruel inconstancy, since faithful kindness prompted him to flee.

(Will, enters with a flagon of wine.)

WILL: I hope this will thee satisfy, for three times thou has sent me out for wine, each time complaining of the taste.

ANNE: I'll be gone.

WILL: No. Stay —. Thou art a gamesome slut, Dear Lucy — why is't that I love thee so well?

ANNE: Because I love not thee.

WILL: *(Dragging her to the bed.)* Nay, thou liest! How could'st thou do those things which we two do together under night's dark coverlet — those wild and stormy expanses of uncharted filth which mark the passing of our hours together — if thou lov'st not me?

ANNE: Why it must follow that if I lov'st thee, I could not do such filth together with thee.

WILL: My sense follows not yours —

ANNE: For I must despise thee to use thee so, ay — marry — for who should play such games as to — *(Producing a whip.)* whip thee— *(Cracks it.)* tie thee up — *(With makeshift bondage apparatus that hangs from bedposts.)* call thee naughty names and romp with thee who had carried the candle of immortal LOVE?

WILL: *(Consumed with lust.)* DO IT!

ANNE: But Women's Affections do evaporate like dew at the sight of red-faced snorting desire, and hath since the old time.

WILL: *(In despair.)* You do wound me to the quick. You laugh at me and scorn me!

ANNE: Nay I do but jest. I do never despise thee, Will.

WILL: Oh, Cruelty was ne'er so fair. And not even so FAIR — and yet I am enslaved.

ANNE: — Though at times I like thee for a good fellow, and a fine sport.

WILL: Fine SPORT! Oh, these words do sound the death knell in my ear! Wilt thou drive me mad! Inconstant woman! On Tuesday last though dids't swear thou lov'd me. I gave thee my purse — ay, and my heart with it, and then on Wednesday thou lov'st me not.

ANNE: I am a woman. We are changeable.

WILL: By troth I see no more in you than in what nature sells, being damaged, on the cheap.

ANNE: I needeth not to listen to this railing. I go, I go. Seek me no more, for I do fly thee. Where's the rest of my hair and my false breasts, too, which wearing, I came hither withal.

WILL: *(Despairing.)* Leave thy wig, and thy false breasts leave too —
And leave me with the better part of you.
As a loathsome disease ever longs for that which makes it sicker, so doth my perverted palette incline to you, foul Leprosy that I adore!

ANNE: Ooooh! Thou sayest the nicest things. Which reminds me — when are you going to put me in one of your plays?

(Oxford enters. Anne, startled, retreats.)

OXFORD: Hello, hello, dear boy. — Forgive me awakening you so late — but I was flipping through the Menaechmi of Plautus, and bethought me it might do well adapted for the Summer Months — set in Syracusa perhaps. Oh — I didn't know you had company!

ANNE: *(Re-emerging, flirts.)* I'm not company. I'm a demon.

WILL: May I present my mistress, Lucy. Lucy, this is Lord O.

OXFORD: Call me O.

ANNE: Call me Abhorred Leprosy. For my Will doth call me so.

OXFORD AND ANNE: HAHAHAHA

OXFORD: *(Aside, approving.)* A hot bitch — by'r'Laken

ANNE: *(Aside, approving.)* A gay blade — by'r'Lord —

WILL: Will you embarrass me before my friend? Will you have some wine, my lord? If my Lady hath not swilled it all?

ANNE: Nay, Will, and I had but a glass — here's a bottle of a fine Rhenish red — shall I heat it up for you Lord O?

OXFORD: Don't put yourself out.

ANNE: Nay, and Will was to it himself to put me out, your Lordship saved me from such a fate by his most portune arrival —

OXFORD: What, gentle Will — throw such a lively lady out into the cold night —

WILL: Truth and lies do alternate like bubbles in a fast disturbed stream — you'll find it best to not believe a word she says, and hope, being ne'er beguiled, converts not into disappointment.

OXFORD: So sour? Sweet Will?

ANNE: Here's a nice hot cup of wine for your lordship — and one for you, my love.

WILL: Call you me LOVE? Unsay it for you mean it not, and do malign the very NAME of love by this misuse.

ANNE: Is he not cruel to me, Lordship?

OXFORD: Ay, most cruel.

ANNE: Well, we women are such fools that we do bend to the one that strikes us. Like as to the spaniel. Who fawns on him who wields the biggest . . . stick.

OXFORD: Upon my soul, Will, a most beguiling wench.

WILL: A wicked wench to wrench a wretch whose fool enough to fall into her fell hellhole.

ANNE: Well, there's my cue.

OXFORD: — a most savage alliteration, Peaceful Will!

ANNE: I'm off home.

OXFORD: It's too late for a lady to be out alone! Only cutpurses, murtherers! I shall guard thee in thy walk and see thee to thy door, lest that thou be bothered — being mistaken for a whore —

WILL: An honest mistake I'll wager . . .

ANNE: Shut UP!

WILL: Leave him be! I see what thou art up to!

ANNE: I WANT him to walk me HOME!

OXFORD: A pleasure. *(To Will.)* Will, this manuscript I leave for thy perusal. If you have any ideas — a line, a speech, a thought, a pungent turn of phrase — that sort of thing —

WILL: Oh, THANK you, Lordship. I'll take a look. By the way, I've finished most of the books you gave me — I've got Lyly, just done Euphues, Sydney, Spenser (and oh, by the way, a-DORED Catullus —)

OXFORD: Hast read that Astrophil and Stella I gave thee?

WILL: Aye, eagerly, and found it most — *(Breaking off, to Anne, who has been flirting with Oxford.)* Strumpet, I forbid thee what thou knowest it is that I forbid thee.

OXFORD: So cloudy with thy lady, Sunny Will?

ANNE: Excuse us, good my Lord. If you would but walk to and fro, I shall be with you presently.

OXFORD: I go to walk to and fro.
(Withdraws.)

ANNE: *(To Will.)* Darest thou tell me what to DO? If you love something, as thou sayst thou do — *(Turns out, beatific.)* then set it FREE and see if it return! *(Gently.)* I will return, Will. Look not so sad, sweet friend. Thou knowst me for what I am, and know I will be true to thee in my fashion.

WILL: Dost thou call me sweet and friend? Thy unaccustomed gentleness maketh me, helpless, to turn my throat up to the butcher's knife.

OXFORD: Will, I'll come to thee tomorrow. Nay, I do but walk her HOME!
(They exit together.)

WILL: Low this blow has laid me. *(Slowly.)* But why have I not the heart to hate them? And in this strain, my thoughts do . . . complicate.
For if my love makes my love one with me,
And my other love be one with me as well,
Than by this 'rithmetic should we not — all Three —
In happy rapture find ourselves to dwell?

If SHE is me — and HE is me — then — why —
Should we not all be one . . . together?
(Stunned.)
What have I said? And . . . how doth it scan?
(He goes to his blank-book, begins to compose.)

SCENE TWO

A little later. Oxford's bedchamber. Anne is waiting for him alone in his bed, suddenly apprehensive.

ANNE: My Lord — what says this motto, stitched into your ancient sheets —

OXFORD: *(Entering, loosely dressed.)* "Semper malefacere — delectatio animi nostri."

ANNE: And say, what does it mean?

OXFORD: *(Moves to her.)* "Ever to do Ill, our sole delight."

ANNE: Perhaps I shall learn Latin. Your ring — what strange figures are those?

OXFORD: Why 'tis a scene of Classical Love — most cunning —

ANNE: Might I see it nearer?

OXFORD: Mmmm hmm.

(He takes it off and gives it to her. She studies it, slides it onto her thumb. Oxford begins to make his moves. They disappear under a sea of writhing sheets. A brief interval. Anne emerges, flushed and tumbled.)

ANNE: *(Aside.)* How strange! I find I do not think upon the children. What hilarity is this! I feel so very far from Stratford — and find I do not miss it!

(She dives energetically under the bedsheet. More strange movements. Oxford emerges.)

OXFORD: *(Aside.)* By Jupiter, I feel sorry for my friend, my gentle Will. For well I know how he burns in love for her. Can it be this is what men call a SCRUPLE? How peculiar!

(Returns to business. Anne emerges.)

ANNE: *(Aside.)* This careless and attractive lord deprives me of all woman's reason! I came to town to woo my husband back, but now I find his image in my mind doth blur! — How odd!

OXFORD: *(Aside.)* I lose my heart for this debauchery —. Can it be a prick of what some call "conscience" that so deactivates my prick? Or is it only the return of the French disease? My dear —

ANNE: My Lord —

OXFORD: *(Getting up, crossing away from bed.)* My friend does love you as his lady —. We shall no further in this affair. "An goodly man is hard to find." Goes the adage. He hath confided to me he burns to marry you.

ANNE: *(Getting up.)* What! His villainy goes farther than I thought! The idiot HATH married me and knows it not.

OXFORD: What say you?

ANNE: He married me and left me for the stage. I, knowing men's desire for fruits which are forbid, did follow him, in this strumpetly disguise. So did I beguile him with promise of abuse. And so, like a sick charm, did I enslave him to me anew.

OXFORD: You're his WIFE? By custom, law of God? Bound to him by Contract most Holy?

ANNE: Ay.

OXFORD: By Priapus, I find my appetite revives! Honor then demands I do the job. Why, e'en now my friend doth feel the horns burst forth upon his brow and knows not why —

(He charges her, she shrieks, he picks her up swings her onto the bed.)

SCENE THREE

A little later. Shakspere's room. Will alone.

WILL: How my forehead aches! I cannot hate my benefactor for I love him. I cannot hate her, for I am her slave. What shall I do! My noble friend and my Fell-Hellhole bed together, and I wish myself (in truth) between them! *(Pause.)* I am confused! Oh, I am on FIRE! The agony! The IRONY! How ist a WHORE's Kiss provokes the lyric art an honest wife could not!

I am driven to the writing-cure that Edward recommends —

"Two loves have I, one of Comfort, one of . . . False hair — ?"

(He buries his face in is hands, disgusted. Oxford come in, somewhat shame-faced.)

OXFORD: Hello.

WILL: *(Stiffening.)* My Lord.

OXFORD: You are angry.

WILL: Nay.

OXFORD: Can't blame you.

WILL: I'm not.

OXFORD: Dost not thou wish to run me through the head?

WILL: And so repay your Lordship's great deserts?

OXFORD: Don't you want to fly at me and tear me all to pieces?

WILL: And thus discharge my debt for all your kindness?

OXFORD: Are you not enraged, isn't your blood boiling! Knowing I did cuck-old thee —

WILL: — 'tis not my place to —

OXFORD: Three times?

WILL: *(Flies at him.)* I WILL KILL THEE FOR IT AND HER TOO!

OXFORD: *(Happily.)* Good lad! To it!

WILL: Urge you me in this bloody course?

OXFORD: I'm BORED! I'm WEARY and SICK of the WORLD! I little care if I kill you or you kill me! 'Tis all one.

WILL: Nay. I cannot kill thee. For you are a sick and melancholy bastard who better needeth counsel than killing.
(Pause. A male-bonding moment.)

OXFORD\WILL: HAHAHAHAHAHAH!

WILL: *(Miserably.)* Oh. Why take her from me!! Thou likest not even GIRLS!

OXFORD: Will, I never can see any bond of love but I must break it. No happy spell but I must unmake it. I can't help it. I'm not proud of it, but there you have it.

WILL: Do you have no thought of Almighty God?

OXFORD: My most BRILLIANT criminality hath done nothing to invite his notice, and sadly I must conclude, He is as dead as my dead father.

WILL: Why 'tis ATHEISM!

OXFORD: It's all the thing 'mongst the better sort at court. What's this? *(Perching on Will's desk, he reads poem.)* "Two loves have I, one of comfort, one of — false hair — ?" Meant to be about your lady?

WILL: *(Embarrassed.)* — and you, my benefactor.

OXFORD: Well, which is which?

WILL: Well, she, of course, of the false hair —
(Oxford removes his wig — his graying hair is cropped quite short underneath. Will slowly rises, irresistibly drawn.)
You TOO?

OXFORD: Beauty's dead fleece, making another . . . gay. Nothing to say?

WILL: *(Enthralled.)* Fair Counterfeit! Do you think I might — ?

OXFORD: Of course.
(Will tries on the wig.)

OXFORD: Why 'tis better on Thee than on rucked, ruined, chapped, old ME!
(They laugh.)

WILL: *(Fondly.)* To me, my Lord, you never could be old.

OXFORD: Call me Friend, rather, sweet Will.

WILL: To me, my friend, you never could be old.

OXFORD: Nay, flatter me in my melancholy and call me "fair friend."

WILL: To me, Fair Friend, you never could be old.

> *(They look out, struck.)*

OXFORD: Oh, wow.

WILL: What?

OXFORD: *(Slowly.)* "To me, fair Friend . . . you never could be old.

> Before . . .time's brutal frost . . . shall touch thy head
>
> — I'd cut thy rosy throat and see thee dead."

I have not writ a sonnet since my YOUTH! What think you —

WILL: Savage. Vicious. Brutal!

OXFORD: DAMN it.

WILL: "tum TUM tum TUM. . . you never can be old,

> for as you were when first your eye — wast beheld —"

OXFORD: Nay. "When first your eye — I — ey'd —" HA!

WILL: That's bold!

OXFORD: *(Modestly.)* Well.

WILL: Ten winters cold have from the forests shook ten summers' pride.

OXFORD: Please. THREE year's constancy in love, maybe but never ten.

WILL: Three beauteous springs to yellow autumn turned —

> In process of the seasons have I seen,
>
> Three April perfumes in three hot Junes burn'd,
>
> Since first I saw you fresh which yet are green.

OXFORD: Now, see, that's the kind of thing that simply ESCAPES me. Let's start another. *(Thundering.)*

> "Were it aught to me I bore the canopy —
>
> With my extern the outward honoring"

WILL: Huh?

OXFORD: You know. Carried the canopy over the Queen.

WILL: Ah. Of course.

OXFORD: *(Softly.)* "Have I not seen dwellers on form and favor

> Lose all, and more —
>
> *(Pause.)*

WILL: *(Glumly, surveying his room.)* — by paying too much rent —"

OXFORD: Get the blank-book. We might play at a verse or two.

WILL: You mean, work TOGETHER on some POEMS? Thou knows't it is my secret pastime!

OXFORD: Thou cans't no more be public with POETRY — being low of birth, than I can with the PLAYS and so forth, being of high. I could, of course, pass them around to the usual toxic fops and inbred idiots. But I can't take them to the Publisher.

WILL: I can.

OXFORD: Good man.

WILL: Posterity's head shall reel with the questions of our authorship! But the spirit of True Poetry shall not be hid!

OXFORD: The spirit of True Poetry is Love, and therefore often pitchy. *(Pause.)* William, I have a love I cannot tell. I seem — to have a block in art. Around, my — *(Gestures vaguely toward chest.)* you know.

WILL: Heart?

OXFORD: There is one for whom I really should like to beget some verses, except I . . . find I'm having difficulty.

WILL: Who?

OXFORD: Oh, let's just call him — H.W. No, better still, W. H. I wouldn't mind your help.

(Moves closer to him. Meditatively. Will is uneasy.)

WILL: I've . . . been . . . improving my use of Ornament — getting a lot more polish —

OXFORD: One can see that. By the way — wherever did you get that jerkin? It really suits you —

(Sits on bed.)

WILL: — I can finally tell a trope from a metaphor, imagine, ME who couldn't tell a . . . dangling modifier —

OXFORD: Sit down, my boy.

WILL: *(Sits uneasily — Oxford beside him.)* — from a — feminine ending —

OXFORD: I want you —.

WILL: *(Panic-stricken.)* NO! No! I'm not that WAY! *(Suddenly intrigued.)* Well — I wouldn't rule it out ENTIRELY — you're a VERY attractive man —

(He half-moves toward Oxford.)

OXFORD: *(Distracted.)* I want you — to write me — something more private and more — simple.

WILL: Oh.

OXFORD: No tapestried chambers — no flowery form, just lines that honor what takes place . . . *(Touches his chest.)* here. Do you know what I mean?

WILL: Yes.

OXFORD: Quite. Well. Enough said. *(Springs up.)* So! Where's thy Lady?

WILL: I was to ask you the same question.

OXFORD: I tossed her out when we were done and bid her go to you.
Came she not back?

WILL: *(Shakes his head.)* " — If you love something set it free and see if —"
(He cannot go on.)

OXFORD: *(Jealously.)* See how you suffer! God WHY cannot I SUFFER! Oh,
a fit of melancholy here or there — a murderous FRENZY or two — but
nothing — *(Surveying Will's wracked form with a kind of wonder.)* like
THAT — !!

SCENE FOUR

Dawn. Anne is on the road back to Stratford.

ANNE: What have I done! My ancient weakness loses me the day! I'm just a
maid who can't say "nay." But neither could I well pronounce "decease"
"desist" or "halt!" So now they bond, and I'm back out on the highway!
I will back to Stratford, to cool my heels and hide my shame. At least let
him still burn for her, which is, of course, myself. I was to have been revealed! He was to have discovered his wife in his slut and so LOVED me.
But now he will discover a slut in his wife and then KILL me. As long as
he thinks me ONLY a whore, he will continue to adore! I am SICK of
men's philosophies. Of this mis-fired adventure, what am I to say — !!
*(She takes Oxford's ring, now on a ribbon around her neck. Looks at it, for
a moment. A slow burn, then a slow smile.)* That I had a wicked and a
sweet night once — that showed me what life might be, if only I had not
been me. *(She exits.)*

SCENE FIVE

*Court. The Reading Group. Elizabeth, Derby, Burleigh, Bacon, Lettice, and
Oxford.*

DERBY: " — For I have sworn thee fair, and thought thee bright
Who art as black as hell as dark as night!"

ALL: Ahh!

(Pause.)

LETTICE: Marvelous!

BACON: *(Moved and somewhat surprised.)* These sonnets, both the sugared and the vitriolic, are so painful and so witty, My Lord of Oxford!

BURLEIGH: And you say they are by William "Shake-speare?" The ACTOR?

ALL: HAHAHAHAH!

OXFORD: *(Not unpleased.)* Why YES! And they were only meant for circulation 'mongst his private friends!

LETTICE: And doth one MAKE private friends at a publick-house!
  Oh, BRILLIANT De Vere, thou pullest not the wool over THESE eyes — 'tis thee, 'tis thee!

OXFORD: Nay, I protest, I protest, I protest, and again I DO protest.
  (Walsingham enters — courtiers murmur.)

ALL: DERBY: Walsingham. LETTICE: There's Walsingham. BACON\BURLEIGH: It's Walsingham.
  (Fanfare. Elizabeth enters, holding a copy of Shakespeare's sonnets. The usual consternation, bowing and scraping)

ALL: DERBY: Her Majesty! BURLEIGH: See how Elizabeth comes! BACON: Great Elizabeth! LETTICE: Untouchable! DERBY: Unknowable! BURLEIGH: Pure! BACON: Remote! WALSINGHAM: REGINA! ALL: The Queen The Queen The Queen!

ELIZABETH: As thou wert, all. Oh. My Lord of Oxford has seen fit to join us.

ALL: HAHAHAHAHA!

OXFORD: Majesty — I —

ELIZABETH: *(To all, ignoring him.)* What hast been up to, this dull and creeping afternoon? Come, all, and say!

LETTICE: Oh your Majesty! We've been reading the private sonnets of William SHAKESPEARE! In edition most unauthorized —
  (All laugh.)

ELIZABETH: I, too, have been reading them. *(They wait. She turns to Oxford.)* And they be most excellently writ.
  (He bows slightly.)

ALL: All: Yes, Yes!

LETTICE: — mine own thought as well!

ELIZABETH: They show more than WIT, 'tis . . . courage.

OXFORD: Really.

ELIZABETH: One — didn't know one had it in One. This sort of thing. Bravo.

ALL: Hail. Kudos. Congratulations. Our Congratulations.

ELIZABETH: To Mister "Shakespeare" of course. Pass it along.

OXFORD: I will.

ALL: BACON: Yes, right. LETTICE: Quite right. BURLEIGH: Yes. WALSINGHAM: Please do. Pass our congratulations along to Mister Shakespeare.

ELIZABETH: But this violence of feeling — of "Love." It astounds and intrigues me. Being a Virgin, of course —

ALL: Of course! Of course! Of course!

ELIZABETH: — I shall rely on you, my seasoned and promiscuous courtiers, to tell me of the truth of such verses.

ALL: LETTICE: Oh, love is the worst. DERBY: Oh, a pain! O 'tis a fever. BURLEIGH: It is to be full of sighs, tears. BACON: 'Tis to be as heavy as lead. WALSINGHAM: 'Tis darkness, hell and blackness all at once.

ELIZABETH: Then why do men and women wish for such a state?

DERBY: Oh there 'tis nothing like it. It maketh the whole world full. 'Tis joy, 'tis transport, madness, to be as light as wind.

ALL: Yes. Yes. That's it, exactly.

ELIZABETH: Most intriguing. To be heavy and light. Full of hope, then cast down with despair. I wonder what it is to love like that. *(Coming forward.)* Ay me. I could wish me a man to love. But I fear I am a marble monument, and not a woman.

BURLEIGH: Oh, how can Your Majesty talk thus a way. All do love her, and would prostrate themselves in gratitude before the Goddess that so bestowed herself in such like way.

ELIZABETH: OH, ARE THERE NONE HERE BUT THEY WILL FLATTER ME?

ALL: LETTICE: Nay! DERBY: No! BURLEIGH: Never! BACON: Oh, absolutely not SO your majesty! WALSINGHAM: Wouldn't —.

ELIZABETH: Ah, my friends, Love doth not its magic make in a hall of REEDS which each their motion take from one another.
(Court looks ashamed of itself. A few throat clearings.)
It seems to me that Love between Two must be akin to War. Adversaries destined to meet from the first of time — longing for the battle and for who will SLAY them!

ALL: BURLEIGH: Absolutely. DERBY: Well said. LETTICE: Indeed. BACON: Just so. WALSINGHAM: Yes.

ELIZABETH: I tire, and you must take your leave. Stand not upon the order of your going. Oxford, stay. A word with you.
(All leave but Oxford and Walsingham.)

OXFORD: Majesty, I —

ELIZABETH: Oh never flinch at me, nor round thine eyes to the exits. It taketh not a brick wall to fall on me.

OXFORD: Your eyes are even as great in farsightedness as they are in beauty. "Even as the pitching cormorant —"

ELIZABETH: Don't be tiresome.

OXFORD: Sorry.

ELIZABETH: I must ask you something. Shakespeare. Is he discreet?

OXFORD: I'd stake my life on it. Has your Majesty a . . . literary . . . project at hand?

ELIZABETH: Hush.

OXFORD: Sir Francis asked me just this question not an hour ago.

ELIZABETH: How now! Doth he think to inflict his *Three Merry Whoresons* upon the public?

OXFORD: He mentioned something to like effect.

ELIZABETH: Rash Sir Francis! But let it be. I'm sending Walsingham to your man. And with him a most rare manuscript.

OXFORD: Hath your Majesty — a play?

ELIZABETH: *(Lays her finger on her lips.)* Not a word.
(He exits.)

SCENE SIX

The Theater. Will enters, distraught, followed by Heminge and Condel in hot pursuit.

WILL: — Nay! I will not lend my name to this *Three Merry Whoresons!*

CONDEL: HAHAHHA. Truly thou art called witty Will!

WILL: It hath not merit. It liveth not, and I cannot see such tripe upon the stage.

CONDEL: Art mad!

HEMINGE: Art insensible of this great and secret honour being offered us?

WILL: Say rather forced upon us! I won't lend him my name — for I have read his lines — and I may tell you plainly. The man hath all the poetry of a mathematician!

HEMINGE: He IS a mathematician. And who art thou to pass judgment on lofty Sir Francis Bacon?

WILL: Am I not William Shakespeare?

CONDEL: Nay!

WILL: What!

CONDEL: Thou art Will Shakspere! — an indifferent actor, capable only of small parts, difficult to hear even from the third ROW!

WILL: Henry, I protest thou useth me with no great justice!

HEMINGE: Nay, Henry, thou art too rough and speak inadvisably. But GENTLE Will, REASONABLE Will, thy name is not thy name to give or Withhold at WILL.

CONDEL: Oxford owns thy name, he can lend it where he listeth!

WILL: He will not do so if he is my FRIEND!

CONDEL: Well, he's NOT! He is an Earl. And he will throw you away when he's THROUGH with you. As long as he pays you, who CARES!

WILL: He won't be through with me. He . . . NEEDS me.

HEMINGE: Oh, yes, we know ALL about it.

WILL: You do?

CONDEL: How you supply him with a JOKE or two . . .

WILL: A "JOKE" or two?

HEMINGE: — the odd bit of "stage business"

WILL: STAGE business — ? Is that what he says?

HEMINGE: — he says you're very good!

CONDEL: — a great hand with a sight-gag.

HEMINGE: A natural clown —

CONDEL: An amusing knave —

HEMINGE: A witty rogue —

CONDEL: A beguiling fool —

WILL: — Clown — Knave — Rogue! — Fool! I — who — wrote *King Richard* while HE was whoring on the Continent!

CONDEL\HEMINGE: Wrote? What? How say you? Rubbish!

CONDEL: *(Hissing.)* He GAVE you the manuscript before he left!

WILL: — "I see a. . . HUNCHBACK. YOU flesh it out." That's all I got from Oxford! Oh how fate hath limed the PIT! I am who I am and none shall ever KNOW it!

CONDEL: Oh, thou makest me MAD! A swollen bladder blown full of alien airs!

WILL: Foist not BACON on me! Or mistake not, I shall run forth and cry the guilty secret to the mob at large although my ears be shortened for it! "Shakespeare" is not some sportive tunic for each slumming lord, who, bored with the getting of bastards — longs to write a play!
(Pause.)

HEMINGE: What is that?

WILL: Unrelieved Blank verse!

CONDEL\HEMINGE: Say YOU! NO!

WILL: — YES!! without end-stop or apology! For I BOIL! OXFORD may be

Shakespeare, or in a desperate hour maybe MARLOWE but never Sir Francis BACON! Besides. The day may yet come when Will SHAKSPERE may be Shakespeare!

CONDEL: *(Threatening.)* Remember. You used to hold horses by the door, my boy, and not so long ago, either!

HEMINGE: *(Threatening.)* And the best of the horse holders, he was, too, wasn't he Henry?

CONDEL: That he was, John. THEY STILL ASK FOR YOU!

HEMINGE: Think, Man, what you're doing . . .

WILL: Oh this I am resolved! Not Walsingham himself could force my hand.

(Lord Walsingham enters.)

HEMINGE: Lord Walsingham!

(All fall to the ground, prostrate.)

WALSINGHAM: You flirt with treason.

ALL: Pardon, Pardon, dear Sir. 'Tis only our way, being rough-speaking men of the theater — 'twas Shakspere only HE that spoke —

WALSINGHAM: Never mind. Shakspere, I agree. Sir Francis is no penner of plays.

WILL: Oh, Sir. You do me honor to admit my taste.

WALSINGHAM: Too long the court hath suffered with his epic poems.

ALL: Exactly. We agree.

WALSINGHAM: Gentlemen, I have for you a most brilliant play that HER MAJESTY herself is most desirous that "Shakespeare" might write. As soon as if he started work today.

HEMINGE: Her Majesty?

CONDEL: The Virgin Queen?

WILL: Who hath writ it?

WALSINGHAM: HER MAJESTY HERSELF — doth wish to see this play performed. At court.

HEMINGE: Of course — of course — . What doth it concern?

WALSINGHAM: It touches matters most near a lady's heart. A lady of considerable spirit and vivacity. Who hath longed long for the man that may match her and o'er master her. Who might have penned it concerneth not me or thee. That She Who Commands the WAVES — SHE who RULETH over the hearts of PRINCES — The DIVINA REGINA, MAGNA MATER, CASTA DIVA herself doth wish to see it performed sufficeth us. See that thou do't shortly.

ALL: AY AY AY.

WALSINGHAM: I need not add that you shall keep my visit and this matter secret.

ALL: NO NO NO.

WALSINGHAM: — or thou shalt to a man be dragged to the Tower there to perform most authentically in thy most final tragedies!

ALL: Well said, Lord Walsingham. HOHOHO What a good WIT hath HE! Oh well said!

(Walsingham exits.)

CONDEL: *(Examining manuscript.)* What have we here — *The Taming of a Shrew.*

HEMINGE: In which the most delicate and spirited Katherine is mated with her true love, the swaggart, brute Petruchio —

CONDEL: Well, there's a part for Dick, anyway! And Geoffrey shall be Katherina, his voice hath just changed — but for a Shrew is no matter.

HEMINGE: And Shakspere as Christopher Sly the Tinker — that starts the story off —

(Geoffrey emerges, claps a low-comedy cap on Will's head)

WILL: — and another thing! nothing but huntsmen, ghosts and clowns! I'm SICK to DEATH of tiny PARTS! Am I not a good PLAYER?

(No one listens to him. A Musical Discord. The show builds up around the protesting Will.)

HEMINGE: Company ON stage — thenk YEW!

(All out. A couple of musicians on stage to add sense of scale. Sounds of tentative musical practice underscore)

HEMINGE: Are all present?

ENSEMBLE: *(Adjusting costume pieces.)* Ay. Ay. Ay.

HEMINGE: Great thanks to all for thine hard week's work. Now nothing doth remain but to let GOOO. To PLAY! Wonderful, everyone — let's just come together shall we, everyone BREATHE — CONNECT —. A short WARM-up please —

(Actors immediately begin to warm up. There's a burst of simultaneous vocalization and arcane physical warm-ups.)

ALL: PLAYER ONE: I am WHOLE I am PERFECT I have every RIGHT to BE here I — \ PLAYER TWO: From the Balls of the Feet to the Tip of the Tongue — \ PLAYER THREE: Rrrotten Rrrichard Rrrotten Rrrichard —\ PLAYER FOUR: Woo Wooo Woo Wee Waw Wee\ PLAYER FIVE: Fourteen Frigging Earls Frighted Philip's Frigate — \ PLAYER SIX: Woozle cock woozle cock woozle cock — *(And so forth.)*

HEMINGE: *(Breaking in quickly.)* That's enough! So everyone mark through any trouble-spots —

(Ten seconds of rehearsal pandemonium. As follows — all at once.)

ACTOR-"CURTIS": Let's h'at Good Grumio —

ACTOR-"GRUMIO": Lend thine ear —

ACTOR-"CURTIS": Here —

ACTOR-"GRUMIO": *(Hitting Curtis.)* There —

ACTOR-"CURTIS": No. Wait. Aren't I supposed to duck.\
(Meanwhile.)

PETRUCHIO: *(To Heminge, while working over Kate, played by Geoffrey.)* Look. — I take her like this and then I PUNCH her, one — and a two — one and a TWO — and then, I SWING her — \
(— and Will is pursuing Heminge. They're momentarily in the clear.)

WILL: *(Over the babble.)* — but what HAPPENS to Sly the TINKER — he hath not a THROUGH line — I don't underSTAND —

HEMINGE: Will, I cannot hear thy problems at this moment — whatever you did last time — do it AGAIN!

WILL: Call you this DIRECTION!

(A fanfare. All genuflect and scurry to places as Elizabeth enters, with Oxford in tow. She greets the house and sits in Royal Box, up among real audience members. The Audience has arrived.)

ELIZABETH: My heart, my heart. I haven't felt like this since the Spanish Armada.

(Hauteboy or trumpet flourish. Derby arrives in audience, late, with a gigantic bonbon that crackles noisily, causing Elizabeth to shoot him a most terrible look.)

WILL: *(Playing to all, in the round. Music under.)* GOOD LORDS and LADIES. A poor, drunken tinker, taken in his cups is gulled by a mighty Nobleman — to think himself a great LORD! Now, as you shall see, I, Christopher Sly, hath awakened — in a chamber hung with silks! Play me this fine play, I tell thee! *(Uncontrollable aside, to Heminge, who's playing Baptista.)* I don't understand why I'm even in the PLAY!

ELIZABETH: *(Stands up, excited.)* Nay, that's not next!

OXFORD: What?

ELIZABETH: Shh!

(Enter Petruchio\Burbage, enter Kate\Geoffrey, opposite sides of stage. Ensemble rings them.)

PETRUCHIO: Good morrow, Kate, for that's your name I hear.

KATE: Well have you heard, but something hard of hearing. They call me Katherine that do talk of me.

ELIZABETH: *(Laughs hard and alone.)* Ay me, I fear to split my stays.

PETRUCHIO: You lie in faith, for you are called plain Kate and Bonny Kate and
sometimes Kate the Curst —

ALL: HAHAHAHAH

ELIZABETH: Ay me —

WILL: *(As Sly.)* Another pint of smallest ALE!

ELIZABETH: *(Enraged.)* What doth the idiot? He hath not another line there!

OXFORD: How say you?

ELIZABETH: Nay, I spoke of nothing. Hush! Petruchio is to TAKE her now.
You shall see!

(Now the company suggests the plot of Shrew *in 60 seconds of brilliantly inventive dumb show. Music and picture hold at moments as actors revolve
around a painted drop — allowing Elizabeth's outbursts to top. See end note
for detailed story-board images.)*

(Music. Action. Petruchio kisses Kate violently.)

ELIZABETH: *(Aroused.)* NOW she shall come to know her keeper's call!

(Music. More action. Kate weeps.)

ELIZABETH: *(Deeply moved.)* Left alone at the altar, oh poor girl!

(Music. Action. Petruchio swings Kate up in his arms.)

ELIZABETH: *(Enthralled.)* SEE how he snatches her away from all the guests!

(Music. Action. The starving Kate is taunted.)

ELIZABETH: *(Thrilled.)* Cut down to SIZE! How like you THAT, my Girl!

(Music. Kate and Petruchio join hands.)

ELIZABETH: *(Ecstatic.)* Ay me! What a story! How will it end!

*(There is a little trill of happy resolve music. Company restores to real time.
Will, in Tinker's nightgown and cap, holding Sly's Ale-Cup is becoming in-
creasingly upset about the tone of this odd and violent play.)*

PETRUCHIO: Lord how bright and goodly shines the moon!

KATE: The moon! The sun — it is not moonlight now!

PETRUCHIO: I say it ist the moon that shines so bright! Take THAT!

(Cuffs her.)

PLAYERS: *(Shocked.)* Ooohhh!

ELIZABETH: *(Excited, loudly.)* YES!

KATE: I know it is the sun that shines so bright —

PETRUCHIO: *(Beating her savagely.)* Now by my mother's son and that's myself,
It shall be moon, or star, or what I list —

*(Audience shocked. Elizabeth delighted. Petruchio pushes Kate down and
rides her like a donkey.)*

KATE: Ay me! Collared like a spaniel and made to crawl on all fours!

PETRUCHIO: Evermore cross'd and cross'd nothing but cross'd!

(Spanking her.)

ELIZABETH: *(Rapturous.)* Do it again! She LIKES it!!

PETRUCHIO: That's my girl. COME KISS ME KATE!

(He kisses her violently, then shoves her downstage. Elizabeth in an erotic haze. Petruchio pulls Kate up to standing.)

PETRUCHIO: Katherine, I charge thee. Tell these headstrong women what duty they do owe their husbands?

(All applaud approvingly. Kate is down front, secretly wrapping her hand for a real fight.)

KATE: Well, I just don't know. *(Pause.)* Let's FIGHT!!!

(Kate and Petruchio go at it again, this time for real. Play is disintegrating. Company is placing bets on combatants, etc. During a momentary strangle-hold —)

ELIZABETH: *(To Oxford, distraught.)* I couldn't think of anything else.

OXFORD: Ah.

ELIZABETH: Something about the ending doesn't quite WORK.

KATE AND PETRUCHIO: *(Back at it.)* Take THAT and THAT and THAT and THAT!

(Will can't stand it anymore.)

WILL: *(Separating them. To Kate.)* Though I am but a drunken tinker, yet I am provokst to say:

Fie fie unknit that threatening unkind brow!

PLAYERS: *(All at once.)* HEMINGE: Nay! What? CONDEL: That's not —
OTHERS: Is that supposed — What's going on —

WILL: — and dart not scornful glances from those eyes

To wound thy governor, thy lord thy king —

PLAYERS: What? What? What? Is SLY the TINKER — he's not in this —

WILL: *(To Kate.)* It blots thy beauty as frosts do bite the meads — confounds thy fame as whirlwinds shake fair buds —

KATE: *(A snarling aside.)* Shut UP — you!

ELIZABETH: *(Standing up.)* WHO IS THAT!

OXFORD: "Shakespeare?" — his PLAY?

ELIZABETH: Oh. Right.

(Oxford pulls her down into her seat.)

WILL: *(Improvising with passion and tenderness.)* A woman moved is like a fountain troubled . . . muddy, ill-seeming, thick, bereft of beauty, and while it is so, none so dry or thirsty will deign to sip or touch one drop of it.

ELIZABETH: *(Simply.)* Kill him.

OXFORD: *(Amused.)* Why? It's good.

(Will takes off his fool's cap. To Kate, who is standing, slack-jawed and astonished.)

WILL: Thy husband is thy lord, thy life, thy keeper

One who cares for thee

And for thy maintenance commits his body

To painful labor both by sea and land

To watch the night in storms, the day in cold,

Whilst thou liest warm at home,

Secure and safe

And craves no other tribute at thy hands

But love, fair looks and true obedience.

Too little payment for so great a debt.

ELIZABETH: *(Deeply touched. To Oxford. Indicates Will.)* Why, such duty as the subject owes the Prince . . . *(Her hand brushes Oxford's sleeve.)* such a WOMAN oweth to her . . . husband —

OXFORD: *(Alarmed.)* But you, though Woman, are also Prince, and can oweth duty to none. Great Virgin Majesty.

ELIZABETH: Yes, yes, yes and so forth!

(She's up. To audience.)

OH, GO GET IT YOU WOMEN! THOSE WHO CAN!

And thank your STARS that YOU are not as I!

(On "I" she beats her metallic bodice.)

Ow!

(Recovers. Inspiration finds her.)

So —

"Vail your stomachs for it is no boot

And place your hand beneath your master's foot —

Yes! YOU! YOU!

(Kate falls startled to the ground and surrenders to Petruchio.)

In token of which duty if he please —

My hand. is. ready —

May it do him ease —"

(She extends her hand searchingly into the great emptiness of the air. A burst of applause from ensemble for the Queen's impromptu performance.)

ALL: Brava Virgin Queen, Eternal Virgin! Huzzah for our Magna Virginia!

(Elizabeth blinks back tears and transport.)

ELIZABETH: 'Tis a most gratifying . . . fantasy.

(Her moment. Applause and music as all exit away but Elizabeth and Will, Heminge and Condel. Elizabeth crosses down to Will.)

Mister Shakespeare —

WILL: *(Bowing deeply, excited, expecting, maybe, to be knighted.)* Your Majesty —

ELIZABETH: — thou art in water most enormously hot!

WILL: Untouchable Goddess, how have I offended?

ELIZABETH: How darst thou alter by thine own actor's whim a work of divine transcription?

WILL: Great Majesty, in all the dimness of mine own humility, it seemed to me the ending needeth — work!

ELIZABETH: How now! Assaulteth me with dramaturgy? Thou Upstart CROW!

WILL: Nay!

ELIZABETH: Where hast thou gathered all thy goodly wit? From which university? Pray? Answer!

WILL: I have taken pains to educate myself, Divine Majesty.

ELIZABETH: That doth proclaim itself. Perhaps in the TOWER you shalt find time for those further studies thou dost evidently still require.

WILL: Oh, send me not to prison — sweet Highness!

CONDEL AND HEMINGE: Oh, please, Mercy, good Majesty — no more shall actor's ad-lib issue from this our stage —

WILL: Strike me dead, for offending, I did not mean it.

ELIZABETH: Well, enough, all. My great success today inclines me to mercy.

ALL: Oh, THANK you, Merciful Majesty.

ELIZABETH: But I do henceforth command that the part of Sly the Tinker be cut most brutally short. Farewell, Good Players.

ALL: Farewell, farewell, Congratulations on thy Great Opening. Shall run a thousand performances (etc.)

ELIZABETH: Watch thy step, Shakespeare, that thou shalt not OVER-step. Forget not that thou are in disgrace till further notice.

(She exits. Pause.)

HEMINGE: I thought that that went swimmingly well!

CONDEL: Quite.

HEMINGE: Be not downcast, Will.

WILL: Disgrace. Disgrace!

MEN: Nay, think not on it. 'Tis a thing of no importance. Nay, whatever worketh.

(They exit.)

WILL: Fortune eludes me, the times collude. I see too late — and what I see I HATE — My name's become a — BRAND!!

(Oxford enters.)

OXFORD: Good morrow, Will! Congratulations on fine work as Sly the Tinker!

WILL: My lord is in a merry mood —

OXFORD: You know that *Timon of Athens* I started yesterday?

WILL: Yes —

OXFORD: I finished it! Except, of course, any changes you care to make. Timon NEEDS something. Give him a speech, will you?

WILL: *(Anguished, to himself.)* — black — white, foul — fair, wrong — right, base — noble — HAH you GODS why this?

OXFORD: Yes. Terrific! Along those lines.

WILL: How liketh the court my poems?

OXFORD: Well, they can't believe that I, Bloody De Vere, can write in such a sugared and gentle vein. I'm a great hit.

WILL: *(Quietly.)* Suspect they that . . . another . . . has a hand?

OXFORD: Of course not. They think that you are really me. But for decency's sake, they speak as if you were really you. That wrote them.

WILL: And if they thought that I were I?

OXFORD: Well. They wouldn't dare approve them, then, of course. Coming from a Player. You know what people are.

(Sir Francis Bacon enters. He has a strange protuberance under his cloak.)

OXFORD: Well, Hello there, Sir Francis!

BACON: Ah. Hullo, De Vere. I was looking for — the lost and found. Perhaps this mild-looking fellow can show me to it. What is thy name, Sirrah?

OXFORD: Thou needst not dissemble thy purpose, Bacon. That bulging man-uscript in thy cloak proclaims it as loud as thou can'st deny — or art thou just glad to see me —

MEN: HAHAHAHAH

(They slap each other on the back.)

OXFORD: Thou hast caught the dread contagion of poetry — and our Mr. Shakespeare here the only physic in the kingdom.

BACON: You're Shakespeare?

WILL: Yes, my Lord!

BACON: I'm here for a . . . friend, actually. He hath a manuscript for a masque — it's not done, entirely. It's wonderful. Really quite wonderful. Methinks it may play a trifle long — Ist six hours — ?

(Enter several more heavily cloaked, hooded and masked figures, followed by more and more and more! Rising babble of excited greetings.)

OXFORD: Why my Lord of Essex! and Lady Lettice too — why 'tis Florio! I know him by his shoes! Derby! Raleigh! How was Bermuda! Kit! How doth Spain?

BACON: Welcome brother MASON! I salute thee most secretively!

(Hooded man and Bacon perform arcane handgrip-ritual.)

WILL: *(Alarmed.)* Lords, Ladies, Masons, and Lone Jesuit! Give me audience! It cannot be possible that all of you seek Will Shake-Speare? There cannot be so much Art!

(They all brandish their manuscripts — and advance on him.)

VOICES: Ay AY AY. I've got a little — its about a — it runs a bit long — I just finished it — It needs work —

DERBY: There's a confirmed bachelor — this is a comedy — who —

WALSINGHAM: It takes place in Venice where —

LETTICE: An Old King is giving away his Kingdom and —

BACON: Hairpox, a happy whoreson, meets Kitty Custance — 'Tis the one from which I read the first act during Shrovetide!

(All gasp, horrified.)

OXFORD: Well, good William Shakespeare — it seems the times have found thee out and thou shalt have a most prolific and unnatural year!

WILL: Year? Decade rather or say two for no man could write so many plays at once — why, who would believe it! We would be at the performing of these plays until 1611 at least!

DERBY: I cannot wait. I must see my play upon the boards!

LETTICE: And so must I!

BACON: I was the first to ere arrive!

WILL: Hath not my Master Heminge a say in what performeth when?

ALL: NO!!!

OXFORD: Why we must all draw lots. There is no other way. And so we shall here create the unreliable chronology of this our "Shakespearean" canon — and flaming missive to the future time —.

ALL: 'Tis well, 'tis well. The LOT the LOT!

BACON: I, anon, shall conduct the drawing and post the list at court.

ALL: 'Tis agreed, 'tis agreed.

OXFORD: And thus shall we so pace our work to that of our supposed man, our stalking horse, our WILL — !!

ALL: Hip Hip Hooray! Honest Will! Our Dumb Man! Our BEARD! Our Shakespeare — Simple Will!

OXFORD: One matter more. One play alone to all, but ten to me!

ALL: Why WHY YOU!

OXFORD: Because I have so many more plays in me that seethe and prick upon the stony shores of my beleaguered brain — as cannot be contained. And beside — this our sweet device — *(He puts his arm around Will.)* was hit upon by me. I share him with you, but on one condition. This I shall always be — more of SHAKESPEARE than any of thee. Leave thee then thy manuscripts in yonder incoming bucket. And make your diverse ways before this our meeting is discovered. *(They do.)* Well, good Will, thou hast thy work cut out.

WILL: My lord —, a question I pray you. If all at court now know that I am a stalking horse, a blind, a BEARD —

OXFORD: Ay, and do greatly LOVE thee for it —

WILL: — Then WHOM do we conspire to confound?
(Pause.)

OXFORD: *(Momentarily stumped.)* Why, I must revolve me upon this question. Farewell. Oh — and you'll take a look at *Timon*, won't you?

WILL: Tell them.

OXFORD: What?

WILL: At court — ! The poems, at least. — TELL them that I am "I" —

OXFORD: Listen. What does it MATTER who wrote them — they're OUT there — for all time. Someone wrote them. Thee, me, we, whoever. 'Tis all one. It's really about the work. Don't you think? Bury my name where my body lies, simplicity, anonymity — oblivion, GOD how I crave it.

WILL: Of COURSE you do! You're already famous!

OXFORD: *(Irritable.)* Look, what are you complaining about. You're set for LIFE aren't you, you bought the NEW place, didn't you — *(Puts his arm around Will — conspiratorially.)* Between ourselves, I've really come to value your contributions.

WILL: Contributions?

OXFORD: You've a knack. I've never denied it.

WILL: A knack?

OXFORD: — A speech here, soliloquy there — some accidental insight into the soul of the common man —

WILL: Accidental!

OXFORD: — or a KING for that matter — I've wondered how you do it, I confess — you lucky natural, you devil, you SAVANT you — How DID you come up with Juliet? All I had was Mercutio.

WILL: You're claiming it all, aren't you. Sir Edward — Bloody De Vere, now Honeyed De Vere, and no one knows why. Well, I QUIT!

OXFORD: Dare you renounce me! What did you expect?

WILL: I thought at least you might sort of raise an EYEbrow when my name came up . . .

OXFORD: Do what?

WILL: — create some mystery, some confusion —

OXFORD: You're joking —

WILL: — a sort of cloudy authorship ISSUE, maybe.

OXFORD: You mean let them suspect that I'm tag-teaming with a low-down small-time bit-player?

WILL: What did you say?

OXFORD: Forget it. You can't really believe anyone's going to hang a laurel wreath on YOU do you? A thing lofty, that is — Myself, may stoop. SLUMMING is a sign of LIFE! But let you come up from Nowhere — with some freakish GIFT! Without precedent! Imagine a humble kitchen garden.

WILL: My Lord has never SEEN a kitchen garden.

OXFORD: Should the root vegetable displace the rose, disorder would run rampant!

WILL: Your allegory is drawn all of rhetoric, nothing of nature.

OXFORD: *(Grabbing him by the jerkin.)* Correct my ALLEGORY! Thou FELLOW! KNAVE! FOOL! Why? What's wrong with it.

WILL: Correct it thyself. If thou cans't. Oh, Lonely! I shall wander the face of the earth!

OXFORD: But Will! I am your PATRON! We have work!

WILL: I shall have lost years!

OXFORD: Your friend!

WILL: I am NO man, and have no friend. No home, no fixed address — I go I go to beg my fortune of the kinder wild beasts! — I know not where I care not where I go I go —

OXFORD: Your Benefactor!

WILL: I care not! I am leaving the theater!!

(Thunderclap — he takes his cloak and exits in a crash of lightning.)

SCENE EIGHT

A storm on a Heath near Stratford. Will enters. He is drunk. A bundled, wretched, hooded servant is with him. Will staggers down to the lip of the stage.

WILL: Blow winds and crack your cheeks! Mountains fart yourselves! SEA puke! and OCEANS vomit yourselves sick upon the shore! Fire unsheathe thy pizzle and piss flames upon the wondering crowds beneath!

COLIN: Hoo hoo hoo. Please Master Will, Colin's a'cold. Come inside now — come in to thy wife!!

WILL: Never! I abjure all roof, all hearth, all comfort! I shall go — into the barn. Colin — come.

COLIN: Oh hoo hoo hoo!

(Thunderclap. Will staggers into the barn, Colin following.)

SCENE NINE

The Barn. Some days later. Anne, Will, and Colin. A picnic. Sounds of chickens, songbirds, and happiness.

ANNE: Here lies the bones of old Doc Burns —

WILL: Whose soul on Satan's fire-pit turns —

COLIN: *(Beating on the ground.)* Hoo Hoo Hoo!! Another, another!

ANNE: When home to heaven Whately goes —

WILL: The devil nippeth at her toes.

COLIN: HEE HEE HEE — Have at it!

WILL: Now I lay me down to sleep —
　　　And pray the Lord to sell my Sheep
　　　But if you cannot sell for ten —
　　　Please bring me back to life again!
　　　(Colin laughs.)

ANNE: Will.

WILL: Anne.

ANNE: I'm sorry for all.

WILL: Nay, I'm sorry.

(They lean in for a kiss. Colin farts.)

ANNE: Leave us awhile, sweet Colin, to those enraptured musings that amorous absence hath so long delayed —

COLIN: HOO HEE HEE HOO!

ANNE: GO!

COLIN: I go, anon, I go. *(Exits.)*

ANNE: Dids't thou — whilst you were away — not that I'd blame you . . .

WILL: Ask not. Dids't thou . . . Not that I'd blame you.

ANNE: Ask not.

WILL: Why not?

ANNE: Thou bid'st ME ask not.

WILL: Well, 'tis different for women.

ANNE: Why.

WILL: All do know why. It just IS, that's all.

ANNE: Oh, goodly answer.

WILL: Dost tart thy tongue at me that late did vow nothing but honey?

ANNE: Nay, forgive me, sweet.

WILL: Of course, my love. How was it that I could not see, in all the betrayals of this world, a good wife who waited for me through my folly? Why Sweet, why doth thy cheek to pale? Where flee thy former roses?

ANNE: It's nothing.

WILL: I shall never leave thee again. Blessed Saint whom I do not deserve!
     (Enter Heminge and Condel.)

WILL: You!

HEMINGE: Afternoon. We happened to be in town —

ANNE: You!

WILL: Good Wife, fetch us some small beer.

ANNE: I go. *(Passing them.)* You — are not welcome here.

CONDEL: Charming woman.

HEMINGE: You look well! Doesn't he look well?

CONDEL: Certainly he doth.

HEMINGE: How goes it?

WILL: Oh, very well. My wife has brought me twins in my two years absence.

CONDEL\HEMINGE: Oh, congratulations. Congratulations.

CONDEL: We'll get right to the point. Things aren't going well back at the playhouse. Awful.

HEMINGE: Terrible.

CONDEL: Couldn't be worse.

HEMINGE: These noble plays are unperformable! And I speaketh as one who hath produced *Scurvy Wives!*

WILL: Why come you all this way to tell this to ME? A self-inflated pig's bladder?

CONDEL: Many things were spoke in haste that were regretted later.

WILL: Ah. *(Pause.)* Really terrible, are they?

HEMINGE: Beyond all believing. One for example, this Lear and his Daughters — by Lady Lettice —

CONDEL: Ghastly!

HEMINGE: Nothing but the reading of a WILL all the way to the FINIS — what MEANS this lady — "my pewter spoon — china-soup dish — my hundred pair of shoes," and on and on and on — a hundred pages!

CONDEL: She said all people of quality 'twould be interested in the extent of the Royal King's possessions.

HEMINGE: We're done if we present it.

(Sits heavily by Will.)

WILL: A pity.

CONDEL: And My Lord of Derby's play!

WILL: Oh?

HEMINGE: *Any Way You Want It.* A "romp"! Two lords ride into the forest, of a Sunday, and there do murder every living thing that moves within its leafy confines. This be the sum and total of its action.

CONDEL: Further he proposeth to incorporate a bear and BAIT it.

HEMINGE: Further, both Lords are named Jock. Because, my lord sayeth, it is his favorite name. *(Pause.)* There is a part for you, if you're interested.

WILL: Ah! Which? A clown, a bumpkin, or a ghost?

HEMINGE: Old Adam. The torturer.

WILL: A Torturer! *(He laughs, its the relaxed laugh of a free man.)* I cannot play a torturer. I love all things living. Why even when I was a lad, when the butchering began in November . . . I would hie me to the forest of Arden — and hide me there.

(Crosses away from them, to his workbench. Picks up a piece of broken harness, turns it absentmindedly in his hands. The men watch him, aware of a change in him.)

CONDEL: Why, Will. I thought thou wast a poacher of deer.

WILL: *(Thoughtfully.)* . . . I was so branded, but truly, I could not kill me one. It irked me so that the poor dappled fools being native burghers in their own city should in their own confines with forked heads have their round haunches gored . . .

HEMINGE: *(To Condel.)* See that's exactly what it needs!

WILL: *(Lost in the sweetness of the memory.)* — Oh, sweet Arden —. You know, really, it was there — in the gentle and flowing breast of nature, that I found my tongue. In trees. My books in running brooks and good in everything.

CONDEL: — a gentler thought was never spoke —

HEMINGE: *(Outburst.)* Will! Come back with us. And bend your thought upon this most vile comedy.

WILL: Apply you to me? Why! Hath no other amusing knave got my knack for STAGE BUSINESS?

CONDEL: I said I was —

HEMINGE: Nay. Nor thy Taste —

CONDEL: Even-ness —

HEMINGE: Diverse brilliancies, handsome turns —

CONDEL: Sweet and piercing touches —

HEMINGE: Unac-COUNT-table vocabulary!

CONDEL: — unexpected use of FISHING terms —

HEMINGE: 'Tis YOU we needeth for our desperate hour! Will!

CONDEL: Friend —

HEMINGE: Fellow!

CONDEL: Partner!

HEMINGE: "Shakespeare!"

(Long pause. Will takes it in, struggling with something in himself.)

WILL: *(Quietly.)* Give the plays to Oxford.

CONDEL: He's not — you.

HEMINGE: Besides. He's got the plague.

WILL: What?

HEMINGE: He lies abandoned at his ancestral home.

CONDEL: Close to death, I've heard. Attended by no one, they say.

HEMINGE: Sorry. Perhaps we should have written.

ANNE: *(Re-entering.)* Here's some BEER, and pickled BEETS and some nice — chickweed pie, how long since you've had THAT!

WILL: I have to leave —

ANNE: How funny you are.

(Heminge and Condel back out.)

CONDEL\HEMINGE: Good-bye, well, Good-bye — wonderful to see you — Will, we'll wait for you at the Inn!

ANNE: What?

WILL: *(To Anne.)* I'm sorry, but something's come up —

ANNE: Something's come UP! Not one hour ago you swore to me that we were one, all distance forgot, that all would be made well to me —

WILL: I'll write — *(Exits.)*

ANNE: You'll write. YOU'LL WRITE! I can't READ! — you BASTARD!

SCENE TEN

Oxford's bedchamber. Oxford lies in bed. He is dying. Wriothesley is with him.

OXFORD: It is too much! I suffer, I burn! A POX upon this PLAGUE!

WRIOTHESLEY: Lie still, you upset yourself and make it worse.

OXFORD: Oh, Henry, curse the fatal infection that doth unknit my bones — I shall die! I shall DIE! *(More conversationally.)* Really, you shouldn't be here, Darling — I'm catching.

WRIOTHESLEY: I am here, and here I do remain, until thine end. Where suffering stops, where rest begins. And there are no devouring worms where you will go. They live all above with us the living.

OXFORD: My fever o'erwhelms me, quip by quip. I cannot think of anything funny. I cannot think of anything at all. A vacant chamber of aching halls. Oh hell. Who's here?

(Will enters.)

WRIOTHESLEY: *(Surprised.)* 'Tis Will —.

OXFORD: I hear my Muse hath fled me for a Country Dwelling.

WILL: My Lord, my noble friend —

OXFORD: Do you weep, sensitive Will, Gentle Will, Usurping WILL, Who has won thy bread, and made thy bed in borrowed fame? Who dare to couple with the Great under cover of thy NAME?

WRIOTHESLEY: Hush, Edward! Why do you abuse him that loves you? Mark how his tears do flow for you —

OXFORD: Dying makes one out of temper, Will. Forgive your friend, and think not ill of me when I am gone.

(Will moves to him. Sinks down next to bed.)

WILL: My Lord — whose friendship gave me everything.

OXFORD: I said that in we two hath Nature's Genius met Art's. But I could not have thought of FALSTAFF!

(He begins choking.)

WRIOTHESLEY: This railing doth further thy infirmity.

OXFORD: Long live thee in thy clarity, friend. And by the way, that was no whore, that was thy wife.

WRIOTHESLEY: Why do you tell him that?

WILL: *(Looking up.)* What is that thou tell'st me?

OXFORD: That darksome, gamesome toothsome bawd that we two did board was thy wife pretending to thee for love's sake — she was thine own.

WILL: *(Can't believe his ears.)* Ahh! Wilt thou destroy the purity of my WIFE and the attraction of my MISTRESS in ONE FOUL REVELATION?

WRIOTHESLEY: Shame, Edward!

WILL: Cuckold me AGAIN, this last upon thy death bed — who cannot even lift thy diseased fig for a CHOIRBOY!?

WRIOTHESLEY: — even upon thy end to twist thy knife —

So foul, so needless, and so cruel a sport?

OXFORD: I know, I know, but it remembereth me what it was to be ALIVE! Remember this, sweet Will. She loved thee well — BEFORE SHE WENT TO BED WITH ME!!! *(He starts laughing, which starts him coughing.)*

WILL: Godspeed. I shall miss your wit and learning, but not your Lordship's cruel humours.

OXFORD: Wait. Will, I had a play I never dared to show.

(He rises unsteadily and crosses to his trunk of manuscripts, D.S. near his writing table. Kneels by it.)

WILL: Why tellst thou me now? When thou hast kick't me shall I love this news or give a damn?

OXFORD: *(Retrieves an old playscript. He handles it tenderly.)* About a man who loves a man and dare not show it. Take it for me, finish it — and proclaim me when I am dead. It's called *Twelfth Night,* in which a boy loves a lord. And almost dies of it.

WILL: *(Uncomfortable.)* Why look you meaningfully upon me?

OXFORD: *(Looks away.)* Unlike my life unlucky, it has a pleasing end where love triumphs. It was something like my story as a boy, and I wish it were told. *(He starts back to his bed.)*

WILL: Why should I do it?

OXFORD: *(With some remaining flourish.)* Because as true as 'tis thou hast great gift for poetry, its also true thou hast no gift for plot. And this *Twelfth Night* has a good plot. *(Gives Will manuscript.)* But call it — *(Weakening.)* what you will.

(Wriothesley helps him to bed.)

OXFORD: That which I fed on, consumest me!! *(His eyes close.)*

WRIOTHESLEY: So far does his disease progress, he stealeth Marlowe's motto. Take him not bitterly, sweet Will. Thy tears wet his hand — that could not shed a tear himself. Thy WORKS shall be when we shall be forgot. Take his trunk of manuscripts, make them live as he could not.

(Will crosses to trunk. Oxford gestures for him to take it. He does. Crosses out of Oxford's chambers, starts up the stairs to the above. He turns out, and from

behind him, the figure of Geoffrey enters — a dream-image of the boy-player that sang in Stratford so many years ago. He stands above.)

GEOFFREY: And so in the mind of man, below as so above

Everything from nothing comes —

To those who — love —.

(Geoffrey looks toward Shakespeare, Shakespeare looks toward audience . . . lights fade.)

END OF PLAY

* NOTE for the staging of *The Taming of the Shrew:*

This scene has certain shape requirements. In order for it to play coherently, it needs to be very specifically scored and detailed. Whatever choices are made in terms of movement, sound, and choreography, they must allow Elizabeth to be the reactive focal point of the scene. She is the organizing element of the hyperactive play beneath — so either by stop-actions, occasional slow-motions, or accidentally placed "gaps" the audience needs to know to look to her for her key moments.

What follows is the essential storyboard of *Shrew's* plot-points to be used for the play within the play. Generally, the strategy might be to tell the story of the Shrew like an old-fashioned silent movie, a musical score providing bursts of 10 seconds or so of Renaissance-style Chase Music, as the players scramble to form themselves into an image from Shakespeare's play. The music\tableau needs to hold briefly, so that Elizabeth can interject, then the company has another 10 seconds of frenetic or acrobatic physical transition, exaggerated character walk, etc. to form into the next tableau. An attractive solution is to use a drop that they constantly rotate around, emerging into different scene-moments, so the movement flow is constant. Elizabeth's interjections have been written to comment on the following moments from Shakespeare's *The Taming of the Shrew.* All of the players can be used for all the images.

(Picking up after Elizabeth's: What doth the idiot? He hath not another line there! He doth overspeak his part!)

OXFORD: What sayeth her Magna Regina?

ELIZABETH: Nay, I spoke of nothing. Hush! Petruchio is to TAKE her now. You shall see!

(Music. Action. Tableau — Petruchio joining Kate in a forced embraced before an exaggeratedly astonished Baptista.)

ELIZABETH: *(Aroused.)* NOW she shall come to know her keeper's call!

(Music. Action. Tableau —Two suitors, one with a broken lute over his head, Tableau — Kate melodramatically weeping, stood up at her wedding — before sniggering Bianca, unhappy Baptista, and perturbed Guests. Petruchio and Grumio lurk.)

ELIZABETH: *(Deeply moved.)* Left alone at the altar, oh poor girl!

(Music. Action. Tableau — Petruchio abducting Kate on his back, as company mimes chase. Grumio holding them at bay.)

ELIZABETH: *(Enthralled.)* SEE how he snatches her away from all the guests!

(Music. Action. Tableau — The taunting starvation of Kate by Grumio — as hidden Petruchio and "servants" watch.)

ELIZABETH: *(Thrilled.)* Cut down to SIZE! How like you THAT, my Girl!
   (Music. Action. Tableau — Kate and Petruchio join hands, a happy procession behind them.)
ELIZABETH: *(Ecstatic.)* Ay me! What a story! How will it end!
   (There is a little trill of happy resolve music. Company restores to real time.)
PETRUCHIO: Lord how bright and goodly shines the moon!
   (And etc.)

BEE-LUTHER-HATCHEE

Thomas Gibbons

PLAYWRIGHT'S BIOGRAPHY

Thomas Gibbons is playwright-in-residence at InterAct Theatre Company in Philadelphia, which has premiered six of his plays: *Pretending to America, 6221, Axis Sally, Black Russian, Bee-luther-hatchee,* and *Permanent Collection.* His plays have also been seen at the National Playwrights Conference at the Eugene O'Neill Theatre Center, off-off-Broadway at Blue Heron Theatre, Northlight Theatre, Florida Stage, Unicorn Theatre, Repertory Theatre of St. Louis, Arizona Theatre Company, Center Stage, and many other theaters. He is the recipient of six playwriting fellowships from the Pennsylvania Council on the Arts, a Roger L. Stevens Award from The Fund for New American Plays, two Barrymore Awards for Outstanding New Play, a Barrie and Bernice Stavis Playwriting Award, and a Pew Fellowship in the Arts.

ORIGINAL PRODUCTION

Bee-luther-hatchee was first produced by InterAct Theatre Company on March 10, 1999. Director Seth Rozin; set by Stephen Dickerson; lights by Peter Jakubowski; costumes by Margaret McCarty; sound design by Seth Rozin and Ron Schindlinger; stage manage, Patricia Sabato. The cast was as follows:

SHELITA BURNS	*Shelita Birchett*
LIBBY PRICE	*Cathy Simpson*
REPORTER / ROBERT	*Russ Widdall*
ANNA/ SISTER MARGARET	*Catharine Slusar*
SEAN LEONARD	*Tim Moyer*

CHARACTERS
LIBBY PRICE

SHELITA BURNS

INTERVIEWER

SISTER MARGARET

ROBERT

ANNA

WOMAN

SEAN LEONARD

The following parts are doubled:

LIBBY PRICE/WOMAN

INTERVIEWER/ROBERT

SISTER MARGARET/ANNA

SETTING
The present. The play takes place in various locations.

BEE-LUTHER-HATCHEE

ACT I

SCENE ONE

A light rises on Shelita Burns sitting at her desk. She is African-American, in her mid-thirties, attractive and well-dressed. She is reading the first page of a manuscript. Across the stage a light picks out Libby Price; she is also African-American. Her face has a peculiarly ageless quality; she could be younger, or older, than one would guess. Something about her clothes — not flamboyance but an oddness of color or combination — unmistakably sets her apart.

LIBBY: I been a drifter all my life.

I never liked stayin' too long in one place. For a little while it would be all right, then one day I'd look at folks and their faces would be gray and transparent — like a Sunday mornin' veil. And I'd know it was time to move on. For a long time I used to wonder what was wrong with people. One day, I realized this must be what the world looks like to a ghost.

I decided I had a different kind of soul. A smoke-soul, I call it. 'Cause the thing about smoke is, you can see it all right, it's real enough — for a second. But try to grab it, your hand goes right through. And a heartbeat later, it's gone.

(Shelita turns the page. Blackout.)

SCENE TWO

In the darkness, applause. Spotlight on Shelita standing at a podium, poised and confident. An award sits on the podium before her.

SHELITA: Thank you. Thank you very much.

It gives me great pleasure to accept the Haywood Award for Nonfiction on behalf of Libby Price. Unfortunately, Libby is unable to be here tonight, but I have a message from her. *(She unfolds a piece of paper.)* "My seventy-two years are weighing too heavy on me to let me come up to New York. But I want to say thank you to the League. All my life I've been talking, but until now I never thought anyone was listening."

(Laughter modulates into applause as Shelita folds the letter.)

If I may add a personal note . . . As editor of the series *Rediscovered Voices,* this award gives me particular satisfaction. For three hundred years the African-American voice has been silenced in this country. Many profound works of literature have been ignored, ridiculed, belittled — or never allowed to see the light of day at all. The purpose of this series is to reclaim those works from the silence.

Now, finally, they are being heard. They are being heeded.

Finally, the silence is lifting.

Thank you.

(Sustained applause. Shelita lifts the award and poses subtly as cameras flash.)

SCENE THREE

Shelita's office at Transit Press in New York. Shelita stands behind the desk, shaking hands with the Interviewer who has just arrived. He is a white man in his late thirties. To one side of the desk is the award. Two chairs are nearby.

INTERVIEWER: Thank you for seeing me, Ms. Burns.

SHELITA: Who says no to the *Times? (She motions him to one of the chairs and comes out from behind the desk to take the other.)* Please sit down, Mr. Clark.

INTERVIEWER: *(Lifting the award for a closer look:)* So this is what it looks like up close. Ms. Price hasn't picked it up yet?

SHELITA: Not yet. Would you like some coffee?

INTERVIEWER: No thanks. I'm allowed three cups a day, and the next one isn't for hours. *(He puts the award back on the desk and takes a notebook and tape recorder from his briefcase.)* Mind if I record this?

SHELITA: Not at all.

INTERVIEWER: *(Into the recorder.)* Interview with Shelita Burns, November 15. *(He looks up at her.)* Why don't we start with a little about your background . . . Where are you from?

SHELITA: Philadelphia.

INTERVIEWER: School?

SHELITA: Princeton.

INTERVIEWER: How did you get into publishing?

SHELITA: Two experiences, really. My junior year I had a summer internship with the university press. Typical editorial assistant chores — copying, a little proofreading. The work itself wasn't very exciting, but the environment was. The *idea* of publishing.

INTERVIEWER: *(With a smile:)* You thought it was glamorous, right? It still has an aura.

SHELITA: I thought it was worthy. *(Pause.)* The next year I was working on my thesis on Zora Neale Hurston. I discovered that most of the other black writers I needed to read — for context, for a sense of her world — well, I couldn't find their books. Particularly the women. Langston Hughes, yes, but not Nella Larsen or Marita Bonner or Jessie Redmon Fauset. Those writers were long out of print.

INTERVIEWER: Last night you used the word "silenced."

SHELITA: If you take away a people's literature, you take away their collective consciousness, their sense of their own unique identity. We've been allowed to have jazz and the blues . . . but very few books.

INTERVIEWER: And that was the genesis of *Rediscovered Voices?*

SHELITA: Yes. After graduating I worked at Random House for a while. I proposed the series to them — the black voice from our arrival in America to the present. Slave narratives, memoirs, novels that had disappeared — the *excluded* voice. They weren't very interested, though. Then I happened to mention it to one of Transit's editors. They invited me to do it here.

INTERVIEWER: It's certainly been a remarkable success.

SHELITA: *(With undisguised pride:)* Eighteen titles published so far, average sales of forty thousand each. We've demonstrated there is an African-American audience hungry for our own stories. Of course, *Bee-luther-hatchee* has done much better — a hundred thousand copies and counting.

INTERVIEWER: It's also the first new title in the series — by a living writer. How did you find it?

SHELITA: It came in over the transom. No agent, no recommendation from anyone.

INTERVIEWER: The classic publishing fairy tale.

SHELITA: I picked it up because of the title. My grandmother used to use the word, but I've never heard it from anyone else. When I read the first page I felt that . . . tingle, you know? The certainty that you're about to read something that will change you. I took the manuscript home and stayed up all night with it.

INTERVIEWER: What do you think accounts for the book's success?

SHELITA: I believe it's the authenticity of Libby Price's voice. It's intensely *personal.* This explains the popularity of memoirs, I think — readers want the particular reality of a lived life.

(The Interviewer nods, then leans forward to change the course of the conversation, his tone slightly puzzled.)

INTERVIEWER: You know, as part of my research for this I thought I'd read some interviews with Libby. And I couldn't find any. Not one.

SHELITA: She hasn't given any.

INTERVIEWER: Why not?

SHELITA: Well, she's seventy-two years old, her health is poor, she lives in a nursing home . . . She doesn't want her life overturned by the media. *(Pause.)* Also, I think the book is her way of making final peace with some things in her life. That extraordinary episode with Robert, for example . . . In any case, that was her condition — no interviews, no book signings, not even a photo on the jacket.

INTERVIEWER: She sounds eccentric.

SHELITA: She'd hardly be the first writer to value her privacy over fame. Look at Salinger, look at Pynchon. It drove our publicity people crazy at first. Now we all feel protective of her.

INTERVIEWER: How is she reacting to the book's success?

SHELITA: I think she's a bit overwhelmed. First the reviews, now the Haywood . . . As a matter of fact, I'm going to present it to her the day after tomorrow. A surprise. I'm looking forward to meeting her.

INTERVIEWER: *(Suddenly alert.)* Wait a minute, *you've* never — ?

SHELITA: No. All our contact has been through the mail. Not even a phone call — she's practically deaf. *(With a smile, she indicates the award.)* She asked me to send *this* to her in the mail. But I want to put it in her hands myself.

INTERVIEWER: Have you thought about what you'll say to her?

SHELITA: I want to tell her how much her book has meant to me. How honored I am to be the one to bring it to the world. *(Pause.)* I want to say to her . . . as a young woman of color to her elder, as a *daughter* . . . that her life has given me an example of courage and dignity — *(She pauses, unexpectedly overcome by emotion.)* I'm sorry, I . . . God, it sounds maudlin.

INTERVIEWER: Obviously many readers feel the same way.

SHELITA: *(Collecting herself.)* You're right. I can't tell you how many letters we've forwarded to Libby. Hundreds, easily. It's a book people take to their hearts.

INTERVIEWER: Any chance I could accompany you?

SHELITA: Come with me? I don't . . .

INTERVIEWER: A brief interview, that's all. No photographer, just me.

SHELITA: I really don't think I could spring that on Libby. I hope you understand.

INTERVIEWER: What's the name of the nursing home?

SHELITA: Sorry, I can't tell you.

INTERVIEWER: Off the record?

SHELITA: It's down South. That's all I can say.

INTERVIEWER: I see. *(Pause.)* Tell me, will there be another book from Libby?

SHELITA: *(With a smile.)* I'm wondering that myself. Another reason for my visit. *(She glances at her watch.)* I'm sorry to cut this short, but I'm due at an editorial conference in a few minutes.

INTERVIEWER: I think I have what I need. Thanks again for seeing me.
(He gathers up his notebook and tape recorder.)

SHELITA: *(Standing:)* If you have any more questions, please feel free to call me.

INTERVIEWER: I will. *(He hands her a business card.)* Here's my number. If you change your mind . . . *(They shake hands.)* Good luck with your meeting. *(He goes. After a moment Shelita makes a tiny gesture of anger.)*

SCENE FOUR

A bar. Anna sits at a table sipping a drink. She is white, in her mid-thirties, well-dressed. A martini is placed in front of the second chair. After a moment Shelita hurries on.

SHELITA: Anna — sorry I'm late. The traffic — !

ANNA: I was afraid you didn't have time for me anymore, what with picking up awards and being interviewed by the *Times.*

SHELITA: Until the story comes out you're still my friend. After that . . . *(They laugh. Shelita sits and sees the drink.)* Is this mine?

ANNA: I ordered for you.

SHELITA: Thanks. *(She takes a sip.)*

ANNA: So when does the story come out?

SHELITA: Next week sometime — he wasn't sure. *(Pause.)* It was so *strange,* Anna. You think you're prepared, you're going to get your points across, and suddenly it veers off in a completely unexpected direction . . .

ANNA: Never trust a journalist. Especially not a good one. He didn't get you to say anything embarrassing, did he?

SHELITA: No. *(Suddenly she takes a deep breath.)*

ANNA: Are you OK?

SHELITA: I just have to catch my breath. I feel like I can't *breathe*. Things are . . . eventful right now.

ANNA: You have a book on the best-seller list. Enjoy it!

SHELITA: There's something else.

ANNA: Really? *(She smiles.)* Have you met someone?

SHELITA: No, it's the same old desert out there. *(She grins, enjoying the suspense.)* I've been offered a job — by one of the big houses. I can't tell you which one, it might jinx it.

ANNA: It's not us, is it?

SHELITA: No. They took me out to lunch today and dropped it on me. Senior editor. More money — a lot more! — a corner office, A-list authors . . . or at least the top of the B-list.

ANNA: Shelita, this is wonderful. You're a *star*. Let's order champagne!
(She turns to signal a waiter.)

SHELITA: No, please, Anna . . . Nothing is definite.

ANNA: Why not? You're taking it, aren't you?

SHELITA: I told them I needed to think about it.

ANNA: What's to think about?

SHELITA: It's not so simple. I'd have to walk away from what I'm doing now — and what I'm doing is important. And it's *mine* — my own series.

ANNA: For a small house that's . . .

SHELITA: "Marginal"?

ANNA: I was going to say "specialized." Come on, Shelita: Transit has a hard time getting its books in the stores, much less getting reviews, *attention* . . .

SHELITA: We're getting attention now.

ANNA: *Bee-luther-hatchee* has put you at the center of things — for a moment. Take advantage of it.

SHELITA: I don't know, Anna, a house like this, it's so . . .

ANNA: "White"?

SHELITA: I was going to say "mainstream."

ANNA: Do they publish any black writers?

SHELITA: A few. They'd like to find more. The black voice is hot right now.

ANNA: So they came to you.

SHELITA: It's just about making money to them, that's all.

ANNA: Well, of *course*.

SHELITA: It's about something else to me. *(Pause.)* I have to admit, though . . . working on Libby's book has made me a little impatient with the past. I want the new. The manuscript no one's read before.

ANNA: They're giving you the chance, Shelita. While they're making money, you can find the next Libby Price. A twenty-five-year-old Libby Price with a lifetime of books to write. And if you do it in a bigger office with a nicer view, what's wrong with that?

(A pause, then Shelita smiles.)

SHELITA: Trees outside my window . . . That would be nice.

(At once Anna motions offstage.)

ANNA: Waiter — a bottle of your best champagne! *(She turns to Shelita with a smile.)* I've always wanted to say that.

(They laugh.)

SCENE FIVE

Libby appears in a spotlight.

LIBBY: Mobile. Tallahassee. New Orleans.

Southern names.

Norfolk. Savannah. Natchitoches.

I been to all them, and a hundred other places most people never heard of.

Budalean. Goldonna. Rosepine. Zebulon.

I've traveled in just about any way you can think of. By car, by bus, by truck, on foot plenty of times. Once in a wagon pulled by a horse, down dirt roads that never turned the page on the twentieth century. Whenever I could afford it, though — not often — I'd travel by train.

Two steel rods hammered into the earth, runnin' straight or curvin' 'round a bend, shinin' in the sun or dull and gray on a cloudy day. You climb aboard and find a seat, and that's where choice ends. The train takes you where the track leads. You can always get off at the next station. But while a train is movin', all you can do is sit back and let it carry you into the future.

SCENE SIX

The Green Lane Residence in Charlotte, North Carolina. Lights up on a small office. Shelita sits in a chair facing the desk. After a moment Sister Margaret enters. She wears conservative, unadorned clothing.

SISTER MARGARET: Ms. Burns?

SHELITA: Yes.

SISTER MARGARET: How do you do. I'm Sister Margaret, the director of Green Lane Residence.

(She takes Shelita's hand.)

SHELITA: Pleased to meet you.

SISTER MARGARET: I must tell you, you've created something of a stir.

SHELITA: Have I?

SISTER MARGARET: It's not every day that we have a visitor who looks like you.

SHELITA: *(Hardening slightly.)* I'm not sure what you . . .

SISTER MARGARET: What you're wearing, I mean. It's obvious you're not from around here.

SHELITA: I see. No, I'm from New York.

SISTER MARGARET: *(Impressed.)* New York!

SHELITA: I hope I'm not upsetting the . . .

SISTER MARGARET: Oh, a bit of excitement is good for the residents. So much of their day is structured. They'll be buzzing about you for the rest of the month. Now then, would you like a tour?

SHELITA: *(Slightly puzzled.)* A tour? No, I don't think so . . .

SISTER MARGARET: *(Sitting behind the desk:)* Although the Residence is operated by the Sisters of Mercy, we're fully licensed by the appropriate state agencies. The facility is inspected twice a year and always receives excellent ratings.

SHELITA: I think there's been some kind of misunderstanding.

SISTER MARGARET: We do have a waiting list, I'm afraid. Are you seeking a place for a parent?

SHELITA: *(Smiling:)* No, no — that's not why I'm here.

SISTER MARGARET: You have a relative here, then?

SHELITA: No.

SISTER MARGARET: Well, now I *am* intrigued. How can I help you?

SHELITA: I'm here to see your star resident.

SISTER MARGARET: Pardon me?

SHELITA: I'm Libby's editor, you see — with Transit Press. I don't know if you've heard — *Bee-luther-hatchee* just won the Haywood Award. It's a major prize, very prestigious. I thought I'd surprise Libby and present it to her in person.

SISTER MARGARET: *(Frowning:)* Libby . . .

SHELITA: I asked to see you because I thought perhaps we could use your office. It would be a little more private. I hope I wasn't being presumptuous. Of course you'd be welcome to stay.

SISTER MARGARET: I'm afraid I don't understand . . .

SHELITA: I have to confess, the real reason for my trip is to finally meet her. She's a remarkable writer — a remarkable *woman.* Have you had a chance to read the book?

SISTER MARGARET: Please, Ms. Burns . . . Who is this Libby?

SHELITA: Libby Price, of course.

SISTER MARGARET: Libby Price? *(She shakes her head.)* There's no one here by that name.

SHELITA: Of course there is. *Elisabeth* Price.

SISTER MARGARET: No, I'm sorry . . .

SHELITA: Sister, as the director you obviously have many administrative responsibilities. I wouldn't expect you to know every resident personally.

SISTER MARGARET: Ms. Burns, at the moment we have exactly eighty-three residents — fifty-seven women and twenty-six men. I've tended to every one of them, their bodies as well as their souls. I know their names, I know how often their children visit — if they visit at all — and I know the precise ratio of hope to despair in each one.

(Pause.)

SHELITA: I apologize, Sister. I didn't mean to suggest —

SISTER MARGARET: No, I'm sorry. One of our residents passed away yesterday. It has an effect.

SHELITA: This must be very difficult work sometimes.

SISTER MARGARET: Yes. But unexpectedly fulfilling, too. People think the most intimate human connection is sex. In my experience it's being an escort to death. *(She spreads her hands.)* Obviously there's been some kind of mistake, Ms. Burns. We have no Libby Price here.

SHELITA: But she's told me she lives here.

SISTER MARGARET: I don't know what else I . . .

SHELITA: She *must* be here.

SISTER MARGARET: You said you've never met this woman. You've spoken to her?

SHELITA: No. But all of her correspondence with the Press gives Green Lane Residence as her address. Here, I have one of her letters . . .

(She looks through her bag, finds an envelope, and gives it to Sister Margaret.)

SISTER MARGARET: Well, there *has* been a mistake. The return address is a post office box. We don't use one of those.

(Pause.)

SHELITA: Does your order have another residence in Charlotte?

SISTER MARGARET: No, we don't. Or anywhere else, for that matter.

SHELITA: *(Quietly, to herself:)* This doesn't make sense . . .

(Pause.)

SISTER MARGARET: Ms. Burns, I don't pretend to know anything about publishing. Apparently you've dealt with this woman for quite some time. Isn't it unusual that you've never met her?

SHELITA: No. We publish writers from all over the world. We may not meet them for years. *(She looks up with a last hope.)* Writers sometimes use pen names. It is possible she's here under a different name?

SISTER MARGARET: But it's clear she isn't. This business with the post office box . . .

SHELITA: Yes . . . Yes, you're right, of course. I don't know what I . . .

SISTER MARGARET: Even putting that aside . . . We strive to provide a dignified and fulfilling environment for people in their last years. Despite our limited resources I think we manage to do that. Unfortunately, we're at close quarters, and one thing residents must surrender when coming here is privacy. It really wouldn't be possible to write a book without everyone knowing. *(Another silence, then she hands the envelope back to Shelita. Gently:)* I'm sorry. I wish I could help you.

SHELITA: Thank you, Sister. *(She puts the envelope in her bag, then stands.)* I won't take any more of your time.

SISTER MARGARET: You've never been in one of these places, have you? A home for the elderly, I mean.

SHELITA: No.

SISTER MARGARET: I could see it in your eyes the moment I walked in. It's disturbing to come face-to-face with what we will eventually become. Endings have none of the promise of beginnings, do they?

(A moment, then Shelita exits.)

SCENE SEVEN

In the darkness a telephone rings. Shelita appears in a light.

SHELITA: Shelita Burns.

(Upstage a light picks out the Interviewer.)

INTERVIEWER: Ms. Burns, this is Brian Clark at the *Times*.

SHELITA: Yes, Mr. Clark. What can I do for you?

INTERVIEWER: You said I should call if I had any more questions.

SHELITA: Yes, it's all right.

INTERVIEWER: I was wondering how your visit with Libby Price went.

SHELITA: *(Caught off guard:)* I — Fine. It went fine.

INTERVIEWER: I'm about to turn in my story, and I thought this would be a nice way to wrap it up. "The editor finally meets her mysterious discovery."

SHELITA: Yes, I see.

INTERVIEWER: It must have been a very emotional moment. For both of you.

SHELITA: I don't think I can . . .

INTERVIEWER: Can I ask what you talked about?

(Pause.)

SHELITA: I'm sorry, Mr. Clark. To say anything more would violate my agreement with Libby.

INTERVIEWER: Yes, I see. You know, I'd really like to talk to her myself. Would you mind asking her about an interview? As I said before, no photographer.

SHELITA: I really don't think I can do that. I gave Libby my word.

INTERVIEWER: Sorry to hear that. *(Pause.)* Well, thanks anyway, Ms. Burns. The story will be in tomorrow's paper.

SHELITA: Thank you. I'll look forward to it.

(The Interviewer disappears. The light holds on Shelita for a moment.)

SCENE EIGHT

The sound of a train whistle receding into the darkness. Libby appears in a spotlight. She wears a faded sweater; a battered suitcase is at her feet.

LIBBY: I never had too much to do with white people.

Growin' up in Charlotte, when I did, that was easy. All the important people in your life were colored — your family, your friends, your neighbors. You went to a colored school with a colored teacher and a colored church with a colored preacher. White folks were around, of course — in the stores and the police and such. But they weren't *close.* You never had to look into their eyes.

You got to be careful with white folks. You can't lie to 'em exactly. But you can't tell 'em the truth either. And always there's a boundary between you and them, which only a fool — or a saint — tries to cross. *(She picks up the suitcase.)* Once in my life — just once — I was that saint. Or fool.

(Robert appears from the shadows behind her. He is wearing a suit and a fedora: an air of modest prosperity. He is white.)

ROBERT: *(Uncertainly:)* Libby . . . ?

(A moment, then Libby turns.)

SCENE NINE

A restaurant. Shelita and Anna are having dinner. A folded section of the New York Times *lies on the table.*

SHELITA: It's outrageous. It's despicable.

ANNA: Why?

SHELITA: What he chose to include. How he presented me.

ANNA: It's a good story. You should be thrilled.

SHELITA: Anna, don't you *see?*

ANNA: No.

SHELITA: What it implies about me. *(She picks up the paper and reads:)* " 'I want to say to her, as a young woman of color to her elder, as a daughter, that her life has given me an example of courage and dignity —' At this point Ms. Burns' eyes clouded over, and she was unable to finish her thought."

(She slaps the paper down.)

ANNA: And that implies — well, what? That you're human, you have emotions? Yes, that is outrageous.

(She smiles, but Shelita refuses to be deflected from her anger.)

SHELITA: Anna, it says that I'm weak and incompetent.

ANNA: It says that you care about the books you publish. What's wrong with that?

SHELITA: "Her eyes clouded over, she was unable to finish her thought —" Don't you recognize the *code?*

ANNA: I recognize the code when I see it. That is not the code.

SHELITA: He could have said, "She left her phrase unfinished" or any one of a dozen other things. He chose a particular combination of words to convey the impression that I'm overly emotional and not quite capable.

ANNA: Why would he do that?

SHELITA: Because he hasn't been given his own column. Because he has the Great American Novel in his desk drawer and can't get it published. Because I'm a black woman, I'm successful, and I have to be put in my place. Pick one.

ANNA: *(Picks up the paper:)* You really believe he did it deliberately?

SHELITA: Well, if he did it unconsciously, it's even worse, isn't it? *(Pause.)* A white person writes about a black person, and those condescending words creep in. Or else it's that bending-over-backwards, look-everyone-*I'm*-not-a-racist tone. You can always tell.

ANNA: *(Noncommittal:)* Hmm. *(She studies the article.)* The picture is good, though.

(Pause.)

SHELITA: Not bad. *(They laugh, Shelita a bit ruefully.)* I'm sorry, Anna, it's just . . . Something very strange happened a couple of days ago. You know I went to Charlotte to meet Libby. At the nursing home.

ANNA: Yes.

(Shelita says nothing.)

ANNA: And — ?

SHELITA: She wasn't there.

ANNA: She moved?

SHELITA: She never lived there. They had no idea who Libby Price was.

ANNA: *(Frowning:)* That's odd . . .

SHELITA: Then I remembered her royalties go to a lawyer in Charlotte. When I called him, he said he couldn't tell me her address. "My client's wishes."

ANNA: But wait — what about the story? *(She picks up the paper.)* Right here. "About her long-anticipated meeting with — "

SHELITA: *(Quoting from memory:)* " — with her reclusive author, Ms. Burns was circumspect. 'It went fine,' she said, and volunteered nothing further. Apparently Libby Price is to remain, at least to everyone else, a tantalizing mystery."

ANNA: But why did he — *(Pause.)* He invented this?

SHELITA: Not exactly . . . He called back the next day and asked about our meeting.

ANNA: And you told him it went fine? Why on earth did you say that?

SHELITA: I don't know . . . He caught me off guard. The words just slipped out.

ANNA: *(In a still voice:)* My God — you lied. *(Suddenly she bursts into laughter.)* You *lied*. To a *journalist*. From the *Times*.

SHELITA: I didn't mean —

ANNA: I'm so proud of you!

SHELITA: Anna —

ANNA: And now you're afraid he'll find out, right? That he'll turn the blinding spotlight of his moral outrage on you? Journalists are lied to all the time, Shelita. They expect it — they *crave* it. After all, if people simply told them the truth, what fun would they have?

SHELITA: I don't care about *him*, Anna. Why did Libby lie to *me*?

ANNA: For the same reason anyone does. She has something to protect. *(She gestures dismissively.)* She's an old woman, Shelita. Allow her a few eccentricities.

SHELITA: I've checked with friends at other houses. *Bee-luther-hatchee* didn't make the usual rounds. Libby sent it to *me*. I worked on it for a year. You know what it's like — you write back and forth, you share things. I even told her about Paul.

ANNA: That *jerk*. *(She shakes her head.)* Men with rings . . .

SHELITA: Libby and I have a relationship.

ANNA: You're her editor, that's all. Don't confuse it with something else.

SHELITA: Like what?

ANNA: Come on, Shelita, it must have occurred to you before now. It's so *obvious*. *(She reads from the article:)* "I want to say to her as a young woman of color to her elder, as a *daughter* —"

SHELITA: What are you — I didn't mean it *literally.*

ANNA: It's the word you used.

SHELITA: *(Angrily:)* This is ridiculous. Libby is not some kind of mother substitute.

ANNA: As long as I've known you — what is it, ten, *twelve* years now? — the subject of your family has been off limits. You never talk about them.

SHELITA: That's not true — I have told you. My father died, my mother left. I was raised by my grandmother. Until I was twelve years old I thought *she* was my mother.

ANNA: A few facts, yes. Then the wall goes up. It's going up *now*.

SHELITA: I don't believe in advertising my pain, Anna.

ANNA: You don't believe in opening up. My parents' breakup was painful for me, and you've heard every last detail. *(Pause.)* Do you remember your mother at all?

(Pause.)

SHELITA: I have a vague memory of someone. *(Her tone is exasperated, but as she continues she is drawn into the memory.)* I was playing in the living room one day — I must have been four or five. My grandmother was upstairs cleaning. And a woman appeared at the screen door.

(Upstage a Woman appears in silhouette.)

WOMAN: Shelita? Is that *you?*

SHELITA: Who are you?

WOMAN: Look how big you got — !

SHELITA: *(Assertively:)* I ain't supposed to talk to strangers.

WOMAN: I ain't a stranger, honey.

SHELITA: The light was behind her — I couldn't see her face. But her voice . . .

WOMAN: I wish you wouldn't look at me like that. Don't you recognize me?

SHELITA: *(Uncertainly:)* No . . .

WOMAN: I recognize you.

SHELITA: There was something in her voice, a tone words can't capture . . .

WOMAN: *(Tenderly.)* I ain't seen you in such a long time . . .

SHELITA: Then my grandmother came down the steps and told me to go to my room. Her voice was quiet but I could see she was upset. Sitting on my bed, I could hear their voices floating up through the floor. Angry words. The door slammed. When I looked out my window I saw the woman walking down the street, fast. I remember staring at her and thinking, turn around, look back. Look at me. I wanted to see her face. But she turned the corner and disappeared.

(The Woman has vanished. After a moment Anna murmurs sympathetically:)

ANNA: Shelita, I'm so . . .

SHELITA: Was it even her? It was a long time ago.

ANNA: Did you ever try to find her?

SHELITA: It's not like an adoption. When people vanish, they don't leave records. *(Pause.)* I hired a private detective about ten years ago. He felt sorry for me, I think — I certainly couldn't afford to pay him much. He never came up with anything, though. *(A moment, then she shrugs.)* So — a story without an ending. And it has nothing to do with Libby.

ANNA: If you say so.

SHELITA: Her book has changed my life, Anna. And she's *alive*. Is it so strange that I want to meet her?

ANNA: Writers can create illusions out of the best part of themselves. What's left over can be . . .

SHELITA: What?

ANNA: A disappointing reality. Leave her alone.

SHELITA: For all I know, she's working on another book. If she is, I want to sign it. Imagine walking into the new job with *that* contract in my pocket!

ANNA: So how are you going to find your reclusive author?

SHELITA: I wrote her a letter about my trip to the nursing home. Asking why she found it necessary to deceive me. *(Pause.)* I wasn't very nice.

ANNA: Any answer?

SHELITA: Not yet.

ANNA: *(Sighing:)* I envy you, Shelita.

SHELITA: Me? Why?

ANNA: Look at us. Two attractive, reasonably successful women — *very* successful, in your case — and what are we doing? Having yet another dinner together. At least *you* have a mystery to solve.

SHELITA: Just call me a Nancy Drew for the new millennium.

ANNA: *(Picking up the paper:)* The *Times* will probably do another story when you *do* find her.

(Shelita takes a drink. Anna's eye is caught by something.)

ANNA: Hmm . . .

SHELITA: What?

ANNA: This last sentence: "Apparently Libby Price is to remain, *at least to everyone else,* a tantalizing mystery."

SHELITA: What about it?

ANNA: Well, it didn't occur to me before. But if you read it in a certain way . . . *(She looks up at Shelita.)* He almost seems to be suggesting that *you* wrote the book.

SCENE TEN

Libby appears in a spotlight. As she continues, lights rise on Shelita reading a letter at her desk.

LIBBY: I apologize for tellin' you I was in the Green Lane Residence. I never thought it would do no harm, and I had my reasons.

I never been to New York City. I don't know anything about it but what I see on TV. Fancy restaurants, expensive stores, Broadway, taxicabs. You got a big life there, an exciting one I'm sure, and it makes me proud to see a black woman livin' that life.

My life is small, Shelita. All I got is a couple of rooms and seventy-two years of memories to fill them. Now you want to come down here with cameras and microphones because of this award I won. You want to put my picture on TV. I know you mean well, I ain't criticizin'. But your big world won't fit in my house. It'll bust the door down and break all the windows. And after you pack up my life and take it back to New York with you, would anything be left for me?

SCENE ELEVEN

A table and two chairs suggesting a room, perhaps a kitchen. Robert enters carrying Libby's suitcase. He drops his hat on the table, puts the suitcase down, then turns.

ROBERT: Libby, come *in* . . .

(After a moment Libby enters, glancing around, her sweater drawn tightly around her.)

LIBBY Such a nice house you got . . .

ROBERT: Here, let me . . . *(He helps her off with her sweater and hangs it over one of the chairs.)* If you want, I can make some tea.

LIBBY: That's all right.

(Pause.)

ROBERT: Shay is still at school. He'll be home in a couple of hours. You'll meet him then.

LIBBY: How old did you say he is?

ROBERT: Just turned nine.

LIBBY: Nine . . . Awful young to be without a mama. When did she die?

ROBERT: Two years ago. She was sick for a year before that.

LIBBY: Two years is a long time. *(For the first time she looks directly at him, with a disconcerting frankness.)* I don't blame you for bein' lonely. *(Pause.)*

ROBERT: Is that what you think this is about, Libby? Loneliness?

LIBBY: I don't know what I'm supposed to think. You ain't told me much.

ROBERT: *(Quietly.)* I guess you're right. The truth is, searching for you was a way of keeping the loneliness out. *(Pause.)* My wife was a religious woman, Libby. Not the preaching kind . . . she just tried to lead a good life. Seeing her waste away made me lose whatever faith I had, but it made her . . . clearer, somehow. Almost luminous. I'd told her about you, a long time ago. One night she said to me, "You have to make amends to that woman. Not for me — for yourself. Promise me you'll try to find her." *(Pause.)*

LIBBY: How *did* you find me?

ROBERT: I had some old papers. One gave your mother's name and address . . . It was a place to start. Wasn't easy, though. You've lived in more places than I can count.

LIBBY: I don't stay too long in a place. Find a job, make a little money, then I'm off again.

ROBERT: I guess you've done all kinds of work.

LIBBY: *(Quietly.)* What ain't I done. *(Pause.)* Didn't people ask why you was lookin' for a colored woman?

ROBERT: My letters were on bank stationery. I always hinted I was trying to locate the owner of an old account. In my experience, most folks try to be helpful when it comes to money.

LIBBY: That must be nice.

(She says this evenly, with neither reproach nor sarcasm. A moment before Robert speaks.)

ROBERT: All the time I spent looking for you, I never really thought about what would happen when this moment came. And you were actually standing here, in my house.

LIBBY: And what does happen?

ROBERT: *(With a shrug:)* I don't know. Maybe the best thing is to just tiptoe past it. *(He smiles, then indicates her suitcase.)* There's a room for you upstairs. End of the hall. Maybe I should take this up.

LIBBY: Do you really believe . . . *(She hesitates.)*

ROBERT: What?

LIBBY: Me livin' here in your house . . . What will folks think?

ROBERT: They'll think a widower needs someone to take care of the house for him — and help take care of his son. Which is perfectly true and nothing unusual.

LIBBY: Must be *angels* livin' in this town, then.

ROBERT: *(Firmly:)* I have a good reputation, Libby. My neighbors trust me with their money — with their *futures*. They've judged my character and haven't found it wanting.

LIBBY: Maybe you never made things complicated for 'em.

ROBERT: Is that how you see yourself? A complication?

LIBBY: I see myself as what I am. A colored woman in the South.

ROBERT: But the South is changing. This Reverend King fellow and all those folks marching with him — they're making people open their eyes. There's a truth in what they're saying.

LIBBY: *(Quietly.)* You make it sound so simple.

ROBERT: The truth *is* simple. And in this house, we'll live the truth. *(Pause.)* Now why don't you sit down? Please. *(A moment, then Libby sits.)* Say my name.

LIBBY: Mister —

ROBERT: No. My *name. (Pause.)*

LIBBY: Robert.

ROBERT: There. *(He smiles.)* Let me make you that cup of tea. Then we can talk.

SCENE TWELVE

Shelita and Anna sit cross-legged on the floor in blue jeans, eating a casual dinner. Cartons of Chinese food and two glasses of wine surround them. Shelita is reading from a letter.

SHELITA: "When I first read the manuscript of *Bee-luther-hatchee*, it was with a profound sense of recognition. I felt that the voice in the book — *your* voice — was speaking directly to my heart. No other book has affected me in quite the same way.

"And I felt something else as well, something deeper and inexplicable: That this voice was, somehow, one that I have always known. How can that be, Libby?

"So you see, I must meet you. Not to invade your world with mine, but to complete a connection that *you* began." *(She glances at Anna, who has been listening silently.)*

I go on to tell her that I'm flying down to Charlotte on Thursday. She can meet me in the hotel lounge at eight. And I'll be alone — no cameras, no microphones. I don't know where she got that idea.

ANNA: And what if she doesn't show up?

SHELITA: Why wouldn't she?

ANNA: What *if?*

(Shelita says nothing.)

ANNA: You want something from her, Shelita. A word, a gesture, *I* don't know. She may not want to give it. You may never know why.

SHELITA: But it's so *arbitrary*, Anna. Libby decides, I'm forced to accept.

ANNA: You can't keep pestering her.

SHELITA: I'm not "pestering" her, I just —

ANNA: You're *obsessed* with her. Can't you see it?

SHELITA: I published her book. She owes me something.

ANNA: Owes you? She's already given you a fucking *best-seller*. *(She is suddenly, vividly angry.)* Because of her you've gotten a story in the *Times*, you've gotten a great job handed to you. A job I'd kill for. Christ, what more do you want?

(A charged silence, then Shelita speaks quietly.)

SHELITA: You don't understand.

ANNA: You're right, I don't. Do you?

SHELITA: I want the real ending.

(Anna is silent.)

SHELITA: As soon as I walked into the nursing home, I knew. Some part of me did. In the day room the residents were watching TV, or reading *People*, or staring out the windows . . . They all looked up at me with a kind of hunger. I couldn't help it, I felt incriminated somehow. And my first thought was . . . This is wrong. Libby's life couldn't have led here. She can't be one of them. *(Pause.)* She'll come, Anna. I know she will.

SCENE THIRTEEN

Libby appears in a spotlight. Her face is animated, girlish.

LIBBY: Bee-luther-hatchee.

My mama used to use that word when I was a little girl. Lord knows where she picked it up — I never heard it from anyone else. I loved the sound of it, the feelin' it made inside me. And I'd misbehave just to get her to say it. She knew what I was up to — it was a game we played. She'd look at me with big, wide eyes. If you ain't careful, she'd say, you gone end up in Bee-luther-hatchee.

Where's that, Mama, I'd ask. Is that someplace like hell? Never you mind, she'd say, and give me a kiss.

But once, I remember, she told me somethin' different. Her face got sad, and her voice was quiet and far off.

Hell ain't the last stop on the track, she said. Most folks think so, but they're wrong. After the passengers get off, after the conductor turns the lights out and leaves . . . you just stay on the train, gal. Bee-luther-hatchee is the next stop after hell.

SCENE FOURTEEN

A room in Shelita's hotel suite. A small table, two chairs. To one side is an end table with a lamp and a telephone; next to it is another chair. A small suitcase sits on the floor, open. After a moment Shelita enters, carrying her bag and a copy of Bee-luther-hatchee. *She throws them on the table, angrily.*

SHELITA: Shit. *Shit.*

(She moves around the room for a moment, agitated, then sits at the end table, picks up the telephone, and dials. Across the stage a light picks out Anna.)

ANNA: Hello?

SHELITA: Hi, Anna. It's me.

ANNA: Oh. Hi. *(Pause.)* Where are you?

SHELITA: Charlotte. My hotel room.

ANNA: Did Libby —

SHELITA: She never showed up. I sat there for an hour — like a fucking *idiot. Alone* except for some creep who kept staring at me. I think he was trying to decide if I was a hooker.

ANNA: Was he cute? *(Pause.)* Sorry — stupid joke.

(Suddenly Shelita's emotion breaks through, bringing her to the verge of tears.)

SHELITA: Why won't she meet me, Anna? *Why?*

ANNA: How much did you have to drink?

SHELITA: Two martinis, that's all. I'm not drunk, I'm *hurt.* It's not fair to *deny* me like this — !

ANNA: Shelita . . .

SHELITA: I wanted to tell her about the new job. Show her how *well* I've done. Like a little girl running to —

(She puts a hand over her eyes.)

ANNA: Come back to New York, Shelita. Forget about Libby, you're just —

SHELITA: *(Regaining her composure.)* You were right, Anna. She doesn't want to see me — I'll never know why. I have to accept it and turn the page.

ANNA: Listen, let's go out tomorrow night. We never really celebrated the new job. My treat.

SHELITA: You don't have to do that, I —

ANNA: Come on, we can go to that new Portuguese place.

SHELITA: All right, that would be nice. What time?

ANNA: Meet you there at eight?

SHELITA: OK.

ANNA: Great, I'll see you then. Bye.

(She hangs up.)

SHELITA: Anna —

(But Anna is gone. Shelita hangs up. She stands, lost for a moment, then goes to the table, picks up the book, and opens it. Suddenly she begins to cry, soundlessly and without force. A moment of utter desolation. She collects herself, setting the book back on the table. She picks up the suitcase, puts it on one of the chairs, and leaves the room. There is a tentative knock on the door. After a few moments it is repeated. Shelita returns, her feet bare now, a drink in one hand and some clothes in the other. She throws the clothes into the suitcase, then takes a drink. Another knock on the door.)

SHELITA: Yes?

(Sean enters. He is white, middle-aged, casually but neatly dressed: corduroys, twill shirt, tweed jacket. A leather satchel hangs from his shoulder.)

SEAN: I'm sorry to bother you. I was wondering if we could talk . . .

(His voice has a faint Southern lilt.)

SHELITA: *(Backing away.)* Hey, hold on . . . You're the guy from downstairs.

SEAN: Yes. I apologize for —

(Shelita stumbles against the table, then, very quickly, grabs a can of Mace from the suitcase and aims it at him.)

SHELITA: Get out. Now.

SEAN: Look, there's no need for that. If you'll just —

SHELITA: *(Fiercely.)* I said *get out.*

SEAN: I'm the person you were waiting for. You are Shelita Burns, right? *(Shelita says nothing. He smiles and shrugs, almost jokingly.)* I'm Libby Price. *(Blackout.)*

END OF ACT I

ACT II

SCENE ONE
Lights up on Libby and Robert sitting at the table.

LIBBY: . . . I heard the door of the car open and the conductor come in to collect the tickets.

I sat real still and tried to be invisible. Usually that ain't too hard with white folks. Except when it comes to money — then you shine like the sun.

He stopped next to me and said, Can I see your ticket? I don't have one, I said. Not lookin' at him. You can buy one from me, he said. He had a nice voice. I said, I don't have the money.

Come with me, he said. Come on. His voice still sounded nice, but there was somethin' different in it.

All the people in the car were starin' at me, I could tell. No one was talkin'. I stood up and followed him all the way up the aisle into the next car . . . the kind that had private compartments.

Please, mister, I said. I know I done wrong. Just let me get off at the next stop.

He grabbed my wrist and started lookin' through the windows of the compartments. You're hurtin' me, I told him. He opened a door and pushed me into an empty compartment. He pulled the shade down on the window. Then he turned around and hit me. Not real hard . . . just enough to *let me know.*

And he said, Since you can't buy a ticket, you'll have to earn your ride.

(She is silent. After a moment Robert speaks quietly.)

ROBERT: How old were you?

LIBBY: *(Shrugs:)* It was a long time ago.

ROBERT: What happened?

LIBBY: You always got to know every last detail, Robert. You take it all in. Is anything gonna be left for me?

ROBERT: Did he . . . ?

LIBBY: Well, what do you think?

ROBERT: I'm sorry. You don't have to tell me. *(Pause.)* Your life is so different from mine.

LIBBY: You ought to be glad about that.

ROBERT: I'm ashamed of it. My world casts a shadow, Libby, and in that shadow is a whole other world I've never truly noticed. I'm just trying to understand.

LIBBY: You think my tellin' you will do that? Let you understand? *(She shakes her head.)* Hearin' about it ain't nothin', Robert. Seein' ain't nothin'. You got to *feel* that conductor's voice when he says "come with me." Feel it in your belly. You got to feel all those white people's eyes burnin' holes in you. You got to feel that big hand grabbin' you. *(With unexpected strength she grabs Robert's wrist and bends it back. He winces with pain, twisting to stay upright in his chair.)* You believe you can do that, Robert? Make yourself *feel* like a Negro woman — just for a second? If you can, I want you to teach that trick to me. 'Cause I'd love to spend one second of my life knowin' how it feels to be pure white — ! *(A moment, then she releases his hand. As Robert rubs his hand, she speaks quietly.)* Time for me to leave, ain't it?

ROBERT: Don't, Libby.

LIBBY: I can't stay here any more.

ROBERT: I went too far, I realize that. It's my fault.

LIBBY: It ain't you. If it was just you . . .

ROBERT: What, then?

LIBBY: It's what I told you when I came here. *(Pause.)* Yesterday, in the grocery store, one of your neighbors called me your whore. To my face . . . like she was spittin' on me. I just stood there, feelin' that word drip down my skin.

ROBERT: *(Angrily.)* Who was it?

LIBBY: What difference does it make? They all think it. I'm just surprised it took a whole year for someone to get up the nerve to say it. *(She regards him levelly.)* You're a nice man, Robert. I might even say a good man. But you don't pay attention.

ROBERT: I don't care that they think.

LIBBY: Really? You don't care?

ROBERT: It's true.

LIBBY: Well, then you won't mind standin' up in that church of yours this Sunday and tellin' everyone who I am. *(Pause.)* "In this house we'll live the truth," you said. Grand words. But there are *three* lives in this house. It ain't just you and Shay. I'm here too.

(A moment, then lights shift to the hotel room, where Shelita and Sean are standing as at the end of Act I. Sean indicates the Mace in her hand.)

SEAN: Would you mind . . . ?

SHELITA: Who the fuck are you?

SEAN: I'd rather not talk with that thing pointed at me.

SHELITA: Tell me your name first.

SEAN: Sean Leonard. Not that my name would mean anything to you. *(Pause.)* I apologize for not introducing myself downstairs. I was working up to it — you saw me! — but you're a formidable figure. What is it about New Yorkers that makes you seem so . . . what's the word . . . finished? Like brushed nickel.

SHELITA: How do you know I was waiting for Libby Price?

SEAN: Also, you picked a public spot. I thought it would be better to talk privately.

SHELITA: I'd like an answer.

SEAN: You told me. In your letter.

SHELITA: I told Libby.

SEAN: Well, yes . . .

(He takes a letter from his pocket and offers it. Shelita unfolds it, still wary.)

SHELITA: How did you get this?

SEAN: You sent it to my post office box.

SHELITA: *Your* box . . . ?

SEAN: Of course. Like all your correspondence. *(Putting his satchel on a chair, he opens it and removes a number of envelopes bundled with a rubber band, which he places on the table.)* The Green Lane Residence was a falsehood, as you've discovered. Although I do have a grandmother who lives there — it's how I know the place. It never occurred to me that you'd *go* there.

(Shelita picks up the bundle and peruses the envelopes.)

SHELITA: I'm not sure I understand, Mr. — Leonard, is it? Are you representing Libby in some way?

SEAN: No, no . . .

SHELITA: I've come a long way to meet her. Would you mind telling me where she is?

SEAN: I'm sorry, I guess I haven't made myself clear . . . *I* wrote *Bee-luther-hatchee.*

(A moment, then, unexpectedly, Shelita laughs.)

SHELITA: Look, I don't know what kind of scam you're trying to work here, what kind of *prank,* but it's late, I've had a long disappointing day, and I'm catching a late flight back to New York. If there is a late flight. So please . . .

(She gestures to show him out.)

SEAN: I thought you might find this hard to accept. I don't blame you.

SHELITA: I'd like to finish packing.

SEAN: If I could just explain how —

SHELITA: I want you to leave.

SEAN: You won't even listen to me?

SHELITA: Come on, Mr. Leonard — did you think I'd be shocked? This is nothing new. Whenever a book makes the best-seller list, some con artist crawls out of the woodwork yelling fraud. "Oh *I* wrote it." "Someone stole my idea."

SEAN: "Con artist" . . . ?

SHELITA: Or racist. *(The humor is gone from her voice.)* Whichever you are, your little game is ridiculous. And offensive.

SEAN: *(Indicates the letters in her hand:)* But what about those?

SHELITA: So you have Libby's letters — if they're genuine. How you got them is a matter for Transit's lawyers. *(She drops the letters on the table.)* And perhaps the police.

SEAN: Shelita, I can —

SHELITA: *Don't call me that.*

(The sharpness of her tone shocks him. After a moment he speaks quietly.)

SEAN: No. Of course not. *(A pause, then he reaches into his satchel.)* Publishing leaves endless paper trails, doesn't it? So much effort to ensure that the *words* — the countless permutations and combinations — are exactly what the author intends. Because words carry the burden of our belief in them. *(He begins to place papers on the table.)* One set of galleys with my corrections. I had them copied before returning them to you. One set of page proofs, also corrected. A copy of the manuscript I submitted to you. *(He holds up a notebook.)* And the original, in longhand. Personally, I could never write on a computer — or even a typewriter. To me the feel of the pen moving across paper is an essential part of the craft.

(He puts the notebook on the table, which is now covered with stacks of paper. Shelita takes them in for a moment.)

SHELITA: This is — *(Pause.)* You're seriously claiming that you wrote the book.

SEAN: Please, look at what I've brought. You'll recognize it — changes you suggested, words we haggled over. Of course, you could ask for a hand-writing analysis. I assure you I'd cooperate. I can also assure you of the results. *(Pause.)* A few minutes, that's all. You're the editor. Next to me you know the book better than anyone. Just look.

(A long moment, then Shelita goes to the table.)

SHELITA: *(A statement:)* You're not going to watch me.

SEAN: *(Indicates her glass:)* I see you've broken into the honor bar. Mind if I have a drink?

SHELITA: *(Gestures:)* It's through there.

(Sean exits. Shelita sits. She slides the pile of galleys over, turns a few pages, then reads one. We hear Libby's voice.)

LIBBY: That morning I got up at four o'clock and packed my bag in the moonlight through the window. I went out into the hall. The house was quiet. I opened the door to Shay's room, just to hear his breathin' one last time. Then I went downstairs and opened the front door. There was a chill in the air, and the stars were clear and steady. I felt like I was the only person in the whole world lookin' at them at that moment. Then I heard the whistle of a train, miles outside town, and I let that sound pull my feet toward the station.

(Putting the galleys aside, Shelita looks through the page proofs until something stops her.)

LIBBY: Shelita — you're right. The word "incandescent" is better here. Sometimes I think you see the picture in my mind clearer than I do!

(Shelita sits motionless for a moment, then opens the notebook.)

LIBBY: I been a drifter all my life.

(Shelita closes it and sits back, eyes closed. During this Sean has drifted back into the room, a drink in his hand. Now he speaks quietly.)

SEAN: You see why I held back from meeting you. What does one say? "This is going to sound crazy, but —" ? "Have I got a surprise for *you* —" ? I thought it best to preserve my silence.

(Pause.)

SHELITA: No photo, no interviews, no phone calls . . . All the *secrecy*. Why didn't I see?

(Pause.)

SEAN: Your letter —

SHELITA: *(Interrupting.)* Congratulations, Mr. Leonard.

(Pause.)

SEAN: I —

SHELITA: I guess you've managed to pull off quite a hoax on all us dumb niggers. Yassuh, sho' nuff!

SEAN: *(Frowning.)* "Hoax"?

SHELITA: Look at how *many* of us you fooled.

SEAN: I object to the word "hoax."

SHELITA: You *object* — ?

SEAN: Look, you're upset, obviously, I expected that. But I'd hoped you would —

SHELITA: No, let's not make *my* response the issue here. The issue is what *you* have done. You submitted a manuscript under a false name. You misrepresented everything about yourself.

SEAN: Only because I knew —

(Shelita's rage finally breaks through. She screams at him.)

SHELITA: You *lied* to me!

(Pause.)

SEAN: Yes. You're right. And that's why I decided to meet you here. To tell you the truth. You — of all people! — deserve to know. And to apologize.

SHELITA: You "apologize." I see. And what words did you come here tonight expecting to hear? "Oh, that's all right, never mind that you deceived me, never mind that you perpetrated a hoax on all your readers, I forgive you"? *(She shakes her head.)* You cannot apologize for this, Mr. Leonard. Not to me and not to them. *(Pause.)* What happens now? A news conference to announce your little stunt to the world?

SEAN: Of course not. Why would I —

SHELITA: No, you're right. You want something bigger, something splashier — an announcement on Rush Limbaugh, or maybe the Klan's Web site —

SEAN: No.

SHELITA: Then what was the fucking *point?*

(Pause.)

SEAN: The point? *(He seems genuinely baffled.)* The point, if I had one . . . was simply to write a good book. And I think I succeeded. It's not a hoax, Ms. Burns.

SHELITA: You're not a seventy-two-year-old black woman named Libby Price. Is this *news* to you?

SEAN: The book moves people. Does who I am change that?

SHELITA: The book is false — *because* of who you are. It has no authenticity.

SEAN: "Authenticity." I see. Then we should dismiss *King Lear* as a hoax because Shakespeare wasn't actually a half-mad old king who divided his realm among his daughters.

SHELITA: I'm not saying —

SEAN: That is what you're saying, don't you see?

SHELITA: Shakespeare never *claimed* to be a king. That is what I'm saying. *(Pause.)* It matters, don't you think? If a book is presented as a memoir, the assumption — the *promise* — is that the author has actually lived the life he's written about. It affects how readers respond to it. How it moves them. So if you suddenly reveal that the book is written by someone else entirely . . . then you've broken the promise. And the book is a hoax. What other word for it is there?

(She regards him levelly, her control regained. After a moment Sean speaks quietly.)

SEAN: I had my reasons, Ms. Burns. Would you have —

SHELITA: Your reasons don't interest me. Tomorrow I'm going to turn this whole mess over to Transit's lawyers.

(She closes her suitcase.)

SEAN: What will they do?

SHELITA: I imagine they'll want our money back, to begin with. The advance, the royalties . . . *(Another point dawns on her.)* And that's why a lawyer is "handling Libby's affairs." After all, you can't cash checks made out to a woman who doesn't *exist*. *(As if speaking the words has finally made the truth palpable to her, Shelita turns away. She stands for a moment, sad and suddenly vulnerable, then gestures at the stacks of paper on the table.)* Please . . . take all this and go.

SEAN: *(Quietly.)* What about you? When this comes out . . .

SHELITA: I'll be embarrassed, Mr. Leonard. My face will be red. But I'll survive.

SEAN: Please, can't we *talk* about this?

SHELITA: There's nothing you can say.

(She picks up the suitcase and leaves the room. A moment, then Sean takes the letter from the table and reads.)

SEAN: "When I first read the manuscript of *Bee-luther-hatchee*, it was with a profound sense of recognition. I felt that the voice in the book — *your* voice — was speaking directly to my heart. And I felt something else as well, something deeper and inexplicable: that this —"

(During this Shelita reappears from the other room, incredulous and angry.)

SHELITA: All right . . .

SEAN: "— this voice was, somehow, one that I have always known. How can that be, Libby? So you see, I —"

SHELITA: All *right*.

(A pause, then he continues deliberately.)

SEAN: "— I must meet you. Not to invade your world with mine, but to complete the connection that *you* began." *(Pause.)* Do you think I didn't feel the same need? To meet the person who brought my book into the world, gave it a life? More than I ever thought possible! *(He holds out the letter.)* This is what persuaded me to come here tonight. It made me realize . . . we have a responsibility for every connection we forge.

SHELITA: "Connection"?

SEAN: Your word, Ms. Burns.

SHELITA: We have no "connection."

SEAN: I misled you, I've admitted that. But if I hadn't come here to meet you, to explain, you would never have known.

SHELITA: And now I *owe* you something?

SEAN: I want you to admit these words mean something.

SHELITA: *(Snatches the letter.)* I wrote them to Libby. Not to you. *(She tears the letter up, then pauses in sudden realization.)* Christ — I told you things. About my life, about *me* — !
(Sickened, she turns away. Sean lets a long moment elapse before speaking.)

SEAN: When you read *Libby's* book, you responded to it. Because it has some measure of emotional truth. You can't deny that now. The letter proves it. All the letters you've been forwarding to me prove it. The Haywood Award proves it.
(A moment, then Shelita exits without a word. Sean gestures in exasperation. Almost immediately she returns, the award in her hands, and puts it on the table.)

SHELITA: Here. Take it and leave.

SEAN: Is that . . . ?

SHELITA: The Haywood, yes. That's why you came, isn't it? Forget this bullshit about "connecting" with me. You just want to claim your prize. Go ahead, pick it up.
(Sean looks at the award for a moment, then lifts it. Shelita claps mockingly.)

SHELITA: Enjoy it while you can. You won't have it long. The Haywood is given to a nonfiction work of outstanding literary merit. I think the League will want it back when they discover the book is a fraud. *(Pause.)* No matter how much "emotional truth" it has. And let's put aside the arrogance of *that* statement.
(Sean, studying the award in his hands, gives no sign of having heard her.)

SEAN: It's heavy, isn't it? Substantial. *(He smiles.)* No matter how often we say that writing well is its own reward — fully believing it! — the truth is we crave the markers that surround it: glowing reviews, awards, *prestige* . . . These things do matter.
(Shelita snorts derisively.)

SHELITA: Now I see. Now I understand . . . You did this for your *career*.

SEAN: My career?

SHELITA: It hasn't been the brilliant success you hoped for, is that it? So you decided you needed something attention-getting.

SEAN: *(Shaking his head:)* No . . .

SHELITA: Oh, I think so. You're right, after all: Your name *doesn't* mean anything to me.

(Pause.)

SEAN: A novel published a few years ago, which sold the usual two thousand copies and was remaindered. A dozen stories in the usual journals no one reads. And the usual part-time teaching jobs. Pretty typical, it's true . . .

(He is unable to disguise a measure of bitterness in his voice. Shelita indicates the award in his hands.)

SHELITA: But now you've been *validated.* Tell me, Mr. Leonard: How does it feel?

(A moment, then Sean carefully puts the award on the table. He looks up at her.)

SEAN: No. Let's not put it aside.

SHELITA: What?

SEAN: My arrogance, as you see it. Your *perception* of arrogance. Suppose a different person had come into this room. Another man, middle-aged like me — but black. Would you feel the same?

(Shelita says nothing.)

SEAN: You'd still have been surprised, of course. Upset, yes, I don't doubt. And angry, I could see that too. But *outraged?* *(He shakes his head.)* No, somehow I don't think so. *(Pause.)* So let's not put aside your perception. It's because I'm white, isn't it?

SHELITA: Yes. It's because you're white. Of *course.*

SEAN: And that means I —

SHELITA: It means you can't understand.

SEAN: *(Gestures to the book:)* But obviously I can.

SHELITA: Do you have any idea how insulting that is?

SEAN: You published the book.

SHELITA: That's not the issue.

SEAN: Of course it is. Because you should have known. If what you say is true, you should have detected a false note. But you believed it.

SHELITA: *(Stung:)* You told a story that isn't yours to tell.

SEAN: Not mine? *(Pause.)* You're saying, then, there's a *list* somewhere. A list of who I can write about. And Libby isn't on the list. How about, then, a French peasant in the tenth century? A man who speaks a different language from mine, wears different clothes and does different work, lives under a different political and social order. Whose understanding of God and his own place in the universe — the universe itself! — is fundamentally different. Are you saying I can comprehend his life simply because we have the same *pigmentation?*

(He stands with his hands spread apart as if to demonstrate the absurdity of her argument. After a moment Shelita speaks quietly.)

SHELITA: Don't you get it, Mr. Leonard? You don't have the *right.*

(Pause.)

SEAN: The "right"? I don't — How can you say that?

SHELITA: How *dare* I say it, you mean. How dare I not recognize your entitlement. *(Pause.)* It's a question of history, you see. Of what has come before. A few hundred years of suffering. Of oppression.

SEAN: I understand that, but —

SHELITA: But it's not *your* history. *(Pause.)* One of the privileges your skin grants you is that you can live outside your past. Dismiss it as irrelevant. But we *breathe* our past. I won't have it dismissed by you.

SEAN: Ms. Burns, while your ancestors were enslaved on a Southern plantation, mine were scratching out a miserable existence on a tenant farm in County Clare. Oh, they were "free," I admit — for all that word meant to them.

SHELITA: It might have meant more than you imagine.

(Pause.)

SEAN: Yes, you're right. That was stupid. *(After a moment he continues, the edge now gone from his voice.)* I'm just asking . . . do we go through the day with an exquisitely calibrated moral slide rule in hand, granting or withholding rights according to some algorithm of suffering? Surely we can acknowledge the past without being ruled by it.

SHELITA: First we have to *own* our past. By telling our story. Ever since you brought us here, white people have been telling our story for us. And look at the stories you tell. *Huck Finn. Amos 'n' Andy.* TV shows about cops bringing down the dealers and the gangs — who all just *happen* to be black. And those stories have the desired effect, don't they? On *us.* A black man can't get a cab after dark because of those stories. A white woman crosses to the other side of the street when she sees a black teenager because of those stories. People assumed I didn't *deserve* to be in Princeton because of those stories. *(Pause.)* I publish *our* stories, Mr. Leonard. The African-American experience. Told in *our* words. *Our* voices. It does not belong to you.

(Pause.)

SEAN: I agree with you. Are you surprised? "The African-American experience" — *(He shrugs.)* I wouldn't know where to begin. I wrote about *Libby.* And if I had written one more absurd racist stereotype —

SHELITA: *(Impatiently:)* Look, don't tell me you're an exception —

SEAN: You accepted Libby's voice — her life, her reality. You *recognized* her.

SHELITA: Don't you understand? It doesn't *matter.*

(Silence. Sean moves away a bit, looking at the stacks of paper on the table, then he shakes his head.)

SEAN: Why is the author more important than the words?

SHELITA: There's nothing else to discuss.

SEAN: *(Gestures at the table:)* Black marks on white paper. Because of them — miraculously! — a world that exists in one mind is recreated in another. Its sights, its sounds, its texture. Something is *communicated.* Yet none of it matters because the hand holding the pen has the wrong color skin. *(He shakes his head.)* This demand that the storyteller be "authentic" . . . what is it really but a fashionable form of prejudice?

(There is a hint of challenge in his voice. After a moment Shelita nods.)

SHELITA: Yes, I see what you're saying. It's perfectly clear. You're saying you've been discriminated against.

SEAN: I'm not —

SHELITA: You're claiming the status of *victim.*

(The scorn in her voice is apparent. She goes on before Sean can reply.)

"Miraculous — !" You just don't want anyone to take away your award.

SEAN: That's not what I —

SHELITA: And there's the money also, let's not forget that.

SEAN: *(Angrily.)* It's not about the fucking money! *(Pause.)* I don't want the book to be dismissed. And forgotten.

SHELITA: No one will *forget* this, I — *(Suddenly she stops as she realizes the implications of his words.)* Wait a minute. Are you — *(Pause.)* Are you actually asking me not to reveal this?

SEAN: *(Quietly:)* What would it accomplish?

SHELITA: I can't believe this —

SEAN: What *really? (He spreads his hands.)* I've read the letters you forwarded. The book has become important to people. Libby resurrects someone in their lives — a mother, an aunt, a grandmother. Themselves. Will you be the one to —

SHELITA: *(Interrupting angrily:)* I won't be a collaborator in this.

SEAN: You already are.

SHELITA: Without my knowledge.

SEAN: No interviews, no photo, no publicity . . . Unusual demands, but you agreed to them. How do you think it will look?

SHELITA: All your letters are in my files. I can prove you lied about your identity.

SEAN: That's true. But *you* lied about meeting Libby. *(Pause.)* I saw the article in the *Times*. That was an unsettling moment, believe me — like discovering a stranger is impersonating you. Then I got your letter, and I realized . . . there was no danger in meeting you. If you expose me, you expose your lie.

(Shelita is very still. He regards her, genuinely curious.)

SEAN: You told that reporter you met Libby Price. Why, Ms. Burns?

(A silence, then Shelita speaks quietly.)

SHELITA: Do you know how the series got started? The idea, I mean? *(Pause.)* I was sitting in the library at Princeton reading W.E.B. DuBois. It was a brilliant fall afternoon, the trees outside the window blazing away — I remember it with perfect clarity. And I came to a sentence: "What if the only record of your having been here is what other people write about you?" *(Pause.)* It was one of those moments — how many of them are there in your life? — when your place in the world snaps into focus. I was suddenly, painfully aware of exactly what *surrounded* me. Shelf after shelf, row after row, floor upon floor . . . the infinite weight and volume of other people's words. And against them, how few of ours. *(Pause.)* The urgency of the moment fades though, doesn't it? I'm in my thirties. The series is successful. I've gotten comfortable . . . I have to remind myself of what I believe. Because you're putting me to the test, aren't you? *(She is looking directly at him, her manner calm, as if the clarity of the situation has focused her.)* And the test is: What am I willing to lose?

(Pause.)

SEAN: Nothing has to be lost.

SHELITA: You're asking me to betray my beliefs.

SEAN: I'm asking you to look *beyond me. (Pause.)* A book offers some truth or it offers nothing. It convinces us or it fails to convince. The writer should be invisible.

SHELITA: I publish writers who were *truly* invisible, Mr. Leonard. Because of the color of their skin — the hand holding the pen. Your "invisibility" is a self-serving choice. It's a *fiction* — just like your book.

SEAN: Wait a moment —

SHELITA: And now you want me to —

SEAN: "Fiction"?

SHELITA: Yes.

SEAN: But that's not true. I never — You think I *invented* Libby?

SHELITA: What are you —

SEAN: Libby is real. As real as you. She lived in our house — when I was a boy.
(*A pause, then Shelita realizes.*)

SHELITA: The boy in the book — Robert's son. That's you . . . ?

SEAN: Shay, yes. That's what everyone called me.
(*Across the stage a light picks out Robert and Libby sitting at the table, their heads turning. Libby rises expectantly, her manner a bit formal.*)

ROBERT: Shay, come on in. Come on — don't be shy.

SEAN: My father and I had been alone in the house for two years. Even the echoes of my mother's voice had faded. Sometimes it was hard for me to remember her face without a picture.

ROBERT: I want you to meet someone.

SEAN: One afternoon, another woman was there.

ROBERT: This is Libby Price. She's going to stay here with us for a while.

LIBBY: Now ain't you a *handsome* young man. I'm pleased to meet you.
(*As she extends her hand, they vanish.*)

SEAN: She became a part of my life, Ms. Burns. A very important part. Surely that gives me some right.
(*Pause.*)

SHELITA: Did you know who she was?

SEAN: Not then. I only knew that she was . . . unfamiliar. Some of my friends had black cooks, nannies, gardeners — I knew them in the way a child knows the adults in his friends' lives. Libby was a new element in my world. One day I asked her where she came from.
(*Libby appears at the table, alone now.*)

LIBBY: You gonna let me fix you this sandwich, or are you gonna chatter?

SEAN: I'm just curious, that's all.

LIBBY: Oh, I been a drifter all my life. Never liked stayin' too long in one place.

SEAN: You're going to stay here, aren't you?
(*The appeal in his voice is undisguised. She considers him for a moment.*)

LIBBY: They teach you about your soul in church, don't they, Shay?

SEAN: Sure.

LIBBY: Well, I'm gonna tell you a secret. (*She takes some matches from her pocket, lights one, and holds it up.*) I got a different kind of soul. Never learned about it in church, never read about it in any book. I got a smoke-soul.

SEAN: There was something in her voice, something that stayed with me . . .

(Libby blows out the match. Smoke curls into the air.)

LIBBY: Now, you can *see* smoke, can't you? It looks real enough. But try to grab it — *(She snatches at the air and holds up a fist.)* — and what do you get? *(Eyes wide, she opens her empty hand and laughs before disappearing.)*

SEAN: When I began the book, they came to me as the right words to begin with.

(Pause.)

SHELITA: It's true, then? The book is true?

SEAN: Of course.

SHELITA: Please, I want to be clear about this. All the stories . . . she told you those?

SEAN: Some, yes.

SHELITA: "Some"?

SEAN: Most she told my father. At night, after I'd gone to bed, they would sit in the kitchen and talk. Well, Libby talked, mostly. Lying there in the dark, I'd hear her voice floating up through the floor. Telling my father about her life.

SHELITA: And he told you. It's *secondhand,* Mr. Leonard. Don't you see? You know what he *chose* to tell you.

SEAN: Please, you don't . . . *(Pause.)* Before my mother died, she used to sit on my bed at night and read to me. All kinds of stories — *Call of the Wild, Treasure Island,* the Hardy Boys. When the story was over, my father would come in and kiss me good night. *(He shrugs.)* He was never a reader. That's how I remember my mother's death, mostly — the stories stopped.

(Across the stage lights reveal Libby and Robert at the table. Libby is speaking quietly, her words not quite audible.)

SEAN: When Libby came they started again. And because I was fascinated by her . . . or maybe because I missed my stories . . . I would slip out of bed, creep down the stairs, and sit on the third step from the bottom. Just outside the kitchen doorway . . .

(He turns his head slightly as if listening to Libby, whose voice now becomes audible.)

LIBBY: . . . . used to say it when I was little. If you ain't careful —

SEAN: . . . where I could hear every word.

LIBBY: — you gone end up in Bee-luther-hatchee. Funny word, ain't it? "Bee-luther-hatchee." Never heard it from anyone else. Who knows where she picked it up?

(Libby and Robert vanish.)

SEAN: Remember what it's like to be nine years old, Ms. Burns? How eagerly you absorb the world? I carried Libby's stories — her voice! — inside me for years. *(A note of exoneration has entered his voice.)* So you see, not fiction at all. As real — as *authentic* — as a life.
(Pause.)

SHELITA: I want to meet Libby. *(Pause.)* I want to know exactly what your arrangement with her is. If there's a contract, I want to see it. I want to see her *signature* on it. I want to know that she's agreed to everything you've done.
(Pause.)

SEAN: Our arrangement is private.

SHELITA: "Private"? *(She shakes her head dismissively.)* No. I want to talk to her. Is she really in a nursing home somewhere? Did you get her to sign something she didn't understand?

SEAN: Why do you —

SHELITA: Does she even *know* about the book?

SEAN: Why do you assume I've cheated her?

SHELITA: *(Relentless:)* You know what you've done, don't you? I mean, you must. "As authentic as a life," yes. But not yours. You appropriated hers, Mr. Leonard.

SEAN: "Appropriated"?

SHELITA: Has your own life been so boring, is that it? So *arid* it's not worth writing about?

SEAN: A writer should write only about himself, is that what you're saying? That's absurd. Life hands you a dozen stories every day. You use the ones that resonate for you.

SHELITA: "Resonate"? Are you really so — *(The anger is rising in her voice.)* Look at who she was, Mr. Leonard. A black woman. In the *South*. What did she have? Not money, not status, certainly not any *power*. What did she have that was truly hers but her own experience? But you invade it, plant your flag, and claim it as your own. And not just her life — you've usurped her *voice* as well, her *identity*. You've —
(She gestures in frustration, then finds the word.)
Colonized. *(Pause.)* You've colonized her life.
(She aims the charge at Sean like a weapon. Surprisingly, he is unfazed.)

SEAN: Well, that word was bound to come up eventually, wasn't it? The unreturnable ace, the knockout punch, the stake through the vampire's heart . . .

SHELITA: *(Angered by his flippancy.)* You don't take me seriously, do you? You *can't.*

SEAN: I did what a writer does, Ms. Burns. I don't apologize for it. And let's be honest, that's not really what bothers you.

SHELITA: Oh? And just what —

SEAN: What bothers you — what *infuriates* you! — is that I did it so well.

SHELITA: Don't flatter yourself, Mr. Leonard. It isn't the real Libby. Is that what you think? It's your *idea* of her, that's all —

SEAN: The "real" Libby?

SHELITA: — a white man's *fantasy.*

SEAN: You didn't even know her. How can you —

SHELITA: I know her in a way you never could.

SEAN: Yes? By virtue of what, exactly? Your Princeton education? Your six-figure job? Your apartment in — where, the Upper West Side?

SHELITA: *(Holding up her hands.)* By virtue of *this.* And everything that goes with it — a history, a culture. Ours, not yours.

SEAN: I *made* Libby real, Ms. Burns. For all those readers — and for you. So real that you could *lie* about her. *(Pause.)* How much more real can a person be?

(Shelita is silent. Knowing he has hit home, Sean gestures at the book on the table.)

SEAN: Now you see why I didn't submit it under my own name. Would you have published it — you or anyone else? Would you even have *read* it?

(After a moment Shelita speaks quietly.)

SHELITA: "What a writer does . . ."? *(She shakes her head.)* No, Mr. Leonard. You went way beyond. And you tell me you didn't have a choice. It's not true though, is it?

SEAN: There was no choice.

SHELITA: You could have written *about* Libby — under your own name. Honestly. Instead, you chose to write *as* her. *(Pause.)* You *chose,* Mr. Leonard. Let's recognize that.

(Pause.)

SEAN: There was another version of the book. A "correct" version. I was the writer, Libby was the subject. The boundary between us was properly observed. After all, I thought, I have her stories. I worked on it every night, conscientiously, for two years. But what came out was — *(He gestures dismissively.)* You can't imagine the frustration of those lifeless words. The inadequacy of "she" to depict Libby . . . the distance that word was powerless to cross. One night I took the manuscript into the backyard and burned it, page by page. *(Pause.)* I had her stories, yes. What I needed was her voice. *(Pause.)* It took me a long time — months! — to step over the boundary. I made every objection: "What right do I have?" "How can I presume to understand the universe inhabited by a black woman?" Finally, I opened a fresh notebook and wrote the word.

(Suddenly, startlingly, Libby's voice comes from the darkness.)

LIBBY: I —

SEAN: A single stroke on a blank page.

LIBBY: — been a drifter all my life.

SEAN: And suddenly Libby was *present.* In me. Guiding my hand. Her thoughts in my mind. Her voice in my mouth.

(Across the stage Libby appears dimly, a silhouette sitting alone at the table. It is her voice we hear voice Sean mouths the words.)

LIBBY: I never liked stayin' too long in one place. For a little while it would be all right, then one day I'd look at folks and their faces would be gray and transparent — like a Sunday mornin' veil. And I'd know it was time to move on.

(Libby vanishes.)

SEAN: *(Quiet, inward:)* How does one person *disappear* into another — glimpse the world through different eyes? "An act of imagination," we say. But what does that mean, really? In the end — *(He looks at Shelita, his hands spread.)* — it's a mystery, isn't it? With no solution. *(Pause.)* It was never my intention to deceive anyone, Ms. Burns. Please believe me. I just wanted people to hear Libby's voice. As I do.

(A silence, broken after a moment by Shelita.)

SHELITA: You didn't send the book anywhere else, did you?

SEAN: No.

SHELITA: You sent it to *me.* Why?

SEAN: I came across some of the titles in your series. Your introduction struck me . . . what you wrote about "the silenced voice." I knew you were the right person.

SHELITA: The one who was gullible enough, you mean.

SEAN: No. The one who was listening.

SHELITA: You used me, Mr. Leonard. You used my credibility, which *matters* to me, as a commodity.

SEAN: Put yourself aside. Look at what I gave you.

(Pause.)

SHELITA: I want to meet Libby.

SEAN: Please, you have to understand —

SHELITA: If she tells me what you've told me, if it's what *she* wants . . .

SEAN: She wants to be left in peace. It may not make sense, but —

SHELITA: I have to hear it from *her*.

SEAN: I'll ask her. But I can't promise anything. Once she makes a decision — *(He shrugs.)* — it's done. Even if someone is hurt by it. I speak from experience.

(Pause.)

SHELITA: The way she left your house, you mean.

SEAN: In my ten-year-old's world, everything was fine. Libby had been living with us for a year.

(Across the stage lights reveal Libby standing by the table. Robert is seated.)

LIBBY: You're a nice man, Robert. I might even say a good man. But you don't pay attention.

SEAN: She was my *friend*.

(Again he turns toward them slightly, as if eavesdropping.)

ROBERT: I don't care what they think.

LIBBY: Really? You don't care?

ROBERT: It's true.

LIBBY: Well, then you won't mind standin' up in that church of yours this Sunday and tellin' everyone who I am. *(Pause.)* "In this house we'll live the truth," you said. Grand words. But there are *three* lives in this house. It ain't just you and Shay. I'm here too. Can you do that, Robert? Tell all them good people the truth?

(Pause.)

ROBERT: You don't . . .

(He says nothing else, his eyes on the floor. The moment passes. Libby shrugs.)

LIBBY: It's the world's weight. Triflin' with it ain't as easy as you think. *I* learned that a long time ago.

ROBERT: *(Quietly.)* I'm sorry . . .

LIBBY: I ain't blamin' you. *(Pause.)* I never should have answered that first letter you sent. Any sensible person would have tore it up. Or burned it.

ROBERT: Why didn't you?

LIBBY: I don't know. Curiosity, maybe. Or maybe I'd just been alone too long. It can make you do dangerous things, can't it? You kept writin' to me. I wasn't used to that — all them *words* bein' sent into my life. And I let myself think — what if everything he says is true? He's offerin' me somethin'. A kind of family. A chance to stop driftin' . . . and be *real*. Like other people.

But it was wrong — I should have seen that from the start. Wrong to hope.

(Robert looks up. Tears are shining on her face.)

LIBBY: It's like a paradise I can't ever have.

ROBERT: Libby . . .

(He stands and embraces her. She allows it, not moving for a moment, then her arms come around his shoulders.)

SEAN: I'd never heard her cry before. So I looked around the doorway, just for a second.

SHELITA: And that's when she saw you.

(Libby's eyes widen. As she pulls away from Robert, the two of them vanish.)

SEAN: I ran up the stairs to my room. Terrified that my father would come up and give me a spanking. But the door never opened. I lay there in the dark, unable to sleep, for a long time. Shocked by what I'd seen.

SHELITA: Your father embracing a black woman.

SEAN: No. My father *failing*. How did you put it? "A moment when your world snaps into focus . . ." *(Pause.)* When I woke up the next morning, Libby was gone.

(Pause.)

SHELITA: What choice did she have?

(Sean looks across at her.)

SHELITA: One reality inside the house, a different reality in public . . .

SEAN: My father was a good man, he tried —

SHELITA: "Good"? How can you — Your father was *weak*.

SEAN: It's so simple for you, isn't it?

SHELITA: The truth *is* simple.

SEAN: I began the book because I wanted to tell Libby's story. Her truth. But for every life that's recorded in words, printed, made *tangible* . . . there are a thousand unwritten lives intersecting it. Each one a separate truth, leading to its own ending.

(Across the stage a light reveals Robert, alone now, sitting at the table with a bottle and glass. He wears glasses and seems older, heavier.)

ROBERT: Do you know where your name comes from, Shay?

SEAN: A few years ago my father drove his car into a tree.

ROBERT: Your great-grandfather. Came over from Ireland during the Famine.

SEAN: Fell asleep, apparently. The coroner found alcohol in his blood.

ROBERT: Said good-bye to his land, where the past is as familiar as your neighbor's face, to come to America. The New World. Where the past . . .

(He pauses, then takes a drink.)

SEAN: *(Quietly:)* He never remarried. He never talked about Libby. He gave no clues.

ROBERT: I've always wanted to see it for myself. Let's go together, what do you say? Father and son. Stroll down narrow country lanes, climb the emerald hills . . . Our name would be acknowledged in the local pubs. *(In a thick Irish brogue:)* "Here's to the Leonards, all the way over from America. Welcome home, lads!"

(His glass raised in a salute, Robert disappears. After a moment Shelita speaks quietly.)

SHELITA: I'm sorry . . .

SEAN: After the funeral I found everything in his desk . . . Requests for information. A list of places where Libby had lived. The letters he'd written that had been returned — "Moved, no forwarding address." Somehow he connected her trail, though, and one of the letters found its way into her hands. *(He looks at his hands as if reading an unseen letter.)* "Dear Libby: You are my sister." *(Pause.)* What we inherit is a kind of puzzle, isn't it? Unconnected facts, bits of information that happen to survive . . . We *imagine* a narrative. Give flesh to shadows. *(He turns to Shelita.)* That's why it's so destructive, Ms. Burns — this impulse you have to lock your experience away, to declare it off-limits to anyone not *like you.* It's understandable, yes. A history of slavery, denial, of lifetimes stolen from you. You feel you're finally claiming what is rightfully yours. But for you to say no, you *may not* imagine, you have no *right* . . . *(He holds the book out to her.)* Who *can* we write about? Who can we write *for?*

(A moment, then Shelita takes the book from him. She sits with it resting in her lap, then shakes her head.)

SHELITA: So much trouble to find her . . . What was he hoping for?

SEAN: He was trying to atone, I think. Acknowledge what had been denied.

(Pause.)

SHELITA: Do you know how they were related — the details, I mean? It's not in here.

SEAN: Libby never told me exactly. I know her mother worked in my grandfather's house as a maid, a nanny, a cook . . . I suppose they had an affair. That kind of thing wasn't uncommon.

SHELITA: An "affair" happens between equals. Obviously it was rape.

SEAN: Rape? I never . . . You're right, of course. *(He shrugs.)* It doesn't make any difference now.

SHELITA: To some people it might make all the difference.

SEAN: Yes. I see that. *(Pause.)* There's a certain *redemption,* I think. What my father began . . . his son completes.

(He takes a drink. After a moment Shelita looks up at him with a frown.)

SHELITA: Wait. Are you saying . . . *(She looks at the book in her hands, then across at the table piled with papers.)* You did this for *him?*

(Pause.)

SEAN: No. No, of course not. I was simply pointing out . . .

(He pauses.)

SHELITA: What? You were pointing out *what? (She stands and moves away, turning the pages of the book.)* Jesus Christ, it's true, isn't it? I never realized . . . He *haunts* the book. His presence is all through it. *(She holds it out.)* This isn't about Libby at all.

SEAN: That's ridiculous . . .

SHELITA: It's just one more book *by* a white man *about* a white man. It's your way of trying to understand *Daddy.*

SEAN: *(Quiet, almost bewildered:)* You insist on reducing everything. One motivation, one meaning —

SHELITA: Where is Libby?

SEAN: The world is complexity, *nuance —*

SHELITA: *(Furiously:)* Fuck you! *I want to meet Libby.*

(Pause.)

SEAN: I'm afraid it's not possible.

SHELITA: "Not possible"? Why not?

(Sean says nothing.)

SHELITA: She's dead, isn't she?

SEAN: I don't know.

SHELITA: Don't tell me that. How can you *not know? (Again, she turns the pages of the book.)* After Libby leaves your house, here — it goes on for another — what, sixty, *seventy* pages. She goes to Mobile, she goes to Charleston . . . You're in touch with her, aren't you? She *told* you about all this.

SEAN: No.

SHELITA: What do you mean?

(He says nothing. Finally she realizes.)

SHELITA: You *invented* it . . . ?

(A charged moment, then she throws the book viciously at him. It strikes his upraised arm and falls at his feet.)

SEAN: When I came to that day . . . the morning Libby left . . . I thought the words would dry up, her voice would stop. But it grew stronger, clearer — free of static — and I kept writing. Exactly as so many writers describe it: The character takes over, the pen simply records.

SHELITA: She isn't a *character*. How can you justify —

SEAN: A life has its own trajectory. You don't need to see the entire arc to be able to describe it.

SHELITA: Did you try to find her? To ask her? Did you even *try?*

SEAN: There was no trail for me to follow. I wrote a few letters, placed some ads. Nothing ever turned up. *(He shrugs.)* After she left our house, it seems, she just . . . disappeared.

SHELITA: *(Quietly:)* Disappeared . . . ?

SEAN: Yes. As people do sometimes. *(Pause.)* There was no ending . . . until I discovered it. Those pages are the *truest* I've ever written.

(Shelita says nothing. Sean picks up the book; it hangs limply in his hands. He makes an attempt at lightness.)

SEAN: That's some arm you have. You broke the spine.

(He puts the book on the table, then picks up his glass and drinks what remains. He stands, hesitates for a moment, then leaves the room.

For a long moment Shelita is motionless. Then she goes to the table, picks up the book, and opens it to the last page. Across the stage Libby appears.)

LIBBY: Last night I had a dream. *(Pause.)* I was sittin' in a train with the lights turned out. No other passengers and no conductor — just me, travellin' through a dark country. After a long time, it seemed, the train pulled into a station. When I got off, the Devil himself was waitin' on the platform. "The last stop was for ordinary sinners," he said.

(Gradually, almost imperceptibly, her voice is overlaid with Sean's, which becomes stronger as Libby's fades.)

LIBBY/SEAN: "Bee-luther-hatchee is special. See all them stars up in the sky? Every one of them is a smoke-soul like you." Out of nowhere a big glass jar appeared in his hand. "I'm gonna put you in this and hang you up there with them. You'll see all them other souls shinin' their sorrow at you forever, but you'll never be able to communicate. Now . . . in you go."

(Now Libby's voice is gone, but she continues to mouth the words that Sean's voice speaks.)

SEAN: And he tried and he tried, but he couldn't get me into that jar. Oh, was the Devil mad! He howled and cursed in a hundred languages. But there was nothin' he could do. Somewhere along the line — who knows how? — I had become *real.* *(Pause.)* That's when I woke up. And I started to laugh.

(Her face glowing joyously, Libby disappears.

Shelita closes the book, anguished, and puts it on the table. A long moment, then she goes to her bag, searches in it, and takes something out as Sean returns.)

SEAN: I should go, Ms. Burns. I have an early class in the morning. *(Tentatively:)* Are we . . . ?

(Shelita is silent for a moment, then speaks quietly without turning.)

SHELITA: Do you know the most satisfying thing about publishing, Mr. Leonard? It's when you walk into a bookstore and see, for the first time, a book you've worked on. Brand new, sitting on a shelf — or even better, on a display table, because that means someone who works there likes it and wants to give it a real chance. You remember the energy you invested in it. The *hope.* And you think: One more story rescued from oblivion. One more . . . *(Her voice trails off.)*

SEAN: You're lucky — to have work you believe in.

SHELITA: Yes, I am. It's a good career. *(Her voice is laced with regret.)* I'll be sorry to leave.

SEAN: Leave . . .?

(In her hand is a business card. She picks up the phone and dials. When she speaks it is clear she is leaving a message.)

SHELITA: Yes, Mr. Clark, this is Shelita Burns from Transit Press. You did a story on me a couple of weeks ago.

SEAN: No, wait. *Don't —*

SHELITA: I don't know how to say this exactly . . . The fact is, *Bee-luther-hatchee* is a hoax. *(Pause.)* There is no Libby Price. *(She glances at her watch.)* It's eleven o'clock on Thursday night. I'll call you tomorrow from my office.

(She hangs up. A pause.)

SEAN: Why?

SHELITA: I told you before, Mr. Leonard . . . it's a question of history.

(A silence. Sean moves across to the table and picks up his notebook. After a moment he speaks quietly.)

SEAN: She might have become one of those lost women you see drifting across a street at three in the morning. Or she might have found a good man, had a child, been *happy* . . . It doesn't matter now what happened, does it? *(He tears a page from the notebook and rips it in half.)* You've killed her. *(He lets the pieces fall to the floor. His hands are trembling visibly. He tears out another page.)* No. *(He rips it in half.)* You've *silenced* her. *(He drops the notebook and picks up a handful of pages.)* All because you can't —*(He throws the pages across the room at Shelita.)* What gives you the *right?*

(Suddenly Sean attacks the table with a frightening ferocity, all control gone, grabbing handfuls of paper and hurling them in all directions. Shelita, terrified, crouches to protect herself.)

SEAN: What are these things? What the fuck *are* they? Just black marks on white paper. They're *nothing* — !

(He sinks to his knees. The floor is completely covered with paper — manuscript, galleys, and page proofs chaotically jumbled together.)

SHELITA: *(Fearfully:)* Get out . . . I'll call the police.

(Sean looks around at the scattered pages. He speaks quietly, almost to himself.)

SEAN: It doesn't matter what they do. Take away the award. Call the book a hoax. *I* know what I've done.

SHELITA: Do you? *Do* you?

SEAN: I wrote a book. And you responded. *(He picks up a page from the mess.)* Eighty-four. *(He picks up another.)* One-fifty-two. *(Another.)* Fifty-eight. *(Another.)* Page one. *(He searches through the papers around him.)* Where . . . ? Where is . . . ? Where . . . ? *(He stops, defeated. His hands are filled with crumpled papers. After a moment he looks up at Shelita.)* Help me find page two.

(Shelita looks across at him, not moving. The faint sound of a receding train whistle. Lights fade.)

END OF PLAY

THE LOVE SONG OF
J. ROBERT OPPENHEIMER

Carson Kreitzer

"Do I dare disturb the universe?"
— *T.S. Eliot, The Love Song of J. Alfred Prufrock*

PLAYWRIGHT'S BIOGRAPHY

Carson Kreitzer's *The Love Song of J. Robert Oppenheimer* won the Lois and Richard Rosenthal New Play Prize, the Barry Stavis Award, and the National Theatre Critics' Steinberg New Play Citation, and it was a finalist for the Susan Smith Blackburn Prize. *Self Defense or death of some salesmen,* inspired by the true story of a prostitute on death row for killing seven johns in what she claimed where seven separate acts of self-defense, has been produced in Providence, Minneapolis, New York, and Los Angeles, and it is published in Smith and Kraus' *Women Playwrights: Best Plays of 2002. Self Defense* finished out Ms. Kreitzer's Women Who Kill triptych, begun in 1993 with *Valerie Shoots Andy,* an investigation of Valerie Solanas' 1968 assassination attempt on Andy Warhol, followed up with *Heroin/e (Keep Us Quiet),* featuring Ellie Nesler, who entered a California courtroom and put five bullets in the man who molested her son. Her play *The Slow Drag,* a jazz cabaret about a woman who passed as a man to play the music she love, enjoyed a three-month run at the Whitehall Theater in London's West End in 1997–1998, following a successful run in London's Fringe and an original Off-Broadway production at The American Place Theatre in 1996. Other work includes *Slither, Freakshow, Dead Wait,* and *Take my Breath Away,* featured in BAM's 1997 Next Wave Festival. Ms. Kreitzer holds a degree in Theater and Literature from Yale University and she has received grants from NYFA, NYSCA, the NEA, TCG, two Jerome Fellowships, and a McKnight Advancement Grant. She is a member of The Playwrights' Center and the Dramatists Guild, and she is currently pursuing an MFA at the Michener Center for Writers in Austin, Texas.

ORIGINAL PRODUCTION

The Love Song of J. Robert Oppenheimer World Premiered at the Cincinnati Playhouse in the Park (Ed Stern, Producing Artistic Director; Buzz Ward, Executive Director), March 22, 2003. It was directed by Mark Wing-Davey; the set design was by Douglas Stein; the costume design was by Catherine Zuber; the lighting design was by David Weiner; the sound design was by Marc Gwinn; the video design was by Rupert Bohle;the dramaturg was Kathleen Tobin; and the production stage manager was Jennifer Morrow. The cast was as follows:

J. ROBERT OPPENHEIMER . . . . *Curzon Dobel*
LILITH . . . . *Judith Hawking*
YOUNG SCIENTIST/ STRAUSS, ETC. . . . . *Jason Bowcutt*
RABI/ J. EDGAR HOOVER, ETC. . . . . *Michael Pemberton*

```
TELLER/ LANSDALE, ETC. . . . . . . . . . . . . . . . . . . . . .Steven Rattazzi
KITTY OPPENHEIMER . . . . . . . . . . . . . . . . . . . . . . . .Blaire Chandler
JEAN TATLOCK/ NURSE/ MOTHER, ETC. . . . . . . . .Carolyn Baeumler
```

The Love Song of J. Robert Oppenheimer was originally developed and presented by Frank Theatre, Minneapolis, Minnesota (Artistic Director Wendy Knox), February 6, 2003, as part of the Playwrights' Center's NewStage Directions program. It was directed by Wendy Knox; the set design was by John Francis Bueche; the costume design was by Kathy Kohl; the lighting design was by Michael P. Kittel; the sound design was by Reid Rejsa; the dramaturgs were Kathleen Tobin and Beth Cleary, and the production stage manager was Spencer Putney. The cast was as follows:

```
J. ROBERT OPPENHEIMER . . . . . . . . . . . . . . . . . . . .Phil Kilbourne
LILITH . . . . . . . . . . . . . . . . . . . . . . . . . . . . . . . . . . . .Maria Asp
YOUNG SCIENTIST/ STRAUSS, ETC. . . . . . . . . . . . . . .Patrick Bailey
RABI/ J. EDGAR HOOVER, ETC. . . . . . . . . . . . . . . .Tom Sherohman
TELLER/ LANSDALE, ETC. . . . . . . . . . . . . . . . . . . . .John Riedlinger
KITTY OPPENHEIMER . . . . . . . . . . . . . . . . . . . . . .Annie Enneking
JEAN TATLOCK/ NURSE/ MOTHER, ETC. . . . . .Gwendolyn Schwinke
```

NOTES ON THE TEXT
The passage from the *Bhagavad-Gita* was translated by Barbara Stoller Miler. The T. S. Elliot misquote in the final scene is intentional.

LILITH
"Adam and Lilith never found peace together; for when he wished to lie with her, she took offense at the recumbent position he demanded. 'Why must I like beneath you?' she asked. 'I also was made from dust and am therefore your equal.' Because Adam tried to compel her obedience by force, Lilith, in a rage, uttered the magic name of God, rose into the air and left him."
> — Robert Graves and Raphael Patti, *Hebrew Mythology*

SOURCES
There are many fascinating books available on J. Robert Oppenheimer and this period in history. Those I found most useful are: *J. Robert Oppenheimer: Shatterer of Worlds* by Peter Goodchild; *The Making of the Atomic Bomb* by Richard Rhodes; *Brotherhood of the Bomb: The Tangled Lives and Loyalties of Robert Oppenheimer, Ernest Lawrence and Edward Teller* by Gregg Herken; *The Day the Sun Rose Twice: The Story of the Trinity Site Nuclear Explosion, July*

16, 1945 by Ferenc Morton Szasz; *Brighter Than a Thousand Suns: A Personal History of the Atomic Scientists* by Robert Jungk; *Robert Oppenheimer: Letters and Recollections* by J. Robert Oppenheimer, et al., and John Else's extraordinary documentary, *The Day After Trinity.*

PLAYWRIGHT'S NOTES
What fascinates me about this story is the intersection of such a dizzying array of subjects: rage, control, the ethics of science in wartime, passing (as a gentile), passing (state secrets), the age-old persecution of the Jews turned modern and efficient with Zyklon B, then given a new twist by the House Un-American Activities Committee. In physics, simultaneous realities can exist at once: The chair is solid; the chair is mostly empty space. When observing an event, the outcome is different relative to your position. This is the truth as I know it: elusive, multifaceted, changing under observation. Also capable of great explosion.

ACKNOWLEDGMENTS
The Love Song of J. Robert Oppenheimer was commissioned with public funds from the Individual Artists Program of the New York State Council on the Arts, and it was written during a Jerome Fellowship at the Playwrights Center in Minneapolis. I would like to thank my dramaturg, Kathleen Tobin, without whom this play would certainly never have been written. I am deeply indebted to many others along the way, most notably the amazing Wendy Knox, who first said, Yeah! Let's do this thing! and Wendy's own Frank Theatre, a wild and enthusiastic bunch of folks, and a great home for a playwright to develop new work. Many thanks to Clubbed Thumb for an early reading, the Playwrights' Center for both long-term and specific production support, the many talented actors who participated in readings and workshops, as well as the fantastic final casts, the marvelous Ed Stern, who believed in this play from very early on, the Cincinnati Playhouse in the Park, and Mark Wing-Davey, the best task-master a playwright could ever wish for, and a true inspiration.

CHARACTERS
 J. ROBERT OPPENHEIMER: Eminent physicist, possible Communist
 LILITH: Pre-Biblical demon, the first woman
 KITTY OPPENHEIMER: Wife
 JEAN TATLOCK: Mistress; also MOTHER/CENSOR/REPORTER/NURSE
 SCIENTIST ONE/RABI: Also GROVES/ SECURITY ONE/ HOOVER

SCIENTIST TWO /TELLER: Also VOICE-OVER/ LANSDALE/ SECURITY TWO
SCIENTIST THREE/YOUNG SCIENTIST: Also SOLDIER/ BRITISH ENVOY/
    STRAUSS

NOTE: Lilith lives in the walls and ceiling, crawling up and across chain-link fence, perching, seething, lunging, curling up to sleep, but never touching the floor. She is only visible to Oppenheimer.
    Asterisks (*) are used to indicate overlapping speeches.

Action is continuous: The scene titles are for reader/performer orientation, and they should not be felt by an audience, except in tone shift or light change.

THE LOVE SONG OF J. ROBERT OPPENHEIMER

ACT I

A faint Los Alamos desert dawn. Oppie appears. He addresses the audience as though it were his clearance board.

OPPIE: *And how should I presume?*

And how should I begin?

You have my file before you.

I trust this board will take into account not only certain political associations of an impassioned youth, but our needs as a country, and what I can do toward the task at hand. Certainly, I have associations with various Communists, my wife and my brother to name two, and I have supported various causes and been a member of nearly every Communist front group on the West Coast, but I have never engaged in anything even resembling subversive activities.

LILITH: *(Shadowing him.)* ssssssubverssssive

OPPIE: I am not ashamed of these political leanings. Only that they came rather late in life for me. They are a young man's politics. I had managed to remain shockingly ignorant of . . . the world and its ways. I read no newspapers, never had a radio.
(Smiles.)
I didn't hear about the stock market crash until a friend told me, six months after.

But events conspired to pull me out of this . . . life of pure scholarship. I had relatives in Germany.

I met a woman, to whom I was engaged for a time,
(Jean appears, shadowy.)
who introduced me to various worthy causes including Spanish relief and the organization of migrant farmworkers at home. I contributed sums of money because I could; I never considered joining the Communist Party because I prefer to do all of my thinking for myself.

I assure you, all this is firmly in my past. Now, in time of war, I only seek to serve my country in the way I best can. As the head of the laboratory

currently being built on the spot I suggested for it, Los Alamos. Beautiful part of the country.
Desolate.

Empty.

The site, I have named
Trinity.
VOICE-OVER: *(Whispered.)* What's a Jew doing naming it Trinity?
OPPIE: Batter my heart, three-person'd God
VOICE-OVER: What?
OPPIE: It's Donne.
YOUNG SCIENTIST: Oppie?
OPPIE: What?
YOUNG SCIENTIST: It's done.
VOICE-OVER: 14 July. Gadget complete. Should we have the chaplain here?
SCIENTIST ONE (RABI): Place your bets, gentlemen. Will we ignite the atmosphere and blow up the world? Or just the state of New Mexico?
SCIENTIST TWO (TELLER): It's not going to ignite the atmosphere! My calculations prove —
SCIENTIST THREE (YOUNG): How do you plan to collect?
VOICE-OVER: Seven.
    Six.
    Five.
    Four.
    (The opening bars of The Nutcracker Suite *are heard over the final numbers.)*
    Three
    Two
    One
    (Flash of light. A tremendous explosion.)
YOUNG SCIENTIST: Is it the end of the world?
OPPIE: Maybe.
    (Lilith laughs. She appears, teeth first, like the Cheshire Cat.)
    That was the first time I saw your face.
LILITH: You must admit.
    It would have been funny.
OPPIE: What?
LILITH: If you had
    ignited the atmosphere.

Consumed the world in a fiery ball.

OPPIE: *(Smiles.)* We were a little bit afraid.

LILITH: shows what you know.

OPPIE: Yes.

We should have been much more so.
(Lilith makes a clicking noise like a lizard.)
An apple falls and hits a man on the head.
Thus begins Newtonian Physics. Which begat Theoretical Physics.
A discipline that ends, with great violence, July 16, 1945. Trinity.

I think this story is a metaphor. And it is knowledge which strikes Sir Isaac on the head.

The Apple of course its time-honored stand in since Eve, the first woman, plucked one from the Tree of Knowledge. And that first sweet bite led to enlightenment. Banishment from the Garden. And eventual death.

LILITH: Sssssssssshhhheeee wass not the firsst.

OPPIE: *(Smiles.)* The early Hebrew tradition holds that there was another woman, before Eve. Made from earth, like Adam. Lilith.

LILITH: Lilit. Lillitû. * Lamashtû. Astarté. Ardat-lili

OPPIE: * But she would not behave.

LILITH: I dared disturb the Universe. God revoked my ssecurity clearance.

OPPIE: So God cast her out.

LILITH: I left.

OPPIE: Made a new one. Eve.

LILITH: From whom all you miserable creatures are descended.

And now here you are again.
A bunch of Jews in the desert.
Arguing esoteric points.

SCIENTIST ONE: You see, it is written

SCIENTIST TWO: It is easier for a camel to pass through the eye of a needle

SCIENTIST THREE: Than to ignite the earth's atmosphere.
(Beat.)

SCIENTIST TWO: *(Concerned.)* Or a very thick piece of yarn.
Through the eye of a needle.

LILITH: What leads a kind man. A gentle man. A scholar. To make the biggest explosion the world has ever seen?

OPPIE: I had a . . . continuing, smoldering fury about the treatment of Jews in Germany.

LILITH: Ssmoldering.

20TH CENTURY

Sound of a train. Oppie and Groves in a train compartment.

OPPIE: *(Smiling.)* Let us go then, you and I. The General and the Scientist.
Still within the speed of the 20th Century ...

GROVES: Strange name for a train, I always thought.

OPPIE: Hurtling toward an uncertain destination

GROVES: New York City.
Though now that you mention it, I would call that an uncertain desti-
nation.
(Beat. He tries to figure out if this is the joke Oppie was making.)
You understand, Dr. Oppenheimer, security is our number one priority.

OPPIE: I thought getting the thing built was your priority.

GROVES: Well, yes, of course —

OPPIE: Then you've got to change the way things are being run. You can't just
compartmentalize these people, have them toiling away in ignorance.
Scientific discovery is built upon the free flow of ideas. You never know
where the winning notion is going to come from. Sometimes the most
unlikely of sources.

GROVES: Dr. Oppenheimer, we simply can't have this top secret information
being discussed out in the open —

OPPIE: YES YOU CAN — If. Instead of isolating each man. Isolate us all.
The entire laboratory is top secret. But within this hermetic seal — no
secrets. Everyone is working on the same problem. Give me thirty scientists, with complete freedom of discussion, and we can make this thing
for you.

GROVES: We can't tell them anything about the project until they've agreed to
work on it. Do you think you can recruit under those circumstances?

OPPIE: Yes. I believe I can.

LILITH: cocky bastard, aren'tcha?

OPPIE: Just practical.
Report to a post office box in New Mexico. Disappear.
And I got them.
Armed with nothing but the ever-growing list of luminaries in
attendance.
Fermi
Bethe

all our brightest graduate students

eventually the thing had a gravitational pull of its own.

LILITH: Creating a new star system?

OPPIE: No. Just . . . a world.

LILITH: A world powered by fury.

OPPIE: Our own world.

LILITH: The fury of the small.

OPPIE: A world of pure discovery.

LILITH: The fury of the cast-out.

(Rabi and Oppie, walking the perimeter fence at Los Alamos.)

RABI: I suppose this is all part of a rich historical tradition.

OPPIE: This, Isador?

RABI: At very regular intervals, there's a panic, and Jews are accused of poisoning the wells.

(Oppie nods.)

Once a century, like clockwork.

OPPIE: I did not think it would happen in this one.

RABI: Chosen People, huh?

OPPIE: So they say.

LILITH: Chosen for the Pogrom. To bake your bread on your very back as you leave one not a home for another not a home.

You know what God does to his Favorites.

He does a Job on them.

oppie oppie oppie.

I could see this coming a century away.

OPPIE: *(To Lilith.)* It's almost funny. In the German university system, all the Jews were forced into Theoretical Physics. The unfashionable end of the University. Less prestige, less pay. Now the greatest minds in the world are coming to us, refugees. Thoughts *smoking* out of their heads.

RABI: Those Nazis have signed their own death warrant.

(Lilith purrs.)

If we can just make the damn thing work.

Before they do.

(A soldier approaches Rabi.)

SOLDIER: Dr. Rabbi?

RABI: Rabi!

(Out.)

MOTHER'S HANDS

OPPIE: Lying awake at night, I think of ... many things. Mostly the critical mass of fissionable material. The critical mass of scientists. Fissionable minds. Will we be able to translate Theory into Practice? In time — ?

Sometimes I remember
my mother's hands
smoothing down my hair.
With the soft kidskin gloves she always wore. To cover a . . . defect in her right hand. It was not fully formed. Missing three fingers.
We never discussed it. It just . . . was.
Soft gloves touching my face. smoothing down my hair.
Sending me off to Dr. Adler's School for Ethical Culture.
(Smiles.)
Ethical . . . Culture.
How young we all were.
To believe in such . . . possibilities.
(Mother appears. Takes off a large, broad-brimmed picture hat. Takes off one glove. Is about to take off the other. Oppie turns to see her. She disappears.)
Once Dr. Adler brought a geologist in to speak to my form. And this man brought with him a great iron contraption, much like a large ice-chipper, and a box of unassuming-looking round brown rocks, only slightly larger than a fist.
He rested one carefully in the contraption, brought the handle down with a sharp CRACK, and there lay the geode, in two halves, inner cavern of crystals sparkling in the first light it had ever seen.
I . . . laughed aloud. With the shock of it. The truth of it.
And I knew. I had got to look harder. To *know* what was inside things.
Mineralogy was my first love.
It set me on a rather direct path . . . to here.
Los Alamos.
Where they question my associations. Read my mail. Listen to every phone call. Listen at the keyhole till I think I will go mad.

KITTY AND THE SECURITY MAN
The Oppenheimer home, Los Alamos. Kitty keeps a man on the doorstep.

KITTY: I suppose I have to ask you in.

LANSDALE: Well, I don't think you want to leave me standing on your doorstep —

KITTY: ah but I do.

LANSDALE: Ahem. I have quite a few questions to ask you, actually. About your husband.

KITTY: *(Smiling.)* Which one?

LANSDALE: Well, now that you bring that up, all of them.

KITTY: In that case I suppose I have to ask you in.

(She disappears. Lansdale looks puzzled for a moment. There is the sound of a cocktail shaker. He follows after her, gingerly.)

LANSDALE: Uh, thank you for taking the time, Mrs. Oppenheimer —

KITTY: *(Reappearing.)* Martini?

LANSDALE: Alright.

Not the type to serve tea, then?

KITTY: I suppose it was your remarkable powers of observation that landed you this security job.

LANSDALE: Touché.

KITTY: Gesundheit. *(She drinks more than a little of her martini.)* You won't find anything against my husband.

LANSDALE: Mrs. Oppenheimer, there is no need to be so adversarial. We're not out to "get" your husband.

KITTY: *(Smiling.)* Oh, please, Mr —

LANSDALE: Colonel. Lansdale.

KITTY: Don't lie to me in my own home. *(Beat.)* Oh, I'm sorry, I suppose this is Government Housing. In that case, you can say anything you please.

LANSDALE: We just need to be as thorough as possible, on a project of this nature. You understand.

KITTY: Very well.

LANSDALE: Perhaps we should start with your first husband.

KITTY: *(Finishes her martini.)* Why not. I did. *(Laughs. Refills her drink from the shaker.)* More martini, Colonel? I made a batch.

LANSDALE: Uh, in a minute. About your first husband —

KITTY: Joe.

LANSDALE: Joe Dallet.

KITTY: sweet man.

LANSDALE: He was —

KITTY: A Communist. Yes. And he's dead. Died fighting the fascists in Spain. Nothing to be ashamed of. I left him because I couldn't take the poverty.

That, perhaps, is something to be ashamed of. My second husband was a mistake. And Robert —

Robert is the man I will spend my life beside. Even if it means coming here and living in a god-damned packing crate being grilled by junior J. Edgar Hoovers no offense meant I hope none taken more martini?

(He nods.)

Robert will make you your thing. To stop Hitler.

You need him for that.

LANSDALE: He will be instrumental in the program, certainly, but there are many scientists —

KITTY: You need him for that.

You will poke and prod and write up your little reports saying his wife's a Communist and she was married to a dead Communist and he believed in subversive ideas like people getting paid a decent wage and having enough to eat but it will all come to nothing because you need him to make this thing work.

But what will you do afterward? That's what I want to know.

What will you do when you don't need him anymore.

LANSDALE: *(Laughing uncomfortably.)* Say, I think I'm supposed to be asking the questions around here.

So your second husband, you say, was not a Communist.

KITTY: No, he was a doctor. And a bore. And not a Communist. *(Beat.)* Do you know why I am answering your questions? And entertaining you in my home with anything like a modicum of propriety? Do you know why?

LANSDALE: Because you love him.

KITTY: *(Surprised.)* Yes.

LANSDALE: I have learned something about human nature. Doing this job.

KITTY: I'm impressed.

(Sound of a door opening.)

Hello, darling. How was the office?

OPPIE: *(Offstage.)* Terrible. I had to fire my secretary.

She misplaced our October cravat order, so we'll never get the merchandise to Gimbels in time for Christmas.

KITTY: *(To Lansdale.)* You see? He tells me nothing. Your Atomic Secrets are safe.

OPPIE: It's a tremendous blow to the Men's Neckwear campaign.

LANSDALE: That's not code?

KITTY: *(Bursts out laughing.)* A joke, Colonel. Not code.

OPPIE: I think the boss may fire me.

You and the children will be destitute.

KITTY: We're already destitute.

OPPIE: *(Entering.)* How can you say that? We've got a bathtub.

Oh, hello Colonel.

LANSDALE: Dr. Oppenheimer.

(Could it be a standoff? No, Oppie de-fuses.)

OPPIE: I trust Kitty has made you feel welcome?

KITTY: Actually, I think I make him a bit nervous.

Don't know why. I'm the one who's been getting the third degree.

OPPIE: The Colonel is just doing his job, my dear. To ensure the safety of the project.

KITTY: Funny kind of a job, if you ask me.

OPPIE: It's a funny kind of a time. But we all do what we can.

LILITH: We all do what we can? What a pious little choirboy.

OPPIE: *(To Lilith.)* It's got to work. I've got to make it work.

LILITH: Why do you stand for this continual invasion?

OPPIE: the alternative is unthinkable.

As many things are unthinkable. Now.

(They are alone.)

It's so quiet here. The desert seems to . . . absorb all sound.

makes the mind spin. Until it lands.

on . . .

my parents' silverware.

If we did not believe, why the two sets of silverware?

One for the milk. One for the meat.

Patterns.

These are the stories we tell ourselves.

These are the rules we live by.

LILITH: easy for you to say

OPPIE: Religion is . . . poetry.

LILITH: tribes and sides. a recipe for bloodshed.

OPPIE: Patterns. Stories of instruction. How we live with one another —

LILITH: no "we" without "they."

OPPIE: And then one day in Germany it's not shattered windows anymore it's not the ghetto anymore it's a sky full of thick black smoke
a cloud of human ash

And you wonder how this chain reaction ever started.

Wartime reparations + unemployment + directionless hatred given direction = critical mass.

And it all breaks apart. Atoms tear open. Your family is incinerated.
(He looks away. A long beat.)
Your colleagues from Leipzig and Munich and Berlin
come here
to live in pasteboard houses in the desert.
(Teller strides onstage, looking for someplace to put his valise.)
OPPIE: Edward! I'm so glad you could make it.

Here we have gathered all the best scientific minds —
TELLER: Well, now that I am here. Yes.

THE GUN METHOD
Oppie stands with a piece of chalk before the assembled scientists.

OPPIE: This is what we know.
Uranium 235 is our fissionable material.
(He begins drawing on the board.)
We believe the critical mass is 15 kilograms. Beyond that, the chain reaction begins — we have a great deal of energy released from the material.

At the moment, we have approximately three tablespoons of Uranium 235. But that's not our worry. Two laboratories at other locations are working full-time to separate out sufficient material. Our job is the design of the device.
(Oppie sketches on the board. We see a cutaway of the bomb "Little Boy.")
The plan thus far: Inside the bomb's casing, we have a modified artillery gun, which fires the uranium shy, like a large bullet, into the subcritical uranium target. When the two subcritical uranium pieces come together, they exceed critical mass, and a nuclear explosion takes place.

Unless the speed is insufficient, in which case surface reactions blow the bomb apart before it goes fully critical.
(The Young Scientist stands up.)
YOUNG SCIENTIST: Oppie — what if. What if we shaped the fissionable material into a hollow sphere.
(Interested, Oppie motions him forward, hands him the chalk. Young Scientist begins to draw excitedly as he talks.)
A hollow sphere . . . . surrounded by explosive.

So that . . . Implosion. Implosion creates the critical mass.

RABI: You might need significantly less fissionable material.

And the assemblage should be almost

RABI AND YOUNG SCIENTIST: Instantaneous!

RABI: Certainly faster than the gun method.

OPPIE: *(Overlapping.)* Yes . . . . yes . . . *(Beat.)* But the explosion is bound to be at least slightly asymmetrical. Might that cause a spurting of the fissionable material at the point of weakness, again blowing the bomb apart before the chain reaction is established?

YOUNG SCIENTIST: *(Somewhat discouraged.)* Well . . . You're right, of course.

It would have to be absolutely symmetrical.

OPPIE: Good.

You work on that.

(The Young Scientist beams.)

We will also continue work on the gun method. Both have possibilities to succeed.

(Teller, who has been scribbling madly for a while, bursts out:)

TELLER The tremendous heat released by *fission* should be sufficient to cause the even greater —

a FUSION reaction. Not just breaking apart — the atoms FUSE to make a NEW ELEMENT, meanwhile they release TREMENDOUS FORCE OF ENERGY.

OPPIE: Yes. I suppose if you could create an environment where you could produce the fusion of two atoms, that would —

TELLER: THAT would be a REALLY BIG BOMB. A SUPER-BOMB.

OPPIE: Yes, well —

TELLER: Beyond Nuclear. A THERMO-NUCLEAR REACTION.

OPPIE: Yes, Edward, but we don't have the nuclear reaction yet. That's really what we're all here to —

TELLER: *(Shrugs.)* An engineering problem.

You will find it.

I will work on my Super.

Deuterium. Deuterium could work . . . .

(They disappear. Oppie remains.)

OPPIE: All these bright minds.

Shining.

LILITH: Glittering. Furious.

OPPIE: *(Shakes his head.)* Catching fire.

Together.

And we have everything we need.

the laboratory

has everything we need.

Money does not curtail the experiment.

None of us. Have ever known this

freedom.

LILITH: freedom?

OPPIE: *(Looks at her.)* Yes.

(Young Scientist recites his letter. Elsewhere, a Censor, poised with a black marker.)

YOUNG SCIENTIST: Dear Mother:

Outside, you can tell a world-class scientist by the Nobel Prize. In here, he rates a Bathtub. The rest of us are, quite literally, the great unwashed.

(Censor looks suspicious, decides to leave it.)

Dr. (mm-mrf) brought his piano.

(Censor wields the marker.)

The weather is gorgeous. I never knew the sky could be so big.

Would love to tell you more, but you know they (mmrf-rf) our mail.

your loving son,

GROVES

GROVES: You said thirty.

Thirty scientists and their families.

What we have here is a city. Six thousand people. On your project.

I've spent half a billion dollars. On your project.

What I want to know is.

Are you any closer? To making it work?

OPPIE: Yes — always closer.

GROVES: Tell me again.

OPPIE: It's going to work.

GROVES: I'm putting that in my report.

(Groves exits, passing an area with Lansdale and the Censor.)

CENSOR: Sir? They won't stop mentioning the censorship in their letters home . . .

GROVES: Well, keep cutting it out.

CENSOR: Yes, sir.

LANSDALE: *(With a sense of humor.)* It's top secret that this place is so secret we need to censor the mail. The censorship itself is somehow not considered a dead giveaway.
(Groves looks at him sharply.)
Sir.

JULIUS

LILITH: Julius.
Julius.
OPPIE: It's just J.
LILITH: It stands for Julius. Your father's name.
OPPIE: It stands for nothing.
LILITH: The tailor's name.
OPPIE: He imported cloth.
LILITH: You called him that. Called yourself the tailor's son. Very sensitive about that.
OPPIE: Yes.
LILITH: You were a spoiled little brat.
OPPIE: *(Smiling.)* There are those who say I still am.
LILITH: It bothered you that the money came from somewhere?
OPPIE: I suppose
LILITH: That it wasn't just shit by God.
That in fact, you came from a long line of cross-legged, squinting Jews. Pushing needle through cloth. Davening closer to the light to see the tiny stitches. Putting their gold in little purses hidden up in the mattress ticking. In case the Pogrom, in case the Cossacks came again. Building up coin upon coin so that Julius could get out.
Come to America.
Do very well.

So that Julius' son could walk down the street, head held high. Never know the squint and stoop that put him there.

GIBSONS
Spot on Kitty.

KITTY: I did as you asked, darling. I had some of the Women over.
I was an excellent hostess.
Cooked up something elaborate.

Gibsons.

They'd just gotten those little cocktail onions in at the PX, and I thought I'd take advantage.

We drank quietly for an hour or so and then everyone went home. It was truly dreadful.

I'll do it again, if you like.

But I think you should get someone else to play Director's Wife.

TELLER REPLACED BY FUCHS

OPPIE: Edward, I'm glad you're here — I've had several . . . requests. I must ask you to stop playing the piano at all hours.

TELLER: It helps me think.

RABI: You know what helps me think? Sleeping! For at least a few blasted hours a night.

TELLER: I'M WORKING.

RABI: Not on our project!

TELLER: I cannot — Look. Here. My Super is of primary importance.

RABI: This is what I've been telling you, Oppie. He's absolutely —
    (Stops himself, finishes:)
    unhelpful.

OPPIE: Well, the British are sending some men over. I'll get you a replacement.
    (Scans some papers.)
    Uh . . . Klaus Fuchs will join your team. Edward, you're all right on your own?

TELLER: Preferably.

OPPIE: Good. Then it's settled.
    (The Young Scientist enters, holding a mangled pipe.)

YOUNG SCIENTIST: Oppie?
    I thought I'd start with a cylinder, since that's easier than a sphere, but implosion is far from even, no matter what I —

OPPIE: *(Cold.)* Have I picked the wrong man for this job?

YOUNG SCIENTIST: I just . . . Maybe. I just don't know if it can be done.

OPPIE: It was YOUR idea.
    YOU make it work.
    (Blackout. Oppie.)

LILITH: Julius.

J.

J. Robert.

Are you angry at him?

Or yoursssssself?

OPPIE: *(Smiles.)* You're worse than my clearance board.

LILITH: They could never get inside your head. Understand what made you tick tick tick tick tick tick tick tick tick. Their inquiry stopped at the ice blue eyes. While I. Have been inside your head a long, long time.

JEAN

Oppie sits, sketching on a pad of paper. Possibly, we see diagrams sketched out behind him.

OPPIE: *(Muttering.)* A hollow sphere of sub-critical material.

Less than 5 percent variation in symmetry of the shock wave.

Otherwise —

(Phone rings. He jumps, picks it up.)

JEAN'S VOICE: Robert. I have to see you.

OPPIE: Jean. I can't.

(An image: Jean. She chases down a few pills with a glass of water.)

JEAN: I must. see you.

(In another area: Two Security Agents become visible, listening in, taking notes.)

Robert.

OPPIE: I'll see what I can do.

(He hangs up the phone. Jean takes a shuddering breath, hangs up. She turns on the radio, it plays a slow, mournful waltz, which she dances vaguely to.)

SECURITY ONE: subject: Jean Tatlock.

SECURITY TWO: That Red tart again.

SECURITY ONE: Dr. Oppenheimer received call at 21:00 hours.

SECURITY TWO: You think she's pumping him for info?

SECURITY ONE: While he's pumping her?

SECURITY TWO: I heard those communist babes are hot.

SECURITY ONE: Yeah?

SECURITY TWO: *Red* hot.

SECURITY ONE: shaddup an transcribe the tape.

LILITH: And did you see her?

OPPIE: Once.

LILITH: And did you inform Security?

OPPIE: It was not. A government matter.

> They informed me, later. Of her suicide.
> *(Jean. She stares at him, smoking a cigarette.)*
> You look beautiful.

JEAN: *(Smiles grandly.)* Thank you. I feel like shit.

> *(Beat.)*
> Didn't think I was ever going to see you again.
> What's so god-damned important that you can't —

OPPIE: I can't tell you.

JEAN: Right.

OPPIE: I have to go back.

JEAN: Your Country needs you?

OPPIE: Yes.

JEAN: And your wife?

OPPIE: You didn't want to marry me —

JEAN: I wasn't pregnant.

OPPIE: you won't let me go.

JEAN: Can't. There is a difference.

OPPIE: As if you'd know. You've never done a thing that wasn't precisely your current whim —

JEAN: That's right. I'm nothing but a spoiled little dilettante with a bleeding heart and a bottle of prescription pills.

> *(Beat. Soft.)*

OPPIE: I have to go back.

JEAN: You can go in the morning.

> Can't you?

OPPIE: Alright.

> *(He goes to her. Strokes her hair. She leans her face against his chest. Lights fade on them.*
>
> *Lilith eats something.*
> *Wipes blood from her mouth in a smear across her cheek. Pulls a tiny bone from her mouth.*
>
> *Laboratory.*
> *The three scientists, muttering and pacing in circles, à la the Marx Brothers.)*

TELLER: Deuterium.

RABI: Deuterium.

YOUNG SCIENTIST: Deuterium.

TELLER: Lithium . . .

RABI: Lithium.

YOUNG SCIENTIST: For him, or the bomb?

RABI: Shhhh.

TELLER: *(Eureka.)* Lithium Deuteride!

    (They all rush to the board and begin calculating.)

    Lithium Deuteride . . . with an atomic bomb ignition of the Tritium . . .

YOUNG SCIENTIST: According to the new calculations, how heavy will this bomb be?

TELLER: *(Does some quick addition in his head.)* 500 tons.

    (Beat. They all consider this.)

    A plutonium-powered superplane to drop it, perhaps.

    Get some engineers on that.

RABI: Perhaps we should return to the problem of fission —

TELLER: *(Banishes him.)* OUT!

    (Oppie. The desert.)

OPPIE: The first time I saw these mountains I was a boy.

LILITH: A city boy.

OPPIE: The world was contained in the pages of a book for me, and here it was opening up before me like . . . the world.

I'd asked him if we could say I was his younger brother.
For the trip.
He said no.

I had worked too hard, at too high a pitch, and my body collapsed. The whole point had been to attend Harvard at sixteen, but . . .

This year. My parents paid my favorite teacher to take an extended trip with me. To the Sangre de Christo mountains. To get back my strength.

It was a wonderful time. On horseback I was . . . fearless.

All went well. Very well. Then one day we had to get an early start, and he had not finished packing. He asked me to fold his coat for him.

Tossed it across the room to me. Bent to continue packing.

My knuckles went white in the cloth.

I said, that's right, give it to the Tailor's son. He'll fold it.

The look of shock. Hurt, even. That I would think such a thing.

I regretted the words the instant they were out of my mouth.

But that doesn't mean they weren't true.

LILITH: As he shook his blonde head, sadly

OPPIE: I never said he was blonde.

LILITH: Was he better than your father, to model yourself on?

OPPIE: Horseback riding down a ravine. Shoulders thrown back.

Never a shrug, never an apology. Who would you choose?

(Another area: Lansdale, handing General Groves a file.)

LANSDALE: Here it is, sir.

(Jean appears in back. She places cushions in front of a bathtub, then begins, slowly and methodically, to take a large handful of pills. Oppie watches this.)

In the last position we captured, we found the laboratory. What was left of it. They were still all working away, in the midst of, well, a lot of rubble, sir. Amazing, when you compare it with what we've got here.

They were questioned over the course of twenty-four hours, all together and separately.

The information is conclusive.

Germany is no longer working toward an atomic weapon.

(Groves is still reading.)

So.

Shall we tell our guys?

GROVES: No.

LANSDALE: No?

GROVES: No. Gotta keep the fire under the jew-boys.

(Jean walks carefully to the bathtub.)

If they don't come up with it, I've sunk over a billion dollars of the Army's money into the biggest dud in history. It's *my* ass on the line.

LANSDALE: Yes, sir.

GROVES: These scientists think small.

Hitler and their calculations working out. That's about it.

(Jean kneels on the cushions.)

They're not going to understand about America's needing to be the most powerfully armed nation in the world.

They're not looking ahead to the next conflict.

Which is likely to be with our Allies, the Soviets.

After the smoke clears.

And they shut down the ovens.

No, we need the little man with the moustache.

He's going to get us our bomb.

Keep a fire under them until it's too late.

LANSDALE: Too late?

(Jean plunges her head into the water.)

GROVES: Soon, there'll be no stopping.

They'll have to *know* if the experiment works.

LANSDALE: *(Startled.)* Experiment?

GROVES: If they get close enough, they'll forget it was ever anything else.

(Groves smiles. A cool, frightening smile. Blackout on them.)

(Jean. Head underwater. For a long time.)

LILITH: How long is she in the bath?

OPPIE: Four days.

Her . . . her father found her.

(With great effort, looks away from Jean.)

A lovely man. A professor of English at Berkeley. When I went to his home, it seemed there were no walls. Nothing but books, everywhere. And the most beautiful girl. He introduced me to her. and she introduced me to . . . many things.

LILITH: Communism.

OPPIE: Yes. And frozen custard on the boardwalk at Coney Island.

LILITH: And the Metaphysics of John Donne.

(A gathering of scientists. Oppie is distracted.)

YOUNG SCIENTIST: I think we should let the Russians know what we've discovered —

RABI: An international sharing of knowledge. Like before the war.

OPPIE: I'm all for the sharing of our knowledge. But it must be done through the proper channels. It's for the President to decide, now. It's not peacetime anymore.

YOUNG SCIENTIST: But it will be again soon. We can go back to our lives, the way things were. Why shouldn't we let the Russians know what we've been doing?

TELLER: *(Incredulous.)* Why? Why shouldn't we just give over what we have?

YOUNG SCIENTIST: But the Russians are our allies.

TELLER: Bah. Allies.

Only when it suits them.

YOUNG SCIENTIST: How can you say that? The Russians suffered more casualties —

TELLER: You did not see the Communists in Budapest.

And this peacetime? That you remember. Is never coming back.

OPPIE: Edward. I don't think there's any reason to paint so grim a picture.

TELLER: hmf.

OPPIE: Roosevelt will make the right decision.

LILITH: The wise and thoughtful Father of a Nation, curling you up for those Fireside Chats.

(Home. Kitty looks genuinely shaken.)

KITTY: What . . . will we do?

OPPIE: We?

KITTY: The country.

OPPIE: I don't know.

THE PRESIDENT IS DEAD

Oppie gives on-site eulogy for President Roosevelt.

OPPIE: When, three days ago, the world had word of the death of President Roosevelt, many wept who are unaccustomed to tears, many men and women, little enough accustomed to prayer, prayed to God. Many of us looked with deep trouble to the future.

We have been living through years of great evil, and of great terror. Roosevelt has been our President, our Commander in Chief, our leader. All over the world men have seen symbolized in him their hope that the evils of this time would not be repeated; that the terrible sacrifices which have been made, and those that are still to be made, would lead to a world more fit for human habitation.

In the Hindu scripture, in the Bhagavad-Gita, it says, "Man is a creature whose substance is faith. What his faith is, he is." The faith of Roosevelt is one that is shared by millions of men and women, in every country of the world. For this reason it is possible to maintain the hope, that his good works will not have ended with his death.

(Turning suddenly to Groves.)

So Truman knew nothing of the Project?

GROVES: Only the President.

(Exiting.)

Don't worry, I'll explain it all to him.

OPPIE: That's not what I'm worried about.

(Kitty accosts him.)

KITTY: I'm glad she's dead.

(Oppie doesn't answer.)

You hear me?

OPPIE: What makes you think I didn't hear.

KITTY: I don't know, I thought maybe you'd hit me or something. Defend her honor.

OPPIE: I'm going out.

KITTY: At least now I know you'll come back.

OPPIE: I would never have left you. I take the marriage vows seriously.

KITTY: AND I DON'T?

OPPIE: Upon third recitation, the words become true? How like a fairy tale.

KITTY: Get out.

> *(When he's at the door.)*

You leave me I'll fuck those kids up like you wouldn't believe.

OPPIE: *If* I leave?

> *(Oppie stalks out. Kitty takes a deep breath. Releases it slowly. Runs a hand through her hair.*
>
> *Outside. Oppie runs into the Young Scientist, holding another badly mangled pipe.)*

YOUNG SCIENTIST: Oppie, I —

OPPIE: FIX IT.

LILITH: those days before Trinity
> you lived on smoke
> down to 115 pounds. Six feet tall, weighing no more than a girl

> I could lift you in a breath

> lived on smoke

> and the bright-burning fires in your head.

OPPIE: yes.

LILITH: fury.

OPPIE: discovery.

LILITH: only hate burns that bright
> don't lie to me
> I could smell it

OPPIE: I don't lie
> to you

LILITH: I know by now the smell of burning hate
> it comes from my heart
> up into my nostrils
> every day
> the sun rises and hits me, smoldering

> *(Laboratory.*

Oppie watches an experiment. Late night, scientists with their shirtsleeves rolled up. There is an aura of holiness to these rituals, this work. Occasionally one glances at Oppie. They are glad he's there. Watching them, watching over them. Under everything the low-level clicks of a geiger counter.

Small pieces of metal are placed, one by one, into a pile. The geiger counter leaps into an alarming fuzz of rapid, almost indistinguishable clicks. The last piece is quickly removed — the geiger counter calms. That piece is replaced by a much smaller piece. And another. And another. The geiger counter starts up again. The last piece is removed. It is replaced by a smaller one. The geiger counter starts up. It is removed. There is some laughter, relief. Numbers are recorded. Oppie smiles, gets his coat. Administers pats on the back on his way out.

Home. Oppie comes in, quietly. It's very late. Kitty is waiting up.)

KITTY: Nonaggression pact?

OPPIE: *(Smiles.)* Alright.

Kids asleep?

KITTY: It's three-thirty in the morning.

OPPIE: Oh.

We were . . . "tickling the dragon's tail."

KITTY: Is it as dangerous as all that?

OPPIE: *(A light laugh, with an edge of wonder. then:)* yes.

KITTY: You're careful?

OPPIE: We're careful.

(He goes to her. They kiss.)

Why this . . . détente?

KITTY: You didn't hear?

OPPIE: We didn't have the radio on . . .

KITTY: Darling, it's . . .

Victory in Europe.

OPPIE: *(A beat.)* Good.

KITTY: Good?

OPPIE: It's not over yet. The focus will shift to the Pacific.

KITTY: Yes. But.

It's a day of great jubilation. They said so on the radio.

(They embrace. Oppie kisses the top of her head.)

OPPIE: Alright. It's a day of great jubilation.

LILITH: LIAR!

KITTY: I'm exhausted. Come to bed?

OPPIE: Yes.

    (She exits.)

LILITH: Well there you go. Hitler is vanquished. Kiss your wife and take her home.

    hmmm?

    oppie oppie oppie

    so Disappointed —

OPPIE: No —

LILITH: Don't lie to me!

OPPIE: It's . . . very complicated.

LILITH: *(Clicks at him.)* complicated?

OPPIE: We — we wanted to have done something! Alright?

LILITH: *(Smiles.)* Yesssssss

OPPIE: perhaps we should have stopped then.

LILITH: but you didn't

OPPIE: no.

LILITH: you worked harder.

OPPIE: Unabated. We did not slack off in our pursuit the atomic bomb.

LILITH: you worked harder.

OPPIE: perhaps.

LILITH: You didn't want the war to end before you'd got your gadget complete.

OPPIE: we were getting very close to success.

LILITH: succcccccessssss

OPPIE: *tantalizingly* close

LILITH: yesssss

    someone had to pay.

OPPIE: *No.* that's not —

LILITH: Come *on* . . .

OPPIE: Practice!

    The theory was impeccable, but we could have overlooked something. maybe —

    We *had* to see . . . if it would work.

SCIENTIST ONE: Implosion's not working.

SCIENTIST TWO: The blast is uneven.

SCIENTIST THREE: The detonating lenses are pitted! The molds didn't work —

SCIENTIST ONE: I did the calculations. It's not going to work.

OPPIE: It's got to. That's all.

REPORTER

An army Press Corps reporter hovers at Oppenheimer's elbow.

REPORTER: I sent out the press releases.

OPPIE: Nothing's happened yet.

REPORTER: I sent three. They'll release whichever one's appropriate.

OPPIE: *(Distracted.)* Ah. Good planning.

REPORTER: One, an ammunition shed accidentally went off. No one was injured.

Two, a large munitions dump accidentally went off. Some people were injured.

Three, there was a freak accident at Dr. Oppenheimer's ranch, where he was hosting a gathering of eminent scientific friends for his birthday.

That one has all of our obituaries.

VOICE-OVER: Dr. Oppenheimer. It's time for the test.

(Teller puts on suntan lotion. Rabi and Young Scientist don dark goggles.)

THE BLAST

VOICE-OVER: Ten.

Nine.

Eight.

Seven. *[etc.]*

OPPIE: A local station broke in on our frequency.

They were playing

(Again, we hear the opening bars of The Nutcracker Suite.*)*

The Nutcracker Suite.

VOICE-OVER: One.

(Slowly, a blast of pure white light. Then the sound, like thunder but continuous, rolling in from a long way away.)

OPPIE: The hundred foot tower we'd constructed to hold it was vaporized.

The heat from the blast melted the sand.

Fused it into a beautiful green glass, which we named Trinitite.

*

It was, of course, highly radioactive.

LILITH: *(* Sings.)* Green glass, greenglass. Green glass, greenglass. green glass.

OPPIE: We did it.

WE DID IT.

LILITH: And you didn't ignite the oxygen in the air

OPPIE: Nitrogen was the concern —

LILITH: well you didn't blow it up

OPPIE: and the thing worked!

    after all that.

    It worked.

    All the calculations

    the fifteen hour days, the eighteen hour days

LILITH: tasting blood on every cigarette from your own gums

OPPIE : the greatest scientific undertaking ever —

LILITH: it worked.

    Ssssssso the next quesstion is.

OPPIE: What do we do with it?

    (Lilith echoes.)

WHAT DO WE DO WITH IT?

YOUNG SCIENTIST: There could be a test, very much like this one, in an un-
populated area of a neutral country, perhaps. And Japanese heads of state
could be invited . . .

OPPIE: *(To young scientist.)* And what if it doesn't go off?

    What if that one's a dud?

    We've invited the Japanese heads of state to witness our embarrassment.

YOUNG SCIENTIST: *(Bright, joking.)* Then we'll just kill 'em all!

OPPIE: I'll bring it up at the committee meeting.

LILITH: And the committee said:

OPPIE: We can propose no technical demonstration likely to bring an end to
the war . . . We find no acceptable alternative to direct military use.

LILITH: mmmmmm.

    and whose words are those?

OPPIE: mine.

LILITH: words out of your head

    like the beautiful explosion

    out of your head

    that was the first time I took notice of you

    oppie

    such a beautiful man

    head so full of poison

    so full of a thing about to explode

OPPIE: The Interim Committee recommends:

1. That the bomb should be used against Japan.
2. That the target should be a military one surrounded by a civilian population.
3. That the bomb be dropped without any prior warning.

(A flash of light. A tremendous explosion.)

LILITH: *HIROSHIMA.*

VOICE-OVER: Phone call from General Groves for Dr. Oppenheimer.

GROVES: *I'm very proud of you and all your people.*

OPPIE: *It went alright?*

GROVES: *Apparently it went with a tremendous bang.*

LILITH: I watched it explode and burn, curling black in the terrible, beautiful heat. The heat from inside your head. I watched the black death and death and death, breathed it in. I breathed Auschwitz, Dachau, Birkenau. Pogrom after century of pogrom. Huddled, whispering in secret in Egypt, marking our doors with the bloody lamb-bone. Begging for a scrap of god's mercy. I watched it burn and burn and burn

and I said *DO IT AGAIN! DO IT AGAIN! DO IT AGAIN.*
(Soft breaths.)
na
ga
sa
ki
(Getting tired.)
make another one.
bigger
(Cries, like a child and not like a child.)
do it again

HIROSHIMA PARTY

Music of a party. Oppenheimer walks out to look at the stars, martini in hand. The young scientist is retching into the bushes.

OPPIE: Little much to drink?

YOUNG SCIENTIST: no, sir. Nothing.

it's just . . .

OPPIE: What?

YOUNG SCIENTIST: That ammunitions ship that blew up in Halifax. 1917. Five thousand tons of TNT.

OPPIE: yes.

YOUNG SCIENTIST: Two and a half square miles destroyed. Four thousand people dead.

Trinity was —

OPPIE: *(Nodding.)* Fifteen thousand tons.

YOUNG SCIENTIST: And Hiroshima is far more densely populated than Halifax in 1917. So the number of casualties —

OPPIE: Don't do the calculations.

YOUNG SCIENTIST: The . . . the Physics.

It's not *theoretical* anymore, is it?

OPPIE: *(Soft.)* no, it's not.

TELLER: *(Enters, drink in hand.)* So — a good show today.

And now it is begun.

LILITH: and when does the next one go down?

OPPIE: The Japanese are so stubborn —

LILITH: Once again, President Truman tells the Japanese to surrender unconditionally or 'expect a rain of ruin from the air, the like of which has never been seen on this earth.'

Reports came through from Hiroshima but they were not believed. So the emperor sssent envoys to ssseeee. The truth. To sseee that a ssingle bomb had leveled his city.

the gathering and relay of this information took 52 hours.

by which time the bomber captain had decided it was time to drop the other

because the weather was just perfect

to dessstroy a city.

80,000 dead in Nagasaki.

Fat Man. Duplicate of the plutonium implosion model
tested at Trinity

What's a Jew doing naming it Trinity?

OPPIE: I'd been reading Donne.

LILITH: Batter my heart, three-person'd God

OPPIE: And another, written just before his death.

"As West and East
in all flat maps — and I am one — are one
So death doth touch the Resurrection."
(Lilith clicks at him.)
And now —

the fallout —

(Young Scientist walks across the stage with a geiger counter. It registers higher and lower, but never silence.)

YOUNG SCIENTIST: We didn't really think about the fallout.

RABI: Didn't really think about the fallout?

YOUNG SCIENTIST: We thought there might not be any fallout.

RABI: How could there not be any fallout?

YOUNG SCIENTIST: We didn't know if it was going to go off.

(Beat.)

RABI: Right.

OPPIE: Cattle started showing up looking as if they'd had a light dusting of snow.

Radiation burns. The hair grew back in white.

All around the test site . . . the ranches we had commandeered. The army had commandeered. Telling people they'd get their land back after the war. Lingering radiation made the water undrinkable.

We'd poisoned the wells.

(Teller bursts in.)

TELLER: We must Immediately begin production for my SUPER. The THERMO-NUCLEAR DEVICE.

OPPIE: They've surrendered. Let's just —

TELLER: It must be done.

OPPIE: get back to our lives. The Universities.

TELLER: IT CAN BE DONE.

Someone will do it.

Therefore, it must be done.

OPPIE: Edward, I don't even know if it *can* be done.

TELLER: IT MUST.

OPPIE: The war is over.

(Lights down to a spot on Oppie.)

The war is over.

Kitty . . . .

what have I done?

KITTY: *(Very gently.)* What needed to be done.

Drink?

OPPIE: Thank you, darling.

(Kitty exits.)

LILITH: *Is it perfume from a dress that makes me so digress?*

OPPIE: Mm?

LILITH: What's in your ticky little mind?

OPPIE: a different time.

When I was less comfortable in a roomful of men and women.

A time when I would just as soon leave a party as —

(A sudden burst of cocktail party music and chatter. Kitty re-enters, wearing an elegant but sexy little cocktail dress, a drink in each hand. She gives him one.)

OPPIE: I'm sorry?

KITTY: I said, it's a great shame I'm married.

OPPIE: Why?

KITTY: Because I find you very attractive, Dr. Oppenheimer.

OPPIE: *(Blushes.)*

KITTY: I'm sorry. Did I shock you?

OPPIE: No . . . no . . .

KITTY: I'm like that. Just blunder my way through any social situation. That's why I make it a point to dress well. It helps people overlook what I've said when we've all sobered up.

OPPIE: I'm not planning on sobering up.

KITTY: Good for you!

OPPIE: No, I mean . . . I'm not drunk.

KITTY: Well, what are you waiting for? The night is young and you're with another man's wife.

OPPIE: I would have to agree with you.

KITTY: Shall we make our way to the drinks, then?

OPPIE: I would have to agree with you that it is a great shame. That you are married.

KITTY: Well, perhaps there's still hope of shocking you, Dr. Oppenheimer.

(She lowers her voice to a stage whisper.)

It's not an incurable state. Marriage.

(She looks to see if he's shocked.)

OPPIE: Robert. Please call me Robert.

KITTY: Kitty.

(She presents her hand.)

Charmed, I'm sure.

OPPIE: I'm not sure of much, right now.

KITTY: Well then.

You must be Charmed.

(Party fades.)

LILITH: A charmed life.

To cause the deaths of so many.

OPPIE: The greatest scientific undertaking . . . ever.

And in the end, it was for this.

A blast with the light of a thousand suns.

Finally brought that . . . Unconditional Surrender.

(Jean appears. Drowned. Oppie starts, takes a step toward her. She opens her mouth to speak. Water pours out. Oppie rubs his eyes, one hand squeezed over them, massaging his temples. She recedes into the shadows.)

I had wanted . . .

We had all wanted.

To know.

What would happen.

LILITH: ssssseeeeeking knowledge?

OPPIE: yes

LILITH: and?

OPPIE: And to stop Hitler, of course. It was of the utmost importance that we find this knowledge before he did.

Knowledge had always been implicitly good. Now this very premise must be questioned.

I have . . . blood on my hands.

What if you

what if you spend your life in pursuit of knowledge and it

unleashes a great destructive force upon the world

and not even on Hitler but on —

what if you spend all your time and thoughts and breath and life creating this great destructive force and you wish you had never unleashed the fury inside those atoms? Let uranium 235 remain sovereign and unbroken. Not opened that box?

LILITH: I've heard all this ssssssomewhere before.

God says

I've got this great idea

I'm going to make a woman

out of dirt

and breathe into her nostrils and look how beautiful

SHE LIVES.

Adam and Lilith, my playthings. I breathed my wet god-breath into their little dirt mouths and look at the mud things walking around naming the beasts, eating the plants.

then Adam says to me LIE DOWN
as if we were not both the same
he says LIE DOWN I WANT TO
and I say, hey, wait a minute here, I'm not saying let's not have fun, but what makes you the one to climb up on top of me? I don't think this is really about sex here I don't think this is about exploring these new bodies with the new wet life breathed in I think this is about you trying to get on top of me
LIE DOWN
I think you want to hold me there
LIE DOWN
He would not stop saying it and his face all red
LIE DOWN
Grabbed both my arms and tried to knock me down in the dirt we'd both come from.

I spoke the sacred name of God and flew up into the sky.

Went off on my own, to the shores of the red sea. Till he thought better of his behavior.
We're all learning here, after all.

But Adam
Adam goes to God and he complains
that I will not lie down and God says

What?

Don't worry, little man
I will make you a new one.

I will rip open your side
and take from you
since you would not take what I made you the first time

(and I thought, made You?)

let me rip a piece from you
close to the heart

now I take this dripping bloody piece of you and I make you a woman
who will lie down. She will do nothing but lie down.
she will lie down for you.

and to me he says
eat their babies.
They are delicious.

Especially the red-brown marrow in the troughs of their white bones.
TELLER: WE MUST MAKE MY SUPER.

Nothing changes. Don't go —
OPPIE: We're going home.

everyone is going home.
(Light on Young Scientist, placing plutonium cubes carefully atop a pile.)
YOUNG SCIENTIST: Before we go

just a few final
(Removes a large cube from the bottom, adds a small one on top.)
calculations
*(Drops the large cube onto the pile. The room is instantly suffused with a blue
glow. The geiger counters go crazy.)*
ah!
*(He knocks this final cube off the pile. The blue glow stops, the clicking is
silenced.)*
YOUNG SCIENTIST: That was a close one!

Did . . . .

did anyone get a reading on that?
(Blackout. Sound of decontamination showers.
*Makeshift hospital: Los Alamos. The Young Scientist lies, oxygen-tented, in a
hospital bed. Sound of labored breathing. Oppenheimer sits at his bedside,
reading from a small book.)*
OPPIE: *Our bodies are known to end,*
but the embodied self is enduring,
indestructible, and immeasurable;
therefore, Arjuna, fight the battle!

As a man discards
worn-out clothes
to put on new ones,
so the embodied self
discards
its worn-out bodies

to take on other new ones.

Weapons do not cut it,
fire does not burn it,
waters do not wet it,
wind does not wither it.

If you think of its birth
and death as ever-recurring,
then too, Great Warrior,
you have no cause to grieve.
(Oppie wipes at his eyes.)

NURSE: Perhaps you should go now, Dr. Oppenheimer. He should rest.

OPPIE: You think I'm keeping him awake?

NURSE: *(Gently.)* I think you should get some sleep, actually.

OPPIE: Oh.

I suppose . . .

That's . . . very kind of you.

(Oppie and the Nurse move away from the bedside.)

NURSE: I thought that Jews had the same Bible, or the first part, anyway.

OPPIE: *(Absently.)* Yes, they do.

NURSE: What was that, then?

OPPIE: One of the sacred Hindu texts.

It's Krishna's instructions to the warrior Arjuna, who . . . hesitates on the battlefield.

NURSE: And you believe that stuff?

OPPIE: I find it . . . beautiful.

There are those who would say that makes it true. I . . . cannot.

(He puts on his coat.)

I can prove it with Matter.

NURSE: What?

OPPIE: Neither created nor destroyed.

(Nurse nods. She's heard this before.)

You . . . You've seen this before.

You've seen men die.

You've seen babies take that first breath into their lungs

(He is desperate, searching.)

You tell me. Is it the same?

Are we never . . . destroyed . . . utterly?

(Nurse looks at him.)

NURSE: You're right, Dr. Oppenheimer.

OPPIE: What?

NURSE: It's a nice idea.

(*Noise. Breathing more labored.*)

NURSE: You'd better go.

(*Nurse disappears. Oppie stares. Light out on the hospital scene.*

Oppie's shoulders collapse. He seems to sink into himself. Covers his face with his hands.

Lilith arrives to collect him.)

LILITH: Oppie.

One death?

You are a sentimentalist.

OPPIE: It's my fault.

LILITH: Many things are your fault.

OPPIE: And the pictures started coming back.

Horrible, horrible things.

(*Mother appears, wearing a kimono. Her back is to us.*)

Kimono burns. The embroidery thread burned the flowers directly onto their skins.

(*Teller appears, crouched over a small seismograph. He stares at it intently.*)

Among the photos brought back from Hiroshima, there was a woman. Severe burns. She was missing three fingers from her right hand.

(*Slowly, elegantly, Mother begins to pull off her gloves.*)

I know it doesn't mean anything.

Still. It struck me.

(*As she removes the second one:*

Blackout.)

END ACT I

ACT II

Teller appears, with a kimono as a dressing gown, over his clothes. He has a basin, a shaving brush, a cake of soap.

TELLER: Ah. If a thing is to be done.
It should be done properly.
(He creates lather, taking time and pleasure with this routine; lathers up and begins to shave with a straight razor.)
You see, Oppie, you are not the only one with a refined sensibility. You do not have a patent on the understanding of beauty.
And certainly not of truth.

I am the one who knows. Who always knew.
I drove Szilard to Einstein, in my old Plymouth, beat up and sputtering, stopping to ask directions of a child along the way. I got him to Einstein, to sign the letter to FDR warning
what the Germans were about to do
While you taught worshipful graduate students the correct wine to choose with dinner.

Who is better equipped to see what is needed?
I know what this country my adopted country, needs.

I will protect this country from Communism. From Fascism. From any threat. Because I am willing to do the ugly thing. First.

I have been accused of being a monomaniac. I ask you. Could a mono-maniac play the piano like this?
(He plays Mozart's Eine Kleine Nachtmusik: *The first two phrases deli-cately, but he cannot resist playing the third with great force and bombast.)*
Ha.
They do not know me.
Or else they underestimate me. All of them. All the thems. Out there, who do not know.

Opje, they say you do not suffer fools gladly. But you do. You suffer them. More gladly than I. I can't suffer them at all. Not at all. No more fools for me. Suffering, I will take gladly. But not fools.
There are so many fools these days.
And Opje, you are the worst.
Because they listen to you.

You make fools of all the rest.

This I will not suffer. My community to be made fools, every one. Fools for Russia. SHE IS DANGEROUS. YOU FOOLS.

A young boy. Is working on a layer cake. Mother Russia, with her Russian Dolls, one inside another inside another inside another. She's got one in the oven. Ja. Uranium wrapped in Lithium Deuteride. Wrapped in Uranium. So on. Frosted in high-impact explosive.

A young boy named Sakharov has no-one telling him to stop. No one telling him, We must not do this thing.

He is building his layer cake. To bring this country to its knees.

Later he will be sorry and sad. He will be a dissident. A fool like you, Opje.

But only after he's made it work.

When all fools get their conscience caught up. After the moment of discovery.

After coition, man sighs. And thinks and is sad.

After it's too late.

The woman understands the moment to hesitate is before, not after.

After is too late.

Does this help me? None at all. Helps me none at all.

I will be alone. All "good" men will turn their backs on me.

Because they say I stabbed you there, Opje.

You should not have turned away.

You knew the knife was in my hand. You should have helped me to wield it. And protect this great country. This country that you profess to love. You should not have turned from me.

From this idea that must now be born. It is in my head. It is in Sakharov's. In layer upon layer in his mind. It was in Klaus Fuchs. The head that he took with him each time he met his Russian contact, in Santa Fe, New Mexico. In a coffee shop in New York. In a pub in London. That big head went along. Full of secrets.

Klaus, he is very good at keeping secrets.

Ja.

And passing them like notes in school. He has a crush on the Soviet Union. As so many of you do. Because you do not know her, Mother

Russia. You do not know she breaks bones. You do not know the gulag is built with them.

This bomb must happen. I have seen it in my mind. It will happen.

And I will be cast out, before that first test. I will watch from the basement of my Berkeley lab, four in the morning, watching the tiny dot of light. The photo-seismograph. At precisely the test time, there is a tiny shudder. I almost think I have not seen it. But I have seen it. A tiny shudder.

The world's first thermo-nuclear reaction.

It is begun.

But that is later.

(He towels the last of the lather off his face.)

Not now.

But soon.

(He exits, revealing Oppie besieged by reporters.)

REPORTERS: *(Overlapping.)* Dr. Oppenheimer!

Dr. Oppenheimer!

(Oppie squints in the newsreel camera light. Nods to one reporter.)

REPORTER: Dr. Oppenheimer, can you tell us what your first thoughts were upon seeing the explosion at Trinity?

OPPIE: We knew the world would not be the same.

A few people laughed. A few people cried. Most people were silent.

I remembered the line from the Hindu scriptures, the Bhagavad-Gita.

Vishnu is trying to persuade the prince that he should do his duty, and to impress him, takes on his multi-armed form and says Now I am become Death, the Destroyer of Worlds.

I suppose we all thought that, some way or another.

LILITH: Dessssssssssstroyer.

OPPIE: I need to make this stop.

Got to make it stop.

I have a responsibility to my country —

LILITH: *Your* country.

Do you really think it's yours?

OPPIE: Of course it is.

LILITH: The Jews have never had a country. Only the clothes on their back.

oppie oppie oppie

so naïve

how does such a smart man

learn so little
from Hissssstory?

OPPIE ADDRESSES THE SCIENTISTS

OPPIE: The experience of war has left us with a legacy of concern. Nowhere is this troubled sense of responsibility more acute than among those who participated in the development of atomic energy for military purposes.

In some crude sense which no vulgarity, no humor, no overstatement can quite extinguish, the physicists have known sin; and this is a knowledge which they cannot lose.

LILITH: pisssssed a lot of people off that time

OPPIE: My first year at Cambridge, I . . . was under a great deal of strain. Over summer's break I went on holiday with friends to Corsica. We were to continue on to Sardinia, but I felt much refreshed and told my companions that I had to return to school immediately, as I'd left a poisoned apple on Professor Blackett's desk.

It was a metaphor. Rotten scholarship, not a nice gift for teacher. A bad paper.

I discovered later that my companions had missed the metaphor and worried that I'd cracked up for good.

LILITH: And now. Did you return?

Dare disturb the University?

OPPIE: How could I? *(Sits, beaten.)* How could I?

PANDORA'S BOX

Rabi enters. Looks at him a moment.

RABI: You should take Princeton.

(With a little shrug, a little smile.)

It's a nice campus.

OPPIE: *(Looks at him.)* Things will never be the same.

RABI: No.

But perhaps . . . better?

(Oppie looks away.)

You remember, in the story. The last thing let out, after all the demons are set loose. The last thing to come out of Pandora's Box is hope.

The horror of this weapon is so shocking a thing —

OPPIE: *(An awakening.)* You're right. People will see. People will have to understand.

LILITH: I always wondered.

With Pandora's Box.

Is Hope a good thing?

Or is that the final evil loosed upon the world.

That no matter what, you are cursed with this

Hope.

That things will turn out alright.

OPPIE: It's so clear — if all the countries of the world agree

never to produce these things again

instead of bombs

we make reactors

energy enough to light the darkness

irrigate the deserts

produce food

energy — the universal currency of production — will barely be an expense.

abundance, plenty, ease

these things are within our grasp

as a people

as a world

(Lilith laughs.)

OPPIE: What?

LILITH: *(Kind.)* You're funny.

OPPIE: It's possible! Right now —

if we don't

lose this chance —

LILITH: not yours to lose

OPPIE: *(Urgent.)* yes

LILITH: It doesn't work.

OPPIE: what do you —

LILITH: It doesn't work.

There is no future of light and harmony and grace.

OPPIE: Maybe you're wrong.

LILITH: *(Shrugs.)* Maybe I am.

OPPIE: Can you see

everything?

LILITH: only flashes.

flashes of light. explosions.

they don't stop.

pain. the smell of blood. Women ripped open by the life inside them.

Thousands of times a day.

smell of gunpowder

smell of iron

smell of ozone

a lightning storm and the ground is soaked with blood

more of you grow out of this blood soaked dirt

there is quiet for a while

and then it starts again

the explosions

blood and crying little wriggling things

with soft sweet bones

the explosions get bigger and bigger

the earth shakes and trembles

she is pitted in her deserts

in her oceans

choking smell of ozone the atmosphere is torn

like a woman's cunt

no time to heal in between

the explosions get bigger and bigger

and then tiny

but they never stop

so small

barely a pinprick

a girl straps explosives to her waist

and walks to the market

a bus splits in two

a marine barracks

an embassy

rhythm like a tapping

like a ticking

of something big

waiting to

explode.

OPPIE: STOP IT.

LILITH: Why do you fight?

OPPIE: IT STOPS. Here.

I will dedicate my life to it.

LILITH: *(Smiles.)* one life . . .

REPORTERS: *(Overlapping.)* Dr. Oppenheimer!

Dr. Oppenheimer!

OPPIE: *(Flooded with newsreel camera light.)* I have been asked whether in the years to come it will be possible to kill 40 million American people in the twenty largest American towns by the use of atomic bombs in a single night. I'm afraid the answer to that question is Yes.

Our only hope lies in international control of this force so great it could mean the death of all civilization.

(To Lilith.)

People will see.

These are not weapons for war. These are weapons to stop war. Make it so hideous a thing it can no longer be contemplated.

LILITH: There is nothing so hideous it cannot be held within the confines of a human skull.

OPPIE: An appeal to people's better nature, the spirit of cooperation, and WHAT'S SO FUNNY?

LILITH: When do you stop being a boy?

OPPIE: I was never a child as a child. I was always . . . this.

(Jean becomes visible, lying down, reading the paper. The calm of a happier time. Oppie starts, composes himself.)

LILITH: She's dead, you know.

OPPIE: I know.

LILITH: Pretty girl.

OPPIE: *(Snaps around to Lilith.)* leave me alone, can't you leave me alone for one damned minute?

(He turns around.)

LILITH: Don't turn your back on me. You will regret it.

(She is gone.)

OPPIE: *(Smiles.)* What's one more?

JEAN: *(Calls, not looking up from her paper.)* What did you say?

(Oppie approaches her, strokes the gentle curve of her side.)

OPPIE: Did you know, in Sanskrit poetry, the poets always make reference to the great beauty of the three rolls of fat at the beloved's waist?

JEAN: What's that mean?

OPPIE: You wouldn't have been considered beautiful at all.

JEAN: Well, it's a good thing I'm not written in Sanskrit.

OPPIE: And lips like ripe bimba fruit.

JEAN: What *could* that mean?

OPPIE: *(Smiles.)* Red!

JEAN: Mmmm.

OPPIE: *(Shrugs.)* Lips like cherries, lips like bimba fruit . . .

JEAN: So the most beautiful women were great fat cows?

OPPIE: Beauty changes. Elizabethan women plucked their hairlines, as a high forehead was considered the zenith of beauty.

Of course, In modern times. You. Are the most beautiful woman in the world.

(Jean makes an amused noise, continues reading.)

OPPIE: What are you reading?

JEAN: *The People's World.*

OPPIE: What people?

JEAN: The workers.

OPPIE: Oh, those people.

JEAN: Those who pick the bimba fruit. Or strawberries.

Did you know the migrant workers call strawberries the Devil's Fruit. It's backbreaking labor, picking them off the ground all day. Bending from sunup to sundown.

OPPIE: Yes, it's terrible, the inequities of the world.

JEAN: *(Sits up, agitated.)* You say that. It's perfectly easy to say that. But are you willing to *do* something about it? There are people who —

Listen. I want you to come to a meeting with me —

(Lights up, harsh, on a Senate Committee Meeting.)

STRAUSS: But what of the Communist Menace?

INSULTS STRAUSS

Oppenheimer testifies before a Senate Committee on the export of isotopes.

STRAUSS: These ISOTOPES, that you claim would be perfectly safe to release to scientists in Norway, many of whom have KNOWN COMMUNIST CONTACTS. Isn't it true these ISOTOPES could be used by a Foreign Power to make their own atomic bomb?

OPPIE: *(Much put-upon by the ignorance around him.)* No one can force me to say you cannot use these isotopes for atomic energy. You can use a shovel for atomic energy. In fact you do. You can use a bottle of beer for atomic energy. In fact, you do. But the fact is that during the war and after the war these materials have played no significant part and in my knowledge no part at all.

(A ripple of laughter in the senate. Strauss turns purple with fury.)

My own rating of the importance of isotopes in this broad sense is that they are far less important than electronic devices, but far more important than, let us say, vitamins, somewhere in between.

(More laughter. Oppie smiles and nods to the room. Strauss, front:)

STRAUSS: I'll get that Jew commie if it's the last thing I do.

(Scene blackout.

glow on Lilith)

LILITH: Ju-lius.

OPPIE: I thought you were gone.

LILITH: *(Shrugs.)* When you don't hear me anymore, then I'm gone.

OPPIE: I long for that day.

LILITH: The great silence? It will come soon enough.

You'll miss my breath in your ear. As you will miss this
Prestige.

This grand role in the International Theater of War.

TELLER: Opje, what is the meaning —

my funding is held up. Now that you have spoken to the committee.
The top men say Yes, we come work on the Super. They call you first, and they don't want to work anymore. Why?

OPPIE: Those men made their own decisions.

TELLER: NO. YOU MADE THE DECISION.

OPPIE: If a man asks my opinion, I give it.

TELLER: Your opinion. Is wrong.

And you are killing me, holding up this funding.

OPPIE: I cannot in good conscience counsel the government to spend billions on a project unlikely to produce practical results.

TELLER: You will kill us all.

(He stalks off.)

LILITH: The man with the Atomic Answers, molding public policy.

OPPIE: It's a matter of where one is called —

LILITH: Personal scientific advisor to the President.

OPPIE: someone had to —

LILITH: Cover of *Life* magazine. Interviews on television. Rushing Einstein for the title of most famous theoretical physicist in the world!

OPPIE: I didn't seek — all this. Before the war theoretical physics was among the most esoteric of all academic disciplines, comparable to Medieval French Poetry or . . . Sanskrit. Akin, almost, to taking the cloth.

But this is not angels dancing on the head of a pin
this is splitting the smallest increment of the head of the pin releasing
the Fury inside
the Fury at this
violation.

or we were the angels
dancing on the head of that pin
that pin that was about to
explode

LILITH: boom.

OPPIE: I did not court this. Fame. I did not seek it out.

LILITH: But you liked it.

OPPIE: I have never claimed to be super-human. I liked it, yes.

LILITH: Yessssssss.

OPPIE: And I had a responsibility. Someone had to tell them. We must not go on from here. There is no need for a bomb fifty, a hundred times the power of the one that leveled Hiroshima.

RABI: But how can we be sure the Russians aren't working toward one? That plan of Teller's, with the addition by Fuchs, could perhaps be workable.

OPPIE: A nuclear explosion as ignition? It will blow itself apart long before the thermo-nuclear reaction is triggered.
And besides, Russia suffered greatly in this war. They need to rebuild first. The only way Stalin could be devoting significant resources to an atomic program would be to starve his people.

RABI: You're right. Only a madman would —

LILITH: And so it was that a madman starved his people to create the magnificent explosion. Left Siberia without electricity so that a handful of young scientists would never be without what they needed to make the big explosion.
and then

THE BRITISH ENVOY

BRITISH ENVOY: Beg your pardon, so sorry to trouble you. But it looks as if we're in a bit of a rough spot, something of a sticky wicket, so to speak.

Chocolate? So nice not to have it rationed anymore, what?

Ahem. It seems our intelligence has uncovered something of a Spy Ring at your Los Alamos, there. Chap by the name of Greenglass, Jewish fellow, seems his contact was Harry Gold, another, well you know. Transmitted the information through a Julius *Rosenberg*. Greenglass' brother-in-law. Keep it in the family, eh? Apparently they're all very gung ho about this classless society for the worker business —

Toffee? They're rather good.

Er, ahem. How did we find all this out? Well, it's a funny story. It's through the . . . eh . . . the fellow we sent you. Klaus Fuchs.

Funny little chap. Glasses.

Yes. It seems he's a Russian Agent.

So sorry, but you know we were a trifle busy, what with the V2's raining down. Perhaps if our allies had been a little quicker to enter the war, there'd have been more time for the paperwork, what?

Turkish Delight?

(At the mentions of the name, Lilith sings an echo: "Green glass. Greenglass." Teller strides on, shoving a large sheaf of papers into Oppie's hands.)

TELLER: Fuchs was there. In the room. HE WAS IN CHARGE OF WRITING UP ALL THE NOTES. A spy! A damned spy among us! Sending all my ideas straight to MOTHER RUSSIA. They stole my country when I was a boy, and now they will STEAL THE VERY IDEAS FROM MY MIND. Fuchs thinks there is possibility to succeed. Ah? And so do the Russians. I need MONEY. I need MEN. a CRASH PROGRAM. NOW. We MUST HAVE THE SUPER.

(Under Teller's rant, Oppie has been looking at his papers, frowning. Gradually, his face relaxes, then breaks into a soft smile.)

OPPIE: *(Muttering.)* X-rays. Trigger the thermo-nuclear reaction almost instantaneously using X-rays.

LILITH: And you said it was

OPPIE: Sweet.

LILITH: Sssssssweeeeeeet.

OPPIE: This . . . this could work.

TELLER: *What?* You now . . . *yes?*

and what of your precious Scruples? Mmmm?

OPPIE: When you see something that is technically sweet, you go ahead and do it and argue about what to do about it only after you have had your technical success.

LILITH: And what *of* your precious scruples?

OPPIE: *(Looks at her.)* The calculations . . . It was . . . beautiful.

TELLER: So you will return then to Los Alamos?

   (Beat.)

OPPIE: No.

   This one's yours.

   (Teller bows curtly, exits.)

LILITH: If a thing is beautiful, it should go on? No matter what the consequences?

OPPIE: It's hard to think of consequences.

   When a thing is so beautiful.

LILITH: Ah yes.

   And the island of Elugelab disappeared beneath the sea.

   To protect against the Communist Menace.

   Embodied for the country as a little Jewish couple from the Lower East Side.

   oh the terror you could inspire with that word

   Rosenberg.

ETHEL

LILITH: Ethel ethel ethel. Ethel didn't know what hit her. Home making latkes. Noodle Kugel. Didn't know U-235 from Saltpeter. Didn't didn't didn't. Didn't know what hitler.

   Except in her blood. Ethel ethel ethel. Her blood remembers the shtetl. Her blood sings
   (She sings softly.)
   Ethel.
   The cossacks have come again.
   As the gas flows like liquid into her lungs.

   They didn't pull her teeth.

   The government of the United States of America does not melt down the gold from the teeth of the Jews it gasses.

OPPIE: She was electrocuted.

LILITH: Mmmmm. All the difference.

   oppie oppie oppie. So ethical. So cultural.
   What do you do when they point the finger at you and say
   HE'S POISONED THE WELL AGAIN.

STRAUSS GETS THE CALL

Ringing. Strauss, wearing a yarmulke, picks up an enormous phone.

STRAUSS: Yes?

    Yes, Mr. President.

    Head of the Atomic Energy Commission?

    Yes, Sir!

    Thank you, Sir!

    (Hangs up phone, clenching the yarmulke in one fist.)

    I'll get that Jew commie if it's the last thing I do!

    (Proclaims grandly.)

    Bring me the head of J. Robert Oppenheimer.

J. EDGAR HOOVER DOES THE DANCE
OF THE SEVEN VEILS

Music: Salome. Light rises on J. Edgar Hoover, his back to the audience, swathed in long scarves. He does the dance of the seven veils, removing one for each charge read. In the end, he is revealed in a sober gray suit and tie.

STRAUSS: Mr. Hoover, I have here a letter I think you will find of interest . . .

    I will read only the salient parts . . .

    the subject is J. Robert Oppenheimer. In the pre-war period, there is evidence that Oppenheimer

    1. Contributed substantial monthly sums to the Communist Party.

    2. Had, and still has, a wife and a brother who are Communists.

    3. Had at least one Communist Mistress.

    During the war, there is evidence that:

    4. He was responsible for employing a number of Communists at Los Alamos

    5. He was a vigorous supporter of the H-bomb program until Hiroshima, Aug. 6, 1945, on which day he personally urged each senior individual working in this field to desist and

    6. He was an enthusiastic sponsor of the A-bomb until the war ended, when he immediately and outspokenly advocated that the Los Alamos laboratory be disbanded.

    After the war, Oppenheimer:

    7. Worked tirelessly to retard the H-bomb program.

    In conclusion, we must realize that

STRAUSS AND HOOVER: More probably than not, Dr. Oppenheimer is an espi-
onage agent under Soviet Direction.

HOOVER: Erect a Blank Wall between this man and any top-secret documents
currently in his purview. Confiscate his filing cabinets. And subpoena
that mistress!

STRAUSS: We can't, sir. She's dead.

HOOVER: A dead red?

STRAUSS: Yes, sir.

HOOVER: *(Sighs.)* I never thought I'd be sorry to hear those words.

OPPIE: Are they talking about Jean?

LILITH: Of course.

OPPIE: Mistress. That's ridiculous.

LILITH: Did you sleep with her?

OPPIE: Yes.

(Jean appears in back, dancing vaguely to the same waltz.)

LILITH: When you were not married?

OPPIE: Yes.

I considered us engaged, but she never —

LILITH: And also, when you were married. To someone else.

OPPIE: yes.

LILITH: Then what was she, if not your mistress?

OPPIE: She was . . . a friend.

LILITH: a friend.

With black hair. And green eyes.

OPPIE: yes

LILITH: and immaculate breeding.

OPPIE: soft cool hands, touching my face.

as if —

(Jean disappears.)

LILITH: Were you a disappointment to her?

OPPIE: Jean?

LILITH: *(Cocks an eyebrow.)* Your mother.

OPPIE: Why?

LILITH: Because you weren't Normal.

OPPIE: *(Smiling.)* I suppose I wasn't, at that.

Gave my first lecture to the New York Mineralogical Society at twelve.
They didn't know I was twelve until I got there. I had submitted a paper,
which they asked me to read.

I suppose my parents were a bit . . . worried. They tried sending me to camp, the next year, but the other boys locked me in an icehouse overnight.

LILITH: Because you were Jewish?

OPPIE: *(Laughs.)* It was a Jewish camp.

Because I was an insufferable little prick, I suppose.

LILITH: And were you a disappointment to Jean?

OPPIE: Oh, yes. I, and the world.

Very much.

LILITH: And in the end, a disappointment to your Government.

Because the Government has ideas about creation, too. Took it upon themselves to create a Scientific Advisor. And he may be a Jew, but he's from this country. Speaks without an accent! And he's tall and elegant and cultured. A wise man, a pretty man. And he makes the bomb that ends the war. A tall bringer of miracles. He unleashes the power inside the tiny things you can't see. These Atoms.

But then he throws his intellect around like a Lariat, knocking things off the shelves. And he tells everyone the Hydrogen Bomb will be bad.
Then you have to throw him out.
get yourself a new one who will
LIE DOWN.

HEARING

Strauss bangs a large gavel.

STRAUSS: Dr. Oppenheimer, you realize this is not a trial.

(Smiles a big smile.)

This is merely a hearing to determine whether your security clearance will be renewed.

OPPIE: I do not believe that there are any new charges against me. I believe these are the same issues that did not stand in the way of my being granted clearance in wartime.

LILITH: when they needed you.

STRAUSS: This is a proceeding in which classified material will be discussed. In the interest of National Security, during such discussions your lawyers, who do not have clearance, will have to leave the room.

LILITH: Ssssecurity.

(Throughout the following, Strauss' monologue is continuous, leaping into the foreground where noted.)

OPPIE: Security would have had us all Separate. Isolated. Ignorant. Speaking
    different languages. But I changed all that. I said
    build us a great rabbit warren. Our minds will breed.
    Lock out the world. Lock us in. Together.
    And they argued, all those bright bright minds.
    Would have been speaking different languages. If not for me. But I
    listened and I smoothed and I interpreted and I moved on to the next
    conflict and we
    kept building
    I made an Orchestra and we
    kept building
    And we reached God.
    And he vaporized the tower. Fused the sand below into beautiful green
    glass that set the Geiger counters clicking like locusts in the desert.
STRAUSS: And also that you caused to be hired various communists, and in
    fact ONLY communists, to work at Los Alamos.
    Rossi Lomanitz
    Joseph Weinberg
    David Bohm
    Max Friedman —
    That a number of graduate students in Dr. Oppenheimer's "inner circle"
    at Berkeley were either Communists or "fellow travelers" —
OPPIE: Is this the part where you peck out my liver?
LILITH: Pro-me-te-O — !
    Don't use references the committee won't get. Only makes them
    ANGRY.
STRAUSS: That in fact his own Brother was a card-carrying member of the
    Communist Party prior to his employment at the top secret Los Alamos
    labs —
OPPIE: All that time. All that money. My god, we could have built another
    bomb with the money spent surveilling me.
    And still. Those secrets walked themselves out.
    Because secrets have no place in Science.
    And Science has no place in War.
LILITH: Science has always been about war.
OPPIE: That's not true.
LILITH: Metallurgy was invented for spearheads, not plowshares.

Discovery is always about getting the one-up on the next guy.

Bigger club. Bigger bomb.

OPPIE: Science is about the free flow of ideas. It knows no borders. It is a*
community of *minds.*

LILITH: *A community of minds that needs the Army to foot the bills. Pay
for the philosophers' keep. And their cyclotrons.

OPPIE: Fuchs didn't . . . *steal* these ideas, he *had* them.

Why, he proposed the alteration to Teller's Super that made the damned
thing workable.

LILITH: You make a bargain with the devil, he's going to come one day and
want your soul. He will organize a committee to get it. Have himself a
Hearing.

JEAN

STRAUSS: That on June 12, 1943, he was followed to the rooms of a known
Communist woman, Jean Tatlock. He did not see fit to inform security,
either before or after this incident —

(Oppie hears these words with a certain shock. Breathes for a moment.)

OPPIE: Surveilled and surveilled and surveilled.

Wartime and beyond.

WHAT IS THIS, RUSSIA?

The last night I spent with a woman who felt Death breathing down her
back. That last night Violated. As they watched the house. Or had it
Bugged.

Our last sad . . . love.

There were tears involved, if I recall correctly. all these years later.

I recall correctly.

I recall . . . everything.

Blue veins across her white skin.

Freckles on her shoulders from the sun.

The curve of her back as she . . . bent to unbuckle a shoe.

Those eyes.

That I had . . . got lost in. Many a time.

Now *she* was lost in them.

Staring out of her face at me, as if

as if I possessed some sort of Answer and when I didn't . . . .

I, who was now no longer lost in the unswimmable green depths of her eyes but Found

in the yellow sand of Los Alamos.

I saw her there, receding from the world.
like a ghost
(Jean appears, wearing a long silk robe.)
But I was of the world now, in the world and I had to serve it. To save it. Not her. Anymore.

Just this one night to hold her thin shaking body in my arms.
As they waked and watched from their cars outside.

No, the security men must not have bugged the house.
Or they would know
We did not speak of Communism that night.
(Jean opens her robe. She wears a petal-pink silk slip. Burns on her body, in the shape of flowers. She opens her mouth — red, yellow, orange petals like flame.)
Make it stop.
please make it stop
(Lilith clicks at him.)

STRAUSS: We will now hear testimony from Isador Rabi. Top-secret matters may be referred to, so would Dr. Oppenheimer's legal team kindly leave the room.

LILITH: as Kitty smokes in the corridor outside
(Strauss monologue out.)

KITTY SMOKES IN THE CORRIDOR OUTSIDE

KITTY: Bastards.
Bastards.
Bastards.
D'you hear that, Joe Dallet? You and your god-damned Party. Your sleek, incomparable Ideals. And I fell for you. In my bright party dress. And then there were no more party dresses, just the Party. Hardly any dresses at all. Left behind comfort and ease, and that vague sense of unease that comes with. Left behind my family's money, as you had. Fighting for the Worker. Fighting against your Father and his fat money, money made striding over the backs of the poor. I fell for you and your sweet

rightness, and love was enough for anything. Married in a plain blue dress at City Hall, and love was enough for anything. Living in a one-room flat with tenement heat and five-cent meals in the greasy restaurant downstairs, because the stove leaked and might blow us all up. And love was not enough, Joe. I missed hot water, and pretty clothes, and steak. And college. So I went back. Sat in that big living room in my pretty dress and the unease settling like an angry saint on my shoulders. Didn't know Mother was intercepting your letters. I thought you were disgusted with my weakness. Finally I broke, wrote begging you to take me back. By then you were fighting fascists in Spain. Said you'd never stopped loving me a day. We were to meet in Paris but instead I got the telegram. And the official condolences of the god-damned Party.

(Smokes.)

A dead man is no good to me, Joe.

Pretty speeches and pretty ideals. You bled to death on a field in Spain. Stalin did not feed his people. There is no free state for the worker.

A dead man is no good to me, Joe. I'll take a gin martini any day. And the love of a man who is here. With his arms around me. At the head of our table, with our children. Leaning down to kiss the top of my hair. You'd like him Joe. You'd say he's good for me.

You hear that? In there?
They're killing him.
This will kill him.

Right now they're asking about his wife and her Party Membership. If he muttered Atomic Secrets in his sleep, would I pass them along to Mother Russia.

(Smokes.)

Mother Russia. If I ever see the old bitch I'll scratch her eyes out.
Tell her to stop killing
my men.

RABI AND TELLER

LILITH: And Rabi says

RABI: This is simply ridiculous. All during Los Alamos and after, you have had men following my good friend, Dr. Oppenheimer. Don't you think if there *was* anything, you'd have found it?

Here you have a guy who is a consultant. If you don't like the advice he gives, don't consult him. Period.

Above all, the man's contribution to this country must be weighed.

There is a real, positive record . . . We have an H-bomb and a whole series of them. What more do you want, mermaids?

LILITH: And Teller says

TELLER: I know Oppenheimer as an intellectually most alert and very complicated person, and I think it would be presumptuous and wrong on my part if I would try in any way to analyze his motives.

STRAUSS: Do you or do you not believe that Dr Oppenheimer is a security risk?

TELLER: I believe that Dr. Oppenheimer's character is such that he would not knowingly and wittingly do anything that is designed to endanger the safety of this country. To the extent therefore, that your question is directed toward intent, I would say I do not see any reason to deny clearance. If it is a question of wisdom and judgment, as demonstrated by actions since 1945, then I would say one would be wiser not to grant clearance.

LILITH: Sssssssssoooo Teller comes back to haunt you. Because you turned your back on his big beautiful explosion.

OPPIE: We had done calculations, but none of us really understood . . . The photos* came back from Hiroshima —

LILITH: *The dead of Hiroshima are NOTHING. I have seen Hissssstory. People fall. You blink and a thousand lie at your feet. They become dirt. Again. Return to that black muck that God shaped me out of. But you —

OPPIE: There was a woman missing three fingers* from her right hand.

LILITH: *I have seen thousands. Hundred thousands. I saw your mother birth you. I should have taken you then. red and squalling but something told me no. this one will be interessssssting. this one will not LIE DOWN. for another century. Thissssssss one will take the rage of the Jews and make it explode.

OPPIE: *(Soft.)* I wanted to know . . . how the world worked.

LILITH: You wanted to KILL.

OPPIE: No.

LILITH: You could have voted for a demonstration.

OPPIE: They wouldn't have gone* for a demonstration . . .

LILITH: *No.

But you could have voted for one.

You suggested Hiroshima.

OPPIE: We gave them a list . . .

LILITH: You suggested Nagasaki

OPPIE: of possible targets that would appropriately demonstrate the

OPPIE AND LILITH: destructive force

(Oppie coughs. Lights another cigarette.)

LILITH: And then you turned your back.

On that sheer beautiful destructive force.

Teller could see in his mind's eye. The bomb ignited by the bomb.
Atomic blast captured and held. Until fusion
the great destructive force that fuels the sun
until fusion happened.

and then it would not be the hundred foot tower you'd built to hold the
bomb vaporized, as at your pretty Trinity. But the whole island it was sitting on. A mile-wide crater in the ocean floor.

HOW BEAUTIFUL

You turned your back on the thing you made happen.

God breathed into my mouth
but he sided with the other one
split him open and took out a rib

I spoke the sacred name of God and I
exploded
with a light as bright as a thousand suns.

CLEARANCE REVOKED

STRAUSS: It is the decision of this Board that the clearance of J. Robert Oppenheimer shall not be renewed.

LILITH: And now you know.

What it is to be cast out.

you will be an old man.
wandering the desert
without the company of your own kind
without the company of your
creation.
(Silence. The desert again. Oppie is alone.)

OPPIE: At least it's quiet.

(He coughs delicately.)

At least I'm at Princeton.

(He coughs again. spits into a handkerchief.)

Beneath the pretty trees.

(Silence.)

But I am forbidden to touch

to teach

to hear

to know

the discipline grows, changes

and I

am on the outside.

Forbidden to enter

the room.

(A silence. Jean appears. Smoking.)

VOICE-OVER: Dr. Oppenheimer? It's time for your test.

JEAN: You don't do a woman any favors, putting her on a pedestal. Just another way to avoid looking her in the eye.

(Oppie looks at Jean.)

OPPIE: Jean —

I'm sorry, I —

JEAN: *(She touches his face.)* Shhhh.

(Smoke rises behind his head.)

You've got to be still while they take the picture.

(Sound of an X-ray. Jean is gone. Silence. He looks for Lilith, but she is nowhere.)

CANCER

VOICE-OVER (INTERVIEWER): Dr. Oppenheimer?

(Oppie looks toward the voice.)

Dr. Oppenheimer, can you tell us what your first thoughts were upon seeing the explosion at Trinity?

OPPIE: *(Tired. He's said this before.)* A line from the Bhagavad-Gita crossed my mind. Krishna assumes his powerful, many-armed form and he says Now I am become Death, the destroyer of worlds.

VOICE-OVER (INTERVIEWER): Dr. Oppenheimer, could you tell us what your thoughts are on what our Atomic Policy should be?

OPPIE: No, I can't do that. I'm not close enough to the facts. And I'm not close enough to the thoughts of those who are worrying about it.

LILITH: All thisssss . . .

It *sticks in your throat*
doesn't it?

OPPIE: *(Coughs, smiles at her return.)* Yes.

LILITH: Where it grows.

taking on a life of its own.

OPPIE: *(Composing a letter.)* My Dear Hans. Thanks for your inquiries as to my health. My cancer is spreading rapidly; thus I am being radiated further, this time with electrons from a betatron.

(Pause. He laughs. Pause. Kitty is watching him from the doorway.)

LILITH: If you do something beautifully, why stop?

(He looks at Lilith.)

The cancer is not thinking of the consequences. It is thinking only of blossoming. growing.

OPPIE: yes.

LILITH: exploding in your bloodstream.

(He smiles.)

OPPIE: Kitty. Darling, please bring me a cigarette.

KITTY: The doctor says no cigarettes.

OPPIE: Kitty, please. Let's be objective. I am dying. Denying myself the pleasure of tobacco is not going to alter that fact.

(Kitty is already lighting two cigarettes. Passes him one.)

Thank you darling.

KITTY: As if I could deny you anything.

OPPIE: Rewriting history already? You used to make a sport of it.

KITTY: Only when you deserved it.

OPPIE: No, less often than that, surely.

KITTY: *(Looks at him. This interchange is very gentle between them.)* Can you eat some soup?

OPPIE: Oh, I don't think so.

KITTY: Some lime ice, then?

OPPIE: *(Smiles.)* Thank you. That sounds lovely.

(She exits.)

OPPIE: I can't help thinking if I'd been able to love Jean the way I love Kitty. The way I have *learned* to see — the real woman standing before me. Not some . . . theoretical ideal.

(In the next room, the phone rings.)

LILITH: She'd still be alive?

OPPIE: I don't know about that. I was going to say, she'd have married me.

KITTY: *(Enters.)* You'll never guess who just phoned.

It's the Government, darling. Those fuckers want to give you a prize now.

OPPIE: Oh, alright. I suppose.

KITTY: Alright?

OPPIE: *(Shrugs.)* Alright.

Will the President give it himself?

KITTY: I'll find out.

(She exits, returns.)

Yes.

OPPIE: Well then. He's a brave young man.

KITTY: As soon as he returns from a trip to Dallas.

(Lilith snorts.)

THE DEVIL

OPPIE: There is a Zen parable.

A man sees a devil in the market. The merchant says, this is an excellent devil, able to do anything you want. For only 20,000 yen, I will give him to you

The man agreed

I must warn you, said the merchant, this devil is no good.

— But you said he was an excellent devil

That's true, the merchant said, but he will always remain a devil. You have to keep him busy every minute. If he has free time, if he doesn't know what to do, then he is dangerous.

Well if that's all, said the man, and he took the devil home.

It went very well.

Each morning, the devil would kneel obediently while the man mapped out his chores for the day. Chop wood, light the stove, prepare my food, clean the house. All day the devil completed his tasks, at night he slept in his bamboo cage. It went on this way for months.

Then one day the man ran into an old friend in town, and they got to drinking sake, one little stone jar after another, and they ended up in the willow quarter. The ladies kept the two friends busy, and the next morning the man woke alone in a strange room. He paid the bill to the women, who looked quite different from what he remembered the previous evening, and hurried home.

From the road he saw smoke.

The devil had made an open fire, and was roasting the neighbor's child on a spit.

(Beat.)

I thought we were cracking open the secrets of the universe.

LILITH: You were.

OPPIE: I thought it would be a geode.

Shining in the first light of discovery.

LILITH: It is a geode filled with blood.

OPPIE: For only two billion dollars of the Army's money. I will give him to you.

I have left a poisoned apple on the desk.

I must go back.

I must go back.

LILITH: There is no back.

Little man. But you know that.

OPPIE: *I should have been a pair of claws*
scuttling the ragged seas

LILITH: Shhh.

it's time.

OPPIE: Science was my passion. my path. my breath. my truest love.

LILITH: and because your love will not behave, does not balance statue-still on that pedestal but blows it to pieces, you turn your back on her?

(Beat.)

OPPIE: No.

LILITH: No. Theory turns to practice.

OPPIE: The photos come back.

LILITH: The radioactivity lingers in half-lives of a billion years.

OPPIE: a lump grows in your throat

LILITH: And you go on.

Cursed and Blessed.

OPPIE: *(Smiles.)* I have heard the mermaids singing

in great howling sandstorms of desert winds and a fireball burst high above the earth.

For a full moment there was just the unbearable brightness. As the sound raced across the desert to catch up.

(Lilith waits.)

For a moment, in utter silence.

It had the light
of a thousand suns.
(Bright

dark

noise

curtain.)

END OF PLAY

LIVING OUT

Lisa Loomer

ORIGINAL PRODUCTION

Living Out was commissioned by the Mark Taper Forum (Gordon Davidson, Artistic Director; Charles Dillingham, Managing Director; Robert Egan, Producing Director) and received its world premiere in Los Angeles, California, opening on January 18, 2003. It was directed by Bill Rauch; the set design was Christopher Acebo; the costume design was by Candice Cain; the lighting design was by Lap-Chi Chu; the original music was by Joe Romano; the sound design was by Jon Gottlieb; the stage manager was Susie Walsh; and the production stage manager was Mary Michele Miner. The cast was as follows:

ANA	*Zilah Mendoza*
WALLACE	*Kate A. Mulligan*
LINDA	*Elizabeth Ruscio*
NANCY	*Amy Aquino*
BOBBY	*Carlos Gomez*
RICHARD	*Daniel Hugh Kelly*
SANDRA	*Maricela Ochoa*
ZOILA	*Diane Rodriguez*

Living Out received its New York City premiere at Second Stage Theatre (Timothy J. McClimon, Executive Director; Carole Rothman, Artistic Director; Christopher Burney, Associate Artistic Director), opening on September 30, 2003. It was directed by Jo Bonney; the set design was by Neil Patel; the costume design was by Emilio Sosa; the lighting design was by David Weiner; the sound design was by John Gromada; the stage manage was Kelly Hance; and the production stage managers were Pamela Edington and Leslie C. Lyter. The cast was as follows:

ANA	*Zilah Mendoza*
WALLACE	*Judith Hawking*
LINDA	*Kelly Coffield Park*
NANCY	*Kathryn Meisle*
BOBBY	*Gary Perez*
RICHARD	*Joseph Urla*
SANDRA	*Maria Elena Ramierez*
ZOILA	*Liza Colón-Zayas*

SOME THOUGHTS ON PRODUCTION

The set is a living room, a kitchen and two children's areas — flexible enough so that the play can go back and forth between an expensive home on the Westside of Los Angeles and a modest apartment on the Eastside. It's essential that the Anglo couple and the Latino couple occupy the same stage space. So sometimes the living room is Ana and Bobby's, and sometimes it's Richard and Nancy's. And sometimes it goes back and forth even within the same scene, allowing us to see overlapping and parallel worlds. In the park scenes, the living room couch becomes a bench. And, in the final three scenes, only a bed is onstage.

In the Taper production, there was a moveable outer ring that brought on key pieces such as crib or a chair — or actors. In the New York production, the living room and kitchen areas were on an inner turntable. So sometimes the couch was downstage — and the kitchen table, chairs and counter were upstage — and sometimes it was the reverse. Jenna's crib was upstage right, and Santiago's bed was upstage left — both behind scrims. A backdrop of palms came in to establish the park, and another backdrop later established a night sky. I will make references to the latter configuration in this text.

However the set is conceived, it should enable scene transitions to be seamless or you lose the rhythm and momentum of the story. Both Ana and Nancy have warm, colorful homes, so please avoid a look that is cold and conceptual.

In terms of tone . . . The play walks a delicate line between funny and tragic. Actors who are innately funny (not broad), who understand timing and irony, but are not afraid to go deep, capture the tone best. Please go for nuance of character and good intentions as opposed to caricature. Every character in this play cares about children and is doing the best they can . . . in their own way.

Music is also key in conveying tone. Percussive sounds are especially helpful in that they are neither comic nor sentimental and can drive the play forward and hint at something darker to come. Contemporary Latin music from Ana's favorite radio station and National Public Radio from Richard and Nancy's house also work well.

A NOTE ON LANGUAGE

Some productions have done the scenes between Spanish-speaking characters — in Spanish. The Spanish translation of those scenes is available upon request from Dramatists Play Service.

CHARACTERS

ANA HERNANDEZ: Early thirties, smart, proud, Salvadoran, a nanny.

NANCY ROBIN: Thirties, a lawyer, a liberal and a new mom.

BOBBY HERNANDEZ: Thirties, Salvadoran, a carpenter. Good sense of humor. Big heart. Still . . . a man who grew up in a war.

RICHARD ROBIN: Thirties or forties, a Public Defender, but offbeat. His liberal politics and ideals are in conflict with his instincts as a new dad.

WALLACE BREYER: Thirties, well-off, helpful, with a charming smile. An excellent manager, sure of her opinions, and eager to share them.

ZOILA TEZO: Forties, Guatemalan, a nanny, a woman who says what she thinks and likes to laugh.

LINDA BILLINGS FARZAM: Thirties, a well-intentioned, sweet, harried mom.

SANDRA ZAVALA: Late thirties, Mexican, a nanny, positive and practical, an amiable survivor with a surprising depth of emotion.

Note: All parts require actors who have true ease with comedy . . . and are equally comfortable with drama.

PLACE
Los Angeles

TIME
The present

LIVING OUT

ACT I

SCENE ONE

In the dark, on the main speakers, we hear an L.A. radio station, perhaps "Estrella," playing a Roc En Espanol song. As lights come up on Ana in her kitchen, the music comes from a little radio there. Ana quickly fixes her hair, glances at her résumé, and sticks it in her purse. As she crosses to Santiago's room, the lights go down in the kitchen and come up there. She kisses her sleeping son good-bye, and the lights go down in his room, as she leaves and heads for her interview. The music changes to transition music on the main speakers, perhaps something percussive, as she crosses to Wallace's living room on the other side of town.

Ana rings the doorbell and Wallace Breyer comes on to greet her. The couch is Downstage Center. An ultramodern chair is Downstage Left.

WALLACE: Zoila — ?

ANA: *(Smiles; eager.)* No — I'm Ana. Hernandez.

WALLACE: Well — *(Surprised and pleased.)* you must be — early! I'm Mrs. Breyer, come in.

ANA: Thank you.

WALLACE: Sit down —

ANA: OK — *(Ana starts to sit on the couch. Wallace points to the chair.)*

WALLACE: *(Smiles.)* No, no, why don't you sit there, Ana? So we can chat — *(Ana sits, sliding back a bit in the ultramodern chair. Wallace takes the couch and takes out her Palm Pilot.)* Now, you were interested in living in or living out?

ANA: Living out *(Eager to get the job.)* The agency told me —

WALLACE: That's all right. I'm seeing both. So. Tell me about yourself. Where are you from?

ANA: Do you know Huntington Park?

WALLACE: No, I meant, where are you — *(Gestures.)* from?

ANA: Oh. I was born in El Salvador.

WALLACE: Good God, everyone is from El Salvador these days! *(Laughs)* What happened to all the Mexicans?

ANA: I — don't know.

WALLACE: *(Smiles.)* No — of course not. Do you have a résumé, Ana?

ANA: Yes. And here is references — *(Wallace rises and Ana hands her the papers.)*

WALLACE: Excellent. *(Wallace remains standing and motions that Ana may sit. Looking over papers:)* So. Let's see. You drive . . . You swim . . . You know CPR . . . Excellent! You worked for the Meyers for three years . . . And the Reillys for four? May I ask why you left those jobs?

ANA: The children I took care of — they started school. So they didn't need a nanny no more.

WALLACE: So there's no problem with my calling for a reference?

ANA: Yes.

WALLACE: There's a problem?

ANA: I mean — no! — if you call — is no problem.

WALLACE: *(Smiles, a bit skeptical.)* Alrightee . . . Well, I have a few questions, Ana, that I always like to ask...

ANA: Good. *(Wallace reads questions from her Palm Pilot, a charming inquisitor.)*

WALLACE: What do you do when the baby cries?

ANA: I . . . go see what's wrong. Maybe his diaper, maybe he's hungry, maybe he just want me to pick him up —

WALLACE: So you would pick him up?

ANA: Yes, of course, I —

WALLACE: Every time he cried? *(Ana hesitates, knowing there's a right and wrong answer here. Finally, she gives up and just says what she thinks.)*

ANA: Yes.

WALLACE: *(Inscrutable.)* I see . . . *(She makes a note in her Palm and goes to the next question.)* And what is your attitude towards discipline?

ANA: Depends —

WALLACE: On what?

ANA: How old is the child?

WALLACE: Oh, say six.

ANA: Me — I like to talk to the child I like to sit down and try to explain —

WALLACE: So you don't use "time outs"?

ANA: Well, sometimes, it's good to take the child to a more quiet place —

WALLACE: Like —?

ANA: His room — or —

WALLACE: The garage?

ANA: No!

WALLACE: *(After a beat; thrilled.)* Excellent! Why don't I tell you just a little about what this job entails before we go on. *(She sits, patting the couch, motioning for Ana to join her. Ana does. Showing photos on her Palm Pilot.)*

ANA: OK.

WALLACE: Now, Jackson needs to be home by eleven for his nap, so that gives you time to fix his lunch and do a little light cleaning — just the kids' rooms and the family room and the kitchen . . . Before you go back for Alex. Now most days Alex has a music or art class or karate or ballet, so you'd just drop her off and pick her up . . . Then just keep them busy with books or puzzles or an art project, and I'm usually home by five or six. How does that sound?

ANA: *(Smiles.)* OK . . . *(Beat.)* But . . . you don't want to say a regular time — like maybe — I work till five?

WALLACE: No. I need someone who's flexible.

ANA: OK . . . *(Beat.)* Do you work near to the house or —?

WALLACE: I don't work, Ana. But, as I said, I need someone who's flexible. Is that a problem?

ANA: No . . . Is just — I have to pick up my son at — *(Wallace sighs.)*

WALLACE: You have a young child?

ANA: Yes — but he's in the after-school program till six and —

WALLACE: I'm sorry, Ana. *(Exasperated.)* I specifically told the agency not to send me anyone with a young child. I don't know what's wrong with those people! *(Wallace exits. A doorbell rings, Linda runs on, Ana turns — and we are in the next interview. Wallace's chair disappears and Linda's comfy one appears downstage right, filled with toys. Linda's a bit of a nervous wreck. She has a baby in her arms.)*

LINDA: Hi! I'm Linda! And this is Jackson!

ANA: Oh! He's beautiful —

LINDA: He's almost asleep. *(Laughs.)* Finally! *(Worried.)* And the agency told you I also have twin boys?

ANA: Yes —

LINDA: Well, sit down, Ana! *(Ana waits for a clue as to where.)* Oh just sit anywhere! Don't mind the toys — *(Dumps toys from chair to floor.)* Just — *(Points to couch.)* Sit! Do you have references?

ANA: Yes. Would you like me to hold him so you can —

LINDA: Oh — would you? *(Linda gives her the baby with some relief and shakes out her arm. Ana gives her the résumé and references.)* Would you like some water or something? Juice?

ANA: OK. *(Linda goes off reading the references. Ana coos to the baby.)*

LINDA: Well, this all looks great! Your last employer just loved you! *(She returns with a kids' juice box, opens it, and sticks in the straw, as she continues.)* And you're available to start right away?

ANA: Yes.

LINDA: Great. You see our last nanny left rather suddenly . . . Seems her mother needed an operation in Guatemala. You don't have a mother in Guatemala do you?

ANA: I am from El Salvador.

LINDA: Great! *(She takes a sip of juice — then remembers and hands it to Ana.)* We've had a couple of nannies from El Salvador, they were wonderful, such hard workers — they were just like members of the family. And I'd love for you to speak Spanish to the twins. I think a second language — in this city — it's just — well, it's like a car really — it's just great. My husband speaks Farsi to the kids — he's from Iran — *(Laughs.)* and frankly I don't understand a word he says — *(Beat.)* When he speaks Farsi, I mean. Gee, I'd love for you to meet the boys. I mean — they're the ones you really have to get a long with. *(Laughs.)* Keep up with, I should say. Have you worked with boys?

ANA: Yes.

LINDA: Then you know how . . . active they can be. Boys are — well, you know if you've worked with them, they're . . . active. *(Bit defensive.)* That's just how boys are.

ANA: *(Laughs.)* I know! That's why they so much fun!

LINDA: *(Thrilled.)* Right! Could you stick around for an hour or so? They're back from the doctor at noon.

ANA: They sick?

LINDA: *(Defensive.)* No, no, they're fine! *(Ana hesitates.)*

ANA: Maybe I could come back tomorrow? I said I would be someplace at twelve.

LINDA: Can't you make a call?

ANA: I'm sorry. *(Beat; just admits it.)* I have to pick up my son from soccer.

LINDA: Oh. You have children?

ANA: Just one in this country. My other son is in El Salvador.

LINDA: *(Dying to make this work.)* Well, can't your husband pick up your child?

ANA: He's working.

LINDA: You don't have a — a mother or something?

ANA: She's in San Francisco.

LINDA: *(Still trying.)* How old is your child?

ANA: Six —

LINDA: Ouch. You know what, Ana? *(Distraught.)* We had a nanny with a young child — she got sick all the time . . . I just can't put myself through . . . I'm sorry, Ana. I need someone who can make my kids a priority. *(Feels awful and hugs Ana.)* But thanks. *(Linda starts to leave. Ana gets up and starts to give back the baby.)* Oh! Right! *(Linda runs back for the baby and exits. A doorbell rings, and Nancy enters with her baby.)*

NANCY: Hi. I'm Nancy Robin.

ANA: Ana Hernandez.

NANCY: *(Warmly.)* Good to meet you. And this is Jenna. She just turned twelve weeks —

ANA: Oooh — she's big! You just have one child?

NANCY: Yes. She's my first. So — I've never had a nanny before — *(Laughs; bit awkward.)* Well — obviously. Do you have kids?

ANA: I have two boys. *(Long beat.)* But they are both in El Salvador. *(They sit down to chat, as their husbands come on, and we move to the next scene.)*

SCENE TWO

Ana's husband, Bobby, sits in the chair downstage right, reading the sports section of La Opinion. *Nancy's husband, Richard, reads the sports section of the* Times *on the couch. The scenes on the Eastside and the Westside are simultaneous, and at times overlap, but each woman clearly speaks to her own husband.*

ANA: *(To Bobby.)* Pues — tengo un trabajo! I got a job!

NANCY: *(To Richard.)* Well — I hired a nanny! *(Richard and Bobby are not pleased, but cover.)*

RICHARD: Great!   BOBBY: Fantástico!

ANA: I only met the woman. She's seems OK —

NANCY: — *(Positive.)* She's a little young maybe, but she seems fairly intelligent, sweet . . .

RICHARD: Well — great —

NANCY: I'll put Jenna down and later we can take her to the park.

RICHARD: OK — *(Nancy exits. Richard thinks. Bobby tries to read the paper.)*

ANA: Where's Santiago?

BOBBY: Next door, playing.

ANA: I promised to take him to the park to play soccer — *(Ana changes her shoes and straightens up.)*

BOBBY: I already took him. *(Laughs; kicks an imaginary ball.)* You should see him — gonna be another Maradona! *(Casually.)* So how much you gonna make?

ANA: Four hundred. And it's only eight hours!

BOBBY: Ten dollars an hour? *(Feels awful, covers.)* Great! Where?

ANA: *(Hesitates.)* Santa Monica.

BOBBY: *(Laughs.)* Santa Monica? You gonna go all the way to the Westside, hour and a half to Santa Monica, and be back to get Santiago by six? What you gonna do, mama? Fly?

ANA: *(Carefully.)* Pues . . . Maybe I'm going to need you to pick him up sometimes —

BOBBY: Oh sí? So you could take care of somebody else's kid instead of your own son?

ANA: I got to go back to work, Bobby —

BOBBY: Why you go to work, Ana? I work — *(She nods.)* Mira, I worked all last month! *(She nods.)* I work when there's work, Ana. That's construction. If the guy I work for got no work, what you want me to do?

ANA: Pues, maybe when you get your papers, I could get my papers — and get a different kind of job.

BOBBY: I told you the lawyer is working on it.

ANA: We just got to save the money for our papers. *(Beat.)* And the money to bring Tomás.

BOBBY: We're going to bring him soon, baby. Can we eat something now?

ANA: Pero — when?! This morning I called El Salvador and my grandmother said he went on a trip with his school —

BOBBY: Sí?

ANA: He hit his head in the pool — my grandmother didn't even call me! But I'm his mother, even if I can't do nothing — I got to know! *(Bobby goes and hugs her.)*

BOBBY: OK, amor. No te preoccupes, we're going to get your son. *(Beat.)* Can we eat something now?

ANA: Sí. *(Bobby goes to the kitchen table, and Ana starts to prepare something to eat. Nancy reenters with the baby's laundry and stands folding it above the couch.)*

NANCY: But, you know, I hate the term "nanny." It sounds so British. Makes me feel so PBS.

RICHARD: Well, if you're not comfortable . . . *(He remains on the couch, helping her fold.)*

NANCY: I heard someone in the park say "babysitter" — but that's not really the truth is it, if it's a full-time job. I've heard "caregiver" too. That sounds warm but not, you know . . . fuzzy. More like a regular job description.

RICHARD: No I meant — if you're not comfortable having a — someone —

NANCY: *(Lightly.)* Well, I have to go back to work, don't I?

RICHARD: Well, how do you define "have to"?

NANCY: *(Laughs.)* If I don't go back I'll get fired?

RICHARD: They can't fire you, you're an attorney, you'll sue.

NANCY: Then I'll be on "The Mommy Track." I won't have a prayer in hell of making partner — *(Laughs.)* And then what have the last sixteen years of my life been for?

RICHARD: I know, sweetie. I understand. *(Beat.)* But you always say the job's unrewarding —

NANCY: I never said it's "unrewarding." I said it's "unfulfilling."

RICHARD: Oh. Sorry.

NANCY: *(Smiles.)* I mean — it may not be as important as the kind of law you practice —

RICHARD: *(Lies.)* Well, that's not true —

NANCY: I mean, I may not be working for the "People" —

RICHARD: Well, people in Hollywood are — people . . .

NANCY: But I'm an attorney — it's what I'm good at, it's what I — do. We talked about all this when I got pregnant —

RICHARD: I know. I just thought we could take this time right now to enjoy —

NANCY: Besides, we're going to need my salary with the new mortgage, honey.

RICHARD: *(Bit tightly.)* Uh-huh . . .

NANCY: And a good preschool costs nine thousand a year . . .

RICHARD: Uh-huh . . . *(Ana brings Bobby his food, and the two scenes start to overlap.)*

BOBBY: Gracias, amor. You got a beer? *(Ana gets Bobby a beer.)*

NANCY: Unless you'd want to consider taking a job with a firm . . .

RICHARD: *(Laughs.)* Defending Halliburton? No thanks!

BOBBY: *(To Ana.)* Gorda, you got chips? *(Ana gets the chips.)*

NANCY: And, you know, honey, several of the studies I've read say it's actually good for a child to see a mother do work she loves —

RICHARD: Well sure. Unless the stress is . . .

BOBBY: *(To Ana.)* Bring a little lemon too, baby, please? *(Ana gets him some lemon.)*

NANCY: *(Laughs.)* Well, that's why we're hiring a nanny! *(Nancy sits next to Richard. Kisses him.)*

BOBBY: *(To Ana.)* Mira, mira, sit down a minute, mama, I ain't gonna bite. *(Bobby pulls Ana down next to him. Richard puts his arms around Nancy.)*

ANA: Mentiroso!

RICHARD: I'm only questioning the timing. *(A last attempt.)* You're still breast-feeding, honey.

NANCY: I'll pump! They have pumps that look like a purse! And she had excellent references, Richard. Plus she has two kids of her own so she's had experience.

RICHARD: Two kids? What if they get sick? How's she going to take care of Jenna? *(Nancy rises and starts to leave, passing Ana and Bobby.)*

NANCY: They're in El Salvador! *(Ana and Bobby exit.)*

RICHARD: Oh. *(Richard follows Nancy off, as Wallace and Linda enter with baby carriages and move to the couch, which becomes the park bench.)*

SCENE THREE

The park. Wallace and Linda sit on a bench.

WALLACE: So how are the boys?

LINDA: Terrific! They're fine! They're much better. *(Nancy enters with Jenna, who is either in her carriage or in a sling.)* Who's that?

WALLACE: She looks familiar. Maybe yoga?

LINDA: Oh — do you think she's the one who just moved into the fixer-upper on Marguerita?

WALLACE: Aren't they tearing that down?

LINDA: Guess not . . .

WALLACE: I love her diaper bag. Let's ask her to sit down. *(Nancy approaches.)*

LINDA: Hi! Sit down! Sit!

NANCY: Oh — thanks. *(She sits.)*

WALLACE: What a pretty baby! *(Wallace turns her own baby toward Nancy.)*

NANCY: Thank you — *(Looks in Wallace's carriage.)* Yours too! *(Looks again.)* Well, not pretty, I mean — handsome.

WALLACE: I'm not big on color-coding babies. I think, in this day and age, a boy should be able to wear salmon.

NANCY: Absolutely. I'm Nancy Robin.

WALLACE: Wallace Breyer.

LINDA: Linda Billings Farzam.

WALLACE: You look familiar. Do you go to Yoga Works?

NANCY: *(Laughs.)* God no. I mean — I'm sure yoga — *(Jokes.)* works — I'm sure it's great —

WALLACE: It's an excellent way to get your body back after a baby.

NANCY: Then I really should go! If I could find the time . . .

WALLACE: Well, yoga actually gives you *more* time.

NANCY: Wow. I'll — look into it. We just moved here.

LINDA: *(Hugs Nancy.)* Well welcome!

WALLACE: *(Looks her over.)* From New York?

NANCY: No, just across town.

WALLACE: *(Underwhelmed.)* Oh.

NANCY: We're over on Marguerita — *(Wallace and Linda exchange a look.)*

LINDA: Oh! You bought that cute house!

NANCY: We just thought it would be a little safer here, you know, now that we have a child.

LINDA: So you just moved — *and* you just had your first child? Ouch!

WALLACE: Talk about stress! Do you have a good Nanny?

NANCY: Yes, our caretaker — care*giver* — seems very nice.

LINDA: Great!

WALLACE: How long have you had her?

NANCY: Oh, we just hired her. She officially starts Friday.

WALLACE: Well, that's smart, so if it doesn't work out you just call over the weekend. Does she read?

NANCY: Well — I assume . . .

WALLACE: And you've watched her with the baby?

NANCY: What do you mean? *(Jokes.)* Stand outside, have a cigarette, and watch through the window? *(Linda laughs.)*

WALLACE: Well, I'm certainly not suggesting you smoke.

NANCY: Of course. I was just joking.

WALLACE: I know. Well, I just like to take a few precautions.

LINDA: After all, it takes a while to get to know someone in any relationship —

WALLACE: Only in this one, right away you're trusting a perfect stranger with your child.

NANCY: So . . . what do you do?

WALLACE: *(Eager to help.)* Well, I just got a new nanny a couple of weeks ago, myself. And, for the first day or two, I'd tell her I was going to yoga or over to Whole Foods, and I'd just watch through the window for an hour. *(She takes a bottled water from her bag and has a drink.)*

NANCY: So, basically, you just . . . watch?

WALLACE: And, maybe for the first week or so, I'll just leave a little cash on the kitchen counter — like I've just — left it, you know . . . And when I get home I'll count it and see how much is gone. If it's just a little change, well, no bigee . . . But if it's a dollar — and she doesn't say anything about having taken it for an emergency . . . *(Wallace takes another drink.)*

NANCY: What?

LINDA: Well, you certainly don't fire her — not if she's good with the children.

WALLACE: But the next time anything is missing, be it a dollar or a hand towel or a yogurt — I'll mention it. Casually. I'll just say "Gee, didn't I buy two cherry yogurts?" And if she doesn't say, "Oh — I took one for lunch" — then I have to fire her. Now, I know that might sound petty — *(Linda tries to understand and support Wallace's position.)*

LINDA: Well, I suppose — if a person can lie about a yogurt — how do you know she won't lie about your child?

WALLACE: See, an older child like Alex — *(Points.)* That's my daughter over there, playing soccer — *(Nancy looks over. Alex is a very competitive child.)*

NANCY: *(Shocked.)* Wow!

WALLACE: An older child can let you know what's going on. But a baby . . .

NANCY: Oh, my God.

LINDA: Did you ask what religion she is?

NANCY: *(Totally taken aback.)* Should I?

LINDA: Well, one of our nannies was Pentecostal — she was very nice . . . But she found one of the twins playing with his — well with his . . . *(She points. Nancy nods.)* And she started telling the twins about this La Llorona person who drowned her own children in the river, and the boys tried to — well, they didn't know what they were doing — they're very good boys — but the dog did wind up in the pool . . . *(Laughs.)* Well, thank God poodles swim!

NANCY: Oh my God, I never thought of any of this —

WALLACE: Because you're a new mother! You're probably totally exhausted and sleep-deprived. Listen, why don't you just get a Nanny Cam and then you can watch the tapes at night when you're relaxed and calm?

NANCY: A — camera?

WALLACE: They come in a little teddy bear. Don't you belong to a Mommy and Me?

NANCY: No — *(Wallace gets out her card and hands it to Nancy.)*

WALLACE: Call me! You get in the right Mommy and Me, you get in the right preschool — *(Calls, firmly.)* Alex! ALEX! *(To Nancy.)* She's got cotillion — *(Nancy sticks the card in her leopard-print diaper bag. Linda checks her watch.)*

LINDA: *(Remembers.)* Oh God — I have to pick up the twins!

WALLACE: By the way, I love your diaper bag.

NANCY: Oh — yours too —

LINDA: Bye.

WALLACE: Bye-bye. *(Wallace and Linda exit. The turntable revolves so the kitchen is now downstage . . . and Nancy, with Jenna in the sling, is in her kitchen for the next scene.)*

SCENE FOUR

Nancy, carefully and guiltily sets a five and a couple of dollar bills on a counter downstage left. Then she sits and works on contracts at the kitchen table. After a beat, Richard enters, dressed for work.

RICHARD: I'm leaving, Nance. *(She's working and doesn't look up.)*

NANCY: *(Warmly, but distracted.)* OK, honey . . .

RICHARD: Hey, maybe we can try that Pan Asian place for dinner — to celebrate your first day back at work.

NANCY: *(Working.)* OK, honey. *(He kisses the top of her head and kisses Jenna.)*

RICHARD: *(Silly voice.)* Bye-bye little boo — *(He starts to leave.)* Have a good one, honey. *(Nancy picks up the phone and dials. Richard notices the small pile of money on the counter.)*

NANCY: *(Into phone; professional voice.)* Diane Machado, please . . . Diane? Nancy.

RICHARD: Hey, Nance — ? *(She stops him with a gesture of her hand. He sees she's on the phone. So he takes a five and leaves.)*

NANCY: *(Into the phone.)* Just wanted you to know I've looked over the contracts and I'll be in by ten . . . Yes, well, I'm thrilled to be back! . . . Love to have lunch! I'm on my way. *(She hangs up and turns to the baby. Horribly torn:)* Mommy's only going out for a little while, Jenna . . . Just an itty-bitty while . . . *(She starts to coo in that embarrassing way mothers do. Ana enters and crosses to the kitchen counter. Startled; cheery.)* Oh — hi! Everything going OK, Ana?

ANA: Fine. I cleaned up her room and made the bottles. Would you like me to take her now?

NANCY: Uh — sure! I should probably get ready to go . . . *(Ana smiles and takes a step toward the baby. Nancy instinctively steps back.)* I think I've told you where everything is . . .

ANA: I think so, Mrs. Robin — *(Ana smiles and moves toward the baby again. Nancy moves away.)*

NANCY: *(Points to a cabinet.)* I told you the nipples and bottles are in there . . .

ANA: *(Points to another cabinet.)* Diaper genie . . . Diapers, wipes . . . thermometer . . .

NANCY: Well, hopefully you're not going to need — *(Remembers.)* Oh Ana! I left a list of numbers by the phone in case of an emergency. My cell, Richard's cell, her doctor, nearest hospital . . . But I'm sure you won't need —

ANA: But I always like to have all the information.

NANCY: Well — *(To Jenna.)* Mommy's just going to the office for a little while, Jenna — *(To Ana; with enormous difficulty.)* Here.
(Ana takes the baby and starts cooing to her in Spanish, holding her comfortably and close.)

NANCY: Well, you do seem to have a touch . . . OK, well, I better — *(Remembers.)* Oh —! *(Nancy goes to the counter.)* I thought I should probably leave you some cash just in case — *(Surprised — and acting "surprised.")* Darn! I'm sorry, I could have sworn I had more money here! *(Nancy waits. Ana says nothing.)* Well, there's a few dollars anyway —

ANA: Thank you. *(Beat.)* Mrs. Robin?

NANCY: Yes?

ANA: I know it's hard to leave her. It was the same for me with — *(Carefully.)* my babies.

NANCY: *(Feels guilty now.)* Oh God. And you had to leave them in another country! I'm just going across town —

ANA: Why don't you call me — every hour? Whenever you like.

NANCY: All right. Thanks. And if she gets hungry, just give her some pureed zucchini — but wash it first with the soap that says — *(She gets the soap and shows it to Ana.)* This green soap right here.

ANA: *(Smiles; covering offense.)* I know how to read, Mrs. Robin.

NANCY: Oh — of course! Of course.

ANA: I went to school. To be a dentist.

NANCY: You're a — dentist?

ANA: I couldn't finish . . .

NANCY: Oh. Of course. Because of your children . . .

ANA: Because of the war.

NANCY: *(Really feels guilty now.)* Right! *(Checks watch.)* Well, I really should go.

Don't want to be late my first day back! I should be home around five. Unless the traffic is bad . . . *(She picks up her purse and briefcase.)*

ANA: *(Worried about Santi; improvises.)* Well — maybe you could call me? Just . . . so I could call my husband? He gets really . . . worried.

NANCY: Sure. And don't worry, if I'm a little late, my husband can always write you a check.

ANA: Oh. *(She turns away and cleans the kitchen table.)* Mrs. Robin . . . do you think you could make it to cash?

NANCY: Cash?

ANA: It's just easier for me to —

NANCY: You don't have a bank account? *(Ana doesn't answer.)* Ana, you're not illegal are you? *(Drops briefcase and purse.)* Oh God, I can't believe I didn't — I was in such a rush to —

ANA: I am getting the green card, Mrs. Robin. Don't worry.

NANCY: Oh good. Do you know when exactly?

ANA: The lawyer say soon.

NANCY: Yeah, well, never believe a lawyer, Ana. *(Laughs.)* I'm a lawyer so you can trust me on that one. Is there a problem?

ANA: They keep changing the laws for amnesty.

NANCY: But if there was a war in El Salvador . . . Good God, a client of ours did a film — they were torturing people — it was horrible! Was it like that in your . . . village?

ANA: *(Again, offended, but answers directly.)* I come from the city, Mrs. Robin. But . . . yes.

NANCY: Gee, this is a little more complicated than I . . .

ANA: Don't worry, Mrs. Robin, my husband is already a resident, so soon as he gets his papers I could get mine.

NANCY: *(Really torn now.)* Well — I really have to get to the office . . . Look — why don't I just make out your check to cash this week. *(She gets her checkbook and starts to write a check. Ana rocks the baby.)* But please — don't say anything to my husband about your, uh, situation. He doesn't need to be concerned with the legal ethics . . . *(She crosses to Ana.)* Here you are.

ANA: *(Smiles; re: baby.)* She's asleep.

NANCY: Wow! What'd you do, slip her a beer?

ANA: No! Claro que no! I would never — !

NANCY: I'm joking! *(Ana tries a little laugh. Nancy hands her the check.)*

ANA: Thank you. *(Glances at check.)* Mrs. Robin, this is more than —

NANCY: I know. Maybe if you have the time this weekend you could get something more — comfortable to wear to work? *(Looks at her tight jeans.)* Just something . . . more comfortable.

ANA: OK.

NANCY: Well — guess I'll just get my phone and go. *(Ana nods. Nancy hurries to Jenna's room. to herself:)* OK. *(She goes to the new Nanny Cam. She makes sure the little teddy bear with the camera in its belly is properly positioned, then looks through its eyes to check focus, panning the room. Then she takes her cell from her pocket and goes to the kitchen.)* OK — I'm leaving now! Bye! *(The baby cries. Nancy hesitates.)*

ANA: She just want her bottle — *(Nancy sighs and quickly leaves the house. A moment later, she appears outside the kitchen window. She lights up a cigarette and watches Ana feed the baby. Then Ana moves with Jenna, and Nancy crouches, then stands on her tiptoes, smoking, and trying desperately to see. Finally . . .)*

NANCY: Oh, let the fucking bear do it. *(She drags on her cigarette and leaves. Ana exits with Jenna, as the scene shifts to the park.)*

SCENE FIVE

The park. Zoila and Sandra come on with the same baby carriages Wallace and Linda used.

ZOILA: Hola! Buenos días!

SANDRA: Hola! Oye, mujer — aquí. *(They sit on the bench.)* Pues, como te trata la señora?

ZOILA: Esta mujer es completamente loca. She tell me give — *("Yackson")* Jackson the — come se llama esta cosa — blanca y — *(She makes a face.)*

SANDRA: Cual cosa?

ZOILA: Esa cosa, tú sabes, the white thing that looks like somebody ate it already — ?

SANDRA: Éste . . . tofu?

ZOILA: Eso es. Tofu. I give it to Jackson for lunch and then I feel so bad I took him out and bought him a doughnut with my own money. You think I give him the rat poison! Mrs. Breyer, she start yelling at me, "Only give him what I tell you!" "His doctor don't want him to eat sugar." What kind of doctor is that? I'm telling you, I got to quit this job.

SANDRA: I worked for a lady once — the kid hit his head on the table, I put sugar on the cut — I got fired.

ZOILA: They don't like sugar! They rather pay a hundred dollars to the doctor. They don't care. Mrs. Breyer — she got so much money, she just leave it around all over the place. Anybody could come in and find it. These peoples got no respect for money. Gringos.

SANDRA: *(To her baby; "Yackson.")* Not you, Jackson. Chulo. Precioso.

ZOILA: *(To her baby.)* Óyeme, Jackson, next time I give you a doughnut, we don't say nothing to your crazy mami. OK, papi? *(To Sandra.)* I got five kids in Guatemala. All of them ate sugar. They're fine. *(Ana enters with Jenna in a carriage.)*

SANDRA: Quíen es?

ZOILA: I seen her walking down the street from me. She think she something 'cause she drive a Altima. Go ahead ask her to sit down. *(Sandra calls out to Ana.)*

SANDRA: Oye — oye, quieres sentarte?

ANA: Sí. Gracias. *(Ana comes and sits.)*

SANDRA: Yo soy Sandra, esta es Zoila —

ANA: Ana. Mucho gusto.

ZOILA: You working on Marguerita, sí?

ANA: Sí.

SANDRA: I work on Alta. In the house with all the fountains?

ANA: Oh! I think I had a interview with the lady you work for.

SANDRA: *(Pleased she got the job.)* Sí?

ZOILA: *(Laughs.)* Esa casa es bien fea. That house is ugly, no? Where those people from?

SANDRA: Pues, the señor is from Iran. *(Zoila looks in Sandra's carriage.)*

ZOILA: Ay! That's why he so dark! Pobrecito. *(To Ana.)* What kind of people you work for?

ANA: Pues — Americanos. *(Zoila and Sandra look in Ana's carriage.)*

ZOILA: Jews?

ANA: Ay no! Americanos. Their name is "Robin."

ZOILA: Mija. Sometime they change the name so you don't know. How much they pay you?

ANA: *(Evasive.)* They pay OK —

ZOILA: Then they not Jews.

SANDRA: Pero los Hindus pay the worst!

ZOILA: I worked for Hindus. They make you sleep in the room with the kids — you never get no sleep!

ANA: *(Laughs.)* You never work for Chinese?

ZOILA: Ay! Los Chinos pay the worst. And they never talk to you.

SANDRA: How about los Italianos?

ZOILA: *(Laughs; imitating Italians.)* All the time screaming! *(They all laugh.)*

ANA: You ever work for Latinos? *(Zoila stops laughing.)*

ZOILA: *(Indignant.)* Please. I do not work for Latinos, I am no slave. I work for Latinos when I come to this country and I had to live in — they wouldn't let me go to school at night to learn English! They was afraid I'd get a better job!

SANDRA: Cubans?

ZOILA: Worse. Colombians. *(To Ana.)* So how much they pay you?

ANA: Pues . . . They pay OK.

ZOILA: You just take care of the one baby?

ANA: Sí.

ZOILA: You clean?

ANA: A little —

ZOILA: How much you make?

ANA: *(Looks in Sandra's carriage, avoiding.)* What a cute baby!

SANDRA: Gracias. Dile gracias, Jackson!

ZOILA: All the boys around here is name Jackson *("Yackson")* It's like Jesus *("Heysoos"). (To Ana.)* You got kids?

ANA: Two. Tomás and Santiago. You?

ZOILA: I got five kids in Guatemala.

SANDRA: And I got two here and my oldest son in Mexico. But I'm bringing him next month!

ANA: Ay, sí? You're lucky!

ZOILA: *(Laughs.)* Not so lucky. She got a husband too. She work all day and she work all night — for the same money! Pues — así es la vida.

SANDRA and ANA: *(Overlapping each other.)* Así es!

ZOILA: You got your kids with you?

ANA: *(After a beat.)* En El Salvador.

ZOILA: It's better. Mira, I brought two of my kids over — they got in gangs, I sent them back. This is no place to raise kids. *(Zoila and Sandra exit in the scene transition and Ana takes Jenna from the carriage.)*

SCENE SIX

Ana is singing a lullaby to the baby later that evening.

ANA: A la ru ru niña, a la ru ru ya . . . *(Moving to Jenna's room.)* Ay, dios mío, your mami is late! *(She puts the baby in her crib. Bear watches.)* Pero, no te preocupes, nena, Ana is here . . . Pero Ana has to go home soon — to her own little boy. Sí! Santiago! *(Remembers.)* That's a secret, Jenna, don't tell nobody. Entonces, duermete con los ángeles, mija. Todo esta bien. *(She picks up the stuffed animals in the crib, one by one.)* You got your little doggy . . . You got your little piggy . . . *(She picks up the teddy bear.)* You got your little teddy bear — *(The teddy bear is too heavy.)* Qué? Mierda! *(She takes the bear out of the room and unscrews its head.)* I know you, puto! *(She takes out the tape.)* You don't need to know about my son, little puto! *(The tape breaks. We hear the front door open. Richard enters — with flowers. Ana quickly runs back to the crib, puts the bear back in place, and sticks the tape in the back pocket of her jeans.)* Mierda. *(Richard calls from the living room.)*

RICHARD: Nancy? *(Ana goes to the living room.)*

ANA: Oh! Good evening Mr. Robin —

RICHARD: Hey! How's it going, Ana?

ANA: Good! *(He nods and smiles. An awkward pause. This is their first real conversation.)*

RICHARD: How's the baby?

ANA: Fine. *(Pause.)* She's sleeping.

RICHARD: *(Jokes.)* Well — that's her job! *(Another awkward pause.)* So . . . Everything going OK?

ANA: Yes, very good. She's a good baby.

RICHARD: Best kid I ever had! *(Ana looks confused. Richard finally calls for help.)* Nancy — ?

ANA: Oh, she still at the office. She call a little while ago and say she sorry, she stuck in a meeting, she be back in maybe one hour.

RICHARD: *(Smiles; covering anger.)* Stuck in a meeting, huh? First day back! *(Puts down flowers.)* OK . . . Well, guess I'll just call for a pizza. What kind do you like? *(He heads for the phone.)*

ANA: Oh — *(Looks at her watch.)* You still need me, Mr. Robin?

RICHARD: Oh — no, no — I can change a diaper, trust me, we took the course. Uh, what time do you work to, Ana?

ANA: Till five.

RICHARD: Jees, and the traffic's a mess. Do you have far to go?

ANA: Do you know where is Huntington Park?

RICHARD: Of course I do! I know Huntington Park. I'm a public defender, I went to a Quinceanera there once for the daughter of a client. Danced my ass off. In fact . . . can you keep a secret?

ANA: I guess . . .

RICHARD: I actually prefer the Eastside. I find it much more soulful. This place? Way too white. *(Ana doesn't know what to say to that.)*

ANA: Well, I guess I better get going. The traffic . . .

RICHARD: Your husband's waiting?

ANA: Yes.

RICHARD: Well, don't keep him waiting. Especially on a Friday night. Have a terrific weekend, Ana.

ANA: You too, Mr. Robin.

RICHARD: Adios! *(Ana smiles and leaves.)* Fuck, Nance . . . *(He turns on the TV with the remote, stands behind the couch a moment and watches the game. Bobby comes on and sits on the couch. Richard puts down the remote, Bobby picks it up and switches to the same game in Spanish. Richard exits, and we are in the next scene.)*

SCENE SEVEN

Bobby's watching the game, as Ana hurries in with groceries.

ANA: Santi está dormido?

BOBBY: Claro.

ANA: Gracias. *(Ana goes to the kitchen and unpacks groceries.)*

BOBBY: We got a paper from the teacher. There's no school not this Monday but the next.

ANA: *(Worried.)* Por qué?

BOBBY: Some holiday, pues, don't ask me — I got to work. Can we eat something now?

ANA: I'm sorry. The señor got home later than —

BOBBY: I called over there, the guy said you left two hours ago.

ANA: You called over there? What did you say?

BOBBY: I said, "Is my wife there?"

ANA: You didn't say nothing about Santi?

BOBBY: *(Laughs, keeping it light.)* No, I knew where Santi was! Santi was with me! 'Cause I'm the one that picked him up from school and took him to play soccer — *(Adds.)* And took him to eat and gave him a bath . . .

ANA: *(Guilty.)* I'm sorry. I'll take him to soccer next week. And tomorrow I'm getting a cell phone, so you can always call me. So you don't need to call over there.

BOBBY: Oh. I don't need to call over there . . . 'cause maybe you ain't gonna be over there? You want to tell me what's goin' on, Ana?

ANA: *(After a beat.)* I told them both my kids was in El Salvador.

BOBBY: *(Rises.)* You told them my son was in El Salvador? Santiago is an American! Why you want people to think I can't take care of my own?

ANA: I had to tell them that! I needed the job! And that's what the agency told me to say.

BOBBY: *(Laughs.)* Claro, agency's got to get their cut!

ANA: Pues, as soon as you get your papers —

BOBBY: I told you my lawyer is working on it! *Ya!*

ANA: I'm going to say good night to Santi —

BOBBY: Go on. But he's asleep.

ANA: What did he eat?

BOBBY: I got him some fries.

ANA: Just fries?

BOBBY: *("What's wrong with fries?")* That's what he ask for! Just fries!

ANA: *(After a beat.)* Maybe we could move a little closer . . . I could pick him up, the schools are better —

BOBBY: What's wrong with the schools right here?

ANA: The air is better . . . Maybe he wouldn't have the asthma . . .

BOBBY: *(Defensive about this.)* Lot of kids have asthma, Ana —

ANA: Around here —

BOBBY: Why you always got to be better? *(Mutters.)* Man, Mama was right. Always got to get the best school, the best doctor . . . Why you got to pay all that money for a car?

ANA: Because I want my child to be safe!

BOBBY: And who's picking him up in the truck while you working late?

ANA: You think I want to work late?

BOBBY: *(Insinuating.)* I don't know . . .

ANA: *(Explodes.)* Sure, Bobby! Sure I rather be washing their underwear than yours! Sure I rather be sweeping their floors! And I rather be taking care of their kid than my own son. I love it, Bobby! *(Imitating.)* "This is the soap, Ana" — "Was it bad in your village, Ana?" "Here, let me give you a little money, Ana, for a nice pair of ugly pants —"

BOBBY: *(Can't help himself.)* I told you those pants was too tight — *(They look at each other a moment. He smiles and hugs her.)* Go say good night to Santi. I'll make myself something to eat. *(Ana goes to Santi's room behind the scrim upstage left and talks to the sleeping boy. Bobby watches.)*

ANA: I'm sorry I missed your soccer, mijo. But if I work hard — for a little while — sabes qué? I could bring your brother! I'll take you to soccer next week. Bueno . . . Duérmete con los angeles, mijo . . . *(Bobby exits.*

Nancy tiptoes into Jenna's room behind the scrim upstage right and fixes her covers. Ana sings.) A la ru ru niño, a la ru ru ya, duérmete mi niño, duérmete ya . . .

NANCY: *(Sings.)* Lullaby, and good night — *(Hesitates, keeps singing.)* I don't remember the wo-ords, but it's Brahms, or Beethoven, so-oo go to sleep, Jenna . . . *(Richard enters. They whisper . . .)*

RICHARD: Everything OK at work?

NANCY: Fine! *(Kisses him.)* I'm so sorry I'm late! *(They start to go to the living room.)* We're going to be meeting with an incredible director next week. French! And I'm the only lawyer at the firm who happens to speak fluent French!

RICHARD: Terrific, Nance. Hey, I got to chat with the nanny when I got home. She seems very nice.

NANCY: Yes . . .

RICHARD: You sound hesitant. *(Nancy goes back to Jenna's room. He follows.)*

NANCY: I'm not hesitant.

RICHARD: Sorry. Ambivalent?

NANCY: No, I like her. It's just — *(Sees the bear.)* Oh shit, we're on tape.

RICHARD: What? *(She picks up the bear and they go to the living room.)*

NANCY: Oh, I got a Nanny Cam —

RICHAR: *(Grabs the bear.)* What!? Why? Is something wrong?

NANCY: No, no! She's wonderful with Jenna. It's just . . . Well . . . She took some money from the counter. Just a five. But —

RICHARD: *I* took a five from the counter, Nancy. You were on the phone — *(Bit loaded.)* You were working. You probably didn't even hear me say we were going to that Pan Asian place tonight to celebrate. *(Mutters.)* Now that we have a nanny . . .

NANCY: Oh God, I'm so sorry.

RICHARD: Honey, I know you're under stress —

NANCY: Maybe I'll try yoga —

RICHARD: Good. And if you don't trust the nanny —

NANCY: "Caregiver" —

RICHARD: Whatever — if you don't trust her, just get rid of her! Because I'm getting rid of this bear! *(He heads for the kitchen area.)*

NANCY: Wait! I haven't watched the —

RICHARD: Taping unsuspecting immigrants!? Who *are* you!? Aren't you a member of the ACLU? Lord Almighty, I'm married to Linda Tripp!

NANCY: Richard — *(She tries to grab it. He holds it too high.)*

RICHARD: I refuse to deal with the LAPD all day and come home to this bear! *(He's heading for the garbage now.)*

NANCY: Well, don't throw it out — it cost two hundred dollars!

RICHARD: I don't care! *(She keeps typing to grab the bear but he keeps it out of her reach.)* Either Nanny goes — or Bear goes. *(He tosses it into the microwave and slams the door. Righteous:)* I won't live in a world with this bear. *(He turns on the microwave and exits fast. Nancy quickly retrieves the bear, drops it in the garbage, and exits.)*

SCENE EIGHT

Ana, Sandra, and Zoila enter the park with their baby carriages. Sandra sneezes.

ANA: Salud —

SANDRA: Gracias.

ZOILA: Sientensé. *(They watch another nanny walk by.)*

ANA: Quién es?

ZOILA: She's from Australia or someplace. I don't understand nothing she says. Don't ask her to sit down. *(They sit. Sandra sneezes again. Zoila leafs through a little magazine.)*

ANA and ZOILA: Salud.

SANDRA: My daughter give me her gripa. Linda keep telling me, "Take her to the doctor! Take her to the doctor!" Then she tell me, don't come tomorrow, she don't want Jackson to catch nothing — *("Et cetera.")* la la la . . . This cold cost me two hundred dollars!

ZOILA: Y those kids you work for? They always got something coming out of their nose. Cómo los aguantas? Those kids never sit down! *(To Ana.)* They got DDT, both of em.

ANA: *(To Sandra.)* They got ADD?

ZOILA: They probably got that too. How much she pay you to take care of them?

SANDRA: Three fifty.

ZOILA: *(To Ana.)* Y how much Mrs. Robin pay you?

ANA: About the same . . . *(To Sandra.)* So where does your daughter go to school?

SANDRA: *(Nods.)* Right over there.

ANA: *(Surprised.)* So . . . you live near here?

SANDRA: *(Avoiding.)* No . . . Pues, there's a lotería . . .

ANA: Sí?

SANDRA: Pues . . .

ZOILA: Oh tell her. She don't got no kids in this country, que le importa —? *(Zoila's cell phone rings.)* Mierda. *(Into phone; brightly.)* Allo? . . . Yes, Mrs. Breyer. OK, but I'm feeding the baby right now . . . OK, no problem, I'm writing it down . . . *(She makes no move toward a pen.)* Wheat-free, sugar-free . . . Barbara's Carob Chip. OK . . . OK . . . *(Holds phone farther away.)* Sorry — what did you say? *(She makes her voice like the phone's breaking up.)* The phone is breaking up — I can't hear you, Mrs. Breyer — *(She fans her magazine to sound like static and gives the phone to Ana so she can hold it even farther away. Yells to phone:)* I can't hear you! I see you in a little while! *(Zoila takes the phone back and hangs up.)* Está vieja puta piensa que soy su cholera. I got to walk over to the Whole Foods. The Mommies and the Mes are coming over. Pues, I got to buy some food anyways 'cause I'm living in now and that woman got nothing in the 'frigerator. Just tofu. Pero, sabes qué? *(Lowers her voice; smiles.)* Mrs. Breyer hides candy bars — in the drawer with her panties!

ANA and SANDRA: No!

ZOILA: Sí! That woman got twenty-two pairs of panties! I got to wash 'em by hand! I don't know why she need silk panties with a old husband like that. I saw him without no shirt — he got more tetas than she have! *(Ana and Sandra laugh.)*

SANDRA: Qué boca!

ZOILA: I'm telling you, I got to quit this job.

ANA: How come you live in?

ZOILA: Because she ask me. And when I said no, I got fired. So I said yes.

ANA: You should have stayed home! One day! She'd change her mind.

ZOILA: Easy for you to say. You got a Altima.

ANA: One day we should all stay home!

SANDRA: Everybody! The waiters, the parking peoples, the cleaners —

ZOILA: Los Americanos be driving around in their dirty clothes — starving. Can't go to a restaurant — there's nobody to wash the plate! You get home, the house is a mess —

ANA: The plants is all dead —

SANDRA: Nobody to deliver you pizza —

ZOILA: And then you got to take care of your own kids! *(They all laugh. Then Zoila rises.)* Pues . . . I see you tomorrow, mijas.

ANA: Primero Dios.

ZOILA: *(To baby.)* Ven, mijo, let's go to the Whole Foods and get a doughnut. *(Zoila exits.)*

SANDRA: Pobrecita. She's older so she don't get offer so many jobs.

ANA: Pobrecita.

SANDRA: And she don't got a license. So the señora don't let her drive the kids. Just the errands — *("Et cetera.")* La la la . . .

ANA: Qué horror. *(Beat; casually.)* So how did you get your daughter in that school?

SANDRA: Oh. The last lady I work for, she let me use her address.

ANA: *(Surprised.)* She lied for you?

SANDRA: She was very nice. The school where I live? The gangs sell drugs in the playground.

ANA: The school where my son goes — the same.

SANDRA: They got gangs in El Salvador?

ANA: No — sí, there's gangs — the kids they deport back from here — but . . . *(Beat; confides.)* Mira. My little one is here. But I told Mrs. Robin . . .

SANDRA: *(Nods, understanding.)* Entiendo. Oye, the only reason I got hired is I got my mother-in-law living with me to watch my girls. How old are your kids?

ANA: Santiago is six. And Tomás is eleven — my son that's in El Salvador.

SANDRA: How long since you seen him?

ANA: Eight years. Last time I seen him he was playing with his little cars. *(Beat.)* But I talk to him every week. I just sent my grandmother the money to get their own phone. Oye . . . please don't say nothing to Zoila. I'm already worried for my job 'cause my son got no school next Monday — so I got to ask the señora for the day off.

SANDRA: Ay no, mija! You're only working a little time there! Tell her you're sick. *(Beat.)* No, then she don't let you come back the next day, la la la . . . *(Beat.)* Tell her your mother is sick. *(Ana looks hesitant. Sandra nods and sneezes. Then she exits, as the scene shifts to the living room.)*

SCENE NINE

Ana is sweeping, preoccupied. Jenna is asleep in her carriage or carrier. Nancy enters with a new hairdo.

NANCY: Hi —

ANA: *(Stops sweeping.)* Oh Mrs. Robin — you change your hair! I like it. It's very pretty!

NANCY: Really? My hair's been so thin since Jenna was born . . .

ANA: Same thing for me with my — children. *(Touches her own hair.)* But it comes back again, see?

NANCY: Well, you have great hair. I didn't have hair like that *before* I got pregnant. And it's that straight, naturally?

ANA: Yes.

NANCY: Boy are you lucky. If I had a dollar for every hour I've spent torturing my hair!

ANA: Torturing — ?

NANCY: *(Mortified.)* Well not . . . "torturing"! Of course I didn't mean to compare straightening my hair to what people in your country had to . . . *(Gets purse.)* OK, I'm leaving. *(Ana starts to sweep.)*

ANA: Oh, Mrs. Robin . . . I wanted to ask you . . . do you like me work late this Friday?

NANCY: Friday? Gee . . . I'm sure my husband would love a night out!

ANA: Because next Monday I don't think I could come.

NANCY: No?

ANA: *(Turned away.)* My mother is sick. I have to go to San Francisco.

NANCY: I thought you mother was in El Salvador —

ANA: No.

NANCY: Oh. I just assumed she was with your children —

ANA: No. My grandmother is with them. My mother is here.

NANCY: Here?

ANA: I mean — in San Francisco. The doctor, he wants her to have an operation . . . *(She gestures, vaguely, to her own body.)*

NANCY: Oh. A hysterectomy?

ANA: Yes!

NANCY: Well, I did have a meeting Monday afternoon with this French . . . When do you think you'll be back?

ANA: Tuesday. I'll be back Tuesday. *(After a beat.)* I'm sorry, Mrs. Robin.

NANCY: No, no, I mean — you only have one mother. I'll just have to change my plans . . . *(Heads for the phone.)* Just this one —

ANA: It's just this one time. *(Sound of baby's cries.)* I'll get her. *(They both head for the baby.)*

NANCY: No, no, I'll get her. *(Ana nods and goes to the other room.)* Shit. *(Nancy gets Jenna and makes a call. Drops voice; instantly professional.)* Diane Machado, please . . . Diane? Nancy. Listen, Diane, something has come up vis-à-vis the meeting Monday — . . . Well, I'm afraid it's a real emergency. You see, my caregiver's mother . . . died . . . and . . . — No, I can't leave her with a strange sitter, actually . . . Well, I can understand how it might see "overprotective" if you're not a mother — . . . No, no, of course I respect your decision to be "child-free"! . . . *(Nods.)* Absolutely. Just this one time . . . Thanks. *(She hangs up.)* Bitch. *(Nancy takes the carriage, as Wallace and Linda come on with theirs, and we move to the next scene.)*

SCENE TEN

Wallace, Linda, and Nancy are in the park with their baby carriages.

WALLACE: *(Smiles.)* Well, I just hope for your sake, she comes back.

NANCY: What — she needs to work, doesn't she?

LINDA: *(Carefully.)* Well, sometimes, when they say their mother is sick in Guatemala . . .

NANCY: San Francisco.

WALLACE: *(Surprised.)* So — she's legal?

NANCY: Well — of course. Yours are legal aren't they?

LINDA and WALLACE: Of course!

LINDA: So you probably don't have to worry. Still . . .

NANCY: What?

LINDA: *(Sensitively.)* Well . . . It's not that they actually lie . . . It's a cultural thing. I had a girlfriend who lived in Mexico for a summer and she explained it to me. See, they don't consider it "lying" — they just don't want you to be unhappy! It's just easier to say, "My mother is sick in Guatemala" than "I just got a job for a dollar more an hour." The thing is they're just such sweet people. Especially the Mexicans.

WALLACE: Well, the Guatemalans are sweeter, if you're talking sweet —

NANCY: How about the Salvadorans?

NANCY: Tough as nails. But they can clean.

LINDA: The thing is, they just may not understand the position they put us in.

NANCY: Well, they have children —

WALLACE: And they're able to leave them in another country — I mean, could you do that?

NANCY: Well, I think you really need to take into consideration the political and economic situation that our caregivers —

LINDA: Well, of course! Of course I do! And I pay Sandra top dollar.

WALLACE: How much do you pay if you don't mind my —?

LINDA: *(Avoiding.)* Top dollar. *(Nancy checks her watch, eager to avoid further discussion.)*

NANCY: Which reminds me — God, I better get home and do some work!

LINDA: What do you do?

NANCY: I'm an entertainment attorney.

LINDA: Oh!

WALLACE: Well, if you have to work, that must be an interesting job.

NANCY: And you?

WALLACE: Oh, my husband and I are on a few boards . . .

LINDA: *(Laughs.)* Oh give me a break. This woman has done more diseases than anyone else in town. She runs, she walks —

WALLACE: *(To Nancy.)* I used to run a museum, actually, but I gave it up when Alex was born.

LINDA: You should see the Thanksgiving decorations she made for our school!

WALLACE: *(Smiles to Nancy.)* I keep trying to get her involved with philanthropic work —

LINDA: Well, get over it. I don't have time to get my roots done.

WALLACE: Find the time, honey. Do. Yoga.

LINDA: *(To Nancy; bit defensive.)* Well. Guess I just have my hands full just being a mom!

NANCY: Of course —

LINDA: I just couldn't imagine not being there the first time one of them crawled, or walked, or said their first word . . . Could you, Wallace?

WALLACE: Oh God no.

LINDA: I mean, why else have kids?

WALLACE: *(Nods.)* Why else have kids? *(The two moms look at Nancy and smile. Nancy tries to smile back. As they exit in the scene transition. Ana enters on the phone.)*

SCENE ELEVEN

Ana is on the phone with Tomás, in a pool of light. Bobby fixes a truck for Santiago in the kitchen.

ANA: Tomás? Soy mami! . . . Me puedes oír, mijo? . . . Cómo estas? . . . Sí? Recibistes el paquete? And the shirt? Does it fit? *(Pronouncing it for him.)* "Hill-finger." *(Laughs.)* I don't know, mijo, they liked to put their name on everything, quien sabe . . . How is school? . . . Then you got to study a little harder, Tomás, so when you come here you know your math . . .

OK, just spend a little more time . . . What are you eating? . . . Bueno, Tomás, pero don't eat too much sugar . . . Pues, tell me something else — . . . *(He's running out of conversation.)* Do you miss me? . . . I miss you up to the sky! . . . You're going to come real soon, mijo. *(Surprised.)* No, no , not for vacation — you're going to come here to live! . . . No, not with abuela. Your great-grandmother don't want to come, mijo, she says she's too old. *(Bobby exits. Pained:)* I know it's hard to leave her. But don't you want to be with Mami? . . . Oye, did you get the pictures I sent you from the beach? With the rides? *(Laughs.) Te gustan?* That's me and my sister-in-law and her friend. *(Pause; fighting tears.)* No mijo . . . I'm the one in the middle. *(She hangs up and walks right into the next scene.)*

SCENE TWELVE

Nancy is making coffee at the kitchen counter downstage left.
Ana enters, still upset by her call with Tomás.

ANA: Good morning, Mrs. Robin.

NANCY: *(Thrilled.)* Ana! I wasn't sure you'd be back — *(Adds quickly.)* so soon! My husband took Jenna out for a run. How's your mother doing?

ANA: She's fine. She always say, "I talk to God, I tell him I see him next year." She's a very stubborn woman.

NANCY: *(Laughs.)* Mine too. She always says, "If Hitler didn't get me, why the hell should I fear God?"

ANA: *(Surprised; blurts.)* Oh! You — Jewish!

NANCY: Uh-huh. Would you like some coffee?

ANA: OK — *(Nancy gets a cup and saucer.)*

NANCY: You sure everything's all right? You seem worried.

ANA: My first son is having a little problem in school.

NANCY: I'm so sorry. Well, anyway, I'm so glad you're back. And I've been thinking . . . Maybe I can be of some help with the, uh, immigration situation. I am a lawyer after all. *(She brings Ana's coffee to the table and starts adding teaspoons of sugar.)*

ANA: *(Surprised, eager.)* You could help with — immigration? *(Then; proud.)* No, no, it's very nice of you, but — *(After three teaspoons of sugar, Ana puts her hand over the cup.)*

NANCY: No, really, I want to help. In fact, I took the liberty of speaking with a friend who gave me the name of an excellent immigration lawyer, and he'd be happy to have a phone conversation with you, no charge. *(Ana thinks for a moment. Her need to get Tomás is more important than her pride.)*

ANA: Thank you, Mrs. Robin. Thank you very much.

NANCY: Ana, please — "Nancy." *(Nancy hands her a piece of paper with the lawyer's name and number.)* Well, now I can get to the office! Oh — I'll probably have to make up for yesterday, so I may not get back till six or seven —

ANA: OK — *(Nancy starts to leave. Ana runs and hands her the cell phone she's left on the table.)* Mrs. Robin —

NANCY: Nancy.

ANA: Nancy. *(Nancy smiles and leaves. The rest of the scene is a collage of time and space over the next few weeks. Lighting and a few costume changes indicate the passage of time. Bobby comes on and sits on the couch. If the set's on a turntable, the living room is now upstage, so the couch faces upstage.)*

BOBBY: Ven, amor, SÁBADO GIGANTE! Ven! Siéntate! *(He turns on the TV to a popular variety show. Ana hands him the paper. In a fine mood.)* What's this?

ANA: Mrs. Robin give me the name of a real good immigration lawyer, Bobby. *(He turns off the TV and moves downstage.)*

BOBBY: So you been talking to her about my business? Who told you could talk to her about my business?

ANA: No! Pues . . . she's a lawyer, Bobby —

BOBBY: So is the lawyer I got, Ana! You told her I was with the guerrilleros? *(Nancy enters and goes to her kitchen counter.)*

NANCY: He was with the guerrillas?

ANA: *(To Bobby.)* Pues — you were fifteen years old, you were with them because they took you before the army did. What difference does it make to the Americanos which side you was on?

BOBBY: *(Laughs; ironic.)* It don't. They gave the guns. We gave the bodies. Americanos probably don't even remember which side *they* was on now! All they know is, "Ay! Where'd all these brown people come from?" *(He gives her back the paper.)* Don't be talking about my business. *(He exits, pissed. Ana straightens up Nancy's kitchen, as we jump in time.)*

NANCY: So the lawyer was helpful?

ANA: I . . . haven't called yet. *(Richard enters, turns on the TV, and sits on the couch.)*

NANCY: Well, don't worry, we'll call together —

RICHARD: Nancy? That program about the development of the brain's on — *(Nancy does not want Richard to find out about any of this.)*

NANCY: Be right there, honey! *(Nancy goes and sits with Richard, as Bobby enters and reads the paper at the kitchen table. Ana sits with Bobby.)*

ANA: He said it's no problem you were with the guerrilleros, Bobby . . . *(Bobby doesn't reply.)* So . . . what's the problem? *(Bobby doesn't reply.)* Is there a problem, Bobby?

BOBBY: The problem is you talking to some woman you work for instead of listening to your husband! *(Richard and Nancy exit.)*

ANA: She's trying to help us, Bobby!

BOBBY: So she don't have to worry about hiring nobody illegal! Tu estas ciega?

ANA: I don't care! I want my papers! And that lawyer you got don't do a damn thing! So I don't care why she's trying to help!

BOBBY: Well, she's helping a lot, Ana. 'Cause you never talk to me like that!

ANA: *(In his face.)* Well, maybe I should have — !

BOBBY: Ya! Cállate! I don't want to hear no more! *(He turns away. Ana gets up, hurt and furious. Nancy goes to her.)*

NANCY: *(Feels awful.)* Ana? I'm so sorry, I — certainly didn't mean to cause you any . . . stress. *(Richard enters, with his briefcase, excited.)*

RICHARD: Hey, Nance, remember that Vet I was defending? I finally got him out of jail and into the VA Hospital, so —

NANCY: *(Interested — but torn.)* That's wonderful! Can you fill me in a second, honey? We're just discussing Jenna's binky —

RICHARD: *(Smiles; covering hurt.)* I'll call you from the car. *(Richard crosses Ana and Nancy as he exits downstage right. Nancy turns back to Ana.)*

NANCY: Ana, I don't want to interfere . . . *(Carefully.)* But this is America, you do have your rights as a woman. *(Ana turns to Bobby.)*

ANA: I got my rights as a woman, Bobby! *(Nancy exits. After a moment, Bobby starts to speak.)*

BOBBY: *(With difficulty.)* I got in a fight. Before we met. when I just come to this country. I was walking down Figueroa. Nighttime. Some gang guys tried to jump me — *(Cries out.)* What do I want to be in a gang for? I just come from a *war*! What do I want to be some punk cholo for? So I went a little crazy . . . The police came — the siren, the uniforms, the sticks . . . I got confused — like I was back there, in El Salvador! And I'm fighting everybody — the army, the cholos — guerrilleros, police — I got confused, m'entiendes? *(Beat.)* And the lawyer told me to make a plea. Guilty.

ANA: Por el amor de dios. Bobby!

BOBBY: The lawyer I got now's been trying to fix things — *(Nancy enters downstage right, holding Jenna, and charges across the stage to the phone.)*

NANCY: *(Incensed by Bobby's predicament.)* So he's got a felony on his record? Let me make a call. *(Dialing.)* Jesus. The criminal justice system in this city. Taking advantage of immigrants who don't even know their basic — *(Into phone; warmly.)* Harv? . . . Nance. How are you? . . . How's Beth? . . . *Oh, no! (No pause.)* Listen, Harv, remember that couple I told you about from El Salvador? *(Ana is between Nancy and Bobby now.)*

ANA: *(Angry.)* She knows people, Bobby!

NANCY: *(Into the phone, laughs.)* No, no, I'm not getting involved . . .

ANA: She's Jewish! *(Nancy talks to Ana, and Ana talks to Bobby with increasing urgency.)*

NANCY: My friend says that any competent lawyer should be able to get it —

ANA: *(To Bobby.)* Expunged.

BOBBY: Sponged?

NANCY: He can get your husband's record sealed —

ANA: *(To Bobby.)* He can do it for a thousand dollars —

NANCY: And once he's a citizen, *you'll* automatically get your papers!

ANA: *(To Bobby.)* And when I get my papers, I could go to El Salvador and get Tomás —

BOBBY: Where we gonna get a thousand dollars?! *(He walks away, upstage. Ana looks at Nancy.)*

NANCY: Well . . . I suppose I could just lend — advance you the money — and you could work it off . . .

ANA: Or maybe you could still pay me every week and —

NANCY: And you could work off a thousand dollar advance in overtime . . .

BOBBY: *(Hates this.)* Overtime!?

ANA: *(To Nancy.)* How much an hour? *(Richard enters, wearing the Rolling Stones T-shirt with the big mouth.)*

RICHARD: *(Trying not to blow.)* Nance — the Stones concert starts in exactly fifty-five minutes. I don't mind missing dinner, but there's a Dodger game downtown and the traffic is going to be — are you kidding me? The traffic — on a Friday night?! Now I am not taking the ten. I am not taking Wilshire. And I sure a hell am not taking —

NANCY: I'm coming right now, sweetheart. *(He looks from Nancy to Ana.)*

RICHARD: Fine. *(He starts to exit, upstage.)*

NANCY: I saw Jagger on the news, he looks great!

RICHARD: Jagger will be dead by the time we get there! *(He exits. Nancy continues to Ana.)*

NANCY: Ten dollars an hour.

BOBBY: *(Continues to Ana.)* And what about Santi?

ANA: *(To Nancy.)* Eleven.

BOBBY: What about his soccer?

NANCY: All right, eleven for overtime.

BOBBY: What about the son you got here!

NANCY: Oh Ana . . . Think you could work this weekend?

ANA: *(To Bobby.)* Santi will have a brother — a family! *(At the end of her rope.)* How else am I going to do it? *(He looks at her pained.)*

BOBBY: Pues —

ANA: I can do it, Mrs. — Nancy.

BOBBY: I'm going out for a little while. *(He leaves.)*

ANA: Anytime you need me extra — I can do it. *(Nancy hands Jenna over to Ana, as the lights fade.)*

END OF ACT I

ACT II

SCENE ONE

When the lights come up, it's three months later. Ana has fallen asleep on the couch with the TV on, and we hear the Spanish station. For a moment, it's unclear which living room she's in, hers or the Robins'. A door opens and closes, waking Ana, and Richard enters.

RICHARD: *(Calls out.)* Ana, I'm home —

ANA: Oh — good evening, Mr. Robin —

RICHARD: *(For the tenth time; smiles. She gets up and turns off the TV.)* Ana, please . . . Richard. Sorry I'm a little late. Client of mind, schizophrenic, got out of the VA hospital — started to direct traffic. Caused a ten-car pileup on Wilshire Boulevard.

ANA: Ay no!

RICHARD: I should've been a personal-injury lawyer. Everything OK here?

ANA: Yes, fine! Guess what happen, Mr. Robin!

RICHARD: I give up.

ANA: Jenna is crawling!

RICHARD: She is? You're kidding! She crawled?

ANA: Yes!

RICHARD: That's amazing! Eight and half months old and she —? Wow. God, I wish I'd seen that! She's been doing that snake thing, lately, but — where did she —?

ANA: Right here. She was trying to get the remote.

RICHARD: *(Laughs.)* Uh-oh. *(He goes to the spot where she crawled. Beat.)* You know, Ana — I have a thought . . . Don't tell my wife. When she gets back from her trip. About Jenna crawling.

ANA: *(Surprised.)* You want me to — lie?

RICHARD: Of course not. Just don't mention it. She's been gone so much these last couple of months . . . She'll feel just awful that Jenna crawled when she wasn't here.

ANA: *(Torn.)* OK . . .

RICHARD: She'll see her crawl when she gets home, right? No harm in her thinking it's the first time . . . *(He goes to the fridge.)* No point in adding to her . . . *(With an edge.)* stress. *(He gets a beer.)* Oh — Ana would you like one before you hit the road?

ANA: A beer? No, no! Thank you —

RICHARD: *(Laughs.)* Oh, c'mon, someone should toast my daughter's first crawl, don't you think?

ANA: Well —

RICHAR: *(Playful.)* Look, I'm your employer and I insist.

ANA: Maybe a juice?

RICHARD: You got it. *(He gets a beer and a glass of juice. Mutters:)* Someone should acknowledge the moment . . . *(Ana looks at her watch. He brings her juice.)* How do they toast in El Salvador?

ANA: "Salud, amor, dinero."

RICHARD: Let's see, I have a little Spanish from high school . . . "Health . . . love . . . money"?

ANA: Yes. But I like how the Mexicans say it . . . "Amor, salud, dinero . . . y el tiempo para disfrutarlos."

RICHARD: I'm sorry, I should have added that I *failed* Spanish —

ANA: "Love, health, money — and the time to . . . to like them" — *(Searches for the right word.)* no — the time to . . .

RICHARD: "Enjoy"? "Enjoy" them?

ANA: Yes.

RICHARD: The time to enjoy them . . . Hell, I'll drink to that! *(He does.)*

ANA: What do you say? "To your health"?

RICHARD: *(Laughs.)* Well, that's what we *say* . . . After all, it wouldn't be nice to say, "To your money!" *(They smile. An awkward pause.)* Wow. That Jenna. What next? *(Beat.)* You know, I had her in the car the other day and I had this Elvis Costello tape on, and she starts cooing along with the song — and I swear she was in the same key! I think that kid has perfect pitch.

ANA: *(No idea what he's talking about.)* Yes?

RICHARD: Well, I was in a band after college —

ANA: *(Can't help but laugh.)* You was in a band?

RICHARD: Shit yeah. Rock 'n' roll. Ana. Never judge a man by his clothes. We played a lot of the clubs in Hollywood. We opened for Seinfeld . . . Lot of guys — *(Ana smiles, but glances at the clock.)* What kind of music do you like?

ANA: Latin music I guess I like the best —

RICHARD: Salsa, Tejano, Cubano . . . ?

ANA: Yes.

RICHARD: You like the Buena Vista Social Club?

ANA: I don't think I been there —

RICHARD: What? Oh — no, no — they're a band! Let me put 'em on for you.

Jenna's crazy about these guys — *(He goes to the cabinet and puts on a CD. "Chan Chan" would be ideal here. If that is not possible, Richard's next line changes to — "Oh, wait — listen to this! This is Cubano too. You have to check this out!")*

ANA: Oh no, I don't want you to go to no trouble —

RICHARD: These guys are like the original — they're like the Beatles of Cuban music. You have to check this out. *(Ana sighs. the music, "Chan Chan" or something similar starts to play.)*

ANA: It's very pretty. *(Richard dances to the music and strums an imaginary guitar.)*

RICHARD: Isn't it? So simple, so pretty . . . *(Listens.)* No synthesizers, no samplers . . . No electronic bullshit. *(Listens more.)* These guys didn't live in fancy houses . . . their cars weren't "retro" — they were *old!* Think these guys get all bent out of shape over air? They just breathe . . . *(Ana sneaks another peek at her watch. Richard keeps grooving.)* What does this part say? *(Ana listens. this is not an easy thing to translate for you boss.)*

ANA: Oh — it's like . . . "The love I have . . . I can't stop —" Cómo se dice . . . "I can't stop drooling for you."

RICHARD: Wow. Heavy. *(Ana worries they're about to hear the whole album. Finally . . .)*

ANA: Well, thank you for playing it for me — *(He's lost in the music and doesn't hear. Louder:)* Thank you for playing it for me! *(The baby cries. She puts her glass on a side table and rises.)* Excuse me — *(He puts his beer down next to her glass and they go to the baby's room. Ana gets Jenna.)* It's OK, Jenna — *(She brings the baby to the couch and rocks her. Richard sits next to her on the arm.)* She's going to go right back to sleep.

RICHARD: Really? How do you know?

ANA: From the cry. *(Ana imitates the exact cry.)*

RICHARD: So . . . simple.

ANA: She's a very easy baby.

RICHARD: *(Surprised.)* She is?

ANA: And she's so smart! She's much smarter than the other babies in the park. I think she even know how to say my name! Only she say, "Ama" —

RICHARD: *(Laughs.)* Gee, hope she's not trying to say, "Mama — " *(She looks up at him and smiles. He looks down at her and smiles . . . Suddenly it's terribly awkward. She hands him the baby and rises, fast.)*

ANA: OK — pues — I see you tomorrow. *(She heads for the door.)*

RICHARD: Listen, it's the weekend for godsake — I'm perfectly happy to take care of my own daughter. Take the . . . tiempo por disfrutarlos.

ANA: Oh no, Mrs. Robin already pay me. I'll be here. *(She exits. the music resumes for several beats, as Richard dances Jenna back to her crib . . . And Bobby enters Santiago's room and watches his sleeping son.)*

SCENE TWO
Ana enters her apartment and calls to Bobby.

ANA: Bobby — ?

BOBBY: *(Entering from Santi's room.)* Sí, mi amorcita! *(He hugs her, spins her around, playful. He has good news.)*

ANA: All these nights I'm working late . . . te sientes solo?

BOBBY: I miss you like crazy, mama. Cada noche.

ANA: Pero, you don't never . . . ?

BOBBY: Qué? What are you asking me?

ANA: No se. When I was working tonight, the señor —

BOBBY: Qué? He tried something? Because if he did, I'm going to go over there right now and — I don't want you working there, that's it. You don't know nothing about men.

ANA: He just seemed a little lonely — with the señora gone.

BOBBY: Do I have to hear about the señor and all his — lonely —

ANA: I'm sorry. *(She tries to kiss him.)*

BOBBY: I'm not in the mood no more.

ANA: OK — *(She flops down on the sofa.)*

BOBBY: *(Smiles.)* I'm telling you, you give up too easy . . . Guess what happen?

ANA: What?

BOBBY: You got to guess!

ANA: OK. The Lakers won?

BOBBY: No.

ANA: The other people won?

BOBBY: I won. I got a job. Full-time!

ANA: You did?

BOBBY: Don't look so surprised! I been telling you! That guy I work for last week, painting his house? He wants me to paint his apartment building — the whole thing! Gonna take me a couple of months! I told him I know how to put carpet, fix the electric, whatever he want. And no weekends — so I could still take Santi to soccer! *(Beat.)* Eleven dollars an hour.

ANA: Eleven dollars! *(He puts his arms around her, dances her around.)*

BOBBY: Eleven dollars so now you could quit your job.

ANA: Bobby, the señora lent me the thousand dollars for the lawyer, I got to work to pay her back —

BOBBY: *(Proud.)* So now *I* can work to pay her back. *(Kisses her on each word.)* Vieja, chula, amorcita . . . He said he's going to need somebody to manage the building, do repairs. And they going to get a free apartment!

ANA: Where?

BOBBY: Pues, Vernon —

ANA: *(Sarcastic.)* By the factories or the recycling plant?

BOBBY: Oh — so now you only want to live on the Westside?

ANA: Y por qué no? Why shouldn't I live there?

BOBBY: I got a good job, Ana! How come you're never happy?

ANA: I'm happy, amor — *(Pause.)* but I'm not going to quit till we get Tomás. One of the nannies from the park? She paid five thousand dollars to a coyote to being her son. They brought him in the wheel well of a truck. I can't quit now!

BOBBY: OK.

ANA: You sure?

BOBBY: *(Smiles.)* Because we gonna save that money in no time. Only thing is, if you late coming home, and I'm working I got to get my sister to get Santi —

ANA: No. I don't want somebody else watching my son.

BOBBY: Just once in a while, amor —

ANA: She's too young.

BOBBY: She's eighteen now! She got her license!

ANA: What kind of car?

BOBBY: Caprice.

ANA: What year?

BOBBY: Mira. She can come to my job and leave the Caprice and take the truck. What do you want me to do Ana? Not take a job?

ANA: *(Beat; sighs.)* OK.

BOBBY: Why don't you call El Salvador in the morning and talk to Tomás. Then I take you and Santi for breakfast. Sunday, if you're not working, maybe we even go to church. But if we go to church, I got to start making up for it tonight . . . *(She smiles. They begin to kiss on the couch, as the set revolves, carrying them off, and night turns to day. In the scene transition, Richard enters downstage left, in jogging clothes. He does a few stretches, jogs across the stage, stops for a cigarette, downstage right, and jogs off . . . as Ana enters the kitchen.)*

SCENE THREE

Ana is straightening up in the kitchen. A public-radio host is doing the subscription drive, laying on the guilt about nonsubscribers getting a free ride.

ANA: *(To radio.)* Cállate, hombre, por favor! *(She changes the station to Latin music and starts to dance. A door opens and closes, and Nancy enters with her suitcase.)*

NANCY: Hi!

ANA: Nancy! You're back early!

NANCY: I got an early plane! I'm just going to run in and see Jenna — *(She hurries to her room.)*

ANA: She's taking her nap — *(Nancy doesn't hear. Ana turns off the radio. Nancy returns, disappointed.)*

NANCY: She's taking a nap.

ANA: She been taking her nap a little earlier. How was your trip?

NANCY: Good! Very good! Tres bien! Oh, Ana — I brought you something from New York — *(She opens her purse and gives Ana a snow globe souvenir from New York.)* Snow. Because you said you'd never seen it.

ANA: Oh, that's pretty! Thank you!

NANCY: And I got some "I Love NY" T-shirts for you to send to El Salvador.

ANA: Ay, Tomás love T-shirts!

NANCY: How about Santiago?

ANA: *(Caught.)* Sí! Tomás a little more 'cause he's older —

NANCY: *(Laughs.)* Right. So tell me everything Jenna did while I was gone. *(Ana hesitates, remembering her secret with Richard.)*

ANA: Oh — Jenna was very good, Nancy — *(Searching.)* She slept — very good.

NANCY: She didn't cry for me?

ANA: No, no —

NANCY: *(Disappointed.)* No?

ANA: Well, the first night —

NANCY: And you didn't call me?

ANA: The next night she was fine —

NANCY: You didn't dress her too warmly for bed?

ANA: Just the one blanket like you tell me.

NANCY: And she ate well?

ANA: Yes, very good — *(Sound of front door opening and closing. Ana starts. Nancy notices.)*

NANCY: Ana, there wasn't a problem . . . ?

ANA: No problem! *(Richard enters in jogging clothes with a bag of groceries.)*

RICHARD: Nance! You're back early! *(He puts down the bag and kisses her.)* Hey, Ana —

ANA: *(Bit awkward.)* Mr. Robin. *(Ana quickly goes to another room.)*

RICHARD: Let me just change out of this sweaty shirt — *(He exits. Nancy takes off her jacket and puts it on the couch — and notices the beer and the glass on the side table. Looking closer, she finds lipstick on the glass.)*

NANCY: Shit. *(Richard returns in a clean shirt and hugs her.)*

RICHARD: How was your trip?

NANCY: Terrific. I had breakfast with that director.

RICHARD: You had breakfast? Great!

NANCY: How was your week?

RICHARD: All right.

NANCY: *(Trying to remain casual.)* Anything happen while I was gone?

RICHARD: What do you mean?

NANCY: Well, I don't know. I just got the sense that Ana is acting a little strange

RICHARD: Maybe she feels a little put upon having worked ten days straight.

NANCY: Oh, I doubt that because she needs the overtime.

RICHARD: *(Beat; smiles.)* All right. I asked Ana not to tell you because I knew how awful you'd feel for having missed it, but — Jenna crawled! *(Nancy looks at him, moved and guilt-stricken — but suspicious.)*

NANCY: Jenna crawled . . . Well, I *am* sorry I missed that . . . *(Calling out; casually.)* Hey, Ana? Could you come in here a sec? *(Ana comes in. Nancy smiles.)* So Ana — Jenna's crawling? *(Ana looks from Nancy to Richard. Richard nods. Nancy notices.)*

ANA: Yes, Nancy.

NANCY: Wow! That's — great. Thanks, Ana. *(Ana leaves but starts to eavesdrop, just out of sight. So we see some of her reaction.)*

RICHARD: That was a really lousy position to put her in.

NANCY: I didn't put her in that position. *I* didn't ask her to lie.

RICHARD: She didn't lie. she simply omitted to —

NANCY: An omission is a lie! You know how I feel about honesty. You know that — no matter what it is — the worst thing you can possibly do is lie to me — *(Ana listens, intently.)*

RICHARD: I was simply trying to protect you because I knew you'd feel bad for having missed your daughter's first crawl.

NANCY: *(Beat; composing herself.)* I know I've been gone a lot lately, Richard . . .

RICHARD: Well, yes, but, it's part of your —

NANCY: I know we haven't had sex in a few — weeks . . .

RICHARD: *(Checks date on watch.)* Well, seven and a half, actually, but who's —

NANCY: Did you have a woman here last night?

RICHARD: A woman!? Nancy, you're jet-lagged —

NANCY: I found some lipstick on a glass —

RICHARD: *(Laughs.)* Oh for godsake, that was probably Ana's.

NANCY: She had a beer?

RICHARD: No, she had a juice. I had the beer —

NANCY: With Ana?

RICHARD: Whoa. Counselor. Am I on trial here? I wanted a little company — something wrong with that?

NANCY: Did you sleep with her?

RICHARD: *(After a beat; deeply pained.)* You know . . . I understand you are under a lot of stress. But I think if you really examine what you just said . . . I think you will have to admit that it is a pretty goddamn racist assumption. *And* classist — *and* sexist too.

NANCY: Yeah, but did you sleep with her?

RICHARD: Jesus, I didn't even want to *hire* a nanny, no less fuck one! *(Ana reacts unable to believe her ears. The baby cries. Ana doesn't know what to do. She takes a breath and runs past them toward the baby's room.)*

ANA: *(Lightly.)* I'll get her —

NANCY AND RICHARD: *(Smile; lightly.)* Thanks! *(They go right back to fight mode.)*

RICHARD: Well, if you think something happened, go ask her. *(Waits.)* Go —

NANCY: Oh, I'm really going to go ask the nanny if my husband . . . *(Beat.)* Well. I guess I'll just have to accept your version of the facts for now — *(Richard grabs a teddy bear among a pile of toys nearby.)*

RICHARD: I know — get a Daddy Cam! *(Ana runs back through toward the kitchen.)*

ANA: *(Lightly.)* Diaper — !

RICHARD: *(Cheery.)* Right over there! Say, Ana, could you do us a favor and take Jenna and run over to The Coffee Bean — *not Starbucks* — and get us five pounds of French Roast?

ANA: OK —

RICHARD: Thanks a lot, Ana.

NANCHY: *(Cheery.)* Thanks! *(Ana grabs a diaper and hurries back to Jenna's room. The argument immediately resumes.)* Because you do know that I intend to keep working, Richard. One of us has to bring in serious money —

RICHARD: Sweetheart — no one has ever asked you not to work. I may have felt you were going back a bit prematurely —

NANCY: To pay the mortgage —

RICHARD: Which I may have felt was a bit high —

NANCY: Well, that's the price you pay for clean air —

RICHARD: Which *I* may have felt was clean enough where we *were*. Where we were happy —

NANCY: The air was not good.

RICHARD: You know what? We cannot afford "good air," Nancy, let's just stop breathing right now. *(He holds his breath.)*

NANCY: And the safety issue?

RICHARD: Let's get guns! Let's get 'em, Nance. I'll get you a twenty-two for our anniversary, you get me a Glock!

NANCY: Richard —

RICHARD: It's a non-issue to me, Nancy, but, what can I say? I'm also the one who nuked the bear! I'm also the one who thinks the Volvo's just a really *ugly* car!

NANCY: *(Emotional.)* What do you want to drive, Richard? You want to drive a VW Bug — convertible? Maybe you'd rather throw a guitar in back or a surfboard — instead of a car seat.

RICHARD: *(Hurt.)* I *had* a car seat! You *took* my car seat — for the nanny's car!

NANCY: *(Furious and fighting tears.)* I know the Volvo's ugly. I know it's not — exciting. But at least it's not a gas-guzzling, fume-emitting SUV! The Volvo may not be fun, it may not be hip, or funky, or sexy or "soulful." *(Starts to break.)* But it's a *family* car, Richard. It's an *honest* car. It's Swedish! And it's fucking safe. *(She rushes out of the room.)*

RICHARD: Fuck. *(Ana, hearing silence, ventures out with Jenna. Richard beats her to the door. Eager to leave:)* Never mind, Ana. I'll just run down to The Coffee Bean myself.

ANA: *(Eager to leave.)* No, no, I'll go to The Coffee Bean!

RICHARD: *(Firmly.)* No. *I'll* go to The Coffee Bean. *(He kisses the baby, feeling awful, and leaves. Nancy reenters.)*

NANCY: *(Hurt.)* Did he — leave?

ANA: Yes. *(Nancy goes to Jenna — overwhelmed with guilt and love.)*

NANCY: Hi Jenna! Hi my baby! I'll take her — *(Takes Jenna.)* Mommy's home, baby, Mommy's here. *(Vulnerable.)* Ana — I'm so sorry if you were put in an awkward position.

ANA: *(Barely controlling her anger.)* Maybe, Nancy . . . you want to find somebody else.

NANCY: Oh no!

ANA: After this week, I have worked off the overtime for the thousand dollars —

NANCY: Ana, please . . . It's just hard when you're away so much to feel . . . in touch. *(Beat.)* I know you understand. *(They look at each other.)*

ANA: *(After a beat; nods.)* I . . . understand.

NANCY: Thank you. Anyway, in the future, please — whatever it is . . . just — let me know what's going on. Never ever feel you have to lie to me. *(Ana nods. Lights fade on the two women. In the scene change, Nancy exits and Ana takes the cloth from the kitchen table that will become a blanket for a picnic in the park.)*

SCENE FOUR

Zoila and Sandra enter with their carriages and meet Ana in the park.

ANA: Hola!

SANDRA: Hola muchacha, cómo estas? *(Ana starts to lay out the blanket on the grass.)*

ZOILA: No. Demasiado gringos. Aquí — *(Ana moves the blanket downstage center.)*

ANA: *(To Sandra, eagerly.)* So what did they ask you on that test?

SANDRA: Everything! What day is Fourth of July? What Thursday is Thanksgiving? How many stars have the flag? How many stripes?

ANA: Ay dios mío! *(Zoila takes out a box of doughnuts to celebrate Sandra.)*

SANDRA: Ay no, mijas!

ZOILA: Ta-da!

ANA: For your citizenship! *(Zoila starts to sing. Ana joins her.)*

ZOILA and ANA: Happy citizenship to you, happy citizenship to you, happy citizenship to Sandra — *(Zoila's cell phone rings.)* Happy citizenship to you.

ZOILA: *(Getting her cell.)* Ay por dios. *(Ana hands out doughnuts. Into phone; charming:)* Allo? . . . *(Sitting down on the grass.)* Yes, Mrs. Breyer, we walking to the doctor right now . . . OK, so I'll drop Jackson off, and then I could go to the Trader Joe's . . . *And* the Savon . . . And The Borders. *(Feeding a bit of doughnut to Jackson.)* OK . . . OK . . . OK . . . OK, Mrs. Breyer, no problem. *(She hangs up. The three of them sit and eat.)* Hija de la gran puta. Now I got to go driving all over Santa Monica. Thank God I don't have a license — she'd send me to Beverly Hills!

ANA: Pero how do you drive without a license?

ZOILA: Carefully. Very carefully. That's why people who don't got a license is better drivers.

ALA: Ésa mujer es una bruja! Why don't you just quit?

ZOILA: Porque my daughter's got her quinceañera next month and I got to send money for the party, the dress, the rings, el cojín . . . Easy for you to say "Quit"! You got a license! Your drive a Altima!

ANA: Mira. I'll tell you how I got my license, OK? I know a guy that works for AT&T and he got to check people's credit with their social security numbers. Now California has a code, lot of people have the same social security, except for the last four numbers.

ZOILA: *(Huh?)* Qué?

ANA: So he can try a number — and if nobody has it — he could give it to you.

ZOILA: Qué?

ANA: Then you go down to the DMV in Huntington Park. On a Saturday — late — when everybody's ready to go home. And you give that number —

ZOILA: But that's — lying!

ANA: *(Matter-of-fact.)* Pues, you need your social security to get a license, you need your papers to get your social security, they don't want to give you your papers — you got to lie.

ZOILA: QUÉ? I could never get a license like that!

ANA: Then go down to Alvarado and buy one! *Y ya!*

ZOILA: Qué horror. What kind of person would do that?

ANA: A person that wants a better job! *(Sandra starts to laugh, then quickly turns it into a cough.)*

ZOILA: *(With contempt.)* Uh-huh. *(Rises; ignoring Ana.) Bueno,* I see you to-morrow.

ANA: Primero Dios —

ZOILA: I see you at the Gymboree, Sandra.

SANDRA: Bueno —

ANA: *(Trying.)* Adios — *(Zoila walks off with great pride. Ana sighs.)* She's never going to quit that job.

SANDRA: Ay, mija, I got to get a new job too. Linda is very nice. But the twins? Yesterday they was playing firemen? They put the couch on fire. And I got three kids when I get home, too! And my son that come from Mexico? Last night he come home with a tattoo! I can't work till seven — he needs his mami now!

ANA: Entiendo. I keep missing Santi's soccer practice because I got to work.

Pero now I don't got to work the overtime no more — and Santi's got his first real game tomorrow night!

SANDRA: Sí?

ANA: He's real good at soccer. And the doctor says it's good for his asthma. You should see him in the uniform! And I sent one to Tomás too!

SANDRA: Qué bueno. You going to bring him real soon.

AHA: I got my appointment next month with immigration! So what did you do when you made your citizenship? You made a party?

SANDRA: It's a long story. I don't want to be boring you . . . *(But she's dying to tell her.)* I went to Texas!

ANA: To Texas?

SANDRA: To see the father of my son.

ANA: Sí?

SANDRA: Ay, mija, I never love nobody like I love this man! *(Makes the sign of the cross.)* God forgive me, not even the husband I got now. *(To baby.)* I love you, Jackson, but not like this!

ANA: But you didn't get married?

SANDRA: We was going to! En Oaxaca. Then, when I was three months pregnant, he say his mother don't want him to marry me 'cause he's Christian and I'm Catholic, and he give me money for the abortion, fíjate! And when my son was born, my father give me money to leave Mexico — rápido! — and I had to leave my son and come here. Híjole, I cried for months, for years!

ANA: Ay no . . .

SANDRA: Then last week, I talked to my cousin in Oaxaca, and she say he moved to Texas. So I called his house, his girlfriend answered the phone — *(Laughs.)* She called me a puta, la, la, la . . . But I got dressed real nice and I took a picture of my son in his uniform — from *Catholic School* —

ANA: *(Incredulous.)* And you went to Texas? *(Sandra nods. Seventeen years of emotions begin to pour out of her.)*

SANDRA: *(With laughter, tears, and triumph.)* And I tell him, "You know what? I have your son!" He thought I come for the child support, but I say — "I'm not after you! I have a happy life and I feel so proud of myself 'cause I got my citizenship now and I sent for our son!" And I showed him his picture! *(With sudden fierceness.)* I say, "I didn't ask for welfare — and I didn't be a prostitute — and I didn't ask you for nothing! I didn't ask you — or my father — *nobody!* I just work every day and I feel so . . .

with my face up." And then I left. He want to take me out to eat, but I say, "No, I'm really happy to see you and I just come to say hi."

ANA: How long were you there?

SANDRA: *(Shrugs.)* About forty-five minutes.

ANA: You went to Texas for forty-five minutes?

SANDRA: Pues, I had the day off. *(Sandra starts to clean up. Ana has been inspired by Sandra's speaking up.)*

ANA: Sabes qué? Maybe I should tell Nancy about *my* son. She's a woman too, no? She's a mother —

SANDRA: *(Shakes her head no.)* They're not like us mija. Wait till you get your citizenship. Then we get cake for you too! *(Checks watch.)* Ooooey — the twins! *(Starts to leave.)* Have a good time at the soccer game tomorrow! Qué juege hasta la quinta chingada! *(Sandra leaves. Ana exits in the other direction.)*

SCENE FIVE

Nancy, in her robe, is looking for aspirin in the kitchen. Ana enters, carrying a bunch of flowers behind her back.

ANA: *(Surprised.)* Nancy! You're not going to your yoga class? *(She puts the flowers in a little vase as Nancy keeps looking.)*

NANCY: No. *(Beat.)* I hate yoga. Frankly, I find lying on the floor listening to the breathing of thirty women who are in better shape than I am extremely stressful. Jenna's asleep. Do we have any aspirin?

ANA: I put it in the medicine cabinet in the bathroom.

(Nancy goes off to get it.)

ANA: We got to get the childproofing for the cabinets, Nancy — it's very dangerous now that Jenna is crawling —

NANCY: *(Guilty.)* I know. I promise I'll call this weekend.

ANA: Can I get you something? Some chamomile tea?

NANCY: Oh, no thanks. It's just a cold. I must have caught something on the plane. I just hope I haven't given it to Jenna. She seems, I don't know, fussy —

ANA: I could make her some tea too —

NANCY: Tea? For a baby?

ANA: I always give it to my — *(Quickly.)* both my kids — when they were babies in El Salvador. But you can call the doctor if you don't —

NANCY: *(Sits.)* Oh Ana, please, I trust you. Make me some tea too. *(Ana puts the flowers on the table.)* What're these for? God, I didn't forget my own birthday, did I?

ANA: I just thought maybe you like flowers . . . *(Nancy's eyes well up.)* I didn't buy them — I just picked them on the street — *(Nancy starts to cry.)*

NANCY: It's not that. It's just . . . so kind of you. It was just a — really kind thing to do. I'm sorry, I don't know why I'm — I didn't get much sleep . . . Jenna was so fussy, and nothing — nothing I did seemed to . . . She just kept crying and crying and crying . . . Richard says she never does that with you. He thinks she's angry I'm gone so much — *(Laughs/cries.)* Well, clearly *he's* angry — you can always tell when he gets really *nice* . . . What am I saying, he has a right to be angry — *(Ana doesn't know what to say so she says what Nancy has said to her.)*

ANA: Well, you got your rights as a woman, Nancy —

NANCY: *(Laughs.)* Rights? I have the right to do it all — and not do any of it very well?

ANA: I know. You got stress —

NANCY: No, *you've* got stress. I mean, you don't even get to see your kids! You know what I should do? I should just call up right now. I should just call up and quit and take care of my own child.

ANA: *(Shocked; blurts.)* Oh no. No Nancy! No!

NANCY: *(Taken aback.)* Wow. You must think I'm a really lousy mother —

ANA: No!

NANCY: I was joking, Ana —

ANA: Oh —

NANCY: But tell me the truth — because I'd quit in a minute — in a second if I thought . . . I mean, I'm her mother, I can fuck her up for life! *(Ana thinks. She decides, for a variety of reasons, but mostly for the sake of her own children . . .)*

ANA: You're a good mother, Nancy. And Jenna is fine.

NANCY: *(Utterly vulnerable.)* You think?

ANA: I think Jenna is . . . a very lucky child. And — you *like* to work —

NANCY: I *do* like to work! I like to work — *and* I love my child! Is that so horrible of me?

ANA: You know what? I like to work too! *(Laughs.)* Ay, don't tell that to my husband. Because, in my country, all the women is suppose to love to stay home. I get depressed if I stay home all the time!

NANCY: I know, I know!

ANA: I tell you a secret, I want to go back to school — *(Quickly adds.)* When Jenna is older —

NANCY: You should! You're a smart woman. *(Puts an arm around her.)* You should go to school and get a real job! Thank you. Thank you, Ana.

ANA: Ay dios mío, I forgot your tea! *(Ana goes and pours tea.)*

NANCY: Aren't you having some?

ANA: OK. *(Nancy takes cigarettes from her purse and lights up.)*

NANCY: I don't do this in front of Jenna, by the way. *(Confidentially.)* Or Richard. *(Nancy sits. Ana gets her tea but doesn't sit. Nancy laughs.)* Oh, Ana, sit!

ANA: OK. *(An awkward moment when the two of them are actually seated together at the table.)*

NANCY: What the hell, let's have some cookies. *(Nancy jumps up, gets a bag of cookies, and offers it to Ana, who takes a cookie. Embarrassed:)* Jees, I certainly didn't mean to get into all that. Let's talk about *your* life for a change. what's happening with your papers?

ANA: I got my appointment next month with the immigration!

NANCY: That's terrific! And you know what? When you kids come, we're having a party. *(Shakes her hips.)* At El Cholo. *(Ana feels so awful that she starts to tell Nancy the truth about Santiago.)*

ANA: Nancy . . . I . . . I want to tell you something. It's a little bit hard. I should have told you before . . . *(The phone rings.)* It's about my kids . . . *(The phone rings.)*

NANCY: They need something?

ANA: No, no — *(The phone rings again. The machine picks up.)*

NANCY'S VOICE on MACHINE: Hi! You've reached Nancy, Richard, and Jenna. Please leave a message.

NANCY: Maybe I just better listen to the — *(Ana nods.)*

DIANE'S VOICE on MACHINE: Nancy, it's Diane calling around eight twenty-seven. It's important, and I'm in the car, so call my cell if you get this before nine — *(Nancy rolls her eyes at Ana.)*

NANCY: Maybe I just better — *(Ana nods. Nancy races to the phone.)*

DIANE'S VOICE on MACHINE: After that I'll be at Disney —

NANCY: *(Into phone; instantly professional.)* Diane? Hi, I just walked in . . . tonight? Gee, I did have plans . . . *(Surprised.)* He did? Dinner?! . . . No, no, I understand . . . Can you hold just a sec — ? *(She covers the mouthpiece and goes to Ana.)* Ana . . . do you think you could possibly do me a huge favor and work late tonight?

ANA: Tonight?

NANCY: I know — it's ridiculously short notice —

ANA: I'm really sorry, Nancy. I can't.

NANCY: *(Surprised.)* You can't?

ANA: No — I already got plans.

NANCY: Oh gee. I'm sorry . . . *(Beat.)* Ana, I know it's awful of me to ask — but could you possibly change them? For the weekend maybe? I'm home all weekend —

ANA: I don't think so.

NANCY: Well, can you tell me what it is? Maybe I can figure a way to —

ANA: No. *(Beat.)* It's a — a family thing.

NANCY: *(In a bind.)* Oh God — *(Into phone.)* Diane? . . . I'm so sorry. I'll have to call you right back. *(She hangs up.)*

ANA: Please don't be angry —

NANCY: No, no, I understand. It's just — this director is just impossible to pin down —

ANA: *(Feeling cornered.)* I already worked off the overtime for the thousand dollars . . . *(She put her cookie down.)*

NANCY: I know that! But Richard's working late — there's really no one else I can call —

ANA: And Jenna is getting a cold —

NANCY: I know! I know. But believe me, my boss does not want to hear about Jenna. And she'll be asleep practically the whole time . . . I'm sure I'll be back by nine. And then I don't have a trip planned for quite a while . . . *(Sits.)* I wouldn't ask if I didn't really need your help, Ana. What if we say sixty dollars for the four hours — ?

ANA: It's not the money!

NANCY: Well, could you possibly just do me a — favor? Just this one time? *(Touches her hand.)* As a . . . friend? *(Ana hesitates for several beats.)*

ANA: I . . . guess I could call my husband . . . *(She starts to get her cell from her bag.)*

NANCY: Could you? Oh thank you, Ana, so much. Oh please — use our phone. *(Ana goes to the phone. Nancy goes to her bedroom.)*

ANA: *(Into the phone.)* Bobby? Listen, the señora asked me to work late . . . I know, I know I promised, but I'll see his next game . . . Porque she got no one else! Please — tell him I'll take him to play soccer on the weekend, tell him I don't got to work all weekend! *(Listens; upset.)* Pues — you can't go? . . . OK, OK, you got to work too, entiendo . . . Your sister? . . . Pues, just make sure she know how to get there, and she got his bag — everything — *(Nancy reenters. Into phone:)* and tell everybody have a good time at the party! Gracias, mi amor . . . Bye. *(Hangs up.)* I can do it, Nancy.

NANCY: You can? Oh, thank you so much! Listen, if you get hungry here's a twenty — *(She puts a twenty on the table.)* Now let's just finish our cookies. Diane can just wait! *(They sit back down.)* Now what did you want to tell me about your kids?

ANA: Oh. *(Beat.)* I told them I sent the T-shirts. They're really excited.

NANCY: Well — good! Listen, Ana, whatever they need . . . *(Takes her hand.)* I mean, you're really part of the family now . . . *(Nancy holds Ana's hand for a moment. Then the two women pick up their cups and sip their tea. In the scene transition. Richard enters and hands Jenna over to Ana, and he and Nancy leave. Sound of a Spanish radio station takes us into the next scene.)*

SCENE SIX

Ana is giving Jenna tea in a bottle. A contemporary love song plays on the Spanish station.

ANA: Así, nena . . . You had enough tea? OK, Jenna . . . That's my good girl. Duérmete con los angeles . . . *(Her cell phone rings.)* Ay. *(She gets her cell and answers.)* Hallo? . . . Qué? . . . I can't understand you Bobby, slow down, the phone is — . . . Qué? *(She turns down the radio a bit. Very still:)* OK . . . OK, Bobby . . . OK. *(She hangs up and dials Nancy's cell.)* Answer — damn you — *(She hears a cell phone ringing and realizes it's Nancy's — in the purse Nancy left behind.)* Mierda! *(The baby starts to cry. She hangs up, grabs her purse, and looks for paper and pen. She scribbles a note and leaves it on the kitchen table. Then she runs out with Jenna. Light change. Richard enters with his briefcase. The Spanish station continues to play. The song is now up-tempo, driving, something like Juanes' "A Dios le Pido.")*

RICHARD: Nancy? *(He sighs and pours himself a drink. Nancy enters with her briefcase and sets it down on the table. She has good news.)*

NANCY: Hi! You just get in? *(She kisses him. He is surprised and pleased.)*

RICHARD: Yeah. Where were you?

NANCY: Dinner. I signed a new client!

RICHARD: Congratulations!

NANCY: I'm just going to run in and get Ana —

RICHARD: Can we have a drink after she leaves? To toast your —

NANCY: Sure! *(She goes to Jenna's room and returns, calling to the bedroom —)* Ana? *(Calls out window.)* Ana? *(Waits.)* Richard — she's not there —

RICHARD: What?

NANCY: Jenna's not here —

RICHARD: Honey, I'm sure there's some good —

NANCY: *(Keeps calling.)* Ana? *(To Richard.)* She'd have called — *(Calls.)* Ana? *(To Richard.)* She'd have left a note — did you see a — ?

RICHARD: Well, I just got home, I didn't —

NANCY: You didn't even notice your child wasn't here? It's ten o'clock! *(Notices.)* Richard — Ana left her jacket —

RICHARD: Nancy, calm down. I'm sure there's some perfectly good reason. Didn't you have your cell?

NANCY: Of course I —

RICHARD: Well, did you check your voice mail? *(Nancy looks in her purse — then sees her other purse and realizes —)*

NANCY: Shit! I changed my purse for the dinner! *(She gets her cell and tries her voice mail as she continues —)* what about *your* cell?

RICHARD: Well, I was in court, I had it turned —

NANCY: Check the machine.

RICHARD: Wait — there's a message — *(He plays it. We hear a bit of a telemarketing call, "Mortgage rates are at an all-time low —" Then he cuts it off.)*

NANCY: *(Listening to voice mail.)* She called my cell — she didn't leave a message — ? *(He finds Ana's note — under a briefcase.)*

RICHARD: *Here. (Reads.)* "Emergency. Gone to hospital. OK." "OK"? What the fuck does that mean?

NANCY: *Whose* emergency? *Where?*

RICHARD: Santa Monica Hospital? St. John's? I'll call. You call Ana's cell. *(They call on their cells. Ana and Bobby appear on opposite sides of the stage — on their cells. The furniture starts to leave the stage. The backdrop changes to a nightscape of the city. Dialogue and sound almost overlap — a fragmented mix of dialogue, light and sound.)*

ANA: *(On cell.)* Bobby?

BOBBY: *(On cell.)* Ana — mira — otra dirección — *(We hear the ringing of phones that Richard and Nancy hear.)*

ANA: *(On cell.)* No te oigo, Bobby —

NANCY: Answer, damn you —

ANA: *(Re: cell.)* Puto Sprint!

BOBBY: *(On cell; louder.)* Martin Luther King Hospital. *(Sound of Ana's cell phone ringing that Nancy hears.)*

ANA: *(On cell.)* OK. OK, Bobby — *(Sound of the information recording, "What city please?" that Richard hears.)*

RICHARD: *(On cell.)* In Santa Monica — for Santa Monica Hospital.

NANCY: Oh God, maybe the tea! *(Sound of cell ringing continues.)*

RICHARD: Tea?

BOBBY: *(On cell.)* Ana?!

ANA: *(On cell.)* El traffico, Bobby — !

NANCY: Doesn't she have fucking call waiting?

BOBBY: Ana —

ANA: Bobby?

BOBBY: Por favor — apúrate! *(We hear the recording, "You have reached Santa Monica Hospital — ")*

RICHARD: *(To Nancy.)* It's a recording, honey — maybe I should call the police.

BOBBY: *(On the cell.)* Pues — don't take the 110!

ANA: *(On the cell.)* Sí, sí — !

NANCY: Richard, no —

RICHARD: Will you let me handle something for a change? *(Ana picks up Nancy's call.)*

NANCY: *(On cell.)* Ana?

ANA: *(On cell.)* Nancy?

NANCY: *(On cell.)* What happened to Jenna!?

ANA: *(On cell.)* Jenna is fine — *(Beat; cries out.)* It's my child, Nancy. *My* child! *(Blackout.)*

SCENE SEVEN

Sound of birds as Zoila and Sandra enter the park from different directions. Sandra has a new carriage. It's a few days later.

ZOILA: Hola — !

SANDRA: Hola. Cómo estas?

ZOILA: Bien. How come I ain't seen you?

SANDRA: Oh — I'm not working for Linda no more, I just got a new job! *(Zoila looks in Sandra's carriage.)*

ZOILA: Oh! *(To baby.)* Hola, chiquitita! *(Surprised.)* Morenita! How much they pay you?

SANDRA: Fifteen dollars an hour! Black peoples!

ZOILA: Fifteen dollars! *(Zoila is speechless for a moment.)* I got to quit my job. Today I got to start looking. *(Vehemently.)* And I'm not going to live in no more. I'm going to live out!

SANDRA: Sí, mija, claro.

ZOILA: I got to get a license . . . *(This reminds her.)* Pero, you hear what happen to Ana?

SANDRA: Ana? What happen? *(They start to walk through the park, pausing from time to time.)*

ZOILA: Qué horror. I heard Mrs. Breyer telling it to the Mommies and the Me's — *(Linda and Wallace enter, Linda with her baby. They walk through the park too. Zoila and Sandra speak to each other, and Linda and Wallace speak to each other — though the two conversations overlap.)*

WALLACE: Linda, she took Nancy's baby —

SANDRA: Qué?   LINDA: What?

ZOILA: She took Mrs. Robin's baby!

SANDRA: Qué!?   LINDA: No!

WALLACE: She was taking care of the baby the other night — and something happened — so she was taking the baby with her to the hospital and —

LINDA: The hospital — ?

ZOILA: Pues, Mrs. Breyer said Mrs. Robin said that Ana said something happen to her son — but that's a lie 'cause her kids are in El Salvador, verdad?

SANDRA: *(Beat; lies.)* Pues, sí . . . Pero —

LINDA AND SANDRA: Why was she at the hospital?

ZOILA: Quíen sabe? Maybe she wasn't at no hospital! That Ana . . . tan misteriosa! Like she think she better or something.

WALLACE: And, it turns out, she *was* illegal after all. Apparently she was a rather mysterious person . . .

SANDRA: Híjole —

LINDA: What? According to Zoila?

WALLACE: Oh Zoila's very reliable.

ZOILA: *(To Sandra.)* You remember how she tell me to lie —

WALLACE: She actually told Zoila to *lie* —

WALLACE: *(Continued.)* — to get her license!   ZOILA: *(Continued.)* — to get my license!

LINDA: Oh my god.

SANDRA: But if it was an emergency . . .

LINDA: Was there a note?

WALLACE: Note shmote, Linda. She took the baby out of the house. She was driving around without a valid license — with Nancy's child! *(At some point in the scene, depending on the set and staging, Linda and Wallace stop to talk on one side of the stage, and Zoila and Sandra on the other. Ana might appear upstage center, looking out a window, her back to us. Bobby might join her briefly, then leave.)*

ZOILA: She's lucky the police didn't stop her.

LINDA: But you said her own child was in the hospital — ?

WALLACE: A child Nancy didn't even know about! A child who was supposedly in El Salvador!

LINDA: *(Cries out.)* What difference does it make?! It's a child! *(A beat of silence.)* Is the child going to be all right? *(The question stops Wallace. She's horrified she never asked.)*

WALLACE: *(Upset.)* I . . . don't know. Nancy was very upset — I just — literally ran into her at Whole Foods. And I . . . Well, I . . . *(Her eyes fill with tears.)* I didn't ask about the child. *(Ana exits.)*

SANDRA: I'll call Ana.

WALLACE: I'll call Nancy.

ZOILA: I got to get Alex —

LINDA: Listen, I have to pick up the twins.

WALLACE: Where's Sandra?

SANDRA: *(To Zoila.)* Pues — cuídate mija . . . *(Zoila nods, and she and Sandra exit in different directions.)*

LINDA: Oh, her father is sick in Oaxaca. She had to go back to Mexico for a little while. *(Wallace sighs.)* No, no, no. Not Sandra. People do get sick in Oaxaca you know! And she loves the boys! The boys are — much better.

WALLACE: Well, if there's anything I can do . . . If you get crazy . . . Just bring the boys over to my house and Zoila can watch them for a while.

LINDA: Thanks. *(Wallace gives Linda a hug. They exit in different directions, as Nancy and Richard's bed comes on, with Richard on it.)*

SCENE EIGHT

Richard is sitting up in bed. The TV is on, though we only see the light it casts. Nancy paces, channel surfing with the remote. We hear bits of infomercials, news . . .

RICHARD: You've got to stop torturing yourself, honey. You've left messages on her voice mail, her machine . . .

NANCY: But if I hadn't asked her to work late —

RICHARD: You were *paying* her to work late —

NANCY: She was doing me a *favor* — as a friend!

RICHARD: No, honey, you were working. *Ana* was working. For all we know she was paying the sister-in-law to take care of her child. Everyone's working and paying someone else to take care of their child — it's insane! It's insane people even have to leave their families to come to this country —

NANCY: *(Feeling guilty about everything.)* Well, we funded the war in El Salvador —

RICHARD: We personally?

NANCY: We pay taxes —

RICHARD: *(Ironic, exasperated.)* So in a couple of years we can hire a nanny from Iraq. *(Beat.)* Nancy. Is it your fault her son had an asthma attack? Is it your fault the sister-in-law took him to the nearest lousy clinic before getting to a real hospital?

NANCY: Doesn't asthma have something to do with . . . stress? If he was expecting his mother and —

RICHARD: Half the kids in this city have asthma! What are we going to do about Jenna? Do you want to call the agency about a new nanny or — ?

NANCY: No! If there's something seriously wrong with her son — I am certainly not going to . . . I'll call Diane and tell her my mother is sick. I'll tell her she needs an operation and I have to fly home to Washington.

RICHARD: Fine. And what if Ana doesn't even want to come back? I'm just saying — I mean — we have options. Maybe we could cut back on our hours. Or hey, if worse came to worse — I mean, we've already made a profit, we *could . . . (Carefully.)* move —

NANCY: After that night?! Do you realize how lucky we are to live near the best hospitals? What if something had happened to *our* child? *(He puts his arms around her.)*

RICHARD: Look . . . Nance . . . If you wanted to stay home — for a while — just for a little while . . . *(This is very hard.)* I suppose I could take a job with a firm . . .

NANCY: Working for Halliburton?

RICHARD: *(Breaks.)* I just — I just want us to be a family! I just want our family. *(Beat.)* Why don't you call the hospital again.

NANCY: Good. *(He gets her the phone. She presses "redial." Looks at watch.)* Oooh God, Jenna's going to be up in like another four hours . . . Great. I'm on hold. Should I just go to the hospital?

RICHARD: I don't know, honey, you really knew her better —

NANCY: *(Pained.)* Did I? Wallace's nanny knew her from the park and apparently there were things I didn't . . . *(She gets a cigarette.)* I mean, can you ever really know someone — who's so — different from you? *(They share a cigarette.)*

RICHARD: Well, you know, I read this article the other day about witnesses . . . ! How 97 percent of what a person perceives about someone else is what they already believe? It's like that Dylan "Ain't no use in talkin' to you, just like talking' to me" —

NANCY: I guess — . . . *(Startled; into phone:)* Yes — I'd like to inquire about a patient. Santiago Hernandez. . . . I'm sorry, I'm having a little trouble understanding your accent . . . No, I'm not a family member, but can you just — . . . *(Immensely relieved.)* So he's no longer a patient? Thank you. Thank you so much. *(She hangs up.)* Well, thank God. *(Richard puts his arm around her. They kiss, tentatively, then again. The baby cries. They look at each other smile, and go off to Jenna's room, hand in hand. Bobby enters in the scene transition and sits on the bed that is now his and Ana's.)*

SCENE NINE

Bobby is sitting on the bed, putting on and lacing up his work boots, slowly and deliberately. After several beats. Ana enters from outside.

BOBBY: Dónde estabas?

ANA: *(Quietly.)* Pues — fuí para un trabajo. *(Bobby is surprised but nods.)*

BOBBY: You went for a job. *(Beat.)* It's only two weeks.

ANA: I got to work . . . *(Bobby continues lacing a boot. Ana takes off her sweater.)*

BOBBY: How did it go?

ANA: OK. *(Pause.)*

BOBBY: You hungry? I got tortillas . . . Queso… *(Ana shakes her head no. She sits on the bed, facing away from him.)* Café?

ANA: No, gracias. *(Pause.)*

BOBBY: Friend of mine told me 'bout a night job over in Hollywood.

ANA: What's the job?

BOBBY: Valet parker. I'm gonna check it out after work. So soon as we pay the hospital, you could take a break for a while. And soon as we get our papers, we go back to El Salvador together and get Tomás.

ANA: Gracias. *(Beat.)* But I think he's better down there with my grandmother.

BOBBY: Ana —

ANA: It's better.

BOBBY: A grandmother is not a mother —

ANA: Sometime . . . a mother is not a mother, Bobby. *(She rises and moves away.)*

BOBBY: Ana, please! Don't turn away from me! — because — it wasn't your fault.

ANA: *(After a beat.)* If I'd picked him up . . . If I'd been there. Like a mother. Like any mother. *(Starts to break.)* I never saw him play soccer, Bobby! Did he play good? Did he look for me? Tell me, Bobby! 'Cause I never saw him play! *(He goes to her.)*

BOBBY: Ana — I'm telling you and you got to listen — because Santi was my son too! *(Cries.)* My son! Mi hijo. M'entiendes? And I'm telling you . . . Let him rest. *(Through tears.)* He's . . . sleeping with the angeles, Ana. Just like you always telling him! Tell him. Dile, amor — *(She tries to bring herself to say the words.)*

ANA: Duérmete . . . Duérmete con los angeles, mijo . . . *(He holds her, lets her cry. Then he sits her down on the bed the bed.)*

BOBBY: You too, amor. You get some sleep. *(Kisses her; rises.)* I'll get dinner for us tonight. *(Nancy enters holding her cell. Bobby gets his jacket. Richard enters.)*

RICHARD: I'm going out for diapers, honey. *(He kisses Nancy.)*

BOBBY: *(To Ana.)* I got to go to work. *(Richard and Bobby exit. Nancy sits at the head of the bed and makes a call. Ana's cell phone rings. Ana takes it from her sweater pocket. They speak from opposite ends of the bed, facing out.)*

ANA: Hallo?

NANCY: Ana?

ANA: Sí?

NANCY: *(Warmly.)* It's Nancy Robin. I . . . I just wanted to see how you were doing . . .

ANA: *(After a beat.)* I'm fine.

NANCY: And your son? We called the hospital and they said he was no longer a patient, so he's doing better? *(Ana realizes Nancy doesn't know.)*

ANA: *(After a long beat; fighting tears.)* Yes.

NANCY: Well, thank God. And you got the check we — ?

ANA: Yes, Mrs. Robin.

NANCY: *(With enormous difficulty.)* Well, as I said in my note, we . . . we decided — we're just going to take care of Jenna ourselves — for now . . . *(Ana nods, but doesn't reply.)* But I just wanted to say how — badly I feel, Ana, about what happened . . . And to thank you for . . . everything. And if you need anything, a reference — anything . . . *(Waits.)* I hope you'll let me know.

ANA: I'm fine. I got another job, Mrs. Robin. *(Nancy nods.)* Kiss Jenna for me . . . *(Nancy nods, fighting tears.)*

NANCY: Well . . . Good luck to you, Ana.
ANA: You too, Mrs. Robin. *(Pause.)* Good-bye.
NANCY: Good-bye. *(The lights fade on the two of them . . .)*

END OF PLAY

INTIMATE APPAREL

Lynn Nottage

PLAYWRIGHT'S BIOGRAPHY

Lynn Nottage's play *Fabulation! or The Re-Education of Undine* recently concluded a sold-out run at Playwrights Horizons. *Intimate Apparel* (Roundabout Theatre Company, South Coast Rep, Center Stage and Mark Taper Forum) is the winner of the coveted 2004 New York Drama Critics Circle Award, Outer Critics Circle Best Play and John Gassner awards, American Theatre Critics/Steinberg 2004 New Play Award and 2004 Francesca Primus Award.

An anthology of her plays, *Crumbs from the Table of Joy and Other Plays* was published by TCG, and includes *Crumbs from the Table of Joy, Las Meninas, Mud, River, Stone, Por'knockers,* and *Poof!* Her plays have been produced and developed at theaters throughout the country, including the Alliance Theatre, The Sundance Institute Theatre Lab, Second Stage, Freedom Theatre, Crossroads Theatre, Intiman, Oregon Shakespeare Festival, Steppenwolf, Yale Rep, The Vineyard Theatre, among others.

She wrote the feature film *Side Streets* (Merchant Ivory Productions) directed by Tony Gerber. The film was an official selection at the Venice and Sundance Film Festivals. She is the recipient of numerous awards, including the prestigious 2004 PEN/Laura Pels Award for literary excellence, fellowships from Manhattan Theatre Club, New Dramatists, and the New York Foundation for the Arts, where she is a member of the Artists Advisory Board. She is also the recipient of a NEA/TCG (1999/2000) grant for a yearlong theater residency at Freedom Theatre in Philadelphia.

Ms. Nottage is a resident member of New Dramatists, a graduate of Brown University and the Yale School of Drama, where she is currently a visiting lecturer.

ORIGINAL PRODUCTION

Intimate Apparel was commissioned and first produced by South Coast Repertory (David Emmes, Producing Artistic Director; Paula Tomei, Managing Director) and Center Stage (Irene Lewis, Artistic Director; Michael Ross, Managing Director) in Costa Mesa, California, opening on April 18, 2003. It was directed by Kate Whoriskey; the set design was by Walt Spangler; the costume design was by Catherine Zuber; the lighting design was by Scott Zielinski; the sound design was by Lindsay Jones; the original music was by Reginald Robinson; the arranger and piano coach was William Foster McDaniel; the dramaturg was Jerry Patch; the associate production dramaturg was Rhoda Robbins; the production manager was Tom Aberger; and the production stage manager was Randall K. Lum. The cast was as follows:

ESTHER	*Shané Williams*
MRS. DICKSON	*Brenda Pressley*
MRS. VAN BUREN	*Sue Cremin*
MR. MARKS	*Steven Goldstein*
MAYME	*Erica Gimpel*
GEORGE	*Kevin Jackson*

Intimate Apparel was originally produced in New York City by the Roundabout Theatre Company (Todd Haimes, Artistic Director; Ellen Richard, Managing Director), opening on April 8, 2004. It was directed by Daniel Sullivan; the set design was by Derek McLane; the costume design was Catherine Zuber; the lighting design was by Allen Lee Hughes; the original music was by Harold Wheeler; the sound design was by Marc Gwinn; the production stage manager was Jay Adler; and the stage manager was Amy Patricia Stern. The cast was as follows:

ESTHER	*Viola Davis*
MRS. DICKSON	*Lynda Gravatt*
MRS. VAN BUREN	*Arija Bareikis*
MR. MARKS	*Corey Stoll*
MAYME	*Lauren Velez*
GEORGE	*Russell Hornsby*

CHARACTERS
ESTHER: Thirty-five, African-American
MRS. DICKSON: Fifties, African-American
MRS. VAN BUREN: Thirties, White American
MR. MARKS: Thirties, Rumanian Jewish immigrant
MAYME: Thirties, African-American
GEORGE: Thirties, Barbadian immigrant

SETTING
Lower Manhattan

TIME
1905

PRODUCTION NOTE
The set should be spare to allow for fluid movement between the various bedrooms. The action should flow seamlessly from scene to scene. The act endings mark the only true blackouts in the play.

Intimate Apparel

ACT I

SCENE ONE: WEDDING CORSET — WHITE SATIN WITH PINK ROSES

Lower Manhattan, 1905. A bedroom. It is simple, unadorned with the exception of beautifully embroidered curtains and a colorful crazy quilt. A clumsy ragtime melody bleeds in from the parlor. In the distance the sound of laughter and general merriment. Esther, a rather plain African-American woman (35), sits at a sewing machine table diligently trimming a camisole with lace. She is all focus and determination.

MRS. DICKSON: *(Offstage.)* Don't be fresh, Lionel. I know your mama since before the war. *(Mrs. Dickson, fifty, a handsome, impeccably groomed African-American woman, enters laughing.)* There you are. Mr. Charles was admiring the bread pudding and I told him that our Esther made it. It seems he has a sweet tooth.

ESTHER: Mr. Charles is overly generous, come, the pudding ain't nothing special.

MRS. DICKSON: And did I mention that our most available Mr. Charles was promoted to head Bellman at just about the finest hotel in New York? Yes.

ESTHER: But he still fetching luggage.

MRS. DICKSON: Not just any luggage, high-class luggage.

ESTHER: And is high-class luggage easier to carry?

MRS. DICKSON: I reckon it is easier to haul silk than cotton, if you know what I'm saying. *(Mrs. Dickson laughs.)* And he sporting a right smart suit this evening.

ESTHER: Yes, it cashmere.

MRS. DICKSON: You can tell more about a man by where he shops, than his practiced conversation. 'Cause any man who's had enough tonic can talk smooth, but not every man has the good sense to shop at —

ESTHER and MRS. DICKSON: Saperstein's. *(Esther laughs. Mrs. Dickson examines the embroidery.)*

MRS. DICKSON: Lovely.

ESTHER: It's for Corinna Mae's wedding night.

MRS. DICKSON: Don't tell me you've been in here all evening? Corinna Mae is getting ready to leave with her fiancé.

ESTHER: I wish I could find my party face. It really is a lovely affair. You done a fine job.

MRS. DICKSON: Come now, it ain't over yet. Put aside your sewing and straighten yourself up. There. You'll have a dance before this evening's out.

ESTHER: Please, Mrs. Dickson, I can't, really. I'll just stand there like a wall-flower.

MRS. DICKSON: Nonsense, I've danced a half a dozen times, and my feet are just about worn out.

ESTHER: If I had your good looks I'd raise a bit of dust myself. Ain't nobody down there interested in me.

MRS. DICKSON: Esther, you're being silly. You've been moping around here for days. What's the matter?

ESTHER: If you must know, I turned thirty-five Thursday past. *(A moment.)*

MRS. DICKSON: Oh Lord, I forgot, child. I sure did. Look at that. With Corinna Mae carrying on and all these people, it slipped my mind. Happy birthday, my sweet Esther. *(Mrs. Dickson gives her a big hug.)*

ESTHER: It's fine. You had all this to prepare for. And I been living in this rooming house for so long. I reckon I'm just another piece of furniture.

MRS. DICKSON: Never. You were a godsend when you come to me at seventeen. Yes. I remember thinking how sweet and young you was with a sack full of overripe fruit smelling like a Carolina orchard.

ESTHER: And now? Twenty-two girls later, if you count Lerleen. That's how many of these parties I have had to go to and play merry. I should be happy for them, I know, but each time I think why ain't it me. Silly Corinna Mae, ain't got no brain at all, and just as plain as flour.

MRS. DICKSON: Your time will come, child.

ESTHER: What if it don't? Listen to her laughing. God forgive me, but I hate her laughter, I hate her happiness and I feel simply awful for saying so. And I'm afraid if I go back in there, she'll see it all over my face, and it's her day.

MRS. DICKSON: There are a number of young men open to your smile. A sour face don't buy nothing but contempt. Why our Mr. Charles has had three servings of your bread pudding.

ESTHER: And he shouldn't have had any. *(Esther laughs.)* He weighs nearly as much as your horse.

MRS. DICKSON: Nonsense, he weighs more than poor Jessup. Shhh. He is a good man, poised for success. Yes.

ESTHER: But he's been coming to these parties for near two years and if he ain't met a woman, I'd bet it ain't a woman he after. I've been warned about men in refined suits. But still, Esther would be lucky for this attention, that's what you thinking. Well, I ain't giving up so easy.

MRS. DICKSON: Good for you. But there are many a cautionary tale bred of overconfidence. When I met the late Mr. Dickson he was near sixty and I forgave his infatuation with the opiates, for he come with this rooming house and look how many good years it's given me. Sure I cussed that damn pipe, and I cussed him for making me a widow, but sometimes we get to a point where we can't be so particular.

ESTHER: *(Snaps.)* Well, I ain't going down there to be paraded like some featherless bird. *(A moment.)* I'm sorry, would you kindly take this down to Corinna Mae?

MRS. DICKSON: I'll do no such thing. You can bring it down yourself. *(Mrs. Dickson starts for the door, but abruptly stops.)* It tough Esther for a colored woman in this city. I ain't got to tell you that. You nimble with your fingers, but all Corinna Mae got be her honey-colored skin. And you good and smart and deserve all the attention in the room, but today's her day and all I ask is that you come toast her as I know she'd toast you. Put aside your feelings and don't say nothing about Sally's piano playing, the girl trying. For God's sake, this a party not a wake.

ESTHER: Let me fix my hair. *(Mrs. Dickson suddenly remembers the letter tucked in her dress pocket and extends it to Esther.)*

MRS. DICKSON: And I thought you might want this letter. It come this morning, I didn't want to forget.

ESTHER: Who'd be writing me?

MRS. DICKSON: *(Reading.)* Mr. George Armstrong.

ESTHER: It ain't someone I know. Armstrong? There was an Armstrong that attended my church, but he dead a long time now. Will you read the letter to me? *(Esther takes the letter.)*

MRS. DICKSON: I got a house full of people. You best remind me tomorrow. And I will see you downstairs, shortly. Plenty of punch left and it better than New Year's, so best hurry. I made certain everybody be leaving this party happy. *(Mrs. Dickson exits. Esther examines the letter, then places it on the sewing table unopened. Lights crossfade, allowing Esther to linger in half-light during George's letter. A Panama bunk. George, a muscular handsome African-Caribbean man, rises from his cot. He wipes mud from his face and bare arms, as he speaks with a musical Barbadian accent.)*

GEORGE: Dear Miss Mills,

My name is George Armstrong. I work in Panama alongside Carson Wynn, your deacon's son. We digging a big hole across the land, they say one day ships will pass from one ocean to the next. It is important work, we told. If importance be measured by how many men die, then this be real important work. One man drops for every twenty feet of canal dug, like so many flies. Carson say if we eat a can of sardines, they'll protect us against the mosquitoes and fever. I say, not as long as we be digging. Lord knows our minds deserve a bit of shade. But ain't such a thing to be had, not here at least. Don't think me too forward, but I thought it would be nice to have someone to think about, someone not covered from head to toe in mud, someone to ward off this awful boredom. Carson speaks so highly of his church that I find comfort in his recollections. I ask if I may write you? And if you so please, I'd welcome your words.

Sincerely,

George Armstrong

SCENE TWO: GARDENIA BALL CORSET — PINK SILK AND CREPE DE CHINE

An elegant boudoir. The silhouette of a naked woman moves gracefully behind a translucent screen. She slides her torso into the fitted lingerie. Esther sits at the dressing table exploring the carefully arranged silver grooming set. She jumps to attention at the sound of Mrs. Van Buren's voice, which betrays the slightest hint of a Southern accent.

MRS VAN BUREN: I feel exposed. I think the straps need to be tightened, Esther.

ESTHER: No ma'am, that's the way it's meant to be, but I'll add a little more fabric to —

MRS. VAN BUREN: No, no, if this is what you made for that singer, it is what I want. All right. I'm coming out. *(Mrs. Van Buren emerges from behind the dressing screen wearing a very low corset embossed with lavender flowers. She's an attractive white woman in her early thirties and attempts to carry herself with great poise and confidence.)* Oh God, I look ridiculous, and I'm behaving absolutely foolishly, but I'm not sure what else to do. Look at me. I've spent a fortune on feathers and every manner of accouterment. *(Es-*

ther begins to tighten the lacing of the corset.) They've written positively splendid things about me in the columns this season.

ESTHER: I'm sure they did.

MRS. VAN BUREN: But does it matter? Has he spent an evening at home? Or even noticed that I've painted the damn boudoir vermilion red?

ESTHER: You look lovely, Mrs. Van Buren.

MRS. VAN BUREN: Ha! I feel like a tart from the Tenderloin. Granted I've never been, but I'm told. Are you sure this is what you made for that . . . singer?

ESTHER: It is identical to the stitching. *(Mrs. Van Buren examines herself in the mirror, at first with disgust, which gradually gives way to curiosity.)*

MRS. VAN BUREN: And you say the French women are wearing these?

ESTHER: So I'm told.

MRS. VAN BUREN: I don't believe it. It hardly seems decent. But I suppose the French aren't known for their modesty. *(She strikes a provocative, though slightly self-conscious pose.)*

ESTHER: Well, it the rage. Some ladies ain't even wearing corsets in private.

MRS. VAN BUREN: Is that true?

ESTHER: Most gals don't like 'em, even fine ladies like yourself. Truth is I ain't known a man to court pain for a woman's glance.

MRS. VAN BUREN: You're not one of those suffragettes, are you?

ESTHER: Oh God no, Mrs. Van Buren.

MRS. VAN BUREN: Indeed. I'd just as soon not tamper in men's business. *(Mrs. Van Buren pours a snifter of brandy.)*

ESTHER: Talk and a nickel will buy you five cents worth of trouble. *(Mrs. Van Buren gulps back the brandy.)*

MRS. VAN BUREN: It's come to this. If Mother dear could see what has become of her peach in the big city. *(Mrs. Van Buren clumsily tugs at the bodice. Esther runs her fingers gracefully along the seam, down the curve of Mrs. Van Buren's waist. Mrs. Van Buren tenses slightly at the sensation of being touched. Distracted, she touches the beading along the corset, in doing so . . .)* Do we really need all of these dangling things?

ESTHER: Oh, I hope you ain't mind, I added a touch of beading along the trim.

MRS. VAN BUREN: It is different.

ESTHER: Do you like it?

MRS. VAN BUREN: I confess, I almost do. It's a bit naughty. *(Giggles.)* Yes, I might even wear it beneath my gown tonight. Do you think anyone will notice? It is the annual Gardenia Ball, quite the event of the season.

ESTHER: So I hear.

MRS. VAN BUREN: And do you know what that means? *(A moment.)* They'll all be there, parading their good fortune. I'll have to smile, be polite, because I'm known for that, but I will dread every last minute, every bit of forced conversation with the Livingstons and the Babcocks. They want to know. All of them do. "When are you going to have a child, Evangeline?" And my answer is always the same, "Why we're working on it dear, speak to Harold." And dear Harry will be in a sour mood for a week. You probably don't even know what I'm talking about. Have you children?

ESTHER. No, Mrs. Van Buren. I ain't been married.

MRS. VAN BUREN: Never? May I tell you something?

ESTHER: Yes. If you like.

MRS. VAN BUREN: I've given him no children. *(Whispered.)* I'm afraid I can't. It's not for the lack of trying. One takes these things for granted, you assume when it comes time that it will happen and when it doesn't who is to blame? They think it's vanity that's kept me childless, I've heard the women whispering. If only I were that vain. But it's like he's given up.

ESTHER: But, you're so beautiful.

MRS. VAN BUREN: You think so?

ESTHER: Yes. I can't imagine he'd ever lose interest.

MRS. VAN BUREN: But he has turned to other interests. Trust me. This will stay between us? I'm told you're discreet.

ESTHER: I just sew, missus. I don't hear anything that I ain't supposed to.

MRS. VAN BUREN: You understand why. I'd rather not be a divorcée, at my age it would prove disastrous.

ESTHER: Do you think there's something wrong with a woman alone?

MRS. VAN BUREN: What I think is of little consequence. If I were *(Whispered.)* brave I'd collect my things right now and find a small clean room someplace on the other side of the park. No, further in fact. And I'd . . . But it isn't a possibility, is it? *(A moment. Suddenly . . .)*

ESTHER: I don't know that I'll marry.

MRS. VAN BUREN: Of course you will, it's just a matter of finding the right gentleman.

ESTHER: Ma'am, I don't want to speak out of turn. But, I been working since I was nine years old with barely a day's rest. In fact, the other evening I was at my sewing machine and I stopped work and all this time had passed, gone. Years really. And I known right there that some things ain't meant to be. And that's all right, ain't it? And I wouldn't have thought no more about it, but then I got this . . . *(Esther stops mid-thought and busies herself with her sewing basket.)*

MRS. VAN BUREN: Yes?

ESTHER: I'm almost ashamed to say it. At my age it foolish, I know.

MRS. VAN BUREN: What is it?

ESTHER: A gentleman . . . A gentleman has taken interest in me.

MRS. VAN BUREN: Really? How wonderful! Is he respectable?

ESTHER: I don't know, I mean, I don't know him actually. I got me this letter from Panama. A man in Panama. He wrote about two weeks back. I been carrying it around since. But, I ain't so sure I should answer.

MRS. VAN BUREN: And why not?

ESTHER: I ain't much of a writer.

MRS. VAN BUREN: Oh —

ESTHER: No, I ain't a writer at all. The fact is I can't read.

MRS. VAN BUREN: Do you have the letter? May I see it? *(Esther hesitates, then pulls the letter from her smock and hands it to Mrs. Van Buren, who quickly peruses it and smiles.)* Panama. He has lovely penmanship, that's important. He isn't careless with his stroke, that's the mark of a thoughtful man. It's a good thing, I believe.

ESTHER: I won't respond, of course, if it ain't appropriate.

MRS. VAN BUREN: Nonsense. He's halfway across the world. I'm sure he is perfectly harmless. A bit lonesome perhaps, that's all.

ESTHER: But, if I have Mrs. Dickson over at the rooming house help me, she'll get all up in my business. And she's got an opinion about everything and I'd rather not be lectured or questioned or bothered. She's just about the busiest . . . in any event, she said to rip it up promptly, a decent woman wouldn't resort to such a dalliance. But as you can see he has taken interest in me.

MRS. VAN BUREN: Would you like me to help you write to him, Esther?

ESTHER: I couldn't ask.

MRS. VAN BUREN: You needn't, I insist.

ESTHER: I never done this before.

MRS. VAN BUREN: Nor have I.

ESTHER: Maybe it ain't such a good idea, Mrs. Van Buren. I ain't really got much to say.

MRS. VAN BUREN: Goodness, of course you do —

ESTHER: *(With conviction.)* No, I don't! I live in a rooming house with seven unattached women and sew intimate apparel for ladies, that ain't for a gentleman's eyes. Sure I can tell him anything there is to know about fabric, but that hardly seems a life worthy of words.

MRS. VAN BUREN: It is a beginning. Come Esther, don't be shy. *(Mrs. Van Buren sits at her dressing table and retrieves a sheet of stationery.)* Now how shall we start?

ESTHER: I don't know.

MRS. VAN BUREN: What sort of things do you like to do?

ESTHER: I . . . I go to church every Sunday, well practically, but I don't really listen to the sermons, I just like the company and the singing of course . . . And on Tuesdays . . . I take the trolley downtown to Orchard Street, and I climb five flights, in darkness, to this tiny apartment. And, when I open the door my eyes are met . . . *(Mr. Marks, a handsome Orthodox Jewish man, enters with a bolt of gorgeous flowing fabric that he proudly displays. Lost in the sweet recollection, Esther resumes speaking.)* He keeps a wealth of fabric in that apartment. He got everything you need, even things you don't know you need —

MRS. VAN BUREN: Esther, you're jumping a bit ahead of yourself. *(Lights fade around Mr. Marks.)* Shall we begin with "Dear Mr. Armstrong —"

ESTHER: Yes. That's good. "Dear Mr. Armstrong —"

MRS. VAN BUREN: "I received your letter —"

(Lights crossfade. George enters in his work clothing. The crossfade should allow time for Esther and George to dwell on the stage together, but only for several moments.)

GEORGE: Dear Miss Mills,

I received your letter. It two months in the coming, so please forgive me, I've already written you twice since. I am most happy to make your acquaintance, and I'm anxious to hear all about you. As for me, I'd like to report on our good progress, but it isn't the case. This canal seem a near-impossible mission, but here we be, digging until day end bathed in mud up to our necks. They say a mad Frenchmen dreamed up this Panama project, and convinced the devil to give him an army of workers. The price, this great fissure across the land that reach right into the earth's belly. Indeed, chaos is a jackhammer away, that's what be said here anyway. But when the great oceans meet and the gentlemen celebrate, will we colored men be given glasses to raise? Today we severed the roots of a giant flamboyant, and watched it tumble to the ground. I stood thigh deep in crimson blossoms, swathed in the sweet aroma of death and wondered how a place so beautiful could become a morgue. But the days aren't all bad. If you take a moment to listen to the forest around us there is so much life just out of sight. And there be men from every corner of the Caribbean, sharing tales around fires, heads light on rum and laughter. But now, I read your letter. I see you sitting at your sewing machine. I hear the sound of the wheel turning, the tiny stitches drawing together the pieces of satin. They got machines here that take six men to operate, and slice through stone like butter. All this wonder and waste, but your letter be the most splendid thing and shall ride in me pocket, until the next.

> Yours Considerately,
> George Armstrong

SCENE THREE: IMPERIAL SILK, EMBROIDERED WITH BLUE THREAD

Another bedroom in a cramped tenement flat. It is small and cluttered with bolts of fabric. Mr. Marks, a handsome Orthodox Jewish man, scrambles to put on his suit jacket as a knock sounds on the door. His worn black suit is missing the top button. With haste, he folds up his bedroll and opens the door breathless. Esther stands in the doorway. She notices the bedroll but chooses to ignore it.

ESTHER: Mr. Marks? Am I too early?

MARKS: No, not at all. Come in. Come in. I've a number of new things to show you.

ESTHER: Good —

MARKS: Ah. Let me get. *(He unrolls an extraordinary length of silk.)* Feel this one. Japanese silk, your special order for the lady on Fifth Avenue. It took me nearly one month to find this very piece I had to go everywhere. Lovely. Yes?

ESTHER: Lovely. Look at how finely embroidered. Beautiful. I never —

MARKS: I have two extra yards left. I give to you for next to nothing. If you'd like.

ESTHER: Next to nothing is too much for me. You know my answer. What will I do with it?

MARKS: Make something lovely for yourself.

ESTHER: It will be wasted on me.

MARKS: You'll never see this again. I guarantee. I'll let our Fifth Avenue lady cover the difference. How about that? I see how much you like. I promise it is very best quality. She don't know what she has, she don't come down here to feel the fabric herself, to feel the difference, the texture, she don't know how remarkable a weave.

ESTHER: I could make a shawl.

MARKS: *(Fishing.)* Or a smoking jacket for your gentleman, perhaps.

ESTHER: *(Bashfully.)* My gentleman? Oh no. *(Esther self-consciously runs the fabric across her face, when releases it.)* You've distracted me, Mr. Marks. You always get me to buy something I don't need.

MARKS: When I see something of quality, I like to share with my favorite customers. Everybody want the same thing. But you want different. I like that.

ESTHER: Thank you. *(Mr. Marks warmly smiles at Esther. She averts her gaze, allowing her eyes to fall on the spot where he's — missing a button. Mr. Marks self-consciously touches the spot.)*

MARKS: Ah, look at that. I have lost a button. *(He returns his attention to the silk.)* I buy at the docks yesterday morning, it come right off the ship from the Orient, I see it and think Esther Mills will like. Of course. Everybody else gabardine, wool, nainsook. *(Flirtatiously.)* But it isn't often that something so fine and delicate enters the store. Look at the way the gold thread is interwoven; a hand took the time to gently wind it through each and every stitch like a magician. It is magnificent, yes. You'll make something exquisite. I can see from your hands that you are blessed with the needle and the thread, which means you'll never be without warmth.

ESTHER: I'm afraid it was either learn to sew or turn back sheets for fifty cents a day.

MARKS: You make it sound too simple. My father sew, my brothers sew, yes, for the finest families. But I don't have the discipline, the fingers. Look at the size of my hands. Like Cirnati, Romanian sausage. I wish for your hands. *(Esther laughs and returns to examining the fabric, reveling in the tactile pleasure of the texture. There is a sensual way Esther regards the fabric. Mr. Marks can't help but notice this. She brings the fabric to her nose and sniffs. Marks watches her with genuine delight.)*

ESTHER: It's fruit dye. Am I right? It smells like —

MARKS: — an imperial palace, it is signed by the artist right there. I wouldn't be surprised if it was created for an empress.

ESTHER: You really want me to buy this, don't you? All right it means I'll go without sugar for a week, will that make you happy?

MARKS: It makes you happy, it makes me happy.

ESTHER: Oh Lord, I do want it. *(Esther affectionately grasps Mr. Marks' hand, he abruptly pulls it away. Esther is taken aback.)* The color won't rub off on you.

MARKS: No, no. I'm sorry. It's not that. Please. My religious belief doesn't permit me to touch a woman who isn't my wife or my relative.

ESTHER: Oh, I see.

MARKS: It is the rabbinical law, not mine.

ESTHER: Your wife must be a happy woman.

MARKS: I am not married. Not yet. My fiancée is in Romania. Um, my family made the arrangement years ago.

ESTHER: Oh? I bet you miss her something awful. *(Marks rubs his hand where Esther touched him. He laughs, a bit self-consciously.)*

MARKS: I haven't ever met her, actually. *(Lights crossfade.)*

SCENE FOUR: HELIOTROPE HANDKERCHIEF

Another bedroom. A canopy bed dominates. Mayme, a strikingly beautiful African-American women (30) sits at an upright piano. She plays a frenzied upbeat rag. Her silk robe is torn, and her face trembles with outrage. Esther bangs on the door, then finally enters carrying a carpetbag.)

ESTHER: I been knocking for ages. Didn't you hear me? What's going on? *(A moment.)*

MAYME: They really do make me sick. Always stinking of booze. And look what he done. It's the only pretty thing I own and look what he done. *(Mayme pulls her torn silk robe tight around her body.)*

ESTHER: That ain't nothing, I can fix it for you.

MAYME: All that pawing and pulling. For a dollar they think they own you. *(Mayme quickly washes her face and privates in a basin.)* You don't approve of me, Esther. I don't mind. Sit. I'm awfully glad to see ya, 'am. When you knocked on the door, I thought Christ almighty, not another one. I'm so damn tired, I don't know what to do. *(Mayme sits down at the upright piano and gracefully plays a slow well-considered rag.)*

ESTHER: Oh, pretty. Did you write that, Mayme?

MAYME: Yeah . . . *(Continuing to play.)* My daddy gave me twelve lashes with a switch for playing this piece in our parlor. One for each year I studied the piano. He was too proper to like anything colored, and a syncopated beat was about the worst crime you could commit in his household. *(Mayme stops playing.)* I woke up with the sudden urge to play it.

ESTHER: You must have gotten a lot of licks in your time.

MAYME: Yeah, baby, I wasn't born this black and blue. *(Mayme picks up a bottle of moonshine and takes a belt.)*

ESTHER: That there the reason you tired, that ignorant oil is unforgiving. Best let it lie.

MAYME: Oh bother, stop playing mother hen and come show me what you got.

ESTHER: Anything else, Mistress?

MAYME: Hush your mouth, you're far too sweet for sarcasm. *(Esther pulls a corset from her bag, it's pale blue with lines of royal blue glass beads ornamenting the bodice, like Mrs. Van Buren's. Touched:)* Is that for me? *(Mayme leaps up from the piano and holds the corset up to her body.)*

ESTHER: I made one just like it for a lady on Fifth Avenue.

MAYME: It's so pretty. This is really for me? No kidding? Can I try it on?

ESTHER: Of course you can.

MAYME: Feel it. It feels like Fifth Avenue, does. You outdone yourself this time, honey.

ESTHER: Stop talking and put it on. *(Mayme gives Esther a kiss on the cheek.)* And look at the flowers, ain't they sweet? It took me a whole day just to sew them on. *(Mayme takes off her robe and puts on the corset.)*

MAYME: For shame. This the prettiest thing anybody ever made for me. Truly.

ESTHER: You know that white lady I talk about sometime, hold on . . . *(Mayme grabs the bedpost, as Esther pulls the corset tight.)* She keep asking me what they be wearing up in the Tenderloin. All that money and high breeding and she want what you wearing.

MAYME: No kidding.

ESTHER: What she got, you want, what you got, she want.

MAYME: Onlies, I ain't got the money to pay for it. *(Mayme models the corset.)* Whatcha think? Do I look like a Fifth Avenue bird?

ESTHER: Grand. You look grand. Mr. Marks say, that satin foulard was made for the finest ladies in Paris.

MAYME: No kidding.

ESTHER: I wasn't going to buy it. But, oh Lord, if he didn't talk me into it.

MAYME: Mr. Marks? *(A moment.)* Who is this Mr. Marks?

ESTHER: He just a salesman. That's all.

MAYME: It sound to me like you bit sweet on him.

ESTHER: Me? Oh no, he a Jew. *(Mayme looks into Esther's eyes.)*

MAYME: And? I been with Jew, with a Turk even. And let me tell ya, a gentle touch is gold in any country.

ESTHER: I see the bodice is bit snug —

MAYME: Is he handsome?

ESTHER: I ain't noticed.

MAYME: Good patient, Esther. Come, he wouldn't be your first, would he?

ESTHER: I ain't listenin'.

MAYME: *(Softening her tone.)* You dear thing. *(Mayme laughs long and hard. Esther doesn't respond.)* No kidding. I can't even remember what it was like. Ain't that something.

ESTHER: Let's not talk about this.

MAYME: Mercy, what you must think of me. *(Mayme, suddenly self-conscious, touches the beading on the corset.)*

ESTHER: And if you must know, I'm being courted by a gentleman.

MAYME: Courted by a gentleman. Beg my pardon. Not that Panama man? Oh come on, don't tell me you still writing him.

ESTHER: He writing me.

MAYME: You'd rather a man all the way across the ocean then down Broadway. Are you expecting him to arrive in the mail like some tonic from a catalogue?

ESTHER: Please don't make sport, Mayme.

MAYME: I'm just playing with you.

ESTHER: *(Wounded.)* I ain't expectin' nothing. *(A moment. Mayme acknowledges Esther's hurt. She caresses her friend's face.)*

MAYME: Sure you are. Sure you are, honey. Who ain't? *(Mayme sits on bed, beside Esther.)* I am a concert pianist playing recitals for audiences in Prague and I have my own means, not bad for a colored girl from Memphis . . . *(Mayme plays a few bars of classical music, perhaps allowing it to become a rag.)* And Madame always takes tea twice a week with her dear friend Miss Esther Mills, who's known in circles for . . . for what? I forget. *(Esther is reluctant to share her dream.)* Come on, Miss Esther, don't be proud.

ESTHER: I own a quaint beauty parlor for colored ladies.

MAYME: Of course.

ESTHER: The smart set. Someplace east of Amsterdam, fancy, where you get pampered and treated real nice. 'Cause no one does it for us. We just as soon wash our heads in a bucket and be treated like mules. But what I'm talking about is someplace elegant.

MAYME: Go on, missie, you too fancy for me.

ESTHER: When you come in Miss Mayme, I'll take your coat and ask, "Would you like a cup of tea?"

MAYME: Why, thank you

ESTHER: And I'll open a book of illustrations, and show you the latest styles.

MAYME: I can pick anything in the book?

ESTHER: Yes.

MAYME: How about if I let you choose?

ESTHER: Very well. Make yourself comfortable, put your feet up, I know they're tired.

MAYME: Shucks, you don't know the half of it.

ESTHER: And in no time flat for the cost a ride uptown and back, you got a whole new look.

MAYME: Just like that? I reckon I'd pay someone good money to be treated like a lady. It would be worth two, three days on my back. Yes, it would.

ESTHER: You think so?

MAYME: I know so.

ESTHER: And if I told you I got a little something saved? I keep it sewed up in the lining of a crazy quilt.

MAYME: On a cold lonely night wouldn't that quilt be a poor woman's dream.

ESTHER: I been saving it slowly since I come North. It for that beauty parlor. I ain't told nobody that. Honest, for true.

MAYME: Where'd you get such a damn serious face?

ESTHER: Why not?

MAYME: Because, we just fooling that's all. I ain't been to Prague, ain't never gonna go to Prague.

ESTHER: But come, is this what you want to be doing ten years from now, twenty?

MAYME: You think I ain't tried to make a go of it. You think I just laid down and opened my legs 'cause it was easy. It don't look like nothing but this saloon is better then a lot of them places, ask anybody. Only last night one of Bert Williams' musicians sat up front, and he stayed through the entire show. You think some of those gals in the big revues didn't start right where I am.

ESTHER: You got this beautiful piano that you play better than anyone I know. There are a dozen church choirs —

MAYME: Let me tell you, so many wonderful ideas been conjured in this room. They just get left right in that bed there, or on this piano bench. They are scattered all over this room. Esther, I ain't waiting for anybody to rescue me. My Panama man come and gone long time now. It sweet that he write you but, my dear, it ain't real.

ESTHER: Yes, he here in my pocket in a cambric walking suit, he has a heliotrope handkerchief stuffed in his pocket and a sweet way about him. He so far away, I can carry him in my pocket like a feather. *(Esther laughs and produces a letter from her apron.)*

MAYME: You're funny. You and your silly letter.

ESTHER: Ain't a week go by without one. It got so I know the postman by name. *(Esther holds out the letter.)*

MAYME: I ain't interested. Put it away.

ESTHER: C'mon Miss Mayme . . . don't be proud, you know you want to read it.

(Esther dangles the letter, threatening to put it away at any moment.)

MAYME: Hell, give it here. *(Mayme snatches the letter and quickly peruses it, allowing herself a smile.)* Ooo.

ESTHER: What it say?

MAYME: Your man got himself a new pair of socks. Wait . . . uh-oh, he askin' what you look like. Ain't you told him?

ESTHER: No. I'm afraid, I ain't known what to say.

MAYME: Tell him the truth.

ESTHER: That I don't look like much.

MAYME: You tell him that you're about as lovely a person as there is.

ESTHER: You know that ain't so.

MAYME: Of course, it is. And what does it matter? You think half the men that come in here bother looking at my face. No ma'am. He don't care about this. *(Mayme grabs Esther's face and gives her a kiss on the forehead. She playfully shows off her physical attributes that are accentuated by the form-fitting lingerie.)* He interested in this, my dear. This is what he's asking about. *(Mayme laughs.)*

ESTHER: I wouldn't dare write about something like that. He Christian!

MAYME: And it's in his weakness that he'll find his strength. Hallelujah! C'mon, I'm just playing with you.

ESTHER: I'm being serious and you got you mind in the gutter.

MAYME: Oh for God's sake, the man just asking what you look like 'cause he want something pretty to think about come sundown.

ESTHER: You reckon? Then will you help me write something? *(Mayme hands back the letter to Esther.)*

MAYME: No, what about your white lady? Why not have her do it? *(A moment. Esther opens her carpetbag.)*

ESTHER: 'Cause I'm asking you, my friend.

MAYME: No, my writing ain't perfect.

ESTHER: Don't bother about the handwriting, we'll tell him I pricked my finger while sewing. He'll understand. Please.

MAYME: Oh. *(Mayme fetches a sheet of paper and a pen and sits on the bed. Es-*

ther sits next to her.) I ain't romantic, I find this silly, really I do. Only 'cause it's you. So, how do I begin?

ESTHER: "Dear George." *(Mayme concentrates, then slowly writes.)*

MAYME: *(Savoring the notion.)* A love letter to a gentleman. Yes, I know. "Dear George, I write you wearing a lavender silk robe with —" *(Esther giggles. Lights crossfade. George enters carrying a lantern, he is soaked through by the rain.)*

GEORGE: Dear Esther,

    Thank you for your sweet words. Your pricked finger delivered the most unexpected lift. It quiet now. The only motion is the rain. The only sound is the rain. It is the white season, and the work all but stop. The rum shop be the onliest business that do prosper. I seen months of hard work lost in an evening and good men befriend the devil overnight. An if I told you it's been months since I've seen a decent woman it wouldn't be a lie. There are caravans of sweet-faced Indian girls offering up their childhood for a half-day's wage. Yes, many men leave here with less than they come. I shan't be one. It isn't appropriate, but I will say it. I crave a gentlewoman's touch, even if only be to turn down my collar or brush away the dirt in the evenings. Indeed, I'd like to meet you as a gentleman. I think much about the suit I will wear, and the colors that your eyes find pleasing. I imagine your cobble stone roads and the splendid carriages on the avenues, and a dry place to sit. I think of you running silk thread between your fingers and find a bit of holy relief, for your letters arrive just in time to ward off temptation.

    Yours Affectionately,

    George

(Lights crossfade to:)

SCENE FIVE: HAND-DYED SILK

Esther's boudoir. Esther sits at the sewing machine, working on a silk camisole. Mrs. Dickson enters carrying a letter, which she hands to Esther.

MRS. DICKSON: I don't trust him, not one bit. He writes too often.

ESTHER: It's open.

MRS. DICKSON: I'm sorry, I opened it by mistake. I didn't mean to, but I'm glad I did.

ESTHER: 'Cause you the landlady don't give you the right to tamper with my things.

MRS. DICKSON: What are your intentions?

ESTHER: We corresponding. That's all.

MRS. DICKSON: I know these kind of men. Sugared words, but let them stick to the page and go no further. He'll steal your common sense, he will and walk away. It just don't seem like you, Esther, you're too practical a girl for this.

ESTHER: Don't set your clock by my habits.

MRS. DICKSON: His tone is very familiar. And I don't approve.

ESTHER: I'm sorry, but I needn't your approval.

MRS. DICKSON: My goodness. I hope you ain't expecting anything to come of this.

ESTHER: And if I am?

MRS. DICKSON: Our Mr. Charles has asked me twice about you this week. I told him he was most welcome to call.

ESTHER: Mr. Charles is a fool and a glutton. And I'm sure he don't even know who I am.

MRS. DICKSON: You are a stubborn little country girl. And very particular. And it wouldn't hurt you to be more receptive.

ESTHER: To who? Mr. Charles? Remember it's me you're talking to, not Doreen or Erma, or one of those other silly open-hearted little gals. And yes, I'm writing letters to a man. And it may come to nothing. But I am his sweetheart twice a month, and I can fill that envelope with anything that I want.

MRS. DICKSON: Yes. It's an innocent enough flirtation, and I had my share in my youth. And believe me when I say I was romanced by many bright and willing young men. *(Mrs. Dickson takes Esther's hand.)* It's potent, I know, but I ain't ashamed to admit that my pride ultimately led to compromise. And if you're not careful, Esther —

ESTHER: DON'T! This quilt is filled with my hard work, one hundred dollars for every year I been seated at that sewing machine. It's my beauty parlor. So you see I don't need Mr. Charles for his good job and position. *(Mrs. Dickson pulls the quilt off of the bed.)*

MRS. DICKSON: You think this is enough? Do you? You think this gonna make you happy when another half dozen girls waltz away in camisoles of your making. When the Bellman's Ball come around another year and you here fluffing ruffles for some girls from Kentucky, who just happy to be wearing shoes.

ESTHER: No, I don't think that. And I'd give this quilt and everything in it to be with someone I care for, I would.

MRS. DICKSON: This man in Panama, he's paper and I'll show how easily he goes away. *(Mrs. Dickson rips up the letter.)*

ESTHER: Mrs. Dickson!

MRS. DICKSON: You'll thank me. *(Mrs. Dickson exits. Esther picks up the pieces of the letter. Lights crossfade to George in Panama as he picks up pieces of fabric.)*

GEORGE: Dear Esther, I opened the letter and these tiny bits of fabric tumbled out onto the ground. Imagine my surprise, gray wool, pink silk and the blue flannel, which I tucked in the back of my shirt this morning — *(Lights crossfade to Marks' boudoir. Marks unrolls a cobalt blue roll of silk. Esther touches the various fabrics — muslin, taffeta, satin, tulle. Marks unfurls a vibrant roll of magenta cloth.)*

MARKS: It is hand-dyed silk, I washed it yesterday and look.

ESTHER: Yes, beautiful.

MARKS: Have you ever seen anything like that?

ESTHER: No.

MARKS: It looks fragile, but feel. *(Esther runs her hand across the blue material and smiles.)* Ah, it will feel even better against your back.

ESTHER: The ladies will like this indeed. You shouldn't have shown me this . . . *(She pulls the fabric around her shoulders. He then wraps a strip of magenta cloth around his shoulders.)*

MARKS: Look at this color.

ESTHER: It look very good on you, Mr. Marks.

MARKS: Does it? *(Esther laughs. Mr. Marks laughs. An awkward moment, fraught with the unspoken attraction that lies between them.)*

ESTHER: Your button?

MARKS: I forget.

ESTHER: If you take off your jacket, I'll sew it on for you.

MARKS: Don't worry. It is fine. *(Mr. Marks buttons the remaining buttons on the coat.)*

ESTHER: It'll take me no time.

MARKS: No. Thank you. Truly. It is fine. *(A moment.)*

ESTHER: Why do you always wear black? You sell all of these magnificent colors, and yet every time I see you, you're wearing black.

MARKS: You ask a very complicated question. It's an act of faith, that is the simplest way I know how to explain. It is one of the many ways that I show my devotion to God. *(A moment.)*

ESTHER: Is marrying someone you don't know another?

MARKS: It is a thousand years of history and struggle behind the answer to that question.

ESTHER: And yet it seems as simple as taking off a jacket. *(A moment.)* I'm sorry, I didn't mean to upset you.

MARKS: You haven't upset me.

ESTHER: If you wrap the magenta, I'll pay you next week.

MARKS: To answer your question, it has always been that way in my family.

ESTHER: But this a new country.

MARKS: But we come with our pockets stuffed, yes. We don't throw away nothing for fear we might need it later . . . I wear my father's suit. It is old, I know, but this simple black fabric is my most favorite. Why? Because when I wear it, it reminds me that I live every day with a relationship to my ancestors and god. *(As Marks turns to wrap the fabric, Esther ever so gently touches the back of his collar. He doesn't register the gesture. Or does he? Lights fade around Mr. Marks' boudoir. Mrs. Van Buren wears a lacy kimono and corset made of hand-dyed magenta silk.)*

MRS. VAN BUREN: Hand-dyed silk? Is it popular?

ESTHER: It will be by fall.

MRS. VAN BUREN: Really? I'll have to weave that tidbit into conversation this evening. My in-laws are coming. The frog and the wart. Oh, and did I tell you? I saw Mr. Max Fiedler of Germany conduct selections from *Don Juan*. I had to endure an encore from the soprano, what was her name? Something Russian, no doubt. I'd rather have gone to the electric show at Madison Square Garden, but you see Harry isn't impressed with electricity. "Miracle upon miracle, but there remain things science will never be a able to give us," he says, so he refrains from enthusiasm. By the way, I bled this morning, and when I delivered the news to Harry, he spat at me. This civilized creature of society. We all bleed, Esther. And yet I actually felt guilt, as though a young girl again apologizing for becoming a woman. *(Mrs. Van Buren sheds her kimono, revealing a low-cut magenta corset with a pale pink camisole beneath.)* Maybe I'll be a Bohemian, a Bohemian needn't a husband, she's not bound by convention.

ESTHER: I don't see why you let him do you this way, missus. If you don't mind me saying. *(A moment.)*

MRS. VAN BUREN: Have you been to the opera? *(Esther, aware that she overstepped, nervously adjusts the bodice.)*

ESTHER: Never.

MRS. VAN BUREN: Oh god, you're lucky. It's one of those things required of me. I'm certain you've found a more engaging means of entertainment.

ESTHER: I actually only been to the theater once.

MRS. VAN BUREN: Really? What did you see?

ESTHER: Nothing special. A blind gal from Alabama sang spirituals. I need you to lift your arms.

MRS. VAN BUREN: Like this? *(Mrs. Van Buren seductively lifts her arms.)* It's pinching me right here. *(Esther stands behind Mrs. Van Buren and wraps her arms around her torso. She runs her fingers along the top of the corset, then reaches in to adjust her breast. Esther tightens the bodice as Mrs. Van Buren continues to speak.)* I've never been to a colored show, I'm told they're quite good.

ESTHER: I suppose.

MRS. VAN BUREN: I should like to see one for myself. You must take me to one of your shows.

ESTHER: And will you take me to the opera next time you go?

MRS. VAN BUREN: I would, if I could. It would be marvelously scandalous, just the sort of thing to perk up this humdrum season. *(Mrs. Van Buren touches Esther's hand with an unexpected tenderness. Esther politely withdraws her fingers.)* It is so easy to be with you. *(Whispered.)* Your visits are just about the only thing I look forward to these days. You, and our letters to George, of course. Shall we write something dazzling to him? Something delicious. *(A moment. Esther seems hesitant.)*

ESTHER: But, if —

MRS. VAN BUREN: What? Why not?

ESTHER: Perhaps something simple this time, I believe there real affection growing.

MRS. VAN BUREN: Yes, one would hope. He seems quite taken.

ESTHER: I don't want him to be disappointed.

MRS. VAN BUREN: And he needn't be. We'll send him your warmth and he'll find you irresistible.

ESTHER: Do you think we could describe this silk? *(Esther runs her fingers down the front of Mrs. Van Buren's silk corset.)* Will you tell him what it feel like against your skin? How it soft and supple to the touch. I ain't got the words, but I want him to know this color, magenta red. What it make you feel right now. It —

MRS. VAN BUREN: The silk? Are you sure?

ESTHER: Yes.

MRS. VAN BUREN: Mercy, if my friends knew I spend the day writing love letters to a colored laborer, they'd laugh me out of Manhattan.

ESTHER: People do a lot of things that they don't ever speak of.

MRS. VAN BUREN: I smoked opium once, with the most proper of women. She dared me and I did it. And you? What have you done? *(A moment.)*

ESTHER: I touched someone, who I knew I wasn't supposed to touch. I touched them because I wanted to, it was wrong, but I couldn't help myself.

(Mrs. Van Buren takes in Esther's words. The lights rise on George sitting on his bunk illuminated by a kerosene lantern. Esther remains on stage in half-light, as if listening to George speaking directly to her.)

GEORGE: Dearest Esther,

It dawn. No work has begun, the morning is still holding the ocean, not yet blue. But I can see past everything green to the horizon. And it is here in half-light that I imagine you. Six months have passed since our first correspondence, and much has changed. A water boy from my parish died, taken by fever two nights past. All their magic machinery and there's nothing could be done for this boy. It got me thinking about his family behind and the wife he'd never meet. He die so easy. Why he? His young life end, and not more than a word from the Yankee chief, 'cept regret that the new boy ain't so quick. This morn I try to remember this small blackened face and cannot even recall his smile, though his hand give me water each and every day since I be here. Why this boy go out my mind, I ask? Tomorrow I too could be sucked into the ground without tears and ride the death train that pass through here five times a day. When I first come, a solid ox was the dreams of this man. But I watch the splendid way the American gentlemen touch their fine machines and laugh away the jungle, and I know what great and terrible things their sleep brings. And yet, your America sounds like a wondrous place, a man such as myself would be willing to surrender much for a taste of the modern world. Yes, I see beyond the tilting palms, through the mangroves and across the Caribbean Sea to where you sit. I kneel beside you at this moment and I tell you, I am a good strong man. What I've come to feel for you can best be described as love. I love you. There is no other way to say it, will you marry me?

Most Adoringly,

George

(Lights crossfade to:)

SCENE SIX: WHITE COTTON BED LINEN

Mayme's boudoir. Mayme hangs a pair of wet stockings on the bedpost.

MAYME: Why ya smiling so big? Close your mouth 'fore your teeth dry out.

ESTHER: He's asked me to marry him.

MAYME: What? No kiddin'.

ESTHER: It in writing'.

MAYME: Show me. *(Esther hands Mayme the letter.)* Our own Miss Esther.

ESTHER: He say he loves me.

MAYME: And do you love him?

ESTHER: As much as you can love a man you ain't seen. I'm thirty-five, Mayme, and he wants to marry me. And there ain't gonna be no more opportunities I'm afraid. I've told him yes.

MAYME: Well, goddamn. I'm sure he's a fine man.

ESTHER: Yes, I suppose. Any man go through this much trouble to court a woman must have his virtues.

MAYME: I reckon.

ESTHER: He write that he arriving next month.

MAYME: That soon . . . you hardly ready.

ESTHER: I know. I'm getting married! Oh God, will you come to witness the ceremony?

MAYME: Me? You want to bring me around your new husband?

ESTHER: It would be nice to have a friend witness.

MAYME: No, I ain't been to church since I was seventeen. It ain't about you, it's just a promise I made to myself years ago. I ain't got nothing to say to God, and it don't seem right to go up into somebody's home and you ain't on speaking terms.

ESTHER: It just a building.

MAYME: Just the same, I'd rather not be reminded. But thank you, my dear, it's a long time since I been invited any place proper.

ESTHER: Me too.

(Mayme laughs and grabs a bottle of liquor.)

MAYME: Hell we ought to celebrate. Somebody give me this gin. It look expensive. Whatcha think? Should I open it?

ESTHER: Sure. Why not.

(While speaking, Mayme pours them each a glass of gin.)

MAYME: You'll be fine. You're about the most sensible gal I know. Enjoy this, honey. It's a splendid feeling. Yes, indeed. I was engaged once. You won't tell nobody. A mortician's apprentice who hated music. Need I say more.

ESTHER: Do you regret not marrying him?

MAYME: Some days. No, some evenings, honey. *(Mayme thrusts her glass into the air.)* But here's to Esther, you will be a beautiful bride, and may happiness follow. *(They toast and drink. Mayme sits at the piano.)* My dear, you're gonna go to socials and other ridiculous functions that married folk attend. Drink lots of lemonade, God forbid, and become an awful gossip. And you know, it won't be appropriate to visit a place like this.

ESTHER: Who say?

MAYME: *(Snaps.)* I say. *(A moment.)*

ESTHER: We friends, ain't no Panama man gonna change that.

MAYME: Well, I hope he is wonderful. *(Mayme starts to play piano.)*
> GIVE ME A MAN THAT'LL COME AND BAKE ME A CAKE. PUT IN SOME SUGAR AND SPICE.
> YES, HE CAN PUT IT IN MY OVEN ANY OL' TIME AND WATCH IT RISE ON UP.
> GIVE ME A MAN THAT'LL COME AND MOW MY LAWN FROM THE FRONT TO THE BACK.
> *(Esther joins in.)*
> YES, HE CAN TEND MY GARDEN ANY OL' TIME AND WATCH IT RISE ON UP.
> A WOMAN NEEDS A HANDYMAN TO TAKE CARE OF HER HOME.
> A WOMAN NEEDS A CANDYMAN WHO'LL FIGHT THE BEES FOR THE COMB.
> *(Esther stops singing, she silently contemplates her decision, uncertain.)*
> GIVE ME A MAN THAT'LL COME AND BAKE ME A CAKE.
> LOAD IT WITH SOME SUGAR AND SPICE.
> YES, HE CAN PUT IT IN MY OVEN ANY OL' TIME AND WATCH IT RISE ON UP.

(Lights crossfade. Esther's boudoir. Mrs. Dickson is packing Esther's suitcase. Esther crosses into her boudoir.)

MRS. DICKSON: Who is going to sit next to me at the table? There is Bertha, but she has no conversation. Oh, I could move Erma down closer, but she and Bertha don't speak. It'll be an absolute mess at the dinner table without you. That's for certain. Oh, it's gonna be a shame to let this room to anybody else. It has so many of your sweet touches. Yes.

ESTHER: You wasn't always pleased with my conversation if I recall.

MRS. DICKSON: Who told you that? Well, they lie. *(Mrs. Dickson holds up a dress.)* Oh no. Not this little frumpy thing, really Esther. My grandmother wouldn't even wear a collar like so and she was a right proud Christian soldier. Yes.

ESTHER: Well, I like it. It's the most refined thing I own. I paid five whole dollars for it.

MRS. DICKSON: You'll scare off your gentleman, and it ain't worth five dollars of misery. You needn't be a prude. Trust me, your man'll have needs, and it's your duty to keep his member firmly at home. Yes.

ESTHER: Excuse me?

MRS. DICKSON: I shan't repeat it. But there ain't no greater disappointment than a husband without much . . . vigor. Believe me, I know. And sometime he gotta be pleasured to ensure your own satisfaction. You understand. I ain't an expert, but I do have some experience. And I'll tell you give and take make for the best of partnerships. Never mind what the minister tells you about decency, what go on between a man and wife be their own business. He will test you and he will try you, but don't let him beat on you, don't take no shit from him, understand.

ESTHER: Mrs. Dickson.

MRS. DICKSON: Excuse me for saying, but if he raises his hand once, he'll do it again. I thought we should have this conversation before you go off. I don't mean to scare you, but I know you come as an innocent and we're friends so I feel I can speak plainly.

ESTHER: Thank you, but I do believe I'm old enough to handle things for myself.

MRS. DICKSON: Just the same, I thought I'd say it. Now whatcha want me to do with this dress?

ESTHER: It that bad?

MRS. DICKSON: Let's just say we'll give it to Deacon Wynn and let the church ladies fight over it. Yes. *(Mrs. Dickson sits on the bed.)* You really going to do this, ain't you?

ESTHER: You didn't expect me to be here for the rest of my life?

MRS. DICKSON: I guess I sort of did. I'm so used to hearing your sewing machine and foot tapping up here. Yes, I reckon I'm going to miss it.

ESTHER: Another gal will move into this room, and by supper you'll be fussing about something new.

MRS. DICKSON: You say that with such certainty. You hurt my feelings, Miss Esther Mills. *(Mrs. Dickson dabs her eyes with a handkerchief.)* Eighteen years is a long time. Yes. I don't reckon I've known anyone else that long. It'll be lonely.

ESTHER: You have plenty of suitors to keep you busy.

MRS. DICKSON: But ain't a working man amongst them. *(A moment.)* You know you don't have to do this.

ESTHER: Yes, I do. I stay on here, I'll turn to dust one day, get swept up and released into the garden without notice. I've finally found someone. Just as you found Mr. Dickson.

MRS. DICKSON: I married him, because I was thirty-seven years old, I had no profession and there wasn't a decent colored fella in New York City that would have me.

ESTHER: But you come to love each other.

MRS. DICKSON: I suppose. He give me some laughs. But you see, my mother wanted me to marry up. She was a washerwoman and my father was the very married minister of our mission. He's there proudly every Sunday, determined to gain God's favor. Marry good. She didn't ever want to be embarrassed of my fingers the way she was of hers. I'd watch her put witch hazel and hot oil on her delicate hands, but they remained raw and chapped and she kept them hidden inside gray wool gloves. In the winter they'd bleed so bad sometimes, but she'd plunge her hands into the hot water without flinching, knead and scrub the clothing clean. Fold and press for hours and hours, the linen, the bedding, the stockings and the britches, sometimes wearing the frayed gloves so as not to leave bloodstains on her precious laundry. She wouldn't even let me help her, she didn't want my hands to show the markings of labor. I was going to marry up. Love was an entirely impractical thing for a woman in her position. "Look what love done to me," Mama used to say. "Look what love done to me." *(A moment.)* So I did what was necessary to gain favor. I allowed myself to be flattered by gentlemen. You understand? Yes, this "pretty" gal done things, un-pretty things, for this marble mantle, gaslights in every room, a player piano and an indoor toilet.

ESTHER: But Mr. Dickson was a good man.

MRS. DICKSON: Bless his broken-down soul. He had fine suits and perfect diction, and was too high on opium to notice that he was married. But I would not be a washerwoman if it killed me. And I have absolutely marvelous hands to prove it. *(Mrs. Dickson laughs, displaying her hands.)* But you have godly fingers and a means, and you deserve a gentleman. Why gamble it all away for a common laborer?

ESTHER: . . . Love.

MRS. DICKSON: Don't you let a man have no part of your heart without getting a piece of his. *(Lights crossfade to George.)*

GEORGE: Dear Esther, I held in the port of Havana, Cuba awaiting passage to

New York City. A passenger come down with cholera. So here I wait fighting patience. We sail tomorrow — *(Crossfade to Mr. Marks' boudoir, where Mr. Marks has just finished a cup of tea. Esther hesitantly enters.)*

MARKS: Miss Mills, where have you been? I thought I'd lost you to a competitor. *(A moment.)* I keep looking out the window at Mr. Friedlander's shop, he's giving away thread with each purchase. Yesterday, stress tonic. Tomorrow, who knows? I saw this morning Mrs. Simons, Mrs. Simons my cousin's wife, go into Mr. Friedlander's. His fabric is inferior, I tell her this. But she wants the stress tonic . . . then go to the pharmacy I say. Where have you been? I've been going crazy. I couldn't bear to lose you to Friedlander.

ESTHER: I'm sorry, I —

MARKS: No, I'm sorry. You've been busy, of course. I thought something might have happened to you.

ESTHER: Don't tell me you were worried about me.

MARKS: Well, yes. I didn't have your address, otherwise I would have inquired about your health.

ESTHER: I'm very well, thank you. *(A moment. Esther smiles. Mr. Marks shyly looks away.)*

MARKS: I found something I think you'll love. *(Excited.)* Do you have a moment?

ESTHER: Yes.

MARKS: I'll get it. *(He fingers through the bolts of fabric, but suddenly stops himself. He struggles for a moment with whether to broach a question.)* I just made tea, would you have a cup of tea with me?

ESTHER: Thank you, that would be nice. *(Mr. Marks clears a chair for Esther. She sits, a bit disarmed by the invitation. Mr. Marks pours her a cup of tea, then one for himself. He sits down on a chair across from her. A moment. He touches the spot where the button is missing.)*

MARKS: Is the tea hot enough? Milk? Would you like sugar, of course?

ESTHER: No, thank you, it's fine. *(Esther smiles.)*

MARKS: You have a lovely smile. *(Esther stops smiling. Mr. Marks stand up, embarrassed by his candor.)* Let me show you the fabric.

ESTHER: Actually, I have a special request. I'll need fabric for a wedding gown, something simple, Mr. Marks. The bride don't got a lot of money to throw away.

MARKS: Satin? Chiffon? Cotton? Silk? Yes. Tulle?

ESTHER: Satin, I think.

MARKS: She hasn't told you?

ESTHER: Silk. (*Mr. Marks pulls down several bolts of fabric. Esther examines each one, her excitement muted.*)

MARKS: That one you're touching is very popular. And the price will please you. Thirty cents a yard.

ESTHER: Twenty?

MARKS: Twenty-five cents. The bride will like.

ESTHER: It's too much. Something less expensive, I'll dress it up with lace and ribbons. (*Esther points to a faded old roll.*) How about this one?

MARKS: It's a wedding. This is for an older woman —

ESTHER: I ain't so young.

MARKS: — the bride's mother perhaps. (*A moment.*) You are getting married?

ESTHER: (*A moment.*) Yes. You seem surprised.

MARKS: (*He is.*) No, no. Not at all. My congratulations. (*Mr. Marks pulls out his finest wedding fabric.*) Please. I'm sure the rich lady who ordered this didn't appreciate the delicacy of the fabric. She gave no thought to who crafted this perfection, the labor that went into making it. How many hands touched it. Look. Beautiful. You deserve to wear it on your wedding day.

ESTHER: It's so beautiful, it looks like little fairy hands made it. It's too fine for me.

MARKS: Come, touch it and then refuse. Please. Touch. (*Marks watches Esther run her fingers across the fabric. He also touches it, sensually. She closes her eyes. He continues to watch her, savoring the moment.*) It is exquisite. Miss Mills, many fine ladies have worn it against their skin, but it was made for you. I know this . . . (*Esther holds the fabric to her face and begins to weep.*) . . . May it be your first gift. (*He wants to offer comfort, but he cannot touch her.*)

ESTHER I won't let you.

MARKS: It would be my pleasure. (*Esther accepts the length of fabric They gaze at each other, neither able to articulated the depth of their feelings. A moment. Esther and Marks exit the stage, as the lights rise on Mayme seated at the piano. She plays a rag. Mrs. Van Buren enters smoking a cigarette and nursing a glass of brandy. She studies her image in the vanity mirror. Marks reenters fiddling with the buttons on his jacket. He takes out a needle and thread and contemplates whether to sew on a new button. Mrs. Dickson enters carrying a wedding veil, she toys with the delicate fabric. George enters in an ill-fitted suit, his best. He moves downstage with the uncertainty of a new arrival. Esther, dressed in a wedding gown, nervously enters. Mrs. Dickson places the veil on Esther's head. Everyone but George and Esther exit.*)

Esther joins George downstage, each of them in a separate pool of light. George and Esther look at each other, for the first time, then look out into the world. There is a flash — as from an old-fashioned flash camera. The sepia tone image is captured. A projected title card appears above their heads: "Unidentified Negro Couple ca. 1905." Blackout.)

END OF ACT ONE

ACT TWO

SCENE ONE: THE WEDDING CORSET — WHITE SATIN EMBROIDERED WITH ORANGE BLOSSOMS

Esther stands in a pool of light, she wears a spectacular white wedding gown. Another pool of light engulfs George, he wears a worn gray dress suit frayed around the sleeves, certainly his best. Lights rise. A spare studio flat, an iron bed dominates the room. George and Esther stand on either side of the bed, which is covered with the crazy quilt. A silence divides them. Finally Esther speaks.

ESTHER: Don't really feel much different. I guess I expected somethin' to be different. It was a nice ceremony. Didn't you think? I wish my family coulda witnessed it all. My mother in particular. When the minister said man and wife I nearly fainted, I did. I been waiting to hear those words, since . . . they nearly took my breath away. Man and wife, and the truth is we barely know each other. I've written you near everything there is to know about me, and here we is and I fear I ain't got no more to say *(Note: George's accent is a touch heavier and more distinctly Barbadian than in the first act.)*

GEORGE: We ain't need to say nothin' now. We got plenty of time for that. It late. *(George takes off his jacket and tosses it across the bed. He loosens his top button. Esther picks up the jacket, quickly surveys the label, then neatly folds it, placing it at the bottom of the bed.)*

ESTHER: Do you wish to bathe? I'll fetch the basin. *(George kneels on the bed and extends his hand to Esther.)*

GEORGE: Why don't yuh come sit by me. Let me see yuh. *(Esther sinks on the bed with her back to George. He gently strokes her cheek. Esther trembles.)* Are yuh afraid of me? Yuh shaking.

ESTHER: Am I? None of this be familiar.

GEORGE: Give yuh hand 'ere. *(Esther gingerly passes her hand to George. He sits next to her, kissing each of her fingers, then places her hand on his crotch.)* See. It ain't scary at all. *(Esther leaves her hand resting on his crotch, uncomfortable. A moment.)* I expected yuh to be —

ESTHER: Prettier

GEORGE: No, I was gonna say —

ESTHER: It's OK, I lived with this face all my life, ain't no surprises. We should say what we think now and get it out of the way.

GEORGE: I suppose from yuh letters —

ESTHER: I described my character. And I think you'll find me truthful. *(George begins to unbutton Esther's dress. She stiffens at his touch.)* You're very handsome. More than I thought and I must say it do make me a little uncomfortable. *(Esther withdraws her hand from his crotch.)* And the other thing I think you must know, I ain't been with a man before. I been kissed and done some kissing, but you know what I'm saying. And it might be awkward on this night, even if we man and wife —

GEORGE: Then we'll make it less awkward. *(George slips Esther's dress off of her shoulders and plants a kiss on her bare back. She's wearing a stunning wedding corset of white satin embroidered with orange blossoms.)* Real nice. Pretty. I like it. *(He runs his fingers across the delicate lace covering her breasts.)*

ESTHER: Wait. I made something for you. *(Esther stands up and quickly fetches the smoking jacket.)* Here.

GEORGE: What it?

ESTHER: It's Japanese silk. Put it on. *(George clumsily pulls the smoking jacket around his muscular body. He clearly isn't comfortable with the delicacy of the garment.)* Careful. *(George explores the jacket with his weatherworn fingers.)* It ain't too small?

GEORGE: Nah. But I afraid, I soil it. *(George removes the jacket and tosses it on the bed. He pulls Esther into his arms.)*

ESTHER: Not yet.

GEORGE: Yuh got somethin' in mind?

ESTHER: Couldn't we wait a bit?

GEORGE: Minister say man and wife.

ESTHER: Please, I'd like to know about your mother or about your birthplace. Bar-ba-dos. Something I don't know. That wasn't in the letters. Something for us, right now. *(A moment.)*

GEORGE: Like what? *(Esther pulls away and picks up the smoking jacket.)*

ESTHER: I come here from North Carolina at seventeen after my mother died of influenza. God bless her loving spirit. My father died two years later, he was a slave you see and didn't take to life as a freeman. He'd lost his tongue during a nasty fight over a chicken when I was a baby, so I never heard him speak, no complaints, no praise, no gentle words, no goodbye. He was . . . silent. Broken really. I come to this city by myself, worked my way North little by little, picking berries in every state until I get here. An old woman in the rooming house teach me to sew intimate apparel, saying folks'll pay you good money for your discretion. It was just about the best gift anybody give me. It was as though God kissed my hand when I first pulled the fabric through the sewing machine and held up a finished garment. I discovered all I need in these fingers. *(A moment.)* I wanted you to know that about me.

GEORGE: My parents were chattel . . . born to children of chattel. *(George takes off his shirt.)* We cut sugar cane and die and that's our tale for as long as anybody could say. Nothin' worthy of retelling, really. I come here so the story'll be different, that I hopin'. Now if yuh don't mind, I spent many nights on a hard wood floor, a bed be long overdue. *(Esther gives him her hand.)* We married. I ain't gonna commit no crime 'ere, a man and wife don't 'ave no quarrel in the bedroom. *(George gently pulls her onto the bed. The lights slowly fade as Esther succumbs to his embrace. Ragtime piano. Mayme and Mrs. Van Buren enter, dressed in their twin corsets. They stand over the wedding bed.)*

MAYME: What is he like? *(George climbs out of bed, he stands in a pool of light and slowly goes through the ritual of dressing. Esther kneels on her bed wrapped in the crazy quilt.)*

ESTHER: He handsome enough.

MRS. VAN BUREN: Come, what did he say when he saw you? *(Esther climbs out of bed. As they speak, if necessary, Mayme and Mrs. Van Buren may help Esther dress.)*

ESTHER: He ain't say much of nothing. He just stood there for a moment regarding me with his eyes. Yellow, cotton and cane eyes. I didn't have no tongue.

MRS. VAN BUREN: He must be something of a romantic. He traveled halfway across the world because of some promise on a paper.

ESTHER: And he still smell of salt and groundnuts. It make me sick and it make me excited.

MRS. VAN BUREN: I was tipsy on my wedding night. I recall being in love with the notion of love, and everything took on a rosy glow. Harry was foolish and confident and I was frightened to death.

MAYME: Is he as we imagined?

ESTHER: Yes, he is sturdy enough and quite a pleasure to behold. His hands thick, stained dark from work. North Carolina field hands. But he got a melodious voice, each word a song unto itself. *(Mayme and Mrs. Van Buren reluctantly retreat into the darkness. Esther and George button their shirts.)* And when he finally fell asleep I placed my head on his chest, and listened for the song of cicadas at dusk, and imagined the sweet aroma of the mango trees and the giant flamboyant with its crimson tears. *(Esther and George stand on either side of the bed, dressed.)*

SCENE TWO: VALENCIENNES LACE

George/Esther's boudoir. A rag plays. George smoothes down his overgrown hair, pleased with himself. His clothing is worn but that doesn't seem to trouble him. Esther takes in George from the corner of her eye, quickly averting her gaze when he glances over. He smiles to himself.

ESTHER: Do you want me to fix you something?

GEORGE: I ain't really hungry, you know.

ESTHER: Where are you going? It Sunday. I promised Mrs. Dickson we'd dine with her this afternoon after the church social.

GEORGE: That woman ask too many questions for me liking.

ESTHER: That's what ladies do. She's just being attentive. *(George grabs his hat and toys with it for a moment. He ventures to speak, but stops himself. Finally:)*

GEORGE: Say Mrs. Armstrong, you got two dollars?

ESTHER: What for?

GEORGE: I need a proper hat if yuh want me to look for real work. It near three months now, and this a farmer's hat I tol'. The rag man wouldn' even give me a penny for it.

ESTHER: Two dollars. That's a lot of money. I tol' you I'd make you a worsted suit. Right smart. *(George gently touches Esther's hand.)*

GEORGE: C'mon, Mrs. Armstrong. Just two dollars.

ESTHER: But this is the last time. Hear? *(Esther, reluctant, goes to the quilt and opens the seam with her scissors. She digs in and pulls out two dollars.)* There.

GEORGE: That all you got.

ESTHER: Yes. Why do you need to go out?

GEORGE: I tell some fellas I stop off for a quick ale, be back 'fore yuh know.

ESTHER: But it Sunday. I'll put on some tea, and sit, let me mend your shirt. You can't go out with a hole in your shirt. *(Esther touches the hole in his shirt.)* What will they say about your wife? I won't hear the end of it from Mrs. Dickson.

GEORGE: She a real madam. "Yuh working, George?" "Oh, nuh?" *(Chupses.*)* I ain't been this idle since a boy in St. Lucy. But that busylickum ain' 'ear nothing. *(Chupses again.)* I got me pats on the back from white engineers, and a letter of recommendation from the Yankee crew chief heself.

*A term in Carribean English that means "sucking teeth."

But 'ere, I got to watch buildings go up left and right, steel girders as thick as tamarind trees, ten, twelve stories high. Thursday last I stood all day, it cold too, waitin' for the chief, waiting to interview. Do yuh have tools, boy? Yes! Do yuh know how to operate a machine, boy? Yes. But 'e point just so to the Irishmen, the German and the tall Norwegian who's at least fifty years plus five. And I got more experience than the lot. I tell 'e so. Next time, 'e say. Next time, George. Can you believe? And when everyone gone, 'e pass me this damn note like it money. *(He hands the note to Esther. She examine it, pretending to read.)* What do you t'ink? *(George watches her ever so carefully . . .)*

ESTHER: I don't know what to say. I suppose he mean what he say. *(She anxiously places the letter on the bed.)*

GEORGE: But what you t'ink? You t'ink what he say true?

ESTHER: Why wouldn't he be truthful? *(Frustrated, George takes off his shirt and tosses it to Esther. He then throws himself across the bed and lights a cigarette. Esther goes about mending George's shirt by hand.)* Did you try over at that butcher's? Like I asked. I know they could use an extra man 'cause it's always crowded in there. Especially on Friday.

GEORGE: I don' know. We'll see.

ESTHER: There are worse things you could do. And I thought maybe we could go to the church social before Mrs. Dickson's.

GEORGE: I ain' a church man, really. *(Esther stops sewing.)*

ESTHER: You do believe, don't you? Why in letters you said —

GEORGE: I say lot of t'ings. *(A moment. Esther returns to sewing. George feels the quilt.)*

ESTHER: Please, I ain't been to a social. I sat up in Saint Martin's for years, and didn't none of them church ladies bother with me until I walked in on your arm, and suddenly they want Mrs. Armstrong over for tea.

GEORGE: Yuh and yuh monkey chaser yuh mean?

ESTHER: Oh that ain't so. Most of them folks ain't been nowhere to speak of. But they are fine people, and who knows where help will come from?

GEORGE: I want to build t'ings, not polish silver or port luggage. Them fine jobs for yuh Yankee gentlemen, but not me. I ain' come 'ere for that! They'll have me a bootblack 'fore long, let the damn Italians blacken their hands, I say. Mine been black long enough. A man at the saloon, smart-looking fella, say the onliest way for a colored man in this country is for 'e to be 'e own man. Have 'e own business, otherwise 'e always be shining the white man nickel. You understand, no? And really, how it look to people. Me, sitting 'ere, waitin' on fortune, you out there courtin' it.

ESTHER: I am your wife, and whatever I got, yours. And George mind your smoking on the bed. The Chinaman two floors down burn up that way. *(George puts out the cigarette.)*

GEORGE: Listen, this fella at the saloon talk about a man sellin' a stable with a dozen strong draft horses. 'E in a bit of debt and need money quick quick. A dozen horses for nothin'. Did you 'ear what I say?

ESTHER: That saloon talk. That man'll take your money to Shanghai. It just a dream, it ain't gonna feed you today.

GEORGE: You t'ink I stupid?

ESTHER: No. But supposin' he honest, where would you get the money for twelve horses?

GEORGE: Where, Mrs. Armstrong? *(George gently strokes the quilt.)* Am I wrong?

ESTHER: My quilt? Never mind with that money. It just there and it gonna stay there.

GEORGE: Yuh a squirrel, for true. That's what yuh call them city rats, no?

ESTHER: A squirrel ain't a rat. That money for my beauty parlor, I told you that.

GEORGE: *(George laughs.)* That funny.

ESTHER: Why's that funny to you?

GEORGE: You ownin' a beauty parlor.

ESTHER: Yes. *(George studies Esther. She self-consciously returns to sewing.)*

GEORGE: Look at yuh. How yuh know pretty from the lookin' glass? *(A moment.)*

ESTHER: *(Wounded.)* I make pretty things. *(George pops up off the bed and takes Esther in his arms.)*

GEORGE: I sorry, Mrs. Armstrong, I ain' know what I say. Yuh be real sweet, if you done up yuh hair, nice. Put a little paint on yuh lips. *(George runs his hand across Esther's mouth. He grabs her and tries to do a quick dance.)*

ESTHER: I ain't that kind of woman.

GEORGE: No, yuh ain'. *(George lets go of Esther's arm. Gently.)* Please, Esther.

ESTHER: No. That eighteen years there.

GEORGE: *(Chupses.)* Yuh vex me so. Where's me shirt?

ESTHER: It ain't finished. *(George grabs the shirt from Esther and puts it on.)* Be careful, you'll tear —

GEORGE: I going o'er to the Empty Cup for an ale. I see yuh later.

ESTHER: That a notorious place.

GEORGE: How yuh know?

ESTHER: I know. (*George chupses dismissively.*) Why are you so cross with me? You got your ale money and enough for God knows what else. Ain't that so?

GEORGE: Yes, it yuh nickel. How do t'ink that make me feel?

ESTHER: I come here with nothing.

GEORGE: Don't look at me so.

ESTHER: I slept in a cold church for nine days, and picked up breadcrumbs thrown to pigeons.

GEORGE: Yes. Yuh done good, but five hundred days digging don' amount to nothing 'ere. It always gray, why it so gray? Work on the Isthmus, it hard, but at least the sun shine.

ESTHER: I know you here 'cause of me, and I want you to be happy. We stood in that church, and promised before God to take care of each other. That means something, even if it gray. You listenin'?

GEORGE: I listenin'.

ESTHER: You got a good arm George Armstrong, and I'd be proud to walk in on it whether it shining shoes or picking cotton.

GEORGE: I just tired of comin' home to put me hand in yuh pocket. (*George grabs his hat and coat. Esther attempts to turn down his collar. He brushes her hand away.*) I off.

ESTHER: What about Mrs. Dickson and the social?

GEORGE: I be back for supper. (*George grabs his coat and exits. Esther picks up George's work letter and crumples it up. Crossfade to Mr. Marks' boudoir. Mr. Marks hums a rag as he searches through the piles of fabric. Esther enters.*)

MARKS: Here it is. Scottish wool, it isn't as expensive as one would think. It is very good.

ESTHER: Are you humming a rag, Mr. Marks?

MARKS: No, it's a Romanian song. I can't remember the words. It is driving me mad.

ESTHER: (*Esther smiles.*) I'm very happy to see that you replaced the button on your suit.

MARKS: (*Proudly.*) You noticed. It was time, don't you think? You wanted Scottish wool, yes?

ESTHER: Scottish wool. Yes. (*Esther feels the fabric.*) It's so heavy. Would you wear a suit made of this?

MARKS: Well, yes. You see how soft it is. I bought it from a gentleman who said it came from his village. He had a wonderful story about his mother caring for the sheep like small children. He said every night she'd tell

them a fairy tale, and each morning give the creatures a kiss and a sprin-
kle of salt. The neighbors would watch and laugh. Watch and laugh. But
come time to shear the animals, what wonderful wool they produced for
his mother. Like no other. *(Esther feels the fabric, lovingly. Mr. Marks revels in her delight.)* He could have been a thief for all I know, but the color
is a lovely coffee, very subtle. Don't you think? So I pay too much, but
not enough for the quality. Ah! Yes. I have something else to show you.
Where is it? Where are you? Here we are. *(Mr. Marks unfurls a roll of
lace.)* I almost let it go last week, but I was waiting for you. I wanted you
to see it.

ESTHER: Oh, yes.

MARKS: I knew you'd like it. *(Elated.)* The wait was worth seeing your smile
again. *(Marks playfully drapes the lace around Esther's neck. They find themselves standing dangerously close to each other. They are so close that they can
inhale each other's words. A moment.)* Miss Mills, if I may say —

ESTHER: Armstrong. *(Esther removes the lace.)*

MARKS: I apologize. I forget. I forget. *(A moment. Mr. Marks takes the lace and
places it on the cutting board.)*

ESTHER: It is pretty, thank you, but today I've come for fabric for a gentleman's suit. Next time.

MARKS: Yes. Just a minute, I have some other wools, gabardine, if you'd like
to see? I have no story for them, but they are sturdy and reliable, will give
you no problems. *(As Mr. Marks turns to search for another bolt of fabric,
Esther gently runs her fingers across the lace. Mr. Marks turns with the dark
drab suit fabrics. Mr. Marks slowly rolls the lace, his disappointment palpable.)* Next time.

ESTHER: Mr. Marks?

MARKS: Yes? *(Esther wants to say something, but she can't quite find the words.)*
Is there — ?

ESTHER: No. No . . I'm sorry . . . I can't do this. *(Distraught.)* I thought I'd be
able to, but I can't. I can't come here anymore. I —

MARKS: Why do you say this? Did I do something to offend, tell me, did I

ESTHER: No.

MARKS: Then

ESTHER: Please, I think you know why. *(A moment.)*

MARKS: How many yards will you need for the gentleman's suit?

ESTHER: Four yards. The Scottish wool . . . and if you would, please wrap the
Valenciennes lace. *(Crossfade to Mrs. Van Buren's boudoir. Light pours into
her room.)*

SCENE THREE: ROSE CHEMISE

Mrs. Van Buren's boudoir. Mrs. Van Buren sits on the bed cradling a snifter of brandy. She's upbeat, almost cheerful. However, Esther is distracted, consumed by her own thoughts.

MRS. VAN BUREN: He's gone to Europe.

ESTHER: I'm sorry to hear that.

MRS. VAN BUREN: You needn't be. It's a relief actually. Some business obligation, I don't expect to see him for months. He'll find ways of prolonging his stay, no doubt. Anyway, I'm considering a visit with friends in Lenox this summer. It'll be good to escape the city. Don't you think? You could come, of course, I'll recommend your services to several women.

ESTHER: I thank you, but I can't. *(Esther drapes the Valenciennes lace over the bedpost.)* Here. I found a strand of lace for your rose chemise. I know it ain't exactly what you wanted, but —

MRS. VAN BUREN: I had all but forgotten. I ordered it over four weeks ago. Four whole weeks. It's not like you to —

ESTHER: I been busy.

MRS. VAN BUREN: Oh? Indeed. How is our Mr. Armstrong?

ESTHER: Good. Well, he . . . good. Work scarce, and he so particular. He wanting, but his pride make him idle. And I try, I do, but he ain't really take to this city.

MRS. VAN BUREN: But he will. I am certain. Oh Esther, it must be wonderful to be in love.

ESTHER: I suppose. *(A moment. Mrs. Van Buren quickly examines the lace, indifferent, she tosses it onto the bed. Esther bristles at her employer's lack of interest.)*

MRS. VAN BUREN: Is everything all right?

ESTHER: Yes.

MRS VAN BUREN: Such a long face so early in the day. I won't allow it. *(Esther doesn't smile.)* Come.

ESTHER: I'd like to settle matters. Please. You ain't paid me in two months and I need the money.

MRS. VAN BUREN: Of course, I hadn't realized. *(Mrs. Van Buren sits at her dressing table. Smiling to herself.)* You know what? I miss writing our letters. I do! I've been absolutely without purpose for months.

ESTHER: *(Snaps.)* Let's not talk about the letters!

MRS. VAN BUREN: *(Surprised.)* Fine, we won't.

ESTHER: I'm sorry, Mrs. Van Buren.

MRS. VAN BUREN: Something is wrong.

ESTHER: No. Nothing. (*Esther sits on the edge of Mrs. Van Buren's bed. She carefully refolds the lace, attempting to hold back tears, but they come anyway.*)

MRS. VAN BUREN: Esther, what is it?

ESTHER: The other day George asked me to read a letter. I took it in my hand and I lied. I lie every day. And I'm a Christian woman. (*Mrs. Van Buren takes Esther's hand and sits down on the bed next to her.*)

MRS. VAN BUREN: We do what we must, no? We are ridiculous creatures sometimes. (*A moment.*)

ESTHER: Do you love Mr. Van Buren?

MRS. VAN BUREN: I am a married woman, such a question is romantic.

ESTHER: But I fear my love belongs someplace else.

MRS. VAN BUREN: And why is that?

ESTHER: I shouldn't say. No, I can't. Perhaps I'm wrong.

MRS. VAN BUREN: Perhaps not. (*Mrs. Van Buren pulls Esther close and plants a kiss on Esther's lips. Esther for a moment gives in to the sensation of being touched, then abruptly pulls away. Shocked.*) I'm sorry. I didn't mean to do that. I'm sorry. Please don't go. I just wanted to show you what it's like to be treated lovingly.

ESTHER: Don't say that. You don't love me.

MRS. VAN BUREN: How do you know? Please. We will forget this and continue to be friends.

ESTHER: Friends? How we friends? When I ain't never been through your front door. You love me? What of me do you love?

MRS. VAN BUREN: Esther, you are the only one who's been in my boudoir in all these months. And honestly, it's only in here with you, that I feel . . . happy. Please, I want us to be friends?

ESTHER: I'm sorry. I can't.

MRS. VAN BUREN: (*Screams.*) Coward! (*A moment.*) I'm sorry. (*Mrs. Van Buren digs into her dressing table drawer and produces a wad of money. She tosses the money on the bed.*) There.

ESTHER: I'm not a coward. (*Esther picks up the money. Crossfade to Mayme's boudoir. Mayme plays a slow seductive rag. George enters, he watches Mayme gracefully regard the instrument. He places money on top of the piano, then straddles the piano bench behind Mayme. He kisses her neck and cups her breasts in his hands. Crossfade to Esther's boudoir. Esther sits alone, waiting. Crossfade to Mayme's boudoir.*)

SCENE FOUR: GENTLEMEN'S SUIT

Mayme's boudoir. Esther enters. Mayme is dressed in a red flowing dressing gown and bubbles over with excitement.

MAYME: I've saved up every penny I have. It's been two months and I want something new, Esther. Simple, this time without all the pronouncement. Something a young gal might wear on her wedding night.

ESTHER: Wedding night? What ain't I heard? I don't believe those words got any place in your mouth.

MAYME: Seriously.

ESTHER: What's going on? C'mon, are you gonna tell me?

MAYME: It ain't nothing really. A fella, perhaps.

ESTHER: I thought you didn't feel nothing for these fools.

MAYME: Nothing ain't never felt so good.

ESTHER: Who is he?

MAYME: He ain't nobody really, but he real sweet. Like a schoolboy almost. We call him Songbird, 'cause he sing to speak. He come in like all them others. Hands crude and calloused, a week's wage in his pocket. But when we done I didn't want him to leave and I asked him to have a drink. Fool drunk up all my liquor, but it ain't bother me. In fact I was fixin' to run out and git some more, but he placed his hands around my waist, real gentle and pulled me close. I actually want him to kiss me, I didn't even mind his sour tongue in my mouth, I wanted him there, inside me. He ain't like a lot of the colored men who pass through here with anger about their touch. He a gentleman. Comes three times a week on schedule like the iceman. He was here last night until midnight, but he don't ever stay later. He just leaves his scent, which lingers until two A.M. or three, and I lie awake until it disappears.

ESTHER: He sounds wonderful.

MAYME: Yeah, I reckon.

ESTHER: What?

MAYME: Whatcha think? He got a wife. Yeah. A rich wife. But she troubles him, he say. Troubles him to no end. You should hear him go on about this poor gal. Made me feel bad for her.

ESTHER: She terrible, I'm sure. But just the same, you on uneasy ground.

MAYME: You find it shocking?

ESTHER: Yes, I find it shocking.

MAYME: Hush your mouth, you wouldn't understand. You want to see what my songbird give me? (*Mayme pulls George's Japanese smoking jacket from beneath her pillow. She displays it proudly.*) And you know me, I don't usually take gifts from men, but when he give me this, it took my breath away. It's so pretty. Look Esther. Feel it.

ESTHER: He give you this?

MAYME: Yup.

ESTHER: He must like you a bunch to give you something so fine.

MAYME: What can I tell you, the man got taste, honey.

ESTHER: I've only seen fabric like this just once before. It's Japanese silk.

MAYME: How'd you know?

ESTHER: It's expensive fabric. Very hard to find. You see the pictures were embroidered by an imperial artist, he signed it there. He give you this?

MAYME: He say I his gal. But this time a little part of me is hoping he telling the truth.

ESTHER: And what about his wife?

MAYME: What about her? I'm sure she just a sorry gal.

ESTHER: How you know she ain't a good person? And he just saying what you want to hear. That his words are a smooth tonic to make you give out what ain't free. How you know his wife ain't good?

MAYME: I don't know. But do it matter?

ESTHER: Yeah it do. You ever think about where they go after they leave here? Who washes their britches after they been soiled in your bed?

MAYME: No, I don't actually. Why would I?

ESTHER: 'Cause there's some poor woman out there waiting, getting up every five minutes, each time a carriage pass the window or a dog bark. Who thinks a great deal of her husband, thinks so much of him that she don't bother to ask questions, she just know that there are places that he go that gentlewomen don't belong.

MAYME: I don't want to hear.

ESTHER: She thinks he's playing cards or simply restless. But still when the door opens and he lies down next to her, that poor stupid woman don't feel angry, because his body is warm and she ain't alone.

MAYME: What?! You troubled because he married? They all married. You ain't completely clean of this business. Truth. No, I don't care to think about those women. I don't care to think about the kind of lives that keep them sitting in their windows, worrying while their husbands —

ESTHER: I pity your heart. You are the worst sort of scavenger. (*Lights rise on George and Esther's boudoir. George stands in a brand-new suit.*)

MAYME: What's the matter with you?

ESTHER: I don't feel so good. That's all.

MAYME: I thought you'd be happy for me.

ESTHER: I think I'm gonna go home, if you don't mind. *(Lights Crossfade. Esther and George's boudoir. George stands in a new wool suit.)*

GEORGE: Yuh t'ink I'd be taken for a Yankee gentleman? I do t'ink so, no? I'd like one them tall hats, whatcha call 'em? Like that fella across the way, yuh know, the one always be talking' about 'e rich brother in Chicago. *(Affecting an American accent.)* Yes, sir my name George Armstrong and I from New York, yes sir, born here. *(George laughs.)* It fit real nice. But, it seem to me that the fellas be wearing' shorter jackets with a touch of color. *(Esther pins George's pants.)*

ESTHER: Sporting fellas, they ain't gentlemen. This Scottish wool. It white folk quality and it'll keep you warm through the winter. There is a lovely story —

GEORGE: Yeah? I'm sure it excitin'. *(Esther runs her hands down George's legs, then adjusts the hem. He does not respond to her touch.)*

ESTHER: Be that way, I won't tell it then. There. You look good, George. Really. Now take off the pants so I can hem them proper.

GEORGE: Nah, don't bother. I need them for this evenin'.

ESTHER: This evening? Why? Don't go out. I bought fresh pork chops from Mrs. Franklin's son. I was gonna smother them in onions, the way you like. But it ain't worth the trouble if you ain't gonna eat. And . . . and I have something for you, I was going to save it for later . . . but . . . *(A moment.)* Do you want to see?

GEORGE: *(Excited.)* Sure.

ESTHER: Close your eyes. C'mon. And don't smile. *(George closes his eyes. Esther puts a rose in her hair and a touch of color on her lips. She nervously slips off her dress, revealing an elaborate corset similar to Mayme's.)* You can open your eyes. *(Esther awkwardly poses, awaiting George's reaction. His disappointment is palpable. He clearly was expecting something else. George chuckles to himself with a mixture of amusement and disgust.)*

GEORGE: What yuh doing?

ESTHER: Don't you like it?

GEORGE: Come, put yuh clothin' on.

ESTHER: What's the matter? Ain't this to your liking? Ain't this what you want? *(Esther places George's hands around her waist.)* Feel it. It satin. See.

GEORGE: No, don't do this Esther. C'mon, this ain' yuh. 'Ear.

ESTHER: *(Timidly.)* If I ain't mistaken, a man has certain obligations. *(A moment.)* Why won't you touch me? *(A moment.)*

GEORGE: You want me to touch yuh?

ESTHER: Yes. *(George grabs Esther around the waist. He plants a heavy hard kiss on her mouth. She nevertheless succumbs to his touch.)*

GEORGE: Like so? You want me to touch you. That all you want of George? You want me to bend and please, so you can feel mighty. No. *(George pushes Esther away.)* 'Least in Panama a man know where 'e stand. 'E know 'e chattel. That as long as 'e have a goat 'e happy. 'E know when 'e drunk, 'e drunk and there ain' no judgment if so. But then 'e drink in words of this woman. She tell 'e about the pretty avenues, she tell 'e plentiful. She fill up 'e head so it 'ave no taste for goat milk. She offer 'e the city stroke by stroke. She tantalize 'e with Yankee words. But 'e not find she. Only this woman 'ere, that say touch me, George. And ask 'e to lie down on what she promise, lie down on 'e stable with a dozen strong horses for the work sites, ask 'e to lie down as they haul lumber and steel. Strong sturdy beasts. They are. 'E lie down, but what 'e get? No, he ain't gonna lie down no more.

ESTHER: Stop it. Why you talking this way?

GEORGE: I t'ink yuh know. *(A moment. George eyes the quilt.)*

ESTHER: No. Please don't ask me again.

GEORGE: But it there dreamin' a fine fine house wit it own yard. It taunt 'e so, 'e can't even show what kind of man 'e be. What 'e hands can do.

ESTHER: No. That half my life. Thousands of tiny stitches and yards of fabric passed through that old machine.

GEORGE: And for what, huh? For it sit?

ESTHER: No.

GEORGE: Stop sayin' no! Ain't you see. If 'e own wife ain't willin' to believe in 'e, who will? 'E stand in work lines that wind around city blocks. But 'e don't have to no more, 'cause 'e know a fella got twelve draft horses and want to sell them quick quick. And 'e buy them and in two years, they'll have enough money for a beauty parlor even. They'll have the finest stable in New York City. People'll tip their hats and pay tribute. They'll call them Mrs. and Mrs. Armstrong. The Armstrongs. Them church ladies will clear the front row just for them. And 'e will —

ESTHER: *(Esther wants to believe him.)* He will what?

GEORGE: 'E will sit with she and nod graciously to the ladies. 'E will come home for supper every evenin'. *(Seductively.)* 'E will lie with she.

ESTHER: Only she? *(George strokes Esther's back tenderly, she savors his touch. He kisses her neck, her back, her shoulders, her breasts. He embraces her, almost too much so. Esther nevertheless surrenders to the unexpected affection.)* Are you telling me the truth? Is this the truth?

GEORGE: Yes.

ESTHER: Please, you're not just saying that. You're not laughing at me are you?

GEORGE: No, I ain' laughin'. *(Finally, Esther breaks the embrace. She hesitates, then tears into the quilt, wrenching it apart with her bare hands. She pulls the money out and examines it, before placing it in George's outreached hands.)*

ESTHER: There. There. There. *(She's almost relieved to be shedding the money. Surprised, George smiles and gathers the money into a pile.)*

GEORGE: So much 'ere. Sweet mercy, look at it all. Good lord, that fella ain' gonna believe it. I gonna place the money square in 'e hand, wipe that silly Yankee grin off 'e lips. I show 'e.

ESTHER: George, it's late, you ain't gotta do this now . . . put it back. It'll still be there in the morning.

GEORGE: Woman, how yuh get so much?

ESTHER: Leave it. Come. George, I said put it back, it'll be there in the morning! . . . *(Esther beckons him to the bed. He looks at her pleading outstretched hand, but instead chooses to fetch a worn bag for the wrinkled money. Esther, humiliated, studies her husband with growing horror. Aghast, she slowly lowers her hand and pulls on her dress.)* George? *(George continues to take unbridled delight in the money.)* George?

GEORGE: *(Snaps.)* What?

ESTHER: *(Whispered.)* Do you love me?

GEORGE: What the matter wit' you? You look as though you seen a duppy.

ESTHER: Do I?

GEORGE: Why yuh look at me strange?

ESTHER: I asked you something.

GEORGE: Yuh my wife, ain't yuh?

ESTHER: Am I? *(Whispered.)* I didn't write them letters.

GEORGE: I didn't hear what yuh said.

ESTHER: *(Louder, almost too much so.)* I said I didn't write them letters. *(George studies Esther with disbelief.)* All this time I was afraid that you'd find me out. This good noble man from Panama. *(Esther retrieves a pile of letters tied with a satin ribbon.)* I have all of your letters here. I look at them every day. I have one that looks as though it's weeping, because the words fade away into nothing, and another that looks as if it's been through a hard day, because there's a smudge of dirt at each corner, and it smells of kerosene and burnt sugar. But I can't tell you what it say, because I don't read. I can't tell whether there are any truths, but I keep them, 'cause George give me his heart, though it covered in mud and filthy, but he give it to me in one of these letters. And I believed him. I believed him! *(A moment.)* But you ain't the man in these letters, because that gentleman would have thanked me. Who wrote them letters, George? Tell me! *(George considers.)* YOU TELL ME!

GEORGE: An old mulatto man. I paid him ten cents for each letter, ten cents extra for the fancy writing.

ESTHER: I ain't really Mrs. Armstrong, am I? I been holding on to that, and that woman ain't real. We more strangers now, than on the eve of our wedding. At least I knew who I was back then. But I ain't gonna let you hurt that woman. No! She's a good decent woman and worthy. Worthy!

GEORGE: Esther! *(George reaches out to Esther.)*

ESTHER: No, don't touch me! *(Esther backs away from George.)*

GEORGE: Please, I ain' a thief. No. They warn't my words, but that don't mean I ain't feel them t'ings. I go now, and I gonna bring yuh back them horses.

ESTHER: I hope they real strong horses.

GEORGE: You'll see. And we'll begin here. *(Lights Crossfade. Mayme's boudoir. Ragtime music plays, fast and furious.)*

SCENE FIVE: SMOKING JACKET

Mayme's boudoir. Mayme is lying on the bed wrapped in the Japanese smoking jacket. She sits up, pours herself a shot of moonshine and slams it back. A knock sounds on the door.

MAYME: Hold on, hold on. *(Mayme opens the door. Esther, calm, enters. Mayme's unable to disguise her surprise.)* Esther. What . . . I got someone coming shortly. You can't stay. *(Mayme nervously wraps the robe around her body.)* I can't put him off. You understand. Come back later and we'll catch up. *(Esther grabs Mayme's arm.)* What's wrong? *(Esther gathers her strength.)*

ESTHER: He gone.

MAYME: Who gone?

ESTHER: George.

MAYME: You ain't serious.

ESTHER: He has another woman.

MAYME: How do you know?

ESTHER: She told me so.

MAYME: She did? Well, she must be a cruel heartless heifer.

ESTHER: You think so?

MAYME: Yes.

ESTHER: But, she ain't. When I left home this morning I intended to do harm to his whore. I was going to march into her room and scratch her face with my scissors. I was going to scar her. Make her ugly. Make her feel what I'm feeling. But, she gonna know soon enough.

MAYME: You gotta go now.

ESTHER: No.

MAYME: Please, we'll talk about it later. I got someone coming.

ESTHER: Do you know what I done? I tore a hole in my quilt and give him my beauty parlor. Half my life bent at the machine, and I give it to him, just like that.

MAYME: Oh, Esther. Why?

ESTHER: I wanted to be held. *(Distracted.)* I thought if . . . He ain't come home last night. I sat at the sewing machine all night trying to make something, I just kept sewing together anything I could find until I had a strip a mile long, so long it fill up the apartment. *(A moment. Mayme runs her fingers along the fabric of the jacket.)* Do you know where he is, Mayme?

MAYME: Why would I know?

ESTHER: Because you're wearing the jacket I give him on our wedding night.

MAYME: How come you ain't say nothing before? *(Mayme, horrified, rips off the jacket.)*

ESTHER: What am I gonna say?

MAYME: Yeah, yeah. Last night Songbird come around the saloon in a new suit with bottomless pockets, throwing dice all night, and boasting of easy money. I ask him where he got the money and he say his luck turn and he was gonna ride it out. If you can imagine that. He was gonna buy himself draft horses. The world changing and he want big strong horses. He made me laugh. He promised to take me out someplace special, but I didn't have nothing nice to wear. And honestly it made me think about how long it been since I done something for myself. Gone someplace like you said, where colored woman could go to put up her feet and get treated good for a change. And I see the dice rolling, and I think Lord, God, wouldn't a place like that be wonderful. But every time the dice roll, that place is a little further away. Until it all gone. And then I put my arms around this man, and I know who he is. He George. And maybe I known all along.

ESTHER: Why didn't you stop him?

MAYME: Because, he belong to me as well. *(Mayme places it in Esther's hands.)* But this yours.

ESTHER: Foolish country gal.

MAYME: No, you are grand, Esther. And I ain't worthy of your forgiveness, nor will forget what you done for me. You ain't never treat me like a whore. Ever. *(George knocks on door.)*

ESTHER: Please don't answer that door. *(George rattles door and knocks.)* Please don't answer.

MAYME: He's going to leave.

GEORGE: *(Knocks and rattles door more urgently, shouts.)* Mayme! *(He rattles door again.)*

ESTHER: LET HIM GO! *(Mayme moves toward the door, Esther grabs her arm.)* Let him go. He ain't real, he a duppy, a spirit. We be chasing him forever. *(George knocks and rattles door even more persistently. Eventually he stops. Silence. Mayme sits on her bed. Esther exits with the smoking jacket. Cross-fade to Mr. Marks' Boudoir, as Esther moves into Mr. Marks' Boudoir.)*

SCENE SIX: JAPANESE SILK

Marks' boudoir. Mr. Marks unfurls a roll of ocean-blue fabric. As he turns, he finds himself facing Esther.

ESTHER: Hello, Mr. Marks.

MARKS: *(Surprised.)* Miss Mills, I'm sorry, Mrs. Armstrong. How have you been?

ESTHER: I seen worse days. And you?

MARKS: I've seen better days. *(He laughs.)*

ESTHER: I've been meaning to stop in. I walked past here a half dozen times trying to get up the courage to come in. You remember you sold me a rather special length of fabric some time ago.

MARKS: Please, remind me.

ESTHER: Japanese silk, with —

MARKS: Of course, I remember it.

ESTHER: Well, I made it into a man's smoking jacket, at your suggestion. *(She holds it up.)*

MARKS: It is very nice, it will please your husband, I'm sure.

ESTHER: I want you to have it.

MARKS: Me? I can't —

ESTHER: Yes, you will. *(Marks accepts the jacket, genuinely touched by the gesture.)*

MARKS: Thank you.

ESTHER: I can't stay. *(Esther begins to leave.)*

MARKS: Wait, one moment. (*He removes his outer jacket, revealing the fringes of his Tallit Katen. He carefully puts on the silk jacket.*) What do you think?

ESTHER: It fits wonderfully. (*Esther takes a step toward Marks, hesitates, then takes another step forward. She raises her hands.*) May I? (*He nervously holds his breath and nods yes. Esther reaches toward Marks, expecting him to move away. She smoothes the shoulders of the garment, then expertly runs her hands down the jacket's lapels, straightening the wrinkled material. Marks does not move. Silence. Their eyes are fixed upon one another, then Esther reluctantly walks away, exiting the boudoir without a word. Marks is left alone onstage to contemplate the moment. A gentle rag plays. Lights crossfade; we're in Esther's original boudoir.*)

SCENE SEVEN: PATCHWORK QUILT

Esther's boudoir. Mrs. Dickson's rooming house. Mrs. Dickson folds laundry, humming a ragtime tune. Esther enters.

ESTHER: The girl downstairs told me I could find you up here.

MRS. DICKSON: My Lord, Mrs. Armstrong. I been telling everyone how you forgot us.

ESTHER: It ain't been that long.

MRS. DICKSON: Feel so. (*The women hug.*) Look at you. I was about to take some tea, come on into the kitchen, I'm glad for the company. These new girls are always out and about. They trouble me so these days, but whatcha gonna do? And I want to hear about everything.

ESTHER: Have you rented this room?

MRS. DICKSON: Why do you ask?

ESTHER: I don't much feel like saying why. If you please, just a yes or no would suit me fine.

MRS. DICKSON: No.

ESTHER: Well then, you won't mind another person at supper this evening. It's Friday and you don't know how I been missing your carrot salad.

MRS. DICKSON: Of course, Esther —

ESTHER: I'm fine. (*Esther takes Mrs. Dickson's hand.*) And I'd love that cup of tea.

MRS. DICKSON: Come on downstairs and we'll catch up. I'll tell you about Corinna Mae, girl's as big as a house, I swear to God. (*Esther barely listening takes in the room.*) She didn't waste any time getting pregnant and already talking nonsense about her man. When they first was married he was good enough for her, but to hear it now you'd think the man didn't have no kind of sense.

ESTHER: I don't care to hear about Corinna Mae.

MRS. DICKSON: Oh, I just thought —

ESTHER: I'd like to sit here for a moment.

MRS. DICKSON: Oh, yes. I gotta bring a few more things in off the line before the sunset, I'll see you downstairs shortly.

ESTHER: Of course. Mrs. Dickson, thank you for not asking. *(Mrs. Dickson lovingly takes Esther's hand, giving it a supportive squeeze. Mrs. Dickson picks up the laundry basket and exits. Esther lightly touches her belly. A moment. She walks over to the old sewing machine and begins to sew together pieces of fabric, the beginnings of a new quilt. Lights shift: sepia tone, the quality of an old photograph. A slow gentle rag plays in the distance. As the lights fade, projected title card: "Unidentified Negro Seamstress. Ca. 1905." Blackout.)*

END OF PLAY

BOOK GROUP

Marisa Smith

For Faith

PLAYWRIGHT'S BIOGRAPHY

Marisa Smith is the owner and publisher of Smith and Kraus Publishers. She has worked in the theater as an actress, director, and producer. *Book Group* is her first play.

ORIGINAL PRODUCTION

Book Group was first presented by Signal and Noise Productions, Faith Catlin, Producer, on August 19th, 2004 at the Eclipse Grange Theater on Thetford Hill, Vermont. The cast was as follows:

Girl	*Elissa Erickson*
Ellie	*Carolyn Bardos*
Mags	*Darri Colton*
Alison	*Alison Franks*
Fiona	*Briana Trautman-Maier*
Stuart	*Jeff Wills*
Richard	*Avi Glickstein*
Isabel	*Elissa Erickson*
Nick	*Michael Lamanna*

Book Group was directed by Faith Catlin. Sets by Russell Schamm; Lighting by Jeff Spielberg; Costume assistant, Heidi Postupack; Manager and Sound design, Chris Boone; Production Stage Manager, David Shaw; Technical Director, Kendall Colton; Design Assistants, Sawyer Cohen and Tom Gleason, Publicity and Program, Bonnie Cornell, Floy Wooten and Kelly Van Zile; Technical Assistant, Peter Kraus.

AUTHOR'S NOTE

Book Group was inspired by my personal experience as a member of a book group. While I hope I've captured the spirit of the warm camaraderie that I have enjoyed for ten years with the five women of my book group, the play is a work of fiction.

CHARACTERS

In order of appearance

GIRL: Ageless

ELLIE: Artist, age thirty-eight, separated from Richard, one child, Isabel, age ten

MAGS: Age forty, bookstore owner, married to George, a bookstore owner, no kids

ALISON: Age twenty-nine, homemaker, married to John, a pediatrician, twin boys, age nine

FIONA: Age twenty-six, administrative assistant, from Wales, married to Stuart, no kids

STUART: Age thirty, from Wales, a physics professor

RICHARD: Age forty, Ellie's husband, a urologist

ISABEL: Played by Girl

NICK: Age thirty, a builder

TIME

Early in the twenty-first century.

PLACE

A small New England college town.

Book Group

ACT I

SCENE ONE   *Anna Karenina* by Leo Tolstoy

Ellie's family/living room. It is warm, sophisticated, and colorful; the walls are hung with her bold paintings. There is a swinging door stage right that leads into the kitchen and stairs upstage left that lead to the second floor.

The back door of the house enters into the family/living room. The house is equipped with a state-of-the-art security system upstage stage right. There is a video screen on the inside of the back door that allows you to see who is ringing the doorbell. There's a big flower arrangement on a side table.

Fiona's kitchen is downstage left. The back door opens into the kitchen. There is a table in the room and a wall of shelves, and a dog bed on the floor. Girl walks on to the set with a camera around her neck, goes downstage center and motions to the light booth in the back of the audience, cueing the preshow music to stop.

GIRL: Good evening. This play takes place in a small New England town. There's a college here, a lake, a ski hill, my old school, and not much else. The play is called *Book Group*. It happens before I was born. Over here, *(Crosses to Fiona's kitchen.)* is where I grew up but tonight you'll see me in this house, *(Crosses back to Ellie's living room.)* Ellie's house, where the book group meets. I play Isabel in the play, Ellie's daughter, but I'm not really Isabel. You'll find out who I am at the end when everything comes together. And don't be too concerned about how old I am . . . think of me as *ageless*. I love to act . . . playing Isabel is *way* fun.

Right now it's the beginning of the twenty-first century in the near future. Remember, I'm not born yet of course. *(Girl crosses stage right to the stack of books that are on a small table next to the swinging door that leads into the kitchen. She picks up the top book and holds it up for the audience to see.)* This month, October, the women in book group are reading *Anna Karenina* by Leo Tolstoy. Tolstoy's words following the title, which are often overlooked, are: "Vengeance is mine, and I will repay." When asked, my mother said that it was her very favorite book.

(Girl exits, Ellie enters through the swinging door holding a bottle of champagne and sets it on the coffee table. She plumps pillows on the couch and

walks to the large flower arrangement on the side table. She spits at the flowers, reads the card, tears it up, and throws it in the wastepaper basket. Sits on couch, picks up Anna Karenina. *The doorbell rings, a trumpet trill. Ellie goes to the door, presses the button on the video screen, and the smiling faces of Mags and Alison fill the screen. Ellie opens the back door.)*

ELLIE: Come in! Come in! *Andiamo!* Where's the birthday girl? I have champagne! I have lots of champagne!

(Mags and Alison enter, Alison holding shopping bag with present and a bag of knitting. The women kiss and greet each other.)

MAGS: I have Grappa! *(Hoisting her bottle and a cake box.)* And the cake!

ALISON: *(To Mags.)* What's Grappa? *(To Ellie.)* Fiona just "rung me" — she's on her way, something about her sconces. I love your pumpkin on the porch!

ELLIE: Pumpkin. Oh, Evil Richard carved it for Isabel and brought it over yesterday.

MAGS: Must be easy for him to carve after all those prostates.

ALISON: What's Grappa?

(Gets out her knitting; she's knitting a purple scarf.)

ELLIE: It's fabulous fermented Italian wine.

ALISON: Isn't all wine fermented?

MAGS: Grappa is super-fermented or something. You can get smashed in a second.

ALISON: Well, count me out 'til later. I don't want to drop a stitch, I'm almost done. I wish you'd stop calling him Evil Richard. What if Isabel hears?

ELLIE: I'll say I was talking about Richard the Second.

MAGS: No tell her that's what Lucy calls Ricky when she's mad.

ELLIE: I don't think we get it.

MAGS: Isabel's never seen *I Love Lucy?* That's like criminal.

ALISON: How's Richard's father doing?

ELLIE: Daddy Dick?

MAGS: I can't believe you have to call him that.

ALISON: Daddy what?

ELLIE: Daddy Dick. I know it's sounds ridiculous but Richard says that it's really an honor — that the grandfather was called Daddy Dick.

MAGS: So when Daddy Dick croaks we have to call Richard that? Or maybe Dr. Daddy Dick?

ELLIE: Never.

MAGS: That's so perfect for a urologist. Like Dr. Killum or Dr. Payne, or that OB who lost his license, Dr. Bovary.

(Starts laughing hysterically.)

ELLIE: We are so grateful that you find yourself amusing Mags.

MAGS: *(Wiping away tears.)* Well, it is funny, you've got to admit. Dr. Daddy Dick! *(Holds her nose and crosses to swinging door headed for the kitchen.)* Paging Dr. Daddy Dick, Dr. Daddy Dick, please come to radiology. *(Exits.)*

ALISON: Is he still in the hospital?

ELLIE: Yeah, it doesn't look good. I love the old coot. He loves me, thinks I'm exotic. I'm the only person he knows whose people didn't come over on the *Mayflower.*

ALISON: Well, you came over on a boat.

ELLIE: Yes, I did, thank you God. Gracias a dio.

ALISON: So, poor Daddy Dick.

(Mags enters through swinging door with a box of crackers.)

MAGS: Not so poor, the guy's loaded isn't he Ellie?

ELLIE: To the gills.

MAGS: So Richard's trust fund will kick in, right?

ELLIE: Yup.

MAGS: I think you have a pretty good reason to forgive the bastard and move on honey.

ELLIE: Are you out of your mind? I want to *kill* him. I don't give a fuck about his frigging trust fund. I hate him, do you understand, *hate.*

ALISON: We understand, sweetie.

ELLIE: He sent me that gargantuan, hideous arrangement. *(Motions to the flowers on the side table.)*

ALISON: What? Why? In heavens name. Gosh, they are beautiful.

ELLIE: Our anniversary. Can you believe it? We're separated and he sends flowers.

MAGS: Keeping all his options open. He's tricky.

ALISON: I think it's sweet.

MAGS: It's kind of sick, actually.

ALISON: I don't know, maybe he was being sincere.

ELLIE: Too weird. I'd throw them away but it would upset Isabel.

ALISON: Where is Isabel anyway?

ELLIE: Dork-pie took her to the movies. Something with French subtitles. He's pushing his heritage on her these days.

MAGS: I forgot he was half frog; that explains it.

ELLIE: Is there any group you *do* like Margaret?

MAGS: I love our book group you know that! And *(Holds up* Anna Karenina.) I *adore* Mr. Tolstoy.

ALISON: We can't talk about the book until after the cake. Party first.

MAGS: You did finish the book, didn't you? *(Sternly.)*

alison: Yes, Mags, I finished.

MAGS: OK, Ladies, check out the merchandise. I know it's corny but I couldn't resist putting on the little whales.

(Opens the cake box to show the women — there are small plastic whales on sticks in a circle in the middle of the cake. The women ooh and ahh at the same time.)

ALISON: Oh my gosh — little whales.

ELLIE: Very kitsch.

ALISON: Because she's from Wales!! I hope it doesn't make Fiona cry or anything.

ELLIE: It's good to cry on your birthday.

MAGS: She's only twenty-six. A baby.

ELLIE: Maybe this is her magic year.

ALISON: What?

ELLIE: My Nana told me that every woman has a year when it all works, when she's at her most attractive and all men are drawn to her.

MAGS: I think I'm still waiting for that ship to come in.

ELLIE: I was twenty-two. That was the year I slept with my professor and the Jesuit boy who was still a virgin.

ALISON: At the same time?

ELLIE: No, of course not. What do you think I am?

ALISON: Ellie, I can't believe it.

ELLIE: It was my year.

MAGS: C'mon Alison, you weren't born married to John.

ALISON: I did get two proposals one year, one from John and one from Barry Royston. I really liked Barry, but he had too much hair on his back and he chewed with his mouth open. *(She laughs; she has a very strange, distinctive laugh.)*

MAGS: I hate it when it sprouts out of their ears.

(They all laugh.)

ALISON: I wonder why they don't have kids yet? Fiona I mean.

MAGS: They're waiting 'til he gets tenure; that's what Fi told me.

ALISON: But they've only been here two years.

ELLIE: He's on some fast track to tenure or something. And the Wales thing will help, you know, for "diversity."

MAGS: Gimme a break. If the college were serious about diversity they'd hire a Republican.

ELLIE: C'mon Mags, we've all heard your "college professors are all Marxist dinosaurs" rant and thank God they are dying out.

MAGS: The world has changed enormously in the past twenty years for Christ's sake!

ELLIE: Listen, I'm on your side, I'm an *immigrant* remember?

MAGS: I know, sweetie.

ELLIE: And I know more about baseball than you ever will!

ALISON: Do you know that there's research out there that what's best for the child is for the mother to be under thirty at the time of conception.

MAGS: What's that supposed to mean?

ALISON: You know, there are more risks as you get older . . . Down syndrome . . .

MAGS: And how old were you pray tell, when the twin baby Jesus' were born, thirteen?

ALISON: Margaret! You'd better behave yourself. I'm armed and dangerous! *(Stands up, points her knitting needles at Mags and starts laughing.)* I'm sorry, maybe I've been with the kids too much this week.

ELLIE: It's OK sweetie.

MAGS: So how old El?

ELLIE: Late twenties.

MAGS: How late?

ELLIE: Twenty-eight.

ALISON: My mother had me when she was forty. And I'm . . . *(All stare.)*

MAGS: You are fine.

ELLIE: *(Staring at Mags.)* Yes, you are more than fine, Al.

MAGS: *(To Alison.)* Aren't you the last of seven or something?

ALISON: Eight, actually.

ELLIE: Catholic.

ALISON: Very.

MAGS: God, a litter.

ALISON: An all-girl litter and I brought up the rear. Look, it's done. *(Holds up her knitting.)* Derek's into purple *(Holds up a wildly purple scarf.)* and William wants red.
(Doorbell rings.)

ELLIE: Wow!
(Ellie goes to the video screen and presses the button, Fiona's face appears.)

MAGS: Purple city!

FIONA: *(Entering.)* Hull-oo. *(Women rush to hide cake, presents.) Je suis ici!* Hullo, hullo, I'm sorry I'm late.

ELLIE: Look at you you — peaches and cream!!!

FIONA: Thank you. You are sweet. What have I missed?

ELLIE: Nothing.

FIONA: Oh my God, I saw Richard at Price Chopper.

ELLIE: He's allergic to supermarkets.

FIONA: He was there with his girlfriend. The nurse.

ELLIE: Stacey Bitch, I mean Stacey Balch. She's a physician's assistant.

MAGS: Barbara Morton works with her and told me that Stacey was a surrogate mom a couple of years ago and had twins that now live in L.A.

ELLIE: *No.*

MAGS: The twins belong to some celebrity and Stacey made a ton.

FIONA: Well, Richard couldn't have been nicer. There, right in the lettuce, he introduced us.

ELLIE: So she was a walking womb.

MAGS: And paid handsomely.

ALISON: The world's going to hell in a handbasket.

MAGS: That's what my father said forty years ago and we're still here, Alison.

ALISON: You *know* what I mean.

ELLIE: So, Fi, where have you been?

FIONA: I got in a bit of a jam at home. Nick came over with the sconces just as I was leaving and we got chatting. He's been having some trouble with his oldest, Nelson —

ALISON: Who's Nick?

ELLIE: Her contractor, you know, from North Stratham.

ALISON: Oh, Nick LaFontaine. I know his other son Tucker — he's in Derek and William's class.

MAGS: Is Nelson the really big fifth grader?

ELLIE: He's very tall for his age.

MAGS: Right Nelson, the one that read all of *Joey Pigza* standing up in the store.

FIONA: Well, Nick had told me last week that he couldn't get a word out of Nelson and he knew that something was bothering him —

MAGS: It's against the local religion to speak, doesn't Nick know that —

ALISON: *Mags* . . .

FIONA: — and I suggested, cause my father used to do this, that he should lie down with Nelson in the dark and just chat, not say "What's on your mind," but just chat, you know, create a nice environment, and eventually it would come out. And on the third night Nelson told him that he really hated karate.

MAGS: And wanted to start ballet.

FIONA: I don't think Nelson wanted to disappoint his parents. Karate is expensive and a real commitment.

MAGS: You definitely should get something off the bill for that.

ALISON: Don't be a snob Mags, he's a very sweet guy. He fixed our roof a few years ago.

ELLIE: Is he local?

MAGS: Of course he's local.

ELLIE: Well, sometimes they move here and pretend they're local.

ALISON: Ellie!

ELLIE: No, it's better for business. Isn't that what you did Mags?

MAGS: I know him; he's from here. LaFontaine, they're a million of them. A close-knit family if you catch my drift.

FIONA: Jesus Mags. Nick is a perfectly nice man.

ALISON: He is, I know. He was positively chatty when he wasn't on our roof. Most of those guys don't even talk.

MAGS: It's against their North-country religion.

FIONA: Mags, you are so mean-spirited. You don't even know the man.

ALISON: Yeah, I thought he was quite smart. John thought he was great.

FIONA: I think Nick went to university, actually.

MAGS: Honey, he did not go to university, actually.

FIONA: How do you know? You're such a snob Mags.

MAGS: Does he only wear a T-shirt when it's twenty below? There, I rest my case. God, George is convinced he's going to get chilblains if he leaves the house without his glove liners.

ELLIE: Quite the hothouse flower, your George.

MAGS: But George has other strengths, as you know.

ALISON: Not this. We know all about George, we know too much, please, spare us.

FIONA: Oh, c'mon, we know that Mags always gets the conversation round to sex eventually. It's so American.

MAGS: Please, your people gave us *AB FAB, Benny Hill,* etcetera!!

ELLIE: God, Mags, did you quit smoking or something?

MAGS: *(Pause.)* Well, smoking, drinking, I, uh, I had to quit.
(Silence.)

MAGS: Well, God, I'm embarrassed, I mean I'm *happy,* but, well . . . I'm pregnant.

(Ellie, Fiona speak together.)

ELLIE: That's wonderful!!

FIONA: Mags, I didn't know you were trying!

ALISON: *(Realizing what she said before.)* I'm sorry Mags, what I said before. I didn't mean you were too old or anything. I was just speaking generally.

MAGS: Don't worry; I'm sure my eggs were hard-boiled at birth anyway.

ALISON: How did this happen!

MAGS: Well, Al, the usual way, at least I think so, unless I was impregnated by some alien. Maybe Stan Morganthau snuck in one night.

(This elicits a huge round of laughter from all the women except Alison.)

ALISON: Who's Stan Morganthau?

ELLIE: The gastro guy who left his wife for that colonoscopy nurse.

ALISON: Gross.

FIONA: You were trying though?

MAGS: Stan and I were.

ALISON/ELLIE: When are you due?

(They look at each other and laugh.)

MAGS: March ninth.

FIONA: A spring baby!

ALISON: I had always hoped we'd have a book-group baby.

ELLIE: If it's a girl you aren't going to name it Dagny are you?

MAGS: I love that idea.

FIONA: Who's Dagny?

ELLIE: That was before your time, Fi. It's from *Atlas Shrugged* by Ayn Rand. *(Incorrectly pronounced Ann.)*

MAGS: *Ayn, Ayn. (Pronounced Aiyn.)*

ELLIE: Yes, Ayn, Ayn.

ALISON: Mags forced us to read all one thousand tedious pages. It was too much for me, way too much. At the time I was reading the *Narnia* series aloud to the twins and one night I had this horrible dream that Ayn Rand was standing naked in my kitchen and she had this big spear, like Athena has in pictures, and her breasts were all droopy and her hair was all wavy and forties. Then C. S. Lewis came in and he had a tux on and he was yelling at her about not being ready on time. I guess they were going to a party or something. It was really scary.

(All are stunned at her presentation.)

ELLIE: What . . . a . . . nightmare.

ALISON: There is no God in that book; Ayn, Ayn is God.

MAGS: It's a masterpiece! Dagny is the main character, she owns a *railroad* and she gets to sleep with all the hunky guys.

ELLIE: So, Mags, you're going to have to give up all your vices now.

MAGS: Right, no wine, no liquor, no coffee —

ELLIE: No smoking?

MAGS: I officially gave that up yesterday.

ALISON: Well, you have to you know. It's a filthy habit. Ellie gave it up for Isabel and her asthma.

MAGS: Don't look at me like that Al, it's not as if I don't *recycle*.

FIONA: No birth control, that's not bad.

MAGS: No libido. But that's OK.

George sees me as a large egg and he's afraid he's going to crack me.

ELLIE: Just tell him to put his glove liners on and proceed carefully.

ALISON: I can't believe you're doing this to Buster.

MAGS: I know, poor baby. How can I ever love a baby as much as I love Buster.

ELLIE: God, you are so dumb sometimes. Buster will survive. He'll learn to share maybe.

MAGS: Buster is a prince.

ELLIE: Buster is an aged, ugly drooling beast!

MAGS: Buster has never drooled in his entire life. He's beautiful. He's intuitive. He's my soul mate —

ELLIE: I know, forgive me, I forgot for a brief second.

ALISON: Does Buster ever wear those booties I knitted for him?

MAGS: Yes, he loved them last winter.

ELLIE: Dog booties?

MAGS: To protect his paws from the salt.

ELLIE: *(Raises her glass.)* To Buster, to Fiona, to Mags. Champagne all around! *(Starts pouring and passing.)*

MAGS: We've got a treat. Ellie, get the plates and forks. *(Mags goes to get the cake in the kitchen.)*

ELLIE: Yes, boss, yes, boss.

MAGS: Oh, shut up.

ALISON: I think that's the hormones talking, it's the hormones.

ELLIE: Are you kidding, you're always like this.

MAGS: *(Re-enters.)* Close your eyes!

FIONA: I really hate a fuss . . .

MAGS: Stop simpering. No bawling. Sugar cures all ills.

MAGS: Ta-da!!!

FIONA: *(Opens eyes.) Whales!!!* Oh, my God, it's beautiful. *(Bursts into tears.)* Oh, you are all so good — I can't believe the whales!

ALISON: Did we make you homesick? I was afraid you'd be homesick.

FIONA: Well, yes, I'm homesick. But you have all been so good . . . *(Fiona raises her glass.)* Here's to us, and to Mags, the Mum to be —

ELLIE: And to you . . .

ALISON: And to Buster.

MAGS: Thanks, Al. *Cin-cin. (Italian, pronounced chin–chin.)*

ALL: *Cin-cin.*

FIONA: *Iech yda. (Welsh, pronounced Yich yuh da.)*

MAGS: Ladies, again.

ALL: *Iech yda.*

(Girl enters from upstage, stands directly in front of them and takes a photo, click, flash.)

SCENE TWO

Later that week. Fiona and Stuart's kitchen. Floor is strewn with dog toys, a couple of leashes hang from pegs near the floor-to-ceiling shelves. Stuart enters with groceries, trips on a dog ball that is in his path, regains his balance.

STUART: *Jesus!*
(Fiona enters, cell phone to her ear, then quickly turns it off as she steps into the room.)

FIONA: Sweetheart.

STUART: I'm never going to Shaw's again at five o'clock. Every bloody friend of yours was there. *(Steps into dog water bowl.)* Oh, Lord. Can't these women shop during the day? *(Starts putting away the groceries.)*

FIONA: Women work now Stuart, it's been decades. We're not all like your mother, you know. *(Cleans up spilled water.)*

STUART: Yes, yes. Maureen and Rachael say hello and what's her name . . . your book group hen with the dog, Barnaby or something.

FIONA: Buster.

STUART: Ah, yes, *Buster. (Uses pronounced American accent.)*

FIONA: It's Mag's dog. She's pregnant you know. Due in March.

STUART: Buster?

FIONA: No, Mags, obviously.

STUART: Isn't she a bit long in the tooth for that sort of thing?

FIONA: She's just forty. That's not terribly old these days. She's quite thrilled and so are we, the book group.

STUART: The hens.

FIONA: Yes, the hens.

STUART: Yes, the hens in the hen club. The one where you are presumably discussing great and not so great literature, but you are really chatting about who fancies who while you get legless.

FIONA: Oh, Stu, really.

STUART: Obviously Mags and George have been at it, Mags issuing orders all the way no doubt.

FIONA: Are you intimidated by Mags?

STUART: Dream on. I hardly notice the woman.

FIONA: Did you say hello at the market?

STUART: No, I grunted at her, and passed wind. Yes, of course I said hello. In fact I told her I was due for a visit to the *Book Nook. (He says the name with contempt and picks up cell phone still on table.)*

FIONA: They inherited the name of the store. *(Takes phone from Stuart and puts it on shelf.)* They had to keep it.

STUART: Right.

FIONA: I took Lucy to the vet. Tom gave me antiseizure medications that should control her episodes.

STUART: I bet that cost a bloody fortune. Really, Fi, that dog has had her day. Christ, she's almost thirteen. Maybe we should think about putting her out of her misery.

FIONA: She's not miserable! Tom said her heart is strong and that she has the muscle tone and energy of a much younger dog!

STUART: Well, that's reassuring.

FIONA: Aren't you happy that we can help Lucy have a better life?

STUART: Lucy is a German Shepherd Fi, she doesn't reflect on the quality of her life.

FIONA: That's not what I'm saying at all and how the hell do you know what she does or doesn't reflect upon! For goodness sake, Stu, if it weren't for Lucy we never would have met.

STUART: That's what I get for letting a dog wee on my bike.

FIONA: You love her don't you?

STUART: Yes, I love Lucy. *(They kiss, Fiona pulls away first and as she turns her back to him, Stuart takes the phone from the shelf and quickly puts it in his pocket.)* At least I'm not losing my sense of humor as I teeter toward senility, which is the first left after the *Book Nook.*

FIONA: You're so terribly amusing dear.

STUART: Did you get to the post office?

FIONA: Oh, God, I forgot. I planned to go during lunch but I had to check out Trinity Hall for the Shayma Manji lecture.

STUART: Yes, that's nice but Fi, I was hoping to hear from Foster Sargent —

FIONA: Excuse me Stuart, but this is an important event for me. Claudio wants me to give the introduction.

STUART: That's splendid Fi. But Foster wrote a letter to the tenure committee on my behalf and was posting me a copy.

FIONA: Couldn't he just e-mail it to you?

STUART: Fiona, the man is practically a hundred. Knowing Foster he rejected e-mail on moral grounds. The bad punctuation would probably kill him. Besides, it's our tradition to write one another the old-fashioned way —

FIONA: I'm sorry. Maybe you could ring him up and he could read it —

STUART: So, you didn't get the Volvo checked then.

FIONA: I had to take Lucy to the vet after work Stu, that was the priority. I can take it in tomorrow.

STUART: I would have done it if I knew you wouldn't have time.

FIONA: Well, I thought I would.

STUART: It's the fact that you always say you'll do something and then you don't.

FIONA: I didn't realize that the Volvo had to be done today. And I had *no idea* you were waiting for a letter. It's rather quaint actually.

STUART: I'm not dictating to you that you *must* take the Volvo in; I asked you if you could and you said yes, so I expected it to be done. And now I'm disappointed, that's all.

FIONA: You're disappointed.

STUART: I'm only being honest here, Fiona. You ask me what you can do for me, which I appreciate. You make yourself feel good for asking. Then you don't do it and when I get upset you get angry and become the victim.

FIONA: I'm not the victim, I'm trying to explain why I didn't have time.

STUART: Yes, well, if you needed to go to the post office for the book group you would have gone, believe me.

FIONA: Don't be so mean, Stu.

STUART: I'm simply stating facts Fiona.

FIONA: I've got a lot on my plate these days. Stu. You have *no* idea what's going on here, at all. You've said two words to Nick in three months.

STUART: The man speaks, I didn't know.

FIONA: You think everyone is an idiot and that you know everything. Well, everyone is *not* an idiot and you don't know shit.

STUART: Is that what you learn at hen club?

FIONA: At least I have friends. You've made no effort in the two years we've been here.

STUART: I've been working my ass off that's why. And what do you call Henry and Walter?

FIONA: Yes, and you come home from golf and rip Henry and Walter to shreds.

STUART: Do you care if I get tenure? Henry and Walter can help you know. Can help *a great deal.*

FIONA: I don't know anymore, I really don't.

STUART: What are we doing then?

FIONA: I never knew you had to have the Volvo looked at *today.* How can you be so upset about something I didn't intentionally do?

STUART: You never do anything bad on purpose. Why can't you take responsibility —

FIONA: What do you want me to do, get down on my knees and beg your forgiveness? Who do you think you are? I didn't shag the FedEx man, or poison your food. Why do you make such a big deal about it?

STUART: You don't give a shit if I get tenure or not do you, you're probably hoping I bloody well don't so we can go crawling back to Cardiff.

FIONA: We wouldn't be crawling back, we'd be going home. Look, I'm sorry about the post office and the car. I'm sorry. I should do what I say I'm going to do, you're right.

Please, let's not fight. I didn't mean to hurt you. *I am* sorry, please.

STUART: Sorry? Sorry! It doesn't mean anything to me anymore. It's just one of your tactics.

FIONA: No, I am, I see your point.

STUART: *(Very angry.)* You'll say anything now to get us back on track.

That's what happens every single time, without fail. Why can't you at least be honest for once.

FIONA: I'm just trying to explain, Stu.

STUART: *No,* you trying to exonerate yourself and be the good little girl.

FIONA: Good little girl, why do you say that!

Why are you so mean? I'm sorry. Really and truly, I'm sorry.

STUART: Fuck your sorry, Fiona. *(He exits.)*

FIONA: *(Crying softly.)* I'm sorry.

GIRL: *(Enters, point her camera at Fiona, then turns to the audience.)* No picture.

SCENE THREE *The Art of Eating by M.F.K. Fisher*

Ellie's living room, the book corner, the little table with the stack of books near the swinging kitchen door.

GIRL: *(Holds up the book.)* November. This month the ladies are reading *The Art of Eating* by M.F.K. Fisher, copyright 1937. On my wedding day, Mags gave me a copy with all her favorite recipes underlined like Tomato Soup Cake and Sardine Pie. Food is love she told me and never believe those people who say food is fuel. They're a lot of them up here, they go running five times a day, rain, shine, plague of locusts, whatever, and look like human whippets. Now I get to play Isabel. *(Girl exits.)*
(Doorbell rings, Alison enters from Ellie's kitchen with oven mitts on her hands and an apron over her clothes. She presses video screen button, Richard's face appears and she buzzes him in.)

ALISON: Hi, Richard!

RICHARD: Flower and child delivery, have no fear.

ALISON: I'm holding down the fort. Ellie had to get more oysters.

RICHARD: You're a true friend Alison. It pains me that the separation means I see less of you and John.

ALISON: *(Isabel enters, running.)* Hello, Izzyboo.
(Richard puts the flowers down and walks into the room.)

ISABEL: Hi, Mrs. Chapman. I gotta call Alyssa. Daddy and I just saw her boyfriend!!! *(Runs upstairs.)*

ALISON: Oh, big news! Those lilies are gorgeous.

RICHARD: They're Ellie's favorites. *(Motioning to the flowers and settling in on the couch.)* I want to thank her for coming to my dad's memorial last week.

ALISON: I'm so sorry Richard. Ellie told us he was a great guy.

RICHARD: Yeah, Ellie really loved Dad and he loved her. Loved her spirit you know. *(Puts head in hands.)* We are all going to miss him. He was bigger than life. Daddy Dick.

ALISON: Oh, Richard. *(Sits next to him on couch, hand on shoulder, comforting him.)*

RICHARD: His journey was cut short, but oh what a ride. *(Getting teary.)*

ALISON: This must be so hard.

RICHARD: It's tough, tough. But I feel that he's still with me, keeping an eye out. *(Pause.)*

ALISON: Will you get to be called Daddy Dick now, Richard?

RICHARD: Oh, I don't know. I don't think I can fill those shoes.

(Starts blubbering, Alison puts her arm around him to comfort him and he falls into her bosom.)

ALISON: Oh, it's so sad Richard, I'm so sorry. There, let it out, it's OK, it's OK.

(Ellie enters.)

ELLIE: *Richard! Alison!*

(Alison and Richard jump up.)

ALISON: Richard was just telling me about his father. And look Ellie, he brought you some flowers.

RICHARD: Forgive the emotion here Ellie, I'm still kind of raw. I wanted you to have the lilies, I know you love them.

ELLIE: Thank you Richard, that was very nice of you. Isabel home?

ALISON: I better check on my chicken. Nothing like dry meat. *(Laughs.)* Bye, Richard, sorry again about your dad. *(Exits through swinging door.)*

RICHARD: Very nice lady Alison. Truly sympathetic.

ELLIE: Isabel home?

RICHARD: Ran upstairs to call Alyssa.

ELLIE: Well, come and pick her up on Saturday around eleven. She has practice at noon.

RICHARD: Thanks again for coming to Dad's funeral Ellie. I know he would have wanted you there.

ELLIE: It was the right thing to do for Isabel.

RICHARD: You know, I could come by a little early on Saturday and maybe we could all go out for breakfast.

ELLIE: Aren't you a little busy for that Richard?

RICHARD: Never for you two Ellie. Not for my two girls.

ELLIE: No, sorry, I have plans. So . . . *(Calls upstairs.)* Isabel . . . Daddy's leaving. *(Very angry.)*

RICHARD: That's OK, I'll call later.

ELLIE: Well, I have book group.

RICHARD: Give my best to the ladies.

ALISON: *(Entering from kitchen.)* Ellie, sorry to interrupt, but your oysters smell kind of funny. Very nice to see you again Richard.

RICHARD: I'm on my way out. Alison, always good to see you. *(Phone rings and plays the song, "Hava-Nagilah.")* HAVE A GREAT ONE! *(He exits.)*

ELLIE: Where's my phone? *(Starts looking for it in a panic, overturning couch cushions, displacing Alison from the couch, unearths Ken doll from under couch cushion and throws him on coffee table. Answers phone.)* M.F.K. Fisher speaking. *The Art of Eating* dinner extraordinaire. Just Alison —

her chicken is in the oven. You'd better be bringing that War Cake. No. Hold on. *(To Alison.)* Didn't Fiona tell you Mags was picking her up?

ALISON: Yes, about seven thirty.

ELLIE: Well, that's what Fi told me. No, just come now. We're starving. Bye, bye. *(Hangs up.)* That's odd, Mags went to get Fiona and Stuart said that she left an hour ago. She has been acting strange. All the traditional signs; a little distant, a little thinner.

ALISON: Signs?

ELLIE: Stepping out signs.

ALISON: Really? Do you think she would? You're right though, she is thinner. That really could mean something. You know, last Tuesday John and I were at this boring cardiology dinner and I got chatting with Andrew Warner — we were talking about renovating, it turns out Nick did some work for them. Said he did a great job, kept right on budget. Was Marjorie happy I asked? You know Marjorie; tall, bushy blonde — She's always at Twin Mountain, red ski-suit?

ELLIE: Yeah, yeah, no-makeup, very animated. Too animated.

ALISON: Right, Marge. Anyway, Andrew kind of giggled, he's really a pompous sort of guy. I've actually heard him use *heretofore* in a sentence. *(Imitates Andrew using the Ken doll as a prop.)* Ah, yes, Marge was very pleased with the work; got quite attached to the crew. Told me she cried a real tear when they left. Ho, Ho, Ho.

ELLIE: That doesn't mean diddly-squat. C'mon, you're close to Fiona. Why don't you just ask her?

ALISON: I've tried. But she's so British, or Welsh, or whatever, that she wiggles right out of my grasp. She immediately shifts the focus off of her to me! *(Doorbell rings.)* The other day she asked me if the twins had benefited from *Hooked on Phonics*. What's with that?

(Ellie goes to the screen, Fiona makes a face in the monitor and Ellie buzzes her in.)

FIONA: Hullo, hullo, I'm sorry I'm late; I have my blasted rabbit. How is every little one?

ELLIE: Mags just called. She was at your house. She was supposed to pick you up . . .

FIONA: *(Very happy and high.)* Oh, my God I forgot. I completely forgot. I was running around doing errands. Stuart was home; what did Stuart say? He knew I had book group tonight; I told him I was coming here directly from work. Oh, heavens. Goodness it's nippy out there. I could really use some red wine I think. Oh, Ellie, look at that. What a marvelous arrangement. My God, it's bloody enormous. Oops, my rabbit, wait while I pop it in the oven. *(She exits through swinging door to kitchen.)*

ALISON: Whoa. Oh, my Lord.

ELLIE: Valium anyone?

ALISON: I'll say. Amazing.

ELLIE: Who's that for? *(Pointing to the scarf Alison's knitting.)*

ALISON: Father Polanski. He's getting out of rehab next month.

FIONA: *(Re-enters, with glass of wine.)* I hope I've not been too bold; but I found the wine open on the counter. Those lilies; it smells like Hawaii!

ELLIE: Tricky Dick. Frankly, I wanted to barf. And I heard that Stacey dumped him. For Steve Linzer, the new orthopod fellow. Apparently he's a hunk.

ALISON: Pediatrics actually. *(Doorbell rings.)* And he's kind of scary-looking I think.

(Ellie, goes to the screen, Mags face appears, Ellie buzzes her in.)

MAGS: *(Entering.)* Yoo-hoo. Yoo-hoo. Should we call the police; is Fiona here?

FIONA: Yes, Mags, sorry for the mix-up. I forgot you were coming I had errands and left before you.

MAGS: So I gathered. I was at your house. I think what's his name is embarrassed that I'm pregnant. He kept stealing weird glances at my belly.

FIONA: Lucy??

MAGS: No, the other one, what's his name, the husband.

FIONA: Stuart.

MAGS: Whatever. *(Setting cake down and noticing flowers nearby.)*
Did I forget a birthday or something?

ALISON: Flowers from Richard. To thank Ellie for going to Daddy Dick's funeral.

MAGS: Yeah, old Daddy Dick bit the dust, I heard.

ALISON: Richard was genuinely upset.

ELLIE: Yes, I walked in on Alison *comforting* poor Richard.

ALISON: He was really sad Ellie, I could tell.

ELLIE: He hated Daddy Dick.

MAGS: He's keeping after you though. The whole flower routine.

ELLIE: Probably steals them from the hospital!

MAGS: Probably!

ELLIE: Come in the kitchen, I need help with the oysters. Bring that cake.

MAGS: It's a brick.

(They exit and Fiona and Alison are left alone.)

ALISON: Fiona, it was the funniest thing. Yesterday I was driving back from

Morrisville and I saw you driving North on Route 4. I honked and waved but you didn't see me.

FIONA: Oh, I thought that might be you. I think I was singing along with Andrea Bocelli! I was on my way to Fresh Pond Pottery.

ALISON: So, are you excited that the renovation is almost done? When do we get to see it?

FIONA: I should have you all over sometime.

ALISON: Is Nick done?

FIONA: Just the finishing touches left.

ALISON: I was chatting with Andrew Warner at this incredibly boring dinner last week and he said that when Nick and his crew were finished with their addition, Marge cried real tears. Isn't that strange?

FIONA: I can see how that happens. You're home, they're there every day — you get to know them.

ALISON: Does Nick have a . . . big crew?

FIONA: Alison.

ALISON: What?

FIONA: Good Lord, I'm not an idiot here.

(Mags and Ellie enter from kitchen.)

MAGS: Who's not an idiot here? Certainly not *moi,* the mater gravitas.

FIONA: No, this isn't about you dear.

ALISON: Just been chatting about Ni —

FIONA: Nothing interesting, we've just been —

MAGS: We are all *dying* to know. Is it the tool belt? Or just the tools in general. *(Laughs, very pleased with herself.)*

FIONA: Margaret!

MAGS: Margaret. *(Imitating her.)* Come clean baby, we've all been excruciatingly patient.

ELLIE: C'mon, cone of silence.

(Beat. They all make a triangle over their heads by lifting their arms over their heads and pressing their palms together.)

FIONA: Oh, bloody hell. Nothing's going on with Nick.

MAGS: Now, no one said anything was going on, did we?

FIONA: Nick and I are friends, just friends.

ELLIE: *(To Alison.)* I need to have the upstairs bath redone; maybe I should call Nick.

MAGS: Well, if you haven't slept with him it's worse than I thought.

FIONA: It is possible to be friends with a man without sex entering the picture.

MAGS: Sex always enters the picture.

ELLIE: Except in the case of Stan Morganthau.

FIONA: Well, I'm not going to put my marriage in jeopardy. Stuart and I took *vows*.

MAGS: In a Catholic Church. That's big time.

ALISON: Are you and Stuart Catholic? I've never seen you at St. Anne's.

MAGS: Fi, maybe you should listen to your body, as they used to say in the seventies. Maybe you want a mate who knows his way around a hacksaw.

FIONA: You know Mags, this is no longer funny, I'm sick and tired of your constant innuendo about me and Nick. We are *not* having an affair,

ELLIE: Ladies, ladies.

ALISON: I think that rabbit is hopping ready! *(Runs into kitchen.)*

MAGS: I thought that was the point of book group; we open our minds to great and mediocre literature, you know, female bonding, recipe swapping, husband swapping — just kidding — pedicures . . .

FIONA: To a point, Mags, to a point.
(Bursts into tears.) Oh, I'm sorry, I'm sorry. I'm just on edge. Stuart and I had another fight . . . about *green beans.*

MAGS: Oh, Jesus, Mary, and Joseph. *(Goes over to her.)* I'm sorry, you are right, I can be a pest.
(They hug, Fiona cries quietly.)

MAGS: Al, get in here.
(Alison pokes her head out from the swinging door.)

MAGS: Ladies, good news, the genetic tests were A-OK.

ALISON: *(Comes running over to the couch.)* That's great, Mags. That's wonderful news.

MAGS: All systems are go. George and I decided that we don't want to know the sex. I'm sure it's a girl though, I just know it is. Little Dagny. *(Pats her stomach.)*

ELLIE: Honey, I hate to burst your bubble but you don't know shit about birthing babies. Should we tell her the truth ladies, Al?

MAGS: You're scaring me.

ALISON: Ellie's just joking. Everything will be fine.

ELLIE: *(Suddenly we hear very loud rock music.)* ISABEL, TURN THAT DOWN THIS MINUTE. I'M HAVING BOOK GROUP!!!
(Women search for their books as the music blares. All four sit on couch, open up their books to the same page, covers facing the audience, as Girl enters from upstairs. Girl stands in front of them and takes a photo, click, flash. Girl crosses downstage center and speaks to the audience.)

GIRL: Of course, I really knew Isabel. She was my babysitter and always called me her little sister. My first memory of her is when I was five years old and she was about fifteen. It was summertime and we were really hot. She filled up the bathtub and put all my goldfish in, I had tons of them, in the tub so they could have a special treat. Then Isabel and I got in and the goldfish swam all around us. That was so neat.

SCENE FOUR

Mid-afternoon, Fiona's kitchen. Soft knock on door, door opens. Nick enters, carrying a clipboard with the name Nick *in big letters written on the back of the clipboard in Wite-Out.*

NICK: Hello? Hello.
(Fiona enters with a plate and a knife. There is celery on the table.)
FIONA: Hullo.
NICK: Is this a good time?
FIONA: No, this is not a good time. Stu and I are going to dinner at Henry Mudge's and I have to make the blasted crudités.
NICK: Listen, last night. I thought I could get away, but I couldn't leave the kids, Kitty was out.
FIONA: I know, she was here.
NICK: Kitty?
FIONA: Kitty.
NICK: She was here?
FIONA: Nick, really. You know she was here; you sent her.
NICK: What?
FIONA: C'mon. You sent her to get the samples
NICK: Well, not last night. I did not send her. I didn't know she was here, I didn't know where she was.
FIONA: Nick, please, it's OK.
NICK: Fiona, I like you.
FIONA: We had a nice chat. I like her.
NICK: No, I *really* like you.
FIONA: I'm going back to school.
NICK: What?
FIONA: Well, I'm going to apply to the MIS program — Master of International Studies. If I'm going to be more than an assistant at the Center I'll need an advanced degree.

NICK: Great.

FIONA: It's the right thing. And my boss is all for it. Stuart got tenure. We're staying, definitely.

NICK: Congratulations.

FIONA: You are released.

NICK: What?

FIONA: You know what I mean. I release you.

(Pause.)

NICK: *(Goes to back door and opens it, looking around.)* It's great to go back to school. I could never stay in.

FIONA: You don't need to go back to school. You're doing what you love.

NICK: My dad always said I could have been an architect.

FIONA: I can't see you in a bow tie.

NICK: Some of those guys are all right.

FIONA: You and Kitty met in grade school.

NICK: She told you that?

FIONA: I didn't realize she grew up here too.

NICK: I don't want to be released.

FIONA: Her dad owned the hardware store.

NICK: I really don't.

FIONA: Or that your father was a doctor.

NICK: I like how it is.

FIONA: Kitty was sweet.

NICK: I like you Fiona.

FIONA: Your youngest is still a baby really.

NICK: I should have come last night.

FIONA: Kitty said Nelson only talks to you.

NICK: Yeah, me and Nels are buds.

FIONA: That's great. *(Kiss.)* You should go.

NICK: But it's Friday and Stu has his senior seminar.

FIONA: Excellent memory, Nicholas. *(Very British.)*

NICK: Nicholas. *(With British accent.)* I love it when you call me that.

FIONA: Nicholas.

NICK: But, I don't just love you for your accent.

FIONA: That was fast. You love me now.

NICK: I just might, Mrs. Timmins.

FIONA: Mr. LaFontaine, do you have a middle name?

NICK: Samuel.

FIONA: Nicholas Samuel LaFontaine.

NICK: You and I . . . we're a lot alike.

FIONA: We are?

NICK: We're old souls. You know some of us are old souls and some of us are new. You are definitely an old soul.

FIONA: How can you tell?

NICK: I can tell . . .

FIONA: Nick . . .

NICK: Nicholas.

FIONA: Nicholas. Stop that! *(He is touching her.)* This isn't a good idea. This has been fun, but now is a good time to stop. You know what I mean.

NICK: Well no, I don't think so. I think it's exactly the wrong time, if you know what I mean.

FIONA: Obviously I like you, you know that, but we're getting too close.

NICK: That's a bad thing?

FIONA: Yes, in this case yes.

NICK: I'm enjoying the dance, ma'am.

FIONA: You know what the Baptists say. About dancing.

NICK: Don't think we're Baptists. Not last time I looked.

FIONA: Nick, I can't do this. I think about Kitty and . . .

NICK: We have nothing to do with Kitty. This doesn't affect Kitty.

FIONA: I'm sure she'd be interested to know that.

NICK: Kitty?

FIONA: Yes, Kitty. Hello, Kitty!

NICK: It's just us. Parallel universes.

FIONA: Parallel universes?

NICK: Exactly. It's just us.

FIONA: I don't know.

NICK: Kitty's mom had a guy for years and years and nobody ever knew.

FIONA: How did you know?

NICK: Kitty told me when he died.

FIONA: So what are you saying, that it would be OK with Kitty if you had a girlfriend?

NICK: You make it sound depressing.

FIONA: Well, it's not terribly uplifting do you think?

NICK: Not your style that's true.

FIONA: I can't be your girlfriend Nick, or your mistress.

NICK: We'll agree to disagree then.

(Pause.)

FIONA: Nick —

NICK: Nicholas.

FIONA: Nicholas, I'm married, I took vows, that means something. I have to be productive, use my brain . . .

NICK: Does this seem wrong?

FIONA: Maybe. It doesn't seem right.

NICK: The nuns got you.

FIONA: Clearly.

NICK: Spoken like a true Catholic.

FIONA: And I've learned the art of lying. And I so hate to do it especially with my friends.

NICK: Your hens.

FIONA: God, Stuart calls them that too. Horrors. The only one I'm honest with is Lucy. Maybe I'll get a puppy to share Lucy's burden.

NICK: Excellent. Lucy will be cool with it.

FIONA: Stuart hates dogs.

NICK: He loves dogs. He loves everything. He just got tenure.

(They laugh.)

NICK: I'll be your puppy. *(Kisses her.)*

FIONA: You are a puppy.

NICK: *(Kissing her etc. as he says all this.)* You're a baby lynx, a fisher cat. *(Puts his hand up her skirt causing her to jump away and grab the kitchen knife.)*

NICK: Whoa!

FIONA: You are bad. You are very bad. *(Playfully extends the knife and moves closer to Nick, points it at his throat.)* Marge Warner. Yes or no?

NICK: No. Absolutely not.

FIONA: Sandra Croydon? She recommended you.

NICK: Give me that. *(Grabs the knife.)* Guess I'm lucky you're not the gun type.

FIONA: What type am I, exactly?

NICK: You're the good type.

FIONA: It's always the good girls, right?

NICK: Yup.

FIONA: You like to get the good girls, I get it. Probably the bad ones see right through you.

NICK: Maybe so, Doctor Freud.

FIONA: Maybe this country-boy act is a bit of a put-on too.

NICK: We all just do what we gotta do.

FIONA: Last week I saw your truck at the middle school while I was there and yesterday I saw you in Shaw's.

NICK: Hey, it's a small town.

FIONA: You're following me.

NICK: Sometimes.

You've always been a good girl, right?

FIONA: Until now.

NICK: Am I the worst thing?

FIONA: Well, I wouldn't put it like that but probably, depending. What's your worst thing? Maybe I shouldn't ask.

(Pause.)

NICK: I'm an angel.

(Kisses her, a long kiss.)

FIONA: Nick, we can't do this.

NICK: Yes, we can.

FIONA: It's not right.

NICK: Just one last time. One perfect time.

FIONA: I don't know.

NICK: The last time, I swear.

FIONA: Nick . . .

NICK: You're right. We are getting too close. This will be it.

FIONA: Promise.

NICK: Promise. One last time. Then you can be a good girl again.

FIONA: Nicholas. *(They kiss passionately.)*

(Girl enters and snaps a photo of Nick and Fiona, click, flash.)

GIRL: Remember, I'm not really ten years old. In fact, I think they make a lovely couple.

SCENE FIVE   *Rabbit, Run* by John Updike

Ellie's living room. It's decorated for Christmas.

GIRL: *(In book corner, holds up book.)* December's literary pick is *Rabbit, Run* by John Updike, published in 1960. Mr. Updike once said that "America is a vast conspiracy to make you happy" and Mags needlepointed it on a pillow. The book group conspired to make each other happy too, they were their own little country.

(Ellie and Richard enter Ellie's living room from the upstairs, Richard first. He carries a huge ski bag and two pairs of skis and boots.)

ELLIE: Now, I know you know all this but I'd feel much more comfortable if I could go over it with you, OK?

RICHARD: *(Smiling, deposits large bag on coffee table.)* Fire away.

ELLIE: OK, here's her albuterol, her inhaler. She shouldn't need it because she doesn't have a cold, but it can be exercise induced so . . .

RICHARD: Got it. I'm familiar with the inhaler. I know the drill.

ELLIE: OK, great. Here's her Nasonex for rhinitis, allergies, one pump twice a day. She does it all the time and won't forget. And here's her new allergy medication, the Claritin wasn't really working anymore so Dr. Wolfe changed it. Here's Benydral, Sudafed, just in case, and an epipen, God forbid she eats something new that she's really allergic to.

RICHARD: El, she'll be fine. We're only going away for a week.

ELLIE: But the lodge could be musty or moldy.

RICHARD: We are going to be outside skiing most of the time.

ELLIE: You could take the portable air clearer.

RICHARD: We could. I suppose I could put it in the car . . . *(Starts to head up the stairs.)*

ELLIE: I guess you don't have to.

RICHARD: Probably not necessary.

ELLIE: Yeah. OK, almost done. Here are hand and feet warmers, you know how cold her extremities always get.

RICHARD: I know. Actually I have a lot of those too. They are great.

ELLIE: You do?

RICHARD: Affirmative.

ELLIE: Wow. Oh, Jesus, I almost forgot! Her Lactaid, she can't leave without her Lactaid. Here, I've got some in the kitchen. *(Starts to exit to the kitchen.)*

RICHARD: *(Grabs her arm gently.)* El, I have tons in the car. I'm lactose intolerant too, remember?

ELLIE: Right. *(Disengages her arm and stares at him.)*
(Pause.)

RICHARD: I think we'll be just fine. Promise.
I'll have my own little pharmacy in my camera bag. In fact, I'll stop at CVS and get one of everything . . .

ELLIE: You know, all this is really necessary Richard.
(Isabel enters with her backpack, ski parka, and hat.)

ISABEL: What's necessary?

RICHARD: I was telling your mother that we are going to stop at the drugstore and get one of everything. *(Smiles at Ellie who doesn't smile back.)*

ISABEL: *(Rolling her eyes.)* Mother, I know what to take. *(Suddenly remembering something.)* Oh! Mister Muffin! *(Runs to get her stuffed animal.)*

RICHARD: Mister Muffin. *(He laughs as they watch her run.)*

ELLIE: Call me from the lodge. I've got book group tonight so I'll be here.

RICHARD: What are the women reading now? What's the syllabus?

ELLIE: Updike, *Rabbit, Run.* Mags' choice.

RICHARD: That's a strange choice for Mags. I'd bet she'd think that Harry . . . Harry, right? — was a total asshole.

ELLIE: No, that's the *simple* way to view him. We have to look at the total Harry, in the context of his world . . . he's isolated, alienated, looking for meaning.

RICHARD: Oh, I see. He's looking for something to hang on to.

ELLIE: He leaves his wife for another woman.

RICHARD: He does come back, right?

ELLIE: Reluctantly.

> *(Pause.)*

RICHARD: Have you thought anymore?

ELLIE: No, not really. I've been working on my show.

RICHARD: I'm patient.

ELLIE: Yup.

RICHARD: Just dinner, that's all. Really.

ELLIE: I know.

ISABEL: *(Re-entering, having heard the end of their conversation.)* Mom, wanna come with us?

ELLIE: Oh, honey. I'd love to. I mean, I would but you know I'm a terrible skier, I wouldn't want to slow you down.

ISABEL: You could just read in the lodge like you always do.

ELLIE: Thanks honey, it's really sweet of you but I think I'd better stay home. I have to hang my show in Wilmont.

ISABEL: The Metawhatever series?

RICHARD: Yes, the Metamorphosis series honey.

Well, let's let your Mother metamorphisize away here.

ISABEL: Alright Mom. *(Goes to hug her.)*

I love you. I'll call you tonight. Don't do drugs. *(This line is obviously something they always say to each other.)*

ELLIE: Don't do drugs.

RICHARD: No, drugs.

> *(Isabel and Richard head toward the door.)*

ELLIE: *(Running to the door and yelling.)* NO OFF-TRAIL SKIING!!!

(Fiona and Mags enter through the open door.)

MAGS: Hey, Izzy.

RICHARD: Ladies.

MAGS: Richard.

FIONA: Richard.

RICHARD: Run, Rabbits, Run! *(He exits, skis leading the way.)*

MAGS: Husband number one certainly has his charms.

ELLIE: Yeah.

FIONA: I know it's a cliche but everyone does make mistakes. Whenever I see him he always asks about you and I know it's genuine. It's not like he's a serial womanizer.

ELLIE: Once was enough, trust me! I can't believe what you just said! What sort of message does that send to Isabel? I don't want her to think it's OK. He cheated on me with an over-sexed nurse for Christ's sake. It's like a bad soap opera.

MAGS: Life is a bad soap opera, El.

ELLIE: Whenever we'd run into her, she was always at gallery openings or fund-raisers and she'd rub up against Richard like she was a cat and he was the goddamn scratching post. I used to think, well that's *odd. Odd, schmodd!*

FIONA: Now, don't bite my head off, and I know that Richard was completely in the wrong here but it might be possible for you to start to forgive him, if you wanted to, for Isabel's sake, if you accepted that there might have been something wrong between you that made him, you know, go astray.

ELLIE: Mags, I'm gonna kill her.

MAGS: OK, OK, hold the phone. El, relax. Richard is a complete and total douche bag and I hate him if you hate him and if it weren't for Isabel . . . but there is Isabel. He is a good father, except for this little episode he's been a pretty good husband.

ELLIE: If George cheated on you'd never look back; you wouldn't even bother cutting off his balls.

MAGS: Well, I don't think so actually.

(Pause.)

MAGS: Years ago, centuries ago, very early in our marriage George, well George, he dallied.

ELLIE: George? *(Incredulously.)*

FIONA: Your George?

MAGS: Yep. I was getting my Master's and only part-time at the store; we had just opened — George was there twenty-four seven, you know, the typical story, she was a clerk, she was around all the time, yada, yada.

ELLIE: I never knew that.

MAGS: Don't worry, in a few years we'll all know everything. It's just a matter of time and a few more cases of Beaujolais.

ELLIE: But I think adultery is still pretty much tops on the shit list though — right up there with murder and coveting thy neighbor's livestock or something.

FIONA: Wife, I think.

MAGS: Wife, contractor, whatever.

FIONA: You're not going to start *this* again are you?

MAGS: It's pretty clear you two are having a thing.

FIONA: We aren't having a "thing."

MAGS: So, it's a relationship then?

ELLIE: Mags, lay off.

FIONA: You really are incredible! You think you know everything, you know *nothing*. You're always dictating something — "try and see the total Harry." Well, fuck Harry, he's a selfish pig —

ELLIE: We can't discuss the book, we aren't all here.

MAGS: OK, point well taken, maybe the total-Harry thing was a tad overreaching but I do know this Fiona, I do know that you aren't the first of Mr. LaFontaine's lady-of-the-manor conquests.

FIONA: Lady of the manor — you are such a bullshitter.

MAGS: Just bear with me on this. Do you know Lydia Caselli?

FIONA: Yes, I know Lydia Caselli. What is it with you? Did you hire a private detective Margaret? Is your life so bereft of interest?

ELLIE: Hold the phone girls. Let's take a breath. I'll go get the *glug*.

FIONA: She's not my mother for Christ's sake.

ELLIE: I know honey, but let's hear what she has to say, it might be useful to you.

FIONA: This is such bullshit.

(*Pause.*)

MAGS: OK, Marion Demming told Doris Mayer that Lydia had an affair with Nick when he did their greenhouse two years ago. Now this is book group confidential and does not leave this room. *Cone of Silence.*

ALL: (*Pause, then they make the Cone of Silence triangle over their heads.*)

FIONA: This is bloody crap. How does Marion know it's not just a rumor?

MAGS: Marion heard it from Helen Lassiter the librarian. Apparently, this is so great, Helen, who's in her seventies, walked up to the top floor, you know, the Tower Room, to close the windows like she always does, people open them up cause it's so hot up there —

ELLIE: Mags.

MAGS: So, poor unsuspecting Helen climbs all the way up to the Tower Room, flicks on the ancient light switch, and voila, there are Nick and Lydia, doing it right under the bronze Indian. Helen was so shocked that her heart went berserk and Nick ended up taking her to the ER.

ELLIE: No.

FIONA: That sounds ridiculous.

MAGS: I know, but Marion's son Bruce was the ER doc on call that night and confirmed to his mother that Helen was brought in.

ELLIE: It's a great story. I've always wanted to do it in the library.

MAGS: Floor's too hard. That kind of thing is for college students.

ELLIE: Or if you're totally gone.

MAGS: Yeah, those were the days, I remember once, when I picked up that cowboy —

ELLIE: Please, not the Amtrak story again.

FIONA: And, Mags, why would Doris tell you anyway, and why now?

MAGS: Doris and my mother went to Vassar together. I give Doris pre-pub copies of books occasionally and she's very grateful.

FIONA: The whole story sounds loony to me. I could use some of your glug Ellie.

MAGS: Me too! Fuck! I can't drink! I hate the word . . . glug.

(Doorbell rings, Ellie presses screen, sees who it is and clicks it off quickly.)

ELLIE: Fi, it's Stu. *(Fiona and Mags stand up, alarmed.)* Does he know you're here? Are you here? Should I let him in?

FIONA: *(Very flustered.)* Yes, yes, let him in, of course, he knows I have book group tonight. He thought I was at a workshop all day but I decided to take Lucy for a long walk in the woods and I only just got back. *(Fiona and Mags frantically neaten up.)*

(Ellie opens door.)

STUART: *(Sees the commotion.)* Ladies, there's no fire! Eleanor, Margaret. Margaret, Eleanor. Fi. I was a bit worried so I went to the school to look for you but it seems your workshop isn't until tomorrow so . . .

FIONA: Yes, I thought it was today but then I found out it was tomorrow so I did some errands and I guess I should have checked in.

ELLIE: And Fi was a great help to me with my Victorian gingerbread house. A real artist with the gummy worms.

STUART: Yes, lovely, well. Anyway, I was trying to find you Fi because when I got home I noticed that Lucy was acting very odd —

MAGS: Oh, no, not Lucy!!!

STUART: — she didn't greet me in the kitchen like she usually does, she was very lethargic so I ran her over to the vet.

MAGS: Oh no. Is she OK? What did Tom say?

STUART: Yes, yes, she'll be fine, but Tom wants to keep her overnight for observation. I did leave a note but I wanted to tell you in person.

FIONA: That was very sweet of you.

STUART: Well, I know how you love poor old Lucy. *(To the ladies.)* Goodness knows she's number one in our house. *(Laughs.)*

ELLIE: Congratulations, about the tenure.

MAGS: Yes . . .

FIONA: Stu . . . *(Whispers.)*

MAGS: Stu, jolly good show and all that.

STUART: Well, I think we're all relieved. And we couldn't take Fiona away from her book group. Fiona tells me you're reading Updike this month. Harry's quite the anti-hero, isn't he? Harry Angstrom wasn't it?

MAGS: Very good —

FIONA: Stu.

MAGS: Stu. Didn't know physics profs. were particularly interested in contemporary fiction per se.

STUART: Well, it's all about relationships now isn't it, when you really think about it? Maybe you ladies can discover Harry's redeeming qualities. I failed to.

ELLIE: Stuart, can I get you a drink? Tea? Coffee?

STUART: That would be smashing. And a visit to the loo would be most helpful.

ELLIE: Be my guest. *(Motions him toward the bathroom upstage left.)*
    (When they are gone.)

MAGS: Gingerbread house? Gummy worms?

FIONA: I was doing errands today, I went to the library.

MAGS: The Tower Room?

FIONA: *Mags!*

MAGS: But I thought you took Lucy for a long walk?

FIONA: Yes, after I did my errands.

MAGS: So she was OK then?

FIONA: Yes, she was fine.

MAGS: Poor old Lucy really took a dive, in what, an hour or so?

FIONA: What is this, am I on trial? Maybe you should cut down on your cop-show obsession.

MAGS: What cop-show obsession?

FIONA: We all know you TiVo all the cops shows

MAGS: I give up.

FIONA: He was checking up on me.

MAGS: I think George and I have some "errands" this evening —

FIONA: *(Stands up.)* I'm serious Mags, I'm getting really sick of —
(Doorbell rings, Ellie and Stuart come back in.)

STUART: It's Grand Central here.

ELLIE: *(Looks at screen.)* Alison.

ALISON: Gosh, it's deadly out there! *(Richard and Isabel follow behind her.)* I went off the road! But, I was rescued, thank God Richard was there! I have to call for a tow.

RICHARD: I found her in a snowbank near Daley's farm.

STUART: Here Alison, use my cell.

ALISON: I tried to slow down and I slid right off, it must have been black ice.

RICHARD: We were on our way back to pick up Mr. Muffin and I recognized her car. Ellie, I'll put some salt on the driveway and Izzy and I can head back to my apartment. It's too icy to travel tonight.

ISABEL: Daddy, you can't go back out. It's too dangerous. Mommy, he can stay here, can't he, please.

ELLIE: Well . . .

ISABEL: The guest room is all clean. Alyssa and I made the beds when you asked us.

ALISON: Maybe we should *all* stay!

ISABEL: Like a slumber party!

ELLIE: At least I've got the glug.
(It's tense.)

MAGS: I'd better call George. *(Clutches stomach.)*
Ouch. Gosh that hurt. I think my water broke. Get the sheets. *(All eyes turn toward her.)* Just kidding! Couldn't resist. This is just so Agatha Christie. Will there be a mur-der, I wond-da??

ALISON: I told John I'd be home by ten! I'm the only one who can do the voices in Harry Potter!

MAGS: The twins will survive.

ISABEL: This is so cool.

ELLIE: I'm going to put everyone to work. Everyone close your eyes.

MAGS: I hate games like this.

ELLIE: *(On her way to kitchen.)* Just shut up for one minute and close your eyes.

(Everyone obeys, and Ellie quickly returns with a partially decorated very large gingerbread house, and she sets it on the table.)

ELLIE: TA-DA.

(ALL ooo and ahhhh.)

FIONA: It's fantastic! I've never seen anything like it!! *(This is the first time she has seen it — Stuart looks at her, Mags glares at her.)* Ellie, how did you do it, it's amazing, the windows are extraordinary!

ELLIE: Fi, *you* were such a big help, Fi.

(Uneasy pause.)

STUART: Guess she had a good contractor.

FIONA: That's right, I was helping.

MAGS: Yes, all afternoon!

FIONA: It was so much fun to decorate.

STUART: Yes, with fun like this why would you want to do anything else?

(All stare at Stuart.)

STUART: I mean, why *would* you want to do anything else, Fiona? You could make a whole village of gingerbread houses now couldn't you? You could make a church, a bakery, a massage parlor, the possibilities are endless aren't they?

RICHARD: Isabel, let's get our stuff out of the car for the slumber party.

STUART: Or maybe Mags has a good idea, doesn't Mags always have a good idea, a *better* idea. What say you Mags, what are your ideas about having a really smashing time?

MAGS: I've got a really great idea, Stu, it's Stu, right?

STUART: Stuart, actually.

MAGS: Stuart, why don't we repair to the kitchen with Mr. Updike and the glug. *(Holds up* Rabbit, Run.*)*

ALISON: John Updike? In the kitchen? That's so funny! Sounds like we're playing *Clue*. I suspect John Updike in the kitchen with the glug!

MAGS: C'mon Al, let's blow this pop stand. *(Mags and Alison exit to kitchen.)*

STUART: And I suspect my very own Fiona with the hired help in the . . . where was it dear?

FIONA: Stuart, you're acting positively insane.

STUART: Insane am I? I'm the crazy one, is that it? My wife is running around, lying to me, going on about *gingerbread houses,* and I'm the insane one, right. I may be a bit dense but I'm not a moron.

FIONA: Can't we talk about this at home, Stu? You're embarrassing me . . .

MAGS: *(Entering from kitchen.)* Stu —

STUART: Stuart!

MAGS: Stu —

STUART: STUART!!!!

MAGS: Stuart, can you possibly spare your wife in the kitchen? We need some help with the glug.

(Mags and Fiona exit to kitchen.)

STUART: *(To Ellie.)* Before we were married, when we were living together, she had one last fling with her old boyfriend, he was a freak, an old hippie, practically a felon. I forgave her, she promised me, but now, I'm not going to let it happen again.

ELLIE: You didn't have to humiliate her!

STUART: You women are truly amazing! Aren't I the one who's being served up the ultimate humiliation?

ELLIE: I really don't know Stuart.

STUART: Hiding behind the old book group "cone of silence" are we? *(Pause, makes Cone of Silence with his hands over his head.)* Maybe you can give me some answers.

ELLIE: Like I said, I don't know.

STUART: Don't know what? Just the fact you say you don't know when I haven't asked you anything specific proves my point.

ELLIE: You're acting like a lunatic.

STUART: Maybe Richard would like to know about that graduate student you had holed up here this summer. What was he, twenty-two?

ELLIE: You are so full of shit Stuart.

STUART: Were you playing Mrs. Robinson or was it more of a *Tea and Sympathy* kind of situation? Now, was he into the spanking thing or was that more your bag? I guess it ended badly when he cuffed you to the bed and took off.

ELLIE: What are you, writing a novel or something?

STUART: Luckily you had Mags on speed dial. Thank God Izzy didn't waltz in. I'm not being judgmental. I'll keep my mouth shut if you tell me just how long Fiona has been —

(Isabel and Richard enter from outside.)

ISABEL: Mommy, mommy, the Nasonex froze in the car.

RICHARD: I told Isabel that we could defrost and reconstitute, kind of like a marriage.

ELLIE: Oh, dear God. *(Sinks onto the couch.)*

RICHARD: Everything OK?

STUART: Yes, Ellie and I were just reminiscing about last summer. How did things work out with that graduate student you were putting up?

ISABEL: Liam?

STUART: I guess.

ISABEL: He was an awesome Frisbee player but he never did the dishes.

(Doorbell rings.)

ELLIE: I'll get it.

(Runs to door, Ellie presses screen, Nick's face appears.)

RICHARD: Need some help with traffic control?

ELLIE: Oh, what the hell. *(Opens door.)*

(Nick enters.)

NICK: Howdy.

ISABEL: Hi.

NICK: *(To Ellie.)* Your walk could use some salt. Almost took a header. Don't wanna get sued by the UPS or anything.

ISABEL: It's Mr. La, Mr. La Fountain I think.

NICK: Close enough, smart kid. *(Ruffles her hair.)* Got all your marbles in there?

(Steps into the room, gets a good look at Stuart who takes a good look at him and heads for the kitchen. Presses on the swinging door but it doesn't budge. Presses harder and as he does so, Mags, Alison, and Fiona enter, smashing Stuart with the swinging door, who reels back holding his head.)

MAGS: Here comes the *glug!* *(Sees Stuart.)* Oh, sorry, sorry. *(Has tray with pitcher of glug and glasses.)*

ALISON: And the Bouche de Noel!!! *(Brings in the chocolate log on a plate.)*

NICK: Ladies. Lovely ladies.

FIONA: *Nick!* *(Fiona has tray with plates and forks.)*

RICHARD: What's going on?

NICK: Service call. Fiona.

(All freeze.)

ELLIE: Nick, to what do we owe the honor?

NICK: Alison called me called on my cell and asked for a tow job. *(Laughs at his own joke, he is a little tipsy.)* Whoops, sorry. *(Gestures toward Isabel.)*

ALISON: I'm sorry, Fiona, he was the only one who answered his phone. *(Scampers over to the coffee table to deliver the Bouche de Noel.)*

NICK: *(To Alison.)* The good news is that *your* car is out but now my truck is stuck. But, no sweat, cause Honk is coming over with his big rig.

ALISON: Honk?

NICK: My big brother. It's Hank, but we call him Honk.

ALISON: I love that, Honk!!! Nick, I'm so sorry about your truck.

NICK: No biggie. Honk'll get me out. Been trying to keep warm out there. *(Holds up a flask and takes a swig.)* Mother's milk. *(Winks in Isabel's direction.)*

ALISON: You must be freezing.

ELLIE: C'mon, I'll give you some coffee.

NICK: Yeah, I could use some joe.

ELLIE: OK, anybody else? *(Sees Stuart, still nursing his head.)* Stuart, a little drinky?

STUART: Scotch on the rocks would be great, with ice.

FIONA: Stu, I'll get you something for your head. *(Exits into kitchen.)*

ELLIE: Richard?

RICHARD: I'll stick with the glug.

(Ellie exits to kitchen.)

MAGS: *(Hisses.)* Richard, keep him in the living room. Alison, I need your help.

ALISON: *(To the men.)* Oh, no. I forgot the schlag for the Bouche de Noel. *(To Nick.)* Schlag, it's German for whipped cream.

NICK: I love whipped cream. *(Nick beams at her as she exits to the kitchen, Mags is holding the door for her.)*

(Stuart heads for the swinging door, but Richard puts his arms out, blocking the way and motions for Stuart to sit in one of the chairs flanking the couch. Stuart acquiesces and sinks into his chair as Richard sits in the other chair. Nick settles in the middle of the couch. The three men size each other up.)

NICK: Any takers for this bouche thing? *(He puts a piece on a plate and digs in.)*

RICHARD: I'm all set.

(Alison enters with a bowl of schlag and a big spoon.)

ALISON: Who will partake? Just a dollop??

NICK: Count me in.

(Alison moves toward Nick to serve him the whipped cream, Nick pats the couch and motions for her to sit down, as Mags enters.)

MAGS: *Alison,* I think something's ringing in your purse.

(Alison sets the schlag on the coffee table near Stuart and runs back into the kitchen.)

ALISON: *(To Nick.)* Enjoy! I hate it when it rings!

NICK: Stu, pass the schlag?

STUART: Sure.

(Stares at him, stands up and starts to reach for the bowl of schlag when

Richard intervenes, grabs the bowl, and hands it to Nick while pressing on Stuart's shoulder and pushing him back into the chair.)

RICHARD: Hey, Nick, I guess I'll have a piece of the bouche.

NICK: All the way?

RICHARD: Yeah, the works.

NICK: You got it.

(Nick prepares the dessert for Richard while Richard keeps an eye on Stuart. Nick gives Richard the plate. Nick and Richard eat while Stuart glowers as the music comes on, lights go down.)

END OF ACT I

ACT II

SCENE ONE

A half an hour later, Stuart and Richard are in Ellie's living room. Pause. Stuart and Richard look at one another.

RICHARD: *(Looking toward the bathroom stage left.)* You OK in there?

NICK: Oh, God. *(Comes into room zipping up his fly.)* Hey, Richard, you're a urologist, right?

RICHARD: Board certified.

NICK: You any good?

RICHARD: I'm OK. *(Suspicious.)*

NICK: *(Reaching for his fly.)* I've got somethin' I want you to check out. *(Drops his pants revealing Christmas boxers.)* Hey, just yankin' your chain. Pretty cool shorts, huh? 'Tis the season and all that. You're a good guy. C'mon, let's go get that coffee.

RICHARD: I'll get it. *(Pushes swinging door open and pops his head in.)*

MAGS: *(From inside the kitchen.)* RICHARD!!!

RICHARD: They're working on it. Pretty brutal weather, huh Nick?

NICK: Hell I've seen worse, a lot worse. We'll definitely get some serious snow.

RICHARD: You've had a busy night.

NICK: People know I got my truck. All they need is my number. *(Holds up cell.)*

STUART: I bet a lot of people have your number.

NICK: Sure, like you.

RICHARD: You a big skier, huh, Nick?

NICK: Shit, no. Where's that coffee? *(Heads toward kitchen.)*

RICHARD: *(Blocking his way.)* It's coming! *(Looking in kitchen.)* Regular? Decafe? Latte?

NICK: *(Peers outside.)* Oh yeah it's really coming down. Little snow, big snow.

STUART: Beg pardon?

NICK: You know, little snow, small flakes, equals big snow, lots of it.

RICHARD: I didn't get it either.

ISABEL: I got it.

NICK: She's a firecracker. Hope that school doesn't make her stupid.

RICHARD: You're preaching to the choir.

NICK: Amen.

ISABEL: Daddy, look. *(Holds up Christmas stocking.)*

RICHARD: *(To Isabel.)* Izzy, did you make this for me?

ISABEL: Yeah, Mommy threw your fuzzy one out.

RICHARD: So, you grew up around here, didn't you Nick?

NICK: Born and raised. I'm the real deal. Live free or die.

STUART: What?

NICK: Live free or die.

ISABEL: Like on the license plates.

STUART: Ah, right.

RICHARD: You've probably seen a lot of changes in this town.

NICK: Nah, not too much. Just more money. More people from the city.

RICHARD: More work for you though.

NICK: Sometimes. But seems these days every jerk with a pickup thinks he's a contractor. It's hard to get those jobs. I've a bid on a barn renovation out to Slate Hill. Flatlanders.

STUART: Flatlanders?

NICK: New Yorkers. Cow stalls to artist studios. He's a writer. She's an "artiste." Looms and shit, kind of half-assed.

STUART: Sounds right up your alley.

NICK: I'll tell you one thing, though. The bars were better in the old days. They're no real bars in town anymore. They've got artsy-fartsy music, frigging blue martinis, whatever that is. The real bars are all out of town. Coffee yet?

RICHARD: Lemme check. *(Goes through swinging door and comes right out.)*

MAGS: RICHARD!!!

RICHARD: Too many cooks in the pot, or something.

NICK: What?

RICHARD: Hey, isn't there a strip club in Barton?

NICK: That's what I hear.

STUART: Is that legal?

NICK: Legal. Hell, yeah. Live free or die Stuart.
  (Pause.)

ISABEL: Look, the snow is like, little balls now.

NICK: That's hail.

ISABEL: I know that.

RICHARD: I hate hail.

ISABEL: It's really coming down. I can hear it!

STUART: Quick, go tell your mother. *(Isabel exits.)*

ISABEL: Mommy, mommy, come and see the hail!
  (Ellie and Mags enter.)

ELLIE: Ohmygod, it is.

MAGS: Hail, that sucks.

RICHARD: Lucky to be snug as a bug in here, huh Izzy?

(Alison and Fiona enter.)

ALISON: Oh, horrible . . . hail.

ISABEL: Snug as a bug! C'mon Daddy, let's sing *our Jingle Bells.* "Crashing through the snow, on a one horse open sleigh, o'er the fields we go, laughing all the way. Bells on bobtail ring, making spirits bright, oh what fun it is to laugh and sing a sleighing song tonight. Oh, Jingle Bells, Santa Smells, Easter's on it's way, oh what fun it is to ride in a three-door Chevrolet!

(Nick playfully goes for Stuart's drink.)

STUART: Stop it!

NICK: Cool out, Stu.

STUART: Bugger off!!

NICK: Just fooling with you Stu. *(Reaches again for Stu's scotch.)*

(Stuart gets angry and lunges at him. Fight ensues. Alison drags Fiona back to kitchen, Mags tries to break up the fight, Isabel jumps into Richard's arms. Stuart loses his balance, grabs Mags and flips her over the couch. Nick grabs Stuart's drink and heads up the stairs. Fiona comes running in, Alison peeks out from the kitchen. All freeze.)

GIRL: *(Steps forward.)* This is what happened — Honk came and pulled Nick out with his big rig, Alison got home in time to do the voices in Harry Potter, Fiona drove Stuart home. Mags drove herself home of course and Richard slept in the guest room, we think.

SCENE TWO

Fiona and Stuart enter their house.

STUART: *(Menacing and drunk, hisses at her.)* This is what you're risking our marriage over, this Neanderthal? Jesus, Fiona, if you're going to cheat on me at least you could do with with a — I don't know, are you blind?

FIONA: Stop it Stu, you're knackered.

STUART: I'm not knickered, I mean kockered, I'm not knick-kockered. Jesus, you aren't going to do this to me again. You'd better figure this out, Fiona, I mean it, figure it out soon, or I'm gone. I mean it this time.

FIONA: We can talk about this later. You're drunk —

STUART: Maybe I should go, maybe this is a sign. Why does this keep happening?

FIONA: Stuart, nothing's happening. Please.

STUART: Do you think I'm a complete idiot?

FIONA: I didn't mean that. I mean, please, let's talk in the morning.

STUART: I don't want to be married to me, I mean you, anymore if you don't want me to be married to me, I mean you married to me.

FIONA: Stuart, I do want to be married to you. Shush, I do.

STUART: What is it then, Fiona? Why are you doing this? It isn't a parlor game, this is it, this is our life. Don't be careless with it.

FIONA: I'm not Stu, I'm not.

STUART: Don't be careless with me.

FIONA: I won't, I won't.

(Girl comes on stage and takes photo, click, flash.)

SCENE THREE   *Madame Bovary* by Gustave Flaubert

Lights up on Ellie's living room. A few weeks later.

GIRL: January. A new year. The book for January is *Madame Bovary* by Gustave Flaubert, copyright 1857. Emma Bovary wanted a Technicolor life and she got a black-and-white one. She thought her life would be like those romantic books she read. My mother told me that there are two things in a woman's life that are even better than books — the moment of giving birth and a perfect love affair. I never understood that until I was much, much older.

(Ellie and Nick enter coming down the stairs from upstairs. Ellie carries an iPod and Nick carries his clipboard.)

NICK: The thing is husbands are good in the short term, but they can't handle your long-term needs. Now I'm talking about the house here, you know. Well, you've got my number.

ELLIE: Yeah, I've got your number all right.

(Doorbell rings, Ellie presses the video screen, Richard's face pops into view.)
(Richard enters.)

ELLIE: My late husband.

RICHARD: I know, I know, I'm sorry. *(Doesn't sees Nick.)* It was this woman at my office. She made me examine her over and over again. Turns out she had this infection you had — *(Sees Nick.)*

ELLIE: Richard, I've got book group and I've got to get ready. Nick, please send me an estimate on the bathroom. *(Glaring at Richard.)* I'll get Isabel. *(She exits through the swinging door.)*

NICK: Good idea, that security system.

Hear about the Sullivan murder up to Lansfield?

RICHARD: Yeah, that was a surprise for around here, wasn't it?

NICK: Well, hell, that shit happens every few years. Some yahoo gets tanked and finds his wife in bed with another man.

RICHARD: I believe she was in bed with her stepfather.

NICK: Stepfather, father, these things are always family related.

RICHARD: Pretty nasty.

NICK: Regular soap opera.

RICHARD: Nick, do you play poker?

NICK: Does a bear shit in the woods?

RICHARD: Great. I'm getting together a group of guys to play every Thursday at my place in town, wanna come?

NICK: I'll be there. Bring your paycheck.

RICHARD: Seven-thirty. You know where I live? *(Nick looks at him.)* Right, stupid question, you know where everyone lives.

(Isabel enters.)

NICK: Howdy.

ISABEL: *(Eyes him warily.)* Hi.

NICK: Little snow, big snow.

ISABEL: Right, I get it.

NICK: I told ya, she's a firecracker.

RICHARD: OK, gotta skedaddle.

(Enter Ellie.)

ELLIE: Izzy wait, here's your Lactaid.

RICHARD: Nick, later. See you soon.

(Isabel and Richard exit.)

ELLIE: Off to the movies.

NICK: The movies. *(Moves toward couch.)*

ELLIE: Yeah.

NICK: Two hours. *(Checks out the firmness of the couch pillows and sits down, makes himself comfortable.)*

(Ellie glares at him.)

NICK: Okeydokey, I've got my assignment. *(Gets up from couch.)*

(Doorbell rings.)

ELLIE: *(Checks her screen and sees Mags, Alison, and Fiona.)* Wow, all of them at once.

NICK: Everything all at once.

(Ellie opens door.)

ELLIE: Come on in girls.

MAGS: *(Entering first.)* Jesus, Ellie, it's raining cats, dogs, and illegal immigrants out there.

NICK: Mrs. Savikas.

MAGS: Mr. LaFontaine, what are you doing here?

(Ellie puts her arms around Mags and Alison and purposely walks them away from Fiona and Nick.)

NICK: Hey, Fiona.

FIONA: Nick.

NICK: How's it goin'?

FIONA: OK. And you?

NICK: Can't complain. Whatcha reading tonight?

FIONA: *Madame Bovary.*

NICK: French.

FIONA: Yes, Flaubert.

NICK: Happy New Year and all that.

FIONA: Yes, Happy New Year to you too.

NICK: Made your resolutions?

FIONA: Not yet, you?

NICK: Well, you know, drink more, sleep less. Nah, I don't believe in them. Nobody keeps them, they're like diets. *(Pause.)* Haven't seen you since the night of the big storm.

FIONA: That's right.

NICK: I think I left some cans of polyurethane in your basement. Can I come over tomorrow and pick 'em up?

FIONA: I don't think that's a good idea.

I'll just put them on the front porch.

NICK: Whoa.

FIONA: I've got to Nick. Like I said, we're getting too close.

NICK: Can I check in on you sometime?

FIONA: I don't know.

NICK: Gotta keep my eye on you, ya' know.

FIONA: I'll be OK.

NICK: Stay away from knives, OK? Lay off the "crudité."

FIONA: OK, I will.

NICK: You and me Fi, old souls. *(He exits.)*

(Mags and Ellie and Alison enter.)

MAGS: Attention uber feminists. Let's start the meeting. Would you like some tea? Ellie is pouring, Darjeeling, the fucking champagne of teas. Fiona, you OK?

FIONA: Just fine.

ELLIE: Mags, maybe you should make a resolution to clean up your mouth before the baby comes.

MAGS: Just pour the tea, love.

ALISON: Good grief! I almost forgot. I brought my bourbon balls. Mags, you can eat them! The bourbon, you know the alcohol in the bourbon bakes out but the flavor remains! Fiona?

MAGS: Fiona, you OK?

FIONA: I'm OK, I think.

MAGS: How's Nick? Is it over?

FIONA: I don't know.

(Ellie and Mags sit staring at her.)

MAGS: Sweetie, he's not the cure.

ELLIE: We have something that might help.

FIONA: What?

ELLIE: When he was here I taped our conversation on Isabel's iPod.

ALISON: Sounds creepy.

MAGS: This will help, Fi, it really will. You have to think that you've been in a fever, delirious.

ALISON: Are we doing an exorcism?

ELLIE: Kind of.

MAGS: Yes, exactly.

Hit it El.

(Turns it on, we hear Nick's voice.)

NICK: The steam attachment is really worth it especially in the winter. Oh, shit, I got gravel in your tub.

ELLIE: Don't worry, that's easy to clean.

NICK: Shoulda taken off my boots.

ELLIE: It's fine.

NICK: This you? Look at those big peepers.

ELLIE: I was so serious.

NICK: Isabel looks like you.

ELLIE: A little, yes.

NICK: But she's a new soul. You're an old soul.

ELLIE: Really, how can you tell?

NICK: Look, that expression is from another time. That little girl is tapped into some pretty deep old knowledge. And you still have that in you somewhere.

ELLIE: Gee.

NICK: Yep. Unexplored territory.

ELLIE: Wow.

NICK: I can spot an old soul. Not many around.

ELLIE: Oh, I don't know.

NICK: Really, it's a pretty special thing. The trick is to access those old truths.

ELLIE: Sounds difficult.

NICK: Gotta be willing to take a plunge.

(Ellie turns off the iPod.)

MAGS: I'll give him credit — he's got an angle.

ALISON: That is a dangerous man.

ELLIE: And the thing was, Fiona, I started to buy it. For a few seconds I believed him.

He needs his fix.

MAGS: Great bourbon balls, Al. Bourbony.

(Girl walks in.)

FIONA: Play it again.

(Ellie starts the iPod again and we hear the tape. Girl takes a photo, click, flash, as the women listen to the tape again.)

SCENE FOUR

Ellie's living room stage right, Fiona's kitchen stage left. Richard and Ellie enter from outside.

RICHARD: We had a very nice dinner I'd say, wouldn't you.

ELLIE: Don't tell Isabel I ate venison.

RICHARD: Your secret is safe with me my dear. *All* your secrets.

ELLIE: I have no secrets.

RICHARD: Everyone has secrets. I think our secrets bind us to one another.

ELLIE: Well, I don't know about that.

Grappa?

RICHARD: Nectar of the Gods, bring it on.

(Ellie exits to the kitchen, Richard checks himself out in the reflection of a

silver bowl on the side table. Lights down at Ellie's, up at Fiona's. Fiona and Stuart are in the kitchen. There is an urn on top of a milk crate, two lighted candles flank the urn and there are some dog toys next to the urn. Stuart is holding a square box.)

FIONA: Do you have them?

STUART: Yes, right here. *(Points to box.)*

FIONA: Oh, poor Lucy. *(Starts to cry.)*

STUART: Sweetheart, we can do this later if you want. I'll just put Lucy —

FIONA: No, everything's ready. I can do this. *(Reaches for box and Stuart gives it to her.)*

STUART: Are you sure?

FIONA: Yes. Now, I thought that as I, I, *pour,* we could recite "The Lord Is My Shepherd."

(Fiona starts to pour the ashes into the urn and begins to recite but Stuart sneezes.)

STUART: Sorry. OK. *(They start reciting again.)* The Lord Is My Shepherd, oh I get it, *shepherd,* smashing! *(They start again.)*

The Lord is my shepherd,

I shall not want;

He makes me lie down in green pastures.

He leads me beside still waters;

He restores my soul.

He leads me in paths of righteousness

for His name's sake . . . *(Continue if necessary.)*

(As they recite lights go down, lights up on Ellie's living room.)

RICHARD: Look, sometimes people just want to have a good time. They don't want the evening to de-volve into a big political discussion where people get overheated and say things they'll regret later.

ELLIE: But that's what adults do — since time began, they sit around the proverbial fire and sound off. But not these adults, no, the only thing they are willing to have an opinion about is whether or not they *love* Meryl Streep or think she's *too technical.*

(Ellie and Richard say "too technical" together and laugh. Lights down, up at Fiona's.)

FIONA AND STUART: *Amen.*

(Stuart puts empty box in the kitchen garbage.)

FIONA: And I have a few of her favorite things — *(Holds them up and gives them to Stuart one by one.)* her ladybug, her pull toy, and her wiggly-giggly ball — *(Fiona shakes the ball back and forth, which causes it to make noise, which causes her to cry some more.)* and I thought that as you put them in the urn — *(Stuart starts putting them in.)* — not yet, Stuart, the music — I'm going to play one of her favorite arias.

(Fiona goes to the CD player and puts Maria Callas singing "Casta Diva" from the opera Norma *on full blast. Stuart takes two solemn paces toward the urn and puts the toys in the urn one by one and has trouble fitting the wiggly-giggly ball in as the lights fade. The music continues and the lights come up on Ellie's living room.* Norma *is also playing in Ellie's house. Ellie enters carrying the bottle of Grappa.)*

RICHARD: Ah, Maria Callas. What an instrument.

ELLIE: At some point I always think of that shit Onasis when I hear this.

RICHARD: Maybe her suffering made her sing better.

ELLIE: Suffering. I don't recommend it. *(She turns Maria Callas off.)*

RICHARD: You know I've been reading this book, the one I told you about at dinner.

ELLIE: The Zeus energy thing or something.

RICHARD: *Iron John.* I think it's fantastic.

I know you think it's a load of crap and some of it is I guess but the guy draws on ancient myths and I think I hit on something.

ELLIE: As long as that's the only thing you're hitting on.

RICHARD: Look, I don't want to make excuses for my past, my past —

ELLIE: Unfaithfulness.

RICHARD: Unfaithfulness. But the first step toward solving a problem is naming the problem.

ELLIE: Yes, we've traveled Via Unfaithful before Richard, many times.

RICHARD: So, we've identified the problem.

ELLIE: No, you've identified the problem. Which makes sense because it's your problem. I don't have that particular problem.

RICHARD: Right. OK, then the next step toward solving the problem is deeply understanding what's causing the problem.

ELLIE: Why does Richard wander, whither does he go?

RICHARD: What drives me to be unfaithful to the woman I love, to the woman that I'm wildly attracted to.

ELLIE: Do I know this woman?

RICHARD: Bear with me. According to this book, and I really buy it, all these years I've been suffering from father hunger.

ELLIE: Father hunger?

RICHARD: What I mean is that I never got enough of my father. Remember he took that job overseas when I was twelve? At that point I was in the process of, spiritually speaking, moving from my mother's house to my father's house.

ELLIE: The house of Daddy Dick?

RICHARD: Into the realm of the father — toward the Zeus energy. Suddenly there was this tremendous black hole and I fell down it. According to the author a boy can't fully become a man until he makes a clean break with the mother and bonds with his father. The Apache Indians actually kidnap their boys at age twelve and the boys don't see their mothers for a year and a half while the men are initiating them into manhood.

ELLIE: Wow, I'm glad Isabel is a girl.

RICHARD: And I lived in an all-female household!

ELLIE: But you loved your mother and sisters.

RICHARD: Yes, of course I did. But that's not what I needed then. I needed a father or an uncle to welcome me into the ancient, instinctive male world. My mother couldn't do that for me.

ELLIE: But this father hunger thing, how does this relate to your, like adultery thing.

RICHARD: Because I didn't go through this male initiation I got stuck. I got stuck in kind of an eternal adolescence.

ELLIE: So you were stunted, that's what you mean, developmentally.

RICHARD: Yes, I was still spiritually in my mother's house! That's why I kept going back to the source of the Great Mother, as it were, to fill up my emptiness!

ELLIE: So, you've been like a serial adulterer because you've been stuck in phase one.

RICHARD: Yes, yes!!! What I really need to do is to discover my own maleness; move into my father's house!

ELLIE: Would that be chez Daddy Dick?

RICHARD: Ellie, I'm serious. This is a breakthrough moment for me! I've diagnosed the illness and I'm going for the cure.

ELLIE: So, what are you you're gonna do? Start an all-male book group?

RICHARD: More like a poker game to start. Ellie, I want to re-commit to you. Officially, in a re-commitment ceremony.

ELLIE: Maybe *you* should be committed.

RICHARD: I want a big celebration, very traditional.

ELLIE: You're kidding, right?

RICHARD: I'm dead serious. I feel completely re-oriented.

ELLIE: Richard, this is very sweet but maybe we should let sleeping dogs lie here. I mean, we seem to be having a very amicable separation.

RICHARD: I don't want to live in a half-assed way! You deserve to live with my total devotion! It's not right for Isabel to live like this. Listen, I know you're scared. I know you're probably thinking that I'll be good for a few months and then go back to my old habits. No, I want to be man enough to resist temptation when it presents itself. That's the point! Anything goes doesn't work anymore.

ELLIE: So basically you're saying that you are ready to grow up?

(Lights down, up on Fiona's kitchen.)

FIONA: *(Holding the urn.)* I remember all those years she chased squirrels and chipmunks and never caught one but never stopped trying.

STUART: She never gave up.

FIONA: She was the happiest creature I ever knew.

STUART: She was indeed.

FIONA: She was so much more than a dog.

STUART: Dear old Lucy. I will miss her, truly.

(Fiona kisses the top of the wiggly-giggly ball in the urn and hands the urn to Stuart, who, following suit, kisses the ball and heads for the garbage.)

FIONA: *Stu!!* (Puts her hands out and Stuart gives her the urn. She puts it on the top shelf of her kitchen shelves.)

STUART: Are you homesick?

FIONA: No, not so much anymore. I'm settling in.

STUART: Would you be happier if we went home?

FIONA: You just got tenure.

STUART: Yes.

FIONA: I thought you loved it here.

STUART: I do.

FIONA: Is there a reason you would want to go home?

STUART: Not exactly.

FIONA: Not exactly?

STUART: I like it here, yes.

FIONA: It's completely over Stu.

STUART: Thank God.

FIONA: How did you know?

STUART: Henry saw you together at the Lakeville diner. *(Pause.)* Are the chips there any good? Are they crisp?

(Lights down. Up on Ellie's living room.)

RICHARD: Yes, I'm ready to grow up.

ELLIE: Why is this night different from any other night? *Mah nish tah-nah ha-lie-la ha-zeh? (The Hebrew phonetic translation.)*

RICHARD: You have to make a leap of faith honey.

ELLIE: Richard, I just don't know. My leaping days may be over.

RICHARD: Then you are ready to die! Are you ready to die?

ELLIE: Heavy artillery Richard, you've got the big guns.

RICHARD: It's all about starting over. Every day we start over.

ELLIE: More Grappa? *(Holds her empty glass out.)*

> *(Lights down, up on Fiona's kitchen.)*

STUART: Your friend Mags had a talk with me, did you know?

FIONA: No, I didn't.

STUART: Yes, she talked to me like, what's the expression, like a Dutch Uncle, right after that dreadful night when I said that if you didn't want to be married to me I didn't want to be married to me either or something like that.

FIONA: God.

STUART: She asked me to consider if I loved you enough to fight for you or if I would just prefer to see you tarred and feathered and hung in the public square.

FIONA: What did you say?

STUART: That a large A on your bosom would be sufficient.

> *(They laugh. Lights down, up on Ellie's living room.)*

ELLIE: You are wearing that blue shirt.

RICHARD: I know.

ELLIE: I love that shirt.

> *(Lights down, up on Fiona's kitchen.)*

FIONA: Let's do something crazy. What's the first crazy thing that comes to your mind?

STUART: Bungee jumping.

FIONA: Crazy realistic.

STUART: Let's jump in the car and drive until we get to the ocean.

FIONA: Polar bear swim!

STUART: I'm in! But, first I have a better idea.

> *(He kisses her.)*

FIONA: That's a really crazy idea.

STUART: Totally insane.

> *(They really kiss. Lights down, up on Ellie's living room.)*

RICHARD: Ellie, can you, can you take this leap of faith? Can you?

> *(Lights down, up on Fiona's kitchen.)*

FIONA: I think that Lucy is here with us.

STUART: I certainly hope not. I don't think there's room in our bed for more than two of us. Especially *this* bed. *(Referring to dog bed).*
(They kiss.)
(Lights down, up on Ellie's living room.)
ELLIE: OK, hell's bells, I'll leap.
(Throws empty Grappa glass over the couch and Richard and Ellie kiss.)
(Girl comes on stage and takes a photo, click, flash, click, flash, of each kissing couple.)

SCENE FIVE   *Excellent Women* by Barbara Pym

Ellie's living room, decorated with pink balloons. Presents wrapped in pink are on the coffee table. Early February.

GIRL: February. Tonight's book is *Excellent Women* by Barbara Pym, copyright 1953. Alison discovered Miss Pym. It was a perfect match for the book group. I grew up thinking that everybody used the words *jumble sale, dustbin,* and *Toad-in-the-Hole.* The book group read all of her books, joined the Barbara Pym *society* and when they were all in their *dotage* visited St. Hilda's college in Oxford. They took to calling themselves the EW BG, *Excellent Woman Book Group.* Their code name was U BUG.
(Ellie, Fiona, Alison, Isabel, and Mags are wildly dancing and Mags is hugely pregnant. Finally all sit on couch and chairs. Isabel on couch between Alison and Fiona.)
ELLIE: Isabel did a search of all the songs that have the word *baby* in them.
ISABEL: And some of them are real slow and can be like, lullabies.
MAGS: Isabel, that's really thoughtful of you.
FIONA: And you made the CD?
ISABEL: But I didn't burn it. Danny did, he's in my homeroom and gets into a lot of trouble. He had fifteen blue slips and if he gets five more he can't go to Boston. What a shame.
MAGS: Ladies, I think I overheard the nurse say something after my last sonogram. I think she said penis. I think I'm having a boy. I was sure it was a girl. But now I think she said penis. I don't know if I can do boys. I don't know the first thing about boys. And George is hardly the camping type.
(Starts to get weepy.)
ALISON: You'll be a great mother. Look how you are with Buster.
ELLIE: You're funny, you're energetic . . .

MAGS: I'm ancient, I'm fat. I have these like barnacles on the bottom of my feet, at least that's what I think they are because I can't see my feet anymore. I can't wear pregnant queen panty hose anymore and they don't make pregnant king. Look at me, I'm a tank, I'm a blimp, my stretch marks go all the way to Alpha Centuri.

ALISON: Boys always love their mother.

MAGS: I was so sure it was a girl.

ELLIE: It's not a little you.

MAGS: I know, I'm the vessel. Frigging humongous vessel.

ALISON: Only 1 percent of women deliver on their due date.

FIONA: Well, three more weeks and we'll know.

ELLIE: Thank you Alison.

FIONA: I'm due September first.

ALISON: What! What did you say?

FIONA: Actually, I'm due, I'm pregnant, I'm due on September first.

ALISON: Wonderful news!

MAGS: I'm shocked, I'm never shocked.

FIONA: It wasn't exactly planned.

MAGS: Birth control failure.

FIONA: You could say that.

ELLIE: No birth control sounds like.

ALISON: Goodness sakes, who cares!

FIONA: I wasn't going to tell. I just found out today.

MAGS: Is Stuart excited?

ELLIE: How did he react?

FIONA: I haven't told him yet. I should have told him first . . . I can't believe I just blurted it out.

ALISON: August thirtieth, August thirty-first, and September first are the most common birthdays in America.

MAGS: Someone put her on TV!

ELLIE: There's no problem about telling Stuart is there?

FIONA: Oh, no. He'll be surprised though.

ELLIE: Surprised?

FIONA: Well, we weren't taking my temperature and all that.

MAGS: So, Stuart's the dad.

FIONA: Stuart is the father. Stuart will be the father. Stu and I are going to raise this child.

MAGS: So Stuart got you pregnant?

FIONA: Didn't you hear what I just said?

MAGS: Doesn't the identity of the sperm matter? What about for medical reasons?

ELLIE: Mags, lay off.

FIONA: Mags never lays off. She's a professional interrogator.

ELLIE: She answered your question, Mags.

FIONA: No, Mags won't be satisfied until the DNA tests are conclusive, right? You won't be happy until you have definitive, rock solid, incontrovertible proof that Stuart planted the seed. You just *have* to know, don't you, so that everything is understandable in your perfect little world. Because you know everything,

ELLIE: Fiona, honey, calm down.

FIONA: You like playing God in our little town don't you?

Well, you are mistaken, very mistaken indeed.

(Everyone is speechless at this outburst. Fiona realizes that she has the "stage" and decides to take full advantage of it.)

FIONA: Now, I have to go to the ladies. While I'm gone Mags, you can make this decision. If you can promise me never to bring up this issue again, I will stay in book group and remain your friend. If you do not cease and desist your harassment I will gracefully depart from the book group and I will no longer be your friend.

(All are stunned into silence, Fiona heads to the upstairs bedroom.)

ISABEL: Wrong way Mrs. Timmins.

FIONA: *(Returning.)* Shit! One more thing. Under no circumstances will I read another Barbara Pym. I don't think that you comparing me to the virgin spinster Mildred was the least bit flattering.

(She exits to the bathroom.)

ELLIE: You compared her to Mildred Lathbury?

MAGS: I love Mildred! She's a riot!

(All sit in silence, staring at Mags, who looks out to the audience as if for guidance. Girl leaves couch and comes down stage to address audience. Women remain on stage.)

GIRL: Fiona returned from the "loo" and Mags promised her that she would never bring up the subject of paternity again. It turned out to be the best thing Mags ever did because three years later Fiona saved her life when Mags choked on a chicken sandwich when they were were driving home from Christmas shopping in Boston. It's the rare person who can perform the Hemlich while you're driving and have everything come out OK.

Mags. *(Girl walks to Mags' side.)* Mags did have a son and named him —

MAGS: Adam.

GIRL: He became a doctor, a neurosurgeon no less, which took the sting out of him not being a girl.

Ellie. *(Girl walks to Ellie's side. Ellie reacts to Girl's words about her.)* Well, Richard tried, he really did, but eventually Ellie left him — his father hunger persisted and he tried to satisfy it with one too many oncology nurses. Isabel, an expert on over-the-counter remedies by age five, became a . . . pharmacist.

Alison. *(Girl walks to Alison's side. Alison looks sheepish.)* When Alison's twins graduated from middle school she took them on a celebratory trip to the Holy Land. While they were walking where Jesus walked Alison fell in love with her Israeli guide, an ex-army Colonel, who looked, as she put it —

ALISON: Like a young Paul Newman.

GIRL: She eventually came home in time for the boys to start high school. John, Alison's husband, didn't say a word and now every summer she returns to Israel to be "re-born."

Fiona. *(Girl walks to Fiona and Stuart's kitchen.)* About Fiona and Stuart. I guess you've figured it out by now. I'm their —

FIONA: — daughter.

GIRL: Dad's still at the college and my mother eventually became the Director of the Center when Claudio retired.

The women soldier on. This winter is supposed to be particularly long — the wooly bear caterpillars were completely brown — so the book group decided to tackle *Vanity Fair.* Mags said first it's sex, then real estate, and then, in the end, it's books.

My name is Anna. Anna Samuel. And this is my story.

(Girl pulls down screen and images appear on screen of the photos the Girl has taken throughout the play. Girl goes back to sit with women on the couch who are chatting silently among themselves as the audience watches the slides. When final slide appears of the four women, all freeze, Girl moves downstage, and, as she did in the beginning of the play cues the music, this time, to begin.)

END OF PLAY

THE STORY

Tracey Scott Wilson

PLAYWRIGHT'S BIOGRAPHY

Tracey Scott Wilson's current work includes *The Story*, which was recently produced at The Public Theater/NYSF starring Phylicia Rashad, and which transferred to the Long Wharf Theatre. Additional productions include *Order My Steps* for Cornerstone Theater's Black Faith/AIDS project in Los Angeles; *I Don't Know Why That Caged Bird Won't Shut Up* and *Exhibit #9*, which was co-produced in New York City by New Perspectives Theatre and Theatre Outrageous; *Leader of the People* produced at New Georges Theatre; a reading of *The Story* at Soho Theatre Writers Centre in London in November 2002; a ten-minute play produced at the Guthrie Theatre in Minneapolis and another ten-minute play commission from the same theater. Tracey has had readings at the New York Theatre Workshop, New Georges Theatre, and the Public Theater.

She is currently writing a new drama about the pitfalls in the history of black leadership. She is writing the book for the musical *The Jubilee Singers* for East of Doheny and has been commissioned by the Public Theater to write a new play. She earned a Van Lier Fellowship from the New York Theatre Workshop, a residency at Sundance Ucross, and is the winner of the 2001 Helen Merrill Emerging Playwright Award. Ms. Wilson holds a Master's degree in English Literature from Temple University.

ORIGINAL PRODUCTION

The Story premiered at the Joseph Papp Public Theater/New York Shakespeare Festival (George C. Wolfe, Producer; Mara Manus, Executive Director; Michael Hurst, Managing Director) in New York City, opening on December 10, 2003. It was directed by Loretta Greco; the set design was by Robert Brill; the lighting design was by James Vermeulen; the original music and sound design were by Robert Kaplowitz; the costume design was by Emilio Sosa; the production stage manager was Buzz Coehn; and the stage manager was Damon W. Arrington. The cast was as follows:

YVONNE . . . . *Erika Alexander*
ASSISTANT/ENSEMBLE . . . .*Kalimi A. Baxter*
LATISHA . . . . *Tammi Clayton*
NEIL . . . . *Damon Gupton*
DETECTIVE/ENSEMBLE . . . .*Michelle Hurst*
JEFF/TIM DUNN . . . .*Stephen Kunken*
PAT . . . .*Phylicia Rashad*

REPORTER/ENSEMBLE ....Susan Kelechi Watson
JESSICA DUNN ....Sarah Grace Wilson

OTHER PRODUCTION

The Story was subsequently produced by the Long Wharf Theatre (Gordon Edelstein, Artistic Director; Michael Stotts, Managing Director) in New Haven, Connecticut, opening on February 11, 2004. It was directed by Loretta Greco; the set design was by Robert Brill; the lighting design was by James Vermeulen; the original music and sound design were by Robert Kaplowitz; the costume design was by Emilio Sosa; and the production stage manager was Buzz Cohen. The cast was as follows:

YVONNE .... *Lizzy Cooper Davis*
ASSISTANT/ENSEMBLE ....*Kalimi A. Baxter*
LATISHA ....*Tammi Clayton*
NEIL .... *Duane Boutté*
DETECTIVE/ENSEMBLE ....*Michelle Hurst*
JEFF/TIM DUNN ....*David Wilson Barnes*
PAT ....*Sharon Washington*
REPORTER/ENSEMBLE ....*Christen Simon*
JESSICA DUNN ....*Sarah Grace Wilson*

CHARACTERS
YVONNE
ASSISTANT/ENSEMBLE
LATISHA
NEIL
DETECTIVE/ENSEMBLE
JEFF/TIM DUNN
PAT
REPORTER/ENSEMBLE
JESSICA DUNN

PLACE
An American city.

TIME
The present.

THE STORY

ACT I

PROLOGUE

DETECTIVE: Please state your full name.

JESSICA: Jessica Alisha Dunn.

DETECTIVE: Your address.

JESSICA: 4600 Sycamore Ave, Glenridge.

DETECTIVE: At approximately 8:00 P.M. were you and your husband driving in the Northside area?

JESSICA: Yes.

DETECTIVE: Your husband was driving the car?

JESSICA: Yes. *(Lights up on Tim, her husband.)*

TIM: Where are we?

JESSICA: I don't know.

TIM: What does the paper say?

JESSICA: The paper says the address. It doesn't say where we are.

TIM: Just let me see it.

JESSICA: No, it won't do any good. You don't know where we are.

TIM: Let me see it. *(She doesn't. Continuing; looking out window.)* I'll ask that guy over there.

(Lights up on a black person in hooded jacket, street clothes.)

JESSICA: No, don't ask anybody in this neighborhood.

TIM: Stop being so racist. What is wrong with you?

JESSICA: Nothing is wrong with me? Do you see where we are?

TIM: Of course, I see where we are. We go to work here every day don't we?

DETECTIVE: You and your husband are . . . were teachers.

JESSICA: Yes, in the Teach America program.

DETECTIVE: You taught at Benjamin Banneker?

JESSICA: Yes, just a few blocks from where . . .

(She cries. Detective gives her tissues.)

DETECTIVE: Would you like . . .

JESSICA: No, no let's just . . . *(To Tim.)* It's not so scary in the daytime. This is night. Very dark night. Let's just go home.

TIM: No. Mom and Dad are probably there already.

JESSICA: Too bad. They'll understand. This is scary.

TIM: If you act terrified, how are we ever supposed to convince Mom and Dad that what we're doing is a good idea? Huh? This was your idea. Dinner in the neighborhood so they can see.

JESSICA: That was before . . . now . . . I want to go home. I want to go home.

TIM: That looks like a ramp.

JESSICA: It does not. *(Pause.)* Tim, I'm really scared.

TIM: Honey, don't be scared. We know this neighborhood.

JESSICA: We don't. How are we going to get back?

(Jessica cries.)

DETECTIVE: Would you like a glass of water?

JESSICA: No, no. I'm alright. I'm alright. There was a gas station. *(To Detective.)* It looked sort of shady, but there were a lot of people around. There was this black gentleman getting gas. *(Lights up on black man in a nice suit. Continuing.)* He had a suit on. He looked . . . conservative.

DETECTIVE: Did you get his name?

JESSICA: No.

DETECTIVE: Do you remember his car?

JESSICA: A BMW or Lexus. It was a nice car. Not flashy. He was playing classical music on his car radio. *(Classical music plays. Continuing.)* Which surprised me. And there was a woman in the car. She was dressed nice too.

(Lights up on a nicely dressed black woman.)

DETECTIVE: A black woman?

JESSICA: Yes. She was wearing a red dress.

DETECTIVE: A red dress?

JESSICA: Yeah. It was red. I remember that. Red is my favorite color.

DETECTIVE: Did she speak to you?

JESSICA: No, she smiled. *(Woman smiles. Jessica smiles back. Continuing.)* I remember that. She smiled at me and she seemed nice.

DETECTIVE: The black gentleman gave you directions.

JESSICA: Yeah . . . but . . . I . . . *(To Tim.)* We're lost again.

TIM: We're not.

JESSICA: We are. He said turn right two blocks back. Tim, we're lost. We are los . . . *(Jessica screams.)* TIM!!!!!!!

(Sound of two gunshots. Then lights up on a television reporter reading from copy.)

REPORTER: "He didn't have to teach. His father, Alex Dunn, a self-made billionaire, told him so. But he did. And last night he wanted to prove to his parents that he was right to do so. So at seven P.M., Tim Dunn and

his wife into got their 1990 Honda Accord and drove downtown to meet
their parents at Alcove, a trendy new Brazilian restaurant located in an
area that has been abandoned and neglected since the 1960s."

JESSICA: I was frozen. Just frozen. He said . . .

DETECTIVE: Who said?

JESSICA: He said . . .

TIM: Please don't! Please don't! We're having a baby!

(Jessica starts crying.)

JESSICA: Please, please. Let this be all. (Pause.) Let this be all.

DETECTIVE: OK . . . (Pause.) OK . . .

REPORTER: "They wanted to show their parents the area had changed. They
wanted to show their parents it wasn't so dangerous. They wanted to
show their parents they were right to turn down lucrative jobs in the private sector to teach poor inner-city students with monumental problems.
They wanted to help." (Police siren and lights. We see black males hand-
cuffed, hands behind back, assuming the position.)

SCENE ONE

*Lights up on a newsroom. Jeff, a white man in his mid-twenties and Yvonne
a black woman in her mid-twenties enter. There are two distinct areas, the
Metro area and Outlook area. Also there should be an "outside area" that sig-
nifies the outside world, people's homes, etc. There should be no blackouts between scenes and the play should move as quickly as possible.*

JEFF: And, finally, I think your desk will probably be over there somewhere.

YVONNE: That's the Outlook section . . . way over there?

JEFF: Yeah, over there. From the wall to that desk.

YVONNE: Small section. Much smaller than Metro, I see.

JEFF: Just as important.

YVONNE: Come on.

JEFF: No, no. It is. Outlook's become the hot section. People are taking it seriously now. With the Dunn murder everyone's looking at it for . . . perspective.

YVONNE: I don't have any perspective on murders committed by black people.

JEFF: We don't know the murder was committed by a black person.

YVONNE: In that neighborhood? Come on now. (Jeff tries to interrupt. Continuing.) Alright, alright. It doesn't matter. Like I told you earlier honey. I
don't plan on being at Ebony/Jet Junior for long. Soon, I'll be at Metro

with you, then onto the national desk then . . . *(Notices Jeff's expression.)* What?

JEFF: First, we can't be so familiar. We have to be professional.

YVONNE: Really? I can't have sex with you in the copy room during lunch? Damn, I asked them that during my interview. They said, it'd be alright.

JEFF: Come on now listen, I told you how things are around here. We just . . . We can't slip up and say honey or baby or anything like that around other people. *(Pause.)* Especially Neil.

YVONNE: Yes, baby, honey, sweetheart, love of my life. Can I call you Jeff or do you want me to call you Mr. Morgan?

JEFF: And you have to be careful with that Ebony/Jet Junior stuff. People don't like that.

YVONNE: People like who? Neil? What's wrong with Neil?

JEFF: Nothing, but I think . . . *(Jeff looks around, making sure they are alone. Continuing.)* One time his sister was dating a white guy and I heard, overheard, he didn't like it very much.

YVONNE: Oh, come on. Is that why we can't be too familiar? Is he going to sic da brothers on us?

JEFF: Yvonne, listen. I don't want people in our business. I'm telling you. Racial politics are very tenuous here. Very. Everybody's edgy. And I think it would be good if you . . . You know, Neil and your boss are very close. He's like second in command over there.

YVONNE: So Pat doesn't like white folks either? She didn't even stay for the rest of my interview. Very tacky. Very unprofessional.

JEFF: She was on deadline.

YVONNE: No, she's . . .

JEFF: I'm just saying. Things are very tenuous. Very.

YVONNE: That Pat reminds me of my cousin Adrienne. Adrienne would come over to my house, pull on my hair and ask me why I always acted so white. So, I asked my daddy why I acted so white and he told me I wasn't acting white, Adrienne just acted like a nigger.

JEFF: OK . . . OK . . . That's a good example right there. Don't ever tell that story to anybody around here . . . ever. OK? Yvonne. I'm serious. Ever.

YVONNE: If Chris Rock said that you'd be rolling on the floor right now. *(Jeff starts to interrupt. Continuing; pause.)* Forget it. Let's just go to dinner. Don't worry about Pat and Neil either. I'll be down with them. I be's more black. I be from the streets. *(Rapping.)*
My name is Yvonne
My game is always on

A reporter from the hood
I really think I should
Up to no good.
(Jeff kisses Yvonne. Then he suddenly stops, and looks around nervously.)
YVONNE: What? What's wrong?
JEFF: I thought I saw somebody.

SCENE TWO
Next day. Neil, a black man in his mid-twenties, and Pat, a black woman in her early forties enter. Jeff is not there.

PAT: You've come at an exciting time. It's crazy, busy. We're redesigning, adding new features.
YVONNE: I thought my desk would be over there somewhere. Isn't the Outlook section over there?
PAT: Most of us are over there but we've run out of desk space so . . . We'll just put you over here for now.
YVONNE: This will be fine, thank you.
PAT: OK . . . Well, I don't know how much they told you about how we work around here. Again, I apologize for leaving in the middle of your interview but . . .
YVONNE: No . . . no . . . that's fine. I understand. You know I've worked for several papers. I'm familiar with the workings . . .
PAT: We work a little different. Outlook works a little different. Listen, if I didn't have to leave that day I would have told you how things are around here for us. I'm sure you've noticed that we are in short supply and for years they tried to stick us in one place. The Metro desk.
NEIL: Every day, the Metro Desk would have a picture of some brother doing the perp walk. Every day.
PAT: Then one day . . . Sorry for interrupting Neil. Then one day . . .
NEIL: About six years ago.
PAT: About six years ago.
NEIL: Somebody got the pictures confused.
PAT: They used a picture of a brother that was taken two years earlier.
NEIL: But nobody noticed because it was just another brother doing the perp walk.
PAT: That's how it was but we complained and cajoled.
NEIL: Pat complained and cajoled.

PAT: And we got Outlook.

NEIL: In the past year alone, we exposed corruption and discrimination in public housing . . .

PAT: And the DMV.

NEIL: And the DMV. *(Yvonne does not respond. Continuing.)* But I've never seen anything like this. This murder has got all the white folks up in arms.

PAT: Yes. *(Pause.)* It's crazy. My son was stopped twice yesterday. I went ballistic. Did you read my column this morning?

YVONNE: No.

PAT: Oh, well, I wrote about it.

YVONNE: I was in such a rush this morning . . .

NEIL: It was a great piece. *(Awkward pause.)*

PAT: Thank you. *(Awkward pause again.)*

NEIL: *(Continuing.)* They stopped me this morning.

PAT: Did they?

NEIL: A random police check of cars, but you know who they were looking for.

PAT: Uh-huh. They don't bother checking out Miss Dunn though.

NEIL: No, of course not. Of course not.

PAT: *(To Neil.)* How's your piece going?

NEIL: Oh, great, great. Some very interesting developments. Very interesting.

PAT: *(To Yvonne.)* Neil, has been checking out the grieving widow.

NEIL: Yeah, you know when a spouse is murdered, the other spouse is always, always a prime suspect.

PAT: Uh-huh. Except when the spouse is white and screams, "A BIG, BLACK MAN DID IT! A BIG, BLACK MAN DID IT!"

(Pat and Neil crack up laughing. Yvonne is not amused at all.)

NEIL: You got that right.

(More laughter. Pause. Yvonne still does not respond. Pat's cell phone rings.)

PAT: Damn . . . I'm sorry. *(Checks phone.)* I have to take this. Please excuse me. Neil, will you take over. Just you know, give her the 411.

NEIL: Alright. No problem. No problem. *(Pat leaves. Continuing.)* So . . . You really impressed everybody in your interview. Harvard. *Summa Cum Laud.* Sorbonne. Two, no four languages right?

YVONNE: *(Not acknowledging joke.)* I learned several languages early on. *(Lights up on Jeff. Continuing; to Jeff.)* He was hitting on me.

NEIL: *(To Yvonne.)* Oh, yes. *Oui, c'est très simple quand vous êtes jeune.* *

(**Yes, it's very simple when you are young.*)

YVONNE: And showing off.

NEIL: You know, I almost went to Harvard.

YVONNE: *(To Jeff.)* First day, I could not believe it. *(To Neil.)* Did you? *(Lights up on Pat.)*

NEIL: *(To Yvonne.)* Told them I was going and everything. *(To Pat.)* She one of them uncertain sisters. *(To Yvonne.)* But at the last minute, I changed my mind. *(To Pat.)* Uncertain to the core. *(To Yvonne.)* I went to Howard instead.

JEFF: *(To Yvonne.)* Maybe you read him wrong.

PAT: *(To Neil.)* Uncertain sister?

JEFF: *(To Yvonne.)* Maybe he was just being friendly.

PAT: *(To Neil.)* What's that?

YVONNE: *(To Jeff.)* I know when a guy is hitting on me. *(To Neil.)* Howard's in Washington right? *(To Jeff.)* His eyes checking me out.

NEIL: *(To Yvonne.)* Right. *(To Pat.)* You see, uncertain sisters . . . *(To Yvonne.)* Harvard seemed too much like Andover. *(To Pat.)* Are always on the defensive. *(To Yvonne.)* I wanted to have experiences I was denied.

YVONNE: *(To Neil.)* You went to boarding school? *(To Jeff.)* Telling me all that personal stuff. *(To Neil.)* I went to Groton. *(To Jeff.)* We just met. *(To Neil.)* Did you like it? *(To Jeff.)* Black men always . . .

NEIL: *(To Yvonne.)* Well, great education. *(To Pat.)* That's what we would call them in college. *(To Yvonne.)* But I left Andover hungry for the black experience. *(To Pat.)* Uncertain sisters. *(To Yvonne.)* Did you like . . . Groton did you say?

YVONNE: I loved it.

NEIL: *(To Pat.)* 'Cause they were uncertain about who they were. Uncertain about their place in the world, and uncertain about why they didn't return your phone calls.

YVONNE: *(To Jeff.)* I just keep telling myself. In a few months I'll transfer. In a few months I'll transfer.

JEFF: I think you have to give it a chance. It's been less than 48 hours.

YVONNE: It's like grammar school all over again and all the cool, black kids hate me. Something in my walk. Something in my talk tells them I'm not "down." I'm not keeping it real. But this is it. This is my real.

JEFF: Just give them a chance. If Neil was hitting on you at least he likes some part of you.

YVONNE: *(To Jeff.)* He cooled down quickly. *(To Neil.)* Listen, I'd really like to get started so . . . if we could . . . we'll talk later?

NEIL: Oh, sure . . . sure. You want to go to lunch. Some of us . . .

YVONNE: I have a lunch date, but I'll call you. *(Pause.)* I'll call you.

NEIL: Oh. OK. Cool. Cool. No problem. No problem.

JEFF: Did you tell him the lunch date was with me?

YVONNE: Yes, and that we were having lunch in a hotel room naked.

JEFF: Tenuous Yvonne. Very, very tenuous.

YVONNE: I saw Pat later. *(Pause.)* She mentioned you.

NEIL: *(To Pat.)* Did she mention me?

JEFF: Me?

PAT: *(To Neil.)* Yes.

JEFF: *(To Yvonne.)* What did she say?

NEIL: *(To Pat.)* What did sister-girl have to say?

PAT: *(To Yvonne.)* Listen, what I was trying to say before we were inter-rupted . . . I don't know what they told you in the interview but . . .

YVONNE: They told me I would start here, but then I would have the oppor-tunity to move on.

PAT: Move onto what? What goals have you set for yourself?

YVONNE: Where do I see myself in five years? I . . .

PAT: Listen, they only really started hiring us six years ago. I been here for ten years. For my first four years I was the only one. *(Pause.)* The only one.

YVONNE: So do all the black reporters work at Outlook?

PAT: No, but a lot of us are there because Outlook gives us a chance to write about the positive things that are happening in our community.

YVONNE: That's very admirable, but I would like to be thought of as a re-porter, not a black reporter.

PAT: Well, we all would, but that's not the reality. *(Yvonne tries to interrupt. Continuing.)* The reality is we are at a paper that has only one black edi-tor, way behind every other major paper in the country. And the reality is this paper was notoriously racist in its portrayal of minorities and the reality is we are fighting to keep a balance in the paper every day. Every day is a battle. Every single day. Listen, where are you from originally?

YVONNE: Boston. Originally.

PAT: Boston. Uh-huh. Home of Charles Stuart.

YVONNE: Who?

PAT: Charles Stuart, the white guy who shot his pregnant wife and tried to blame it on a brother. A couple of my cousins were arrested in that raid.

YVONNE: Oh, that was . . . years ago. The eighties.

PAT: Uh-huh. And the Dunn murder was only last week.

YVONNE: But that's not . . . I mean . . . You don't really think that's the same type of situation do you? I mean they . . . the Dunns were teachers in the community. They were trying to help the community. *(Pat looks at her incredulously.)* Boston is not that bad . . . My family . . .

PAT: *(To Yvonne.)* Boston is Mississippi 1963.

YVONNE: (To Pat) I . . .

PAT: *(To Yvonne.)* Boston is Mississippi 1963 and this paper is Alabama. Understand?

YVONNE: No, I'm sorry. I really don't understand how it could be that bad here. How . . .

PAT: Your generation just doesn't grasp the sacrifices made on your behalf and . . .

YVONNE: *(To Jeff.)* God, if I had a dollar for every time an old black person said that to me . . . *(To Pat.)* Uh-huh.

PAT: And it's true. A lot more doors are opened, but we still have to be twice as good, twice as smart, and twice as strong to go through them. Especially here.

YVONNE: You sound like my father. An A wasn't good enough for him. He wanted to know why it wasn't an A+.

PAT: Yes, my father was the same way. When I was growing up we lived next door to this cardiologist, Dr. Summit. Dr. Summit treated white patients. It was amazing to see whites coming into our neighborhood. I think they were mostly white trash, but still, in those days . . . Anyway, Summit was admired by everybody, but he wanted none of our pride. Black pride. He wouldn't accept it. He thought of himself as an exception to the black race instead of part of it. He sent his children off to private schools. They weren't allowed to speak or play with us when they came home. Everyone else in the neighborhood was a part of Jack and Jill. You know Jack and Jill?

YVONNE: I've heard of it.

PAT: Jack and Jill where the black elite meet, but, as I said, Dr. Summit didn't want his family thinking of themselves as black.

YVONNE: Until . . .

(Pause. Pat looks at her.)

PAT: Until . . . one of Dr. Summit's white patients died. There was an inquiry. He lost his license, his practice, everything.

YVONNE: Sad.

PAT: Yes. Some people in the neighborhood were overjoyed that he got his due, but my father wouldn't hear of it. He helped Dr. Summit get back on his feet. Now he owns a very successful medical supply company. He and my father are best friends.

YVONNE: Oh. *(Pause.)* Not sad then.

PAT: No. Not sad at all. *(Pause.)* Summit learned, and you will too, that, in the
end, when it all hits the fan, community is all you have. That's what Outlook is about. Community.

JEFF: What about me though? What'd she say about . . .

NEIL: What about me though? What'd she say about . . .

YVONNE: *(Continued.)* She said . . .

PAT: She said . . . *(Continued. To Yvonne.)* The reality is the most loved person
at the Metro Desk is a white, ivy league trust-fund baby who knows
nothing about us and is not for us.

JEFF: She said that?

YVONNE: *(To Pat.)* I sense some tension between us. Is it because of Neil? I
know you two are close. I didn't mean to be short with him. I am a team
player. There is no need for him to be intimidated by me. I hope to have
lunch with him soon. *(Pause.)* Sometime soon.

JEFF: She really said that?

NEIL: She really said that?

YVONNE: *(Pause.)* Yes.

PAT: *(Pause.)* Yes.

SCENE THREE

*Lights on Jessica Dunn. She is in spotlight answering reporters' questions. We
don't see the reporters, but we hear loud, anonymous questions.*

JESSICA: No, I don't . . . Three months tomorrow . . . No, no it was a wonderful experience. Until . . . I don't know. It was hard sometimes. Please . . .
I . . . No, we had a good marriage, a great marri . . . Who said? What??
Lawsuit? Who would I sue? For what? Who has money around there? I
don't know. I'm sorry about the arrest . . . Those false arrests. But he was
black . . . I'm sure. A black male. He was . . . I can't help that . . . I
won't . . . NO!!! NO!!! NO!!! I won't be giving anymore interviews. Please
don't bother my parents. No more . . . No more . . . No more . . .
*(Lights up on Detective. During the following, Detective and Jessica only
speak to each other. Neil only speaks to Jessica.)* You have to stop them from
bothering me.

DETECTIVE: OK. OK. Just . . .

JESSICA: No, no. I have rights. I have rights. I'm not a suspect here. I'm not a
suspect. They just keep . . .

NEIL: Neil Patterson, *The Daily.*

JESSICA: They distort the facts.

NEIL: Your husband was heir to an oil fortune, but you grew up very poor, correct?

JESSICA: And twist everything.

NEIL: Sources have told me you wanted to quit teaching, your husband did not. Is that correct?

JESSICA: I'm sick of it. It's making me sick.

DETECTIVE: I just . . . I'm sorry. I can't control the press.

JESSICA: They don't understand.

NEIL: Why would you go to dinner in such a dangerous neighborhood without getting accurate directions?

JESSICA: They don't try to understand.

NEIL: How could you get lost six blocks . . . six blocks from your job?

DETECTIVE: Maybe you should hire a lawyer.

NEIL: And is it also true that you and your husband separated a month before the murder?

JESSICA: Then everybody will think . . .

NEIL: Didn't your husband take out a life insurance policy one month before . . .

DETECTIVE: Think what?

NEIL: Don't you stand to inherit a considerable amount of money now?

DETECTIVE: Think what?

SCENE FOUR
Pat hands Yvonne a memo after each of the following lines.

PAT: There's a community center opening up. I want you to cover that.

YVONNE: *(To Jeff.)* I'm dying inside. Just dying.

JEFF: Every reporter goes through a rough time at first. You know that.

PAT: There's a new after-school program at the Southside Community Center. Look into it.

YVONNE: *(To Jeff.)* I had four drinks at lunch today. Cosmopolitans.

JEFF: That's not good. That's not good at all.

PAT: The East Side Community Center is celebrating their tenth anniversary. Be there by two.

YVONNE: *(To Jeff.)* If I don't get transferred soon . . . Death or alcoholism. Those are the options. Death . . . Alcoholism. Death by alcoholism.

JEFF: Just . . . .

YVONNE: There are better stories out there. This is not what I signed up for. They're driving me crazy. *(Lights up on Pat.)*

PAT: *(To Yvonne.)* The Northside Community Center just hired a new director. Interview her.

YVONNE: *(To Jeff.)* You know how many community centers I been to? I never went to a community center once before I got this job. Not once. There was one down the street from us. My father wouldn't let us near it. Now I know why. They're all the same. Every one of them.

(Lights up on chorus women in spotlights. Each woman should have similar mannerisms.)

LIGHT ONE: We hope to create an environment where our children can feel safe and . . .

LIGHT TWO: . . . they can see the positive brothers and sisters who work in the community because . . .

LIGHT THREE: Our families need help and we're the only ones giving it to them. Recent government cutbacks have . . . .

YVONNE: Every one the same. The same. These pristine brick and stone structures located near liquor stores, 99 cent shops, and churches. Inside, it's like a hospital because you get the feeling that there are all these rules and things are going on that you'll never really understand. And the community center director. Always black. Always female. Always.

LIGHT ONE: Eloise Brown.

LIGHT TWO: Ellen Turner.

LIGHT THREE: Jacquelyn Joseph.

YVONNE: Sometimes attractive. Sometimes not. Sometimes stylishly dressed. Sometimes not. But always, always, always . . . A look on their faces as if they've seen the war. Up close. And they carry the wounds around in their bodies. All the time. *(Pause.)* All the time. And the students. *(Chorus women turn into teenage girls.)* Not children. Not close to it. The only thing young about them is their faces. Perfect baby skin. Smooth, unblemished cocoa-colored perfection. But underneath . . . they've not only seen the war, they're in it. But they're too scared to be sad. So they just act amused. And what's worse, every time I bring a story back, Pat edits it to death. She says it's not positive enough.

PAT: *(To Yvonne.)* Are you sure about your sources here?

JEFF: *(To Yvonne.)* She says that? Not positive enough?

YVONNE: *(To Pat and Jeff.)* Yes.

PAT: *(To Yvonne.)* Because according to my research. *(To Neil.)* Her work is sloppy. *(To Yvonne.)* This center was open two years ago, not four. *(To*

Neil.) Very, very sloppy. *(To Yvonne.)* They've had three directors in the past year. Not two. And they actually had an 8 percent increase in federal funds. Not a decrease.

JEFF: *(To Yvonne.)* What do you say?   NEIL: *(To Pat.)* How does sister-girl respond?

YVONNE: *(To Jeff.)* What can I say?   PAT: *(To Neil.)* What can she say?

YVONNE: *(To Jeff.)* I take the story back and put in a lot of "positive" adjectives. Strong black men, blah, blah, blah. Asset to the community, blah, blah, blah. Strong black women, blah, blah, blah.

PAT: *(To Neil.)* She types in my corrections like a secretary.

JEFF: *(To Yvonne.)* You don't debate?

NEIL: She doesn't put up a fight?

YVONNE: *(To Jeff.)* No.

PAT: *(To Neil.)* No.

YVONNE: I tried to fight . . . once . . .

PAT: This one time though . . . She tried to say something when I told her . . . *(To Yvonne.)* Your writing is very biased.

YVONNE: Biased how?

PAT: You editorialize. I've noticed it creeping into a lot of your news stories.

YVONNE: Editorialize which stories? The one about community center number three? Or community center number seven.

PAT: You've written more stories than that. *(Yvonne tries to speak. Continuing.)* That profile of Congresswoman Watts . . . *(Pat looks for story. Finds it.)* You wrote . . . You wrote. . . um . . . "Congresswoman Watts came into the room smartly dressed but disoriented. Although she didn't want to comment on the recent Senate investigation against her, clearly it was on her mind." How do you know that?

YVONNE: I could tell.

PAT: Did you ask her?

YVONNE: She refused to comment.

PAT: Well, you should put it like that. This makes her seem . . . suspect.

YVONNE: But she is under suspicion.

PAT: So are half a dozen other congressmen.

YVONNE: I wasn't writing about half a dozen other congressmen. I was writing about her. A black female. That's the real issue right? You know what? Whatever. *(To Jeff.)* I realized there's just no point. I'll transfer soon.

JEFF: Yvonne . . .

PAT: *(To Neil.)* No way is she going to make it.

YVONNE: No, Jeff, I stumbled across a story today. The story.

PAT: *(To Neil.)* Despite her scoop.

JEFF: *(To Yvonne.)* What?

NEIL: *(To Pat.)* Scoop?

(Lights up on Latisha, a seventeen-year-old black girl.)

YVONNE: *(To Jeff.)* Another assignment about a community center. Another one. As soon as I got there I decided I was going to quit. Just sit at home until a position in Metro or National opened up, but then . . . I saw this girl. *(To Pat.)* This girl was different.

PAT: *(To Yvonne.)* Uh-huh. Go ahead.

NEIL: *(To Pat.)* What's so different about her?

YVONNE: *(To Pat and Jeff.)* You're not   PAT: *(To Neil.)* You're not going to
going to believe this.   believe this.

JEFF: Yvonne, what?   NEIL: *(To Pat.)* What is it?

YVONNE: *(To Jeff.)* She's in da hood, but not of it. *(To Pat.)* She was different from the girls I usually meet. A very high IQ. I'm sure.

LATISHA: *(During this scene she only speaks to Yvonne.)* My parents were activists from the sixties.

YVONNE: *(To Pat and Jeff.)* She was witty, ironic, smarter than her years.

LATISHA: Hence the pseudo African name. *(Pointing to herself.)* Latisha.

YVONNE: *(To Pat and Jeff.)* I liked her right away.

LATISHA: The "revolution" ate them alive. My daddy became an alcoholic. My mother was one for a while too but, she recovered . . . from that.

NEIL: *(To Pat.)* So?

PAT: *(To Yvonne.)* What's so remarkable . . .

JEFF: . . . about that?

YVONNE: *(To Pat and Jeff.)* No, no . . . but listen. She's a straight "A" student.

PAT: *(To Yvonne.)* And?

NEIL: *(To Pat.)* And?

JEFF: *(To Yvonne.)* Yes, but . . . That's not that hard to do in that neighborhood is it? *(Yvonne gives Jeff a look.)* You know what I mean . . . *(Pause.)* I shouldn't have said that.

YVONNE: She speaks perfect Italian. We conversed for several minutes. *(To Latisha)* Quando avete imparato italiano?

LATISHA: *Circa un anno fa. È una lingua bella.*

YVONNE: *Sì, certamente.*

LATISHA: *Spero di andare in Italia un giorno.** (*When did you learn Italian? Around one year ago. It is a beautiful language. Yes, certainly. I hope to go to Italy one day.)*

YVONNE: She taught herself.

LATISHA: I get bored, so I just read stuff. The only thing my dad ever gave me was books. Tons and tons of books, so I read and read and read and read. Whatever I can, you know.

YVONNE: That and German too.

LATISHA: *Deutsch ist sehr musikalisch.*

YVONNE: *Rufen Sie mich an, wenn Sie überhaupt üben möchten.*

LATISHA: *Danke, ich werde.* * (*German language is very musical. Call me if you would like to practice at all. Thank you, I will.*

YVONNE: *(To Pat and Jeff.)* So we're talking, and talking, and talking.

LATISHA: I don't tell anybody around here, of course. Nobody in school either. Not even my teachers. They would make a big deal and single me out. I just want to do my time and get out. No trouble.

YVONNE: *(To Latisha.)* You shouldn't be ashamed of being smart.

LATISHA: Yeah . . . I . . .

YVONNE: I mean, ever. Those idiots . . .

LATISHA: Idiots?

YVONNE: Who make fun of you because you're bright.

LATISHA: My friends. Some of them are my friends.

YVONNE: Oh . . . I . . .

LATISHA: I mean, they don't mean to . . .

YVONNE: They're not your real friends. I know what you're going through.

PAT: *(To Yvonne.)* What did you talk about?

JEFF: *(To Yvonne.)* What did you talk about?

YVONNE: *(To Pat.)* Private matters.

YVONNE: *(To Jeff.)* She thought . . . . LATISHA: *(To Yvonne.)* I thought . . .

YVONNE: *(Continued.)* I grew up rich.

JEFF: *(To Yvonne.)* I thought you grew up rich too.

LATISHA: You remind me of the rich kids at my school.

YVONNE: *(To Jeff.)* We were very well off. *(To Latisha.)* No, I wasn't rich at all. *(To Jeff.)* But I didn't want Latisha to know that. I was afraid she would shut down. *(To Latisha.)* Borderline ghetto, my father used to call it.

LATISHA: I live in one of those neighborhoods. The first six blocks are great. The seventh is a shit-hole.

YVONNE: *(To Latisha.)* People made fun of me before I went to boarding school. Even my own sister. Oreo. Wonderbread. Black Cracker. I heard it all. One time this kid, Jon-Jon, he sprayed white paint all over my face while we were on the school bus. I ran home crying, but my father wouldn't let me feel sorry for myself. He told me to scrub my face and go right back to school and I did.

LATISHA: God, I could never.

YVONNE: *(To Latisha.)* I was scared as hell, but my father told me I had to show them that I could not be stopped, could not be intimidated, and I tell you Latisha those ignorant niggers I went to school with never amounted to a damn thing. My sister got pregnant in the eighth grade by the same boy who sprayed paint on me. She called me a few days ago to ask me for money. I reminded her of that day on the bus. *(Pause.)* Then she was the one crying. *(To Pat and Jeff.)* I encouraged her. I made her feel her hard work would be rewarded.

PAT: *(To Yvonne.)* I have an appointment at three.

YVONNE: *(To Pat and Jeff.)* And suddenly, out of the blue, she tells me.

LATISHA: I'm in this gang.

NEIL: *(To Pat.)* Oh, Lord.   PAT: *(To Yvonne.)* Oh, Lord.

PAT: *(To Yvonne.)* Here we go. More pathology.

NEIL: *(To Pat.)* What gang?   PAT: *(To Yvonne.)* What gang?

YVONNE: *(To Latisha.)* What gang?   JEFF: *(To Yvonne.)* What gang?

LATISHA: The AOBs. We dress like guys and roll people.

YVONNE: Roll people?

LATISHA, PAT, AND JEFF: *(To Yvonne.)* That means rob.

YVONNE: *(To Pat.)* I know what it means. *(To Jeff.)* Latisha told me what it means.

LATISHA: We dress like brothers so we won't be ID'd, and rob Korean groceries and stuff, but no one ever catches us cause we look like any other brother on the street. That's where we got the name from. The AOBs. Any Other Brother. The po-po . . . .

PAT: *(To Yvonne.)* The what?   YVONNE: *(To Latisha.)* The what?

JEFF: *(To Yvonne.)* The what?   NEIL: *(To Pat.)* The what?

YVONNE: *(To Jeff.)* You should have seen Pat's face when I explained it to her.

YVONNE: *(To Pat.)* That means cop.   LATISHA: That means cop.

PAT: *(To Yvonne and Neil.)* Must be a recent slang.

YVONNE: *(To Pat.)* No, I don't think so.

LATISHA: The cops ain't looking for no girl so we don't get caught. *(Pause.)* Until now. Now, we kinda worried. Kinda in trouble.

YVONNE: *(To Latisha.)* Why?

LATISHA: Yo! You can't tell nobody. And I mean nobody.

YVONNE: *(To Latisha.)* No, no, I won't.

LATISHA: I'm telling you I'll jack you up for real.

YVONNE: *(To Latisha.)* I won't tell.

LATISHA: *(Pause.)* We capped that teacher.

PAT AND JEFF: *(To Yvonne.)* What?

NEIL: *(To Pat.)* What?   YVONNE: *(To Latisha.)*What?

JEFF: *(To Yvonne.)* She said that?   NEIL: *(To Pat.)* She said that?

LATISHA: *(Continued.)* I . . . I think . . . I think . . . my girl did which is as
good as me doing it cause we one. You know what I'm saying?

JEFF: *(To Yvonne.)* Wait . . . wait . . .

NEIL: *(To Pat.)* Wait . . . wait . . .

JEFF: Two seconds ago she was speaking . . .

PAT: *(To Yvonne.)* Did she say that in Italian or German. Maybe Dutch.

YVONNE: *(To Pat and Jeff.)* She said it in English. She changed just like that.
Got all street and hard. Then someone walked in and Latisha shut down.
Became a young, scared girl. Before I left she came up to me and . . .

LATISHA: Please, please don't tell anybody anything I told you.

YVONNE: I . . .

LATISHA: No, please, you know, we got to talking and I got carried away. I
shouldn't have said anything.

YVONNE: Latisha, you know I'm a reporter. *(Pause.)* I'm a reporter.

LATISHA: No! No! Listen, I was just talking to you. I mean you look kinda out
of place here. Like me. Like I feel all the time. *(Yvonne tries to interrupt.
Continuing.)* So I chatted you up but really. I . . . Look, if you tell I will
be in real trouble for real and I don't mean with my mother either. My
girls will hurt me. Really hurt me.

YVONNE: Latisha . . .

LATISHA: And kill me. I'm telling you. Just . . . you can't say anything. Alright?
Alright?

YVONNE: OK . . . OK . . .

JEFF: *(To Yvonne.)* What did Pat have   NEIL: *(To Pat.)* What did you say?
to say?

PAT: Have you told anyone else?

YVONNE: No.

NEIL: *(To Pat.)* Anyone?

PAT: *(To Yvonne.)* The police?

YVONNE: No.

PAT: *(To Yvonne.)* Well, that's good. I think this story is about a sister suc-
cumbing to the image. Used to be just young brothers but now thanks
to MTV and I'm ashamed to say, BET, we've got the gangster bitch to
contend with. . . . This girl . . . These girls have succumbed to the image.

JEFF: *(To Yvonne.)* What?!

JEFF: *(Continued.)* *(To Yvonne.)* That's not the story.

NEIL: *(To Pat.)* What about my story?

YVONNE: *(To Jeff.)* I didn't think so either. *(To Pat.)* Listen, I don't know anything about all that.

PAT: *(To Neil.)* I don't know . . . .

YVONNE: *(To Pat.)* I mean I don't know why these girls are forming these gangs. I'm not examining the sociological ramifications because above all else this is a crime story.

NEIL: *(To Pat.)* What do you mean you don't know?

YVONNE: *(To Pat.)* A horrible crime has been committed.

JEFF: Good for you Yvonne.

NEIL: *(To Pat.)* That's fucked up.

YVONNE: Thank you. I laid into her I did. *(To Pat — self-righteously.)* We can talk about image and social responsibility later. It's a crime story.

PAT: *(To Yvonne.)* Uh-huh. *(To Neil.)* I have to follow up on this Neil.

YVONNE: *(To Pat.)* Just a crime story.

PAT: We don't have the facts.

NEIL: *(To Pat.)* What about my research?

PAT: *(To Yvonne.)* We don't know the circumstances of this so called murder.

NEIL: *(To Pat.)* I'm telling you those Dunns are not all they seem.

PAT: *(To Yvonne.)* That Dunn woman was half-Italian . . .

JEFF: *(To Yvonne.)* Half-Italian?

PAT: *(To Yvonne.)* If these girls did commit these crimes . . .

JEFF: She said that?

NEIL: Pat, just give me a chance . . .

PAT: *(To Yvonne.)* I want to explore the circumstances.

NEIL: *(To Pat.)* . . . to follow my leads.

YVONNE: *(To Pat.)* We're not a social service agency.

PAT: *(To Neil.)* I have to do this.

YVONNE: *(To Pat.)* It's a crime story first.

PAT: *(To Neil.)* I have to.

YVONNE: *(To Pat.)* Save analysis for later.

NEIL: *(To Pat.)* No.

YVONNE: *(To Pat.)* But it's a crime story now.

NEIL: *(To Pat.)* I'm writing my story.

YVONNE: *(To Pat.)* That's how I'm writing it.

PAT: *(To Yvonne and Neil.)* Not for me you're not.

JEFF: You can write it for Metro.

YVONNE: *(To Jeff.)* I thought so.

NEIL: *(To Pat.)* Oh, no?

YVONNE: *(To Pat.)* Then I'll write it for someone else.

PAT: *(To Yvonne.)* Alright then . . .

NEIL: *(To Pat.)* Someone else will want my story.

PAT: *(To Yvonne.)* You can pursue your story. *(Pause.)* For Outlook. *(To Neil.)* I'm going to pursue Yvonne's story.

NEIL: *(To Pat.)* Well, goddamn.

YVONNE: *(To Pat.)* Excuse me?

NEIL: *(To Pat.)* You don't have to do anything you don't want to, Pat.

PAT: *(To Yvonne.)* Pursue your story. *(To Neil.)* I don't control the news.

YVONNE: *(To Pat.)* Thank you.

PAT: *(To Neil.)* We have a responsibility. You know that.

NEIL: *(To Pat.)* You wanted my story a week ago. You wanted it before uncertain sister arrived.

PAT: *(To Neil.)* Listen Neil . . . *(To Yvonne.)* But I'm going to have Neil cover this AOB story as well.

YVONNE: *(To Pat.)* What? *(Continued.)* *(To Pat.)* You can't.

JEFF: *(To Yvonne.)* She can't.

PAT: I will.

NEIL: *(To Pat.)* Alright.

YVONNE: You have to transfer me, Jeff. You have to.

JEFF: I can't.

NEIL: *(To Pat.)* I'll do it.

SCENE FIVE

Lights up on Jessica watching infomercial. Deeply depressed she looks like she hasn't left the house or showered for days.

SCENE SIX

Lights up on Neil, Pat, Yvonne, Jeff.

YVONNE: *(To Jeff.)* I'm fine. I'm fine. But I don't trust Neil.

JEFF: *(To Yvonne.)* Don't worry about Neil.

PAT: *(To Neil.)* This is your story.

NEIL: *(To Pat.)* It's going to get ugly.

JEFF: *(To Yvonne.)* You can handle him.

JEFF: *(To Yvonne.)* You've got the upper hand.

NEIL: *(To Pat.)* She's got the advantage.

YVONNE: *(To Jeff.)* I told Pat everything.

PAT: *(To Neil.)* I told you everything she told me.

JEFF: *(Continued. To Yvonne.)* She doesn't know that.

NEIL: *(To Pat.)* How do you know she told you everything?

JEFF: *(To Yvonne.)* Neither does Neil.

PAT: *(To Neil.)* You're a good reporter.

JEFF: *(To Yvonne.)* You're a great reporter.

PAT: *(To Neil.)* Don't sell yourself short.

JEFF: *(To Yvonne.)* Remember that.

PAT: *(To Neil.)* We're counting on you.

JEFF: *(To Yvonne.)* Good luck, honey.

> *(Neil and Yvonne go to opposite sides of the stage. In center of stage are several characters. When characters are speaking on the telephone, spotlight goes on them. Scene begins with the sound of a phone ringing several times.)*

YVONNE: Hi, my name is Yvonne Robinson. I'm a reporter for the *The Daily.*

NEIL: Neil Patterson. I work for *The Daily.*

YVONNE: I spoke to you last week at the community center.

NEIL: Sister, I was hoping you could help me out a bit.

> *(During the following the Black Woman speaks only to Yvonne.)*

BLACK WOMAN: You were supposed to interview me, but you didn't.

> *(During the following the Black Female speaks only to Neil.)*

BLACK FEMALE: What is it?

YVONNE: Yes, well. I apologize for that.

NEIL: The Northside Community Center?

YVONNE: I'd like to talk to you now.

NEIL: I understand you worked there.

BLACK WOMAN: I liked it.

BLACK FEMALE: It was a job. You know, paid the bills.

YVONNE: Uh-huh.

NEIL: Uh-huh.

YVONNE: And the girls. What was it like working with them?

NEIL: . . . mentoring the little sisters.

BLACK WOMAN: Like I said. I liked it.

BLACK FEMALE: It was alright. You know, alright.

YVONNE: You keep talking in the past tense. Did you quit your job?

NEIL: Can you be a little more specific . . . *(Trying a new approach — ghetto.)* Can you break that down for me, sister?

BLACK WOMAN: They closed the center this morning.

BLACK FEMALE: No notice or nothing. I got bills to pay. You know anybody hiring?

YVONNE: Closed? Just like that?

NEIL: Are you sure?

BLACK WOMAN: There was a note on the door. Closed.

BLACK FEMALE: I can type real good. They must need a typist at a newspaper.

BLACK WOMAN: I called and called . . .

YVONNE: *(To Jeff.)* . . . And called.

NEIL: *(To Pat.)* . . . Went by there.

YVONNE: Nothing.

NEIL: Nothing.

YVONNE: *(To Jeff.)* Just a note on the door.

NEIL: *(To Pat.)* Closed.

PAT: *(To Neil.)* That's strange.

JEFF: *(To Yvonne.)* Weird. Really weird. *(Continued.)* *(To Yvonne.)* What school does Latisha go to?

NEIL: *(To Pat.)* Do you know what school Latisha goes to?

PAT: *(To Neil.)* She didn't say.

YVONNE: *(To Jeff.)* I didn't think to ask. It was just so fast.

PAT: *(To Neil.)* Yvonne said something about . . .

YVONNE: *(To Jeff.)* I know her parents grew up in Philly.

JEFF: *(To Yvonne.)* That's a lead?

NEIL: *(To Pat.)* Oh, OK. I'll call all the black people in Philly and ask them if they know a sister named Latisha.

YVONNE: *(To Jeff.)* I was just saying.

PAT: *(To Neil.)* You don't have to be a smart-ass. *(Pause.)* See if you can contact some of the other students from the Center.

JEFF: *(To Yvonne.)* Maybe they have her home number.

PAT: *(To Neil.)* The students are who you should be talking to anyway.

(Sound of the phone ringing.)

YVONNE: . . . *The* . . .

NEIL: . . . *Daily* . . .

YVONNE: . . . Few . . .

NEIL: . . . Questions . . .

YVONNE: I understand your daughter went . . .

NEIL: . . . to the after-school program . . .

(During the following the Mother speaks only to Yvonne.)

MOTHER: No, you're mistaken.

(During the following the Female speaks only to Neil.)

FEMALE: I guess she did. I don't know.

YVONNE: Isn't your daughter named . . .

NEIL: You don't know?

MOTHER: She goes to the program on the Southside. It's less dangerous over there.

FEMALE: She ran up out of here about three weeks ago. I ain't seen her since.

YVONNE: How do you know that?

NEIL: Oh . . . I'm very sorry to have bothered you. I hope you . . . um . . . Sorry to have bothered you, sister. Good-bye.

MOTHER: My girlfriend's daughter goes there. Is that what you're writing about cause they've been closing down a lot of these shady community centers.

(Phone rings. During the following the Assistant speaks only to Neil.)

NEIL: Hello there sister. Listen, I was wondering if you could help me out a bit.

ASSISTANT: A listing of all our students named Latisha? Who is this again?

YVONNE: Ever heard of any gang activity at these centers?

NEIL: Well, sister, I'm sure someone as qualified as yourself can help me.

ASSISTANT: I don't think you're authorized to have that type of information. What's this about anyway?

MOTHER: What?! No?! I can't speak for the Northside though. I don't know anything about them.

ASSISTANT: Well, I can tell you we don't have any students named Latisha. I can tell you that.

NEIL: You sound familiar sister. Did you go to Howard? Are you a member of the Deltas?

(Yvonne dials number.)

ASSISTANT: Come on brother, you trying to flirt.

(A phone rings. A woman answers.)

FRIEND: *(During the following she speaks only to Yvonne.)* Yes, my daughter went to the Northside Community Center.

ASSISTANT: You don't even know what I look like. *(Pause.)* What you look like?

FRIEND: She liked the program. She liked the other girls.

ASSISTANT: The AO what?

FRIEND: What's this story about anyway?

ASSISTANT: The AOBs? I have never heard of anything like that.

FRIEND: My daughter is not in a gang, and she doesn't know anything about gangs. Why don't you all ever write about something positive?

ASSISTANT: I'm sorry. I can't help you. I'm not a Delta. Good-bye.

NEIL: *(To Pat.)* I don't know . . .

YVONNE: *(To Jeff.)* I'm so tired.

NEIL: *(To Pat.)* Something is not right here. A girl like Latisha, speaks several languages, smart.

YVONNE: *(To Jeff.)* I should be able to transfer now. Not after the story.

PAT: *(To Neil.)* So what are you saying?

JEFF: *(To Yvonne.)* If you get the story they'll have to transfer you. If someone else gets it . . .

NEIL: *(To Pat.)* I've been asking around. Plenty of Latishas. No Latisha like that. A girl like that would stand out to somebody, even if she was trying to hide it.

PAT: *(To Neil.)* So what are you saying?

YVONNE: *(To Jeff.)* If someone else gets it?!

NEIL: *(To Pat.)* I don't know what I'm saying.

YVONNE: *(To Jeff.)* Don't play psychological games with me.

NEIL: *(To Pat.)* I think my original story about the wife is still valid.

YVONNE: I get enough of that shit from Pat and Neil.

JEFF: Yvonne, honey.

PAT: Neil . . .

JEFF: This story will make your career.

PAT: This story will make your career.

NEIL: Alright, alright.

YVONNE: Alright, alright.

YVONNE: *(To Jeff.)* I will find this girl.

NEIL: *(To Pat.)* I will get the story.

YVONNE: *(To Jeff.)* Wherever she is.

NEIL: *(To Pat.)* Whatever it is.

PAT: I'm sure you will.

JEFF: I have total confidence in you.

PAT: But I think you should try a different approach.

JEFF: We need to get a little more creative here.

PAT: Sister-girl probably knows more than she let on.

JEFF: You know put together you two probably have opposite sides of a puzzle.

PAT: So use your extraordinary Howard U charm to . . .

JEFF: I think if you were nice to him, a little nicer, you could probably find out a lot.

NEIL: What do you mean?

YVONNE: What are you suggesting?

YVONNE: Sleep with him?   NEIL: Sleep with her?

JEFF: No!!!!!   PAT: No!!!!!

JEFF: (*To Yvonne.*) God! What? Just have dinner or something.

PAT: (*To Neil.*) Why would you even go there? Just hang out with her casually, find out what you can.

JEFF: (*To Yvonne.*) It won't be that hard.

PAT: (*To Neil.*) It will be easy.

(*Yvonne and Neil go to the middle of the stage.*)

JEFF: (*To Yvonne.*) Meet somewhere nice.

PAT: (*To Neil.*) That new place on Ivy is really nice.

JEFF: (*To Yvonne.*) Be polite.

PAT: (*To Neil.*) Hide your contempt.

NEIL: (*To Yvonne.*) Hello sister.

YVONNE: (*To Neil.*) Neil, I'm glad you could come.

PAT: (*To Neil.*) Dance around the topic.

JEFF: (*To Yvonne.*) Be sweet.

NEIL: (*To Pat.*) Uncertain sisters love it when you pay.

YVONNE: (*To Jeff.*) Black men like him love to show off by buying expensive dinners.

PAT: (*To Neil.*) See?

JEFF: (*To Yvonne.*) You know what you're doing.

NEIL: (*To Yvonne.*) Would you like some wine?

YVONNE: (*To Neil.*) Sure, whatever you recommend.

NEIL: (*To Yvonne.*) Oh, no. Please. You do it. Ripple was a delicacy in my house. (*To Pat.*) Uncertain sisters like it when you're humble. Show you're beneath them.

YVONNE: (*To Jeff.*) It will be good if I compliment him. (*To Neil.*) Listen, I was going through some of the story archives. I loved your story on . . . (*To Jeff.*) I'll have to find something.

NEIL: (*To Pat.*) I have to stay away from the hint of anything sexual. Uncertain sisters don't like flirting unless they're in control. Then, I'll make it seem like I'm on her side. (*To Yvonne.*) You know . . . I hate to say it, but Pat . . .

YVONNE: (*To Neil.*) What?

NEIL: (*To Yvonne.*) She's really been trying my nerves lately.

PAT: (*To Neil.*) That's good. Make me the common enemy.

YVONNE: (*To Jeff.*) I'll invoke the name of THE MAN. (*To Neil.*) I was really naive when I started work. I'm starting to sense a lot of racism. Subtle racism.

JEFF: Yeah, that's fine but, don't mention my name and the word *racism* in the same sentence.

NEIL: *(To Yvonne.)* It's been frustrating. *(To Yvonne.)* I really wish . . . I really wish . . .

YVONNE: *(To Neil.)* My own community makes me feel like a stranger. It's just a shame that . . .

NEIL: *(To Yvonne.)* We should be working on this story together.

YVONNE: *(To Neil.)* We should be working on this story together.

NEIL: *(To Pat.)* Then she'll tell me things because uncertain sisters love to give advice.

YVONNE: *(To Jeff.)* That's where he'll slip up, giving me advice.

NEIL: *(To Pat.)* Not a bad idea.

YVONNE: *(To Jeff.)* Not bad at all.

PAT: Thank you.

JEFF: Thank you.

(Lights change. Yvonne and Neil introduce each other like they did at beginning of previous scene. Light change indicates time passing. Yvonne and Neil's body language indicate that things went very, very, very badly.)

NEIL: *(To Pat.)* She was late.

YVONNE: *(To Jeff.)* I almost lost my nerve.

NEIL: *(To Pat.)* I started to leave.

YVONNE: *(To Jeff.)* He was pissed.

NEIL: *(To Yvonne.)* I thought you weren't coming.

YVONNE: *(To Neil.)* I got lost. Sorry.

NEIL: *(To Pat.)* That was a lie. I knew it.

YVONNE: *(To Jeff.)* I stayed in the parking lot for twenty minutes, trying to talk myself into it. It was a stupid idea. Stupid, stupid, stupid.

NEIL: *(To Pat.)* I remained cool. *(To Yvonne.)* Would you like a drink?

YVONNE: *(To Neil.)* No.

NEIL: *(To Yvonne.)* No? But you look hot . . .

PAT: *(To Neil.)* Uncertain sisters don't like the hint of anything sexual.

NEIL: *(To Yvonne.)* I mean . . . You're sweating pretty nastily over there.

YVONNE: *(To Neil.)* Well, it's hot in here.

JEFF: *(To Yvonne.)* Black men like him love to show off.

YVONNE: *(To Neil.)* Hey, listen. You know. I will have a drink.

NEIL: *(To Pat.)* Jekyll and Hyde this sister. *(To Yvonne.)* OK. What would you like?

YVONNE: *(To Neil.)* You pick.

NEIL: *(To Yvonne.)* OK. Well, let's see what we have here. The ninety-five white looks . . .

PAT: *(To Neil.)* Uncertain sisters love it when you're humble . . . .

NEIL: *(To Pat — recalling earlier statement.)* . . . show you're beneath them. Show you're beneath them. *(To Yvonne.)* Hey, what do I know. Ripple was a delicacy in my house. *(Dead silence from Yvonne. Continuing; to Pat.)* Bitch, has absolutely no sense of humor.

YVONNE: *(To Jeff.)* Ripple? I haven't heard that joke since *Sanford and Son.* *(Awkward silence between them. Long pause.)* Oh . . . Oh . . . I read that story you wrote. I went through the archives and I read that story you wrote about the black firemen. It was . . . uh . . . brilliant.

NEIL: *(To Pat.)* I couldn't believe uncertain sister was trying to put one over on me. *(To Yvonne.)* It was alright.

YVONNE: No . . . no, better than that. I loved that you . . .

NEIL: It was alright.

YVONNE: Fine.

(Long awkward pause between them.)

NEIL: So . . . .

YVONNE: So . . .

NEIL: How's the story coming?

YVONNE: What story?

(Yvonne and Neil both laugh awkwardly, fake.)

PAT: Make it seem like . . .

NEIL: *(To himself. Recalling advice.)* . . . I'm on her side. *(To Yvonne.)* You know, I hate to say it but Pat . . .

YVONNE: Yes?

NEIL: Has really been trying my nerves lately.

YVONNE: Yeah, she's a real bitch.

JEFF: Yvonne, Jesus . . .

NEIL: *(To Pat.)* I wasn't expecting her to say that.

YVONNE: *(To Jeff.)* I wasn't even thinking. *(To Neil.)* I'm sorry. It just . . . I'm tired . . . I'm tired. *(To Neil and Jeff.)* It just slipped out.

JEFF: He'll slip up when he tries to give you advice.

YVONNE: *(To Neil.)* You know my own community makes me feel like a stranger.

NEIL: Yeah, well . . . When someone goes someplace for the first time that's how they usually feel. Like a stranger.

YVONNE: Did you write the book on blackness, 'cause I must have missed it.

NEIL: OK . . . Let's cut the bullshit.

YVONNE: Let's. You have no right to that story.

NEIL: What story?

YVONNE: That's real funny. You have no right to that story.

NEIL: I don't know of any story. I know of an alleged girl named Latisha and an alleged gang called the AOBs, but I have not seen anything even remotely resembling a story yet.

YVONNE: OK . . . OK . . . And how is that wife–mob connection story of yours holding up? Have you put the grand conspiracy together yet?

NEIL: I know what you came here to do!

YVONNE: I know what you came here to do!

NEIL: You're trying to bullshit me.

YVONNE: You're trying to bullshit me.

NEIL: Stop doing that. You can't even speak an original sentence.

YVONNE: No, you're the one who can't speak an original sentence.

NEIL: I know what you're trying to do.

YVONNE: I know what you're trying to do.

NEIL: You better stop that.

YVONNE: No, you better stop that.

(*Neil and Yvonne storm off into areas where Jeff and Pat are.*)

NEIL: (*To Pat.*) Stupid . . .

YVONNE: (*To Jeff.*) Stupid . . .

YVONNE AND NEIL: Stupid idea.

PAT: (*To Neil.*) If you were a better reporter . . .

JEFF: (*To Yvonne.*) . . . you wouldn't have to do this.

NEIL: Fuck you.

YVONNE: Fuck you.

(*They storm off. Then sound of a phone ringing. Yvonne picks up phone.*)

YVONNE: I'll talk with you tomorrow, Jeff.

(*Lights on Latisha.*)

LATISHA: This is not Jeff. It's me, Latisha.

JEFF: Latisha!?

YVONNE: Latisha?!

LATISHA: I heard you were looking for me.

YVONNE: Well, yeah.

JEFF: Yvonne, don't go.

LATISHA: Meet me at the Northside in one hour.

YVONNE: (*To Jeff.*) I have to go.

LATISHA: I'll give you the 411.

JEFF: No.

YVONNE: *(To Latisha.)* Alright.

JEFF: Let me go with you.

YVONNE: *(To Jeff.)* No, no, she said . . .

LATISHA: You best come alone. I mean it.

JEFF: Don't be stupid. I'm going.

YVONNE: *(Continuing.)* I'm leaving now Jeff.

JEFF: Yvonne . . .

YVONNE: *(To Jeff.)* I'll call you later.

JEFF: Yvonne! Yvonne!

> *(She hangs up the phone. Jeff calls back. No answer. He runs out the door with his coat on. After a moment there is the sound of the phone ringing. Then lights up on Neil and Pat. Pat and Neil speak only to each other unless otherwise indicated.)*

NEIL: *(Answering phone. Sleepy.)* Hello.

PAT: Neil . . .

NEIL: Pat, I'll talk to you tomorrow.

PAT: No, you won't . . . listen . . .

> *(Lights up on Yvonne and Jeff. Yvonne falls into Jeff's arms crying. Latisha speaks only to Yvonne.)*

JEFF: Shit, Yvonne. Where were you? I looked for you for two hours. I . . .

PAT: She got the story.

LATISHA: Did you come alone? I told you to come alone.

NEIL: What?

JEFF: What's wrong honey? What happened?

YVONNE: She's a baby.

PAT: She went right over my head to trust-fund baby in Metro.

NEIL: She can't do that.

PAT: She did. They did.

YVONNE: Just a baby.

PAT: They didn't call me or anything, Neil. The night reporter in Metro, the brother with the gray hair just phoned me.

LATISHA: Listen, I heard you were looking for me and I have to tell you something.

PAT: Yvonne sent in a rough draft an hour ago.

NEIL: I'm not believing this.

JEFF: It's alright, honey.

PAT: Believe it.

JEFF: It's alright.

PAT: I have the draft right here. "Confessions of a Girl Gang Member," by Yvonne Robinson.

JEFF: Just tell me what happened.

NEIL: Read it to me.

PAT: *(Reading from copy.)* "In many ways she is like any other teenage girl around the country, concerned with boys, her hair and clothes."

YVONNE: *(To Jeff.)* She was scared and nervous. I asked her . . . *(To Latisha.)* Is someone threatening you? Are you in . . .

PAT: *(Reading from copy.)* " . . . but her sweet baby face and soft brown eyes hide a deeper truth."

LATISHA: Don't use my real name. Call me Sadeeka.

PAT: *(Reading from copy.)* "Sadeeka (not her real name) speaks several languages fluently. She is at the top of her class, and she is in a gang."

LATISHA: We don't wear no colors or nothing like that. No gang signs either. We lay low. We know who we are and we stick together.

PAT: *(Reading from copy.)* "Up until a few weeks ago, Sadeeka and her gang, the AOBs, committed what they considered to be petty crimes in the Northside area."

LATISHA: Don't nobody care when you rob black people. It don't make the news.

PAT: *(Reading from copy.)* "But then a Teach America teacher named Tim Dunn made a wrong turn."

LATISHA: I ain't mean to do it. He just looked like an easy mark.

PAT: *(Reading from copy.)* "And then Sadeeka's life changed forever."

LATISHA: You won't tell them who I am, will you?

YVONNE: *(To Latisha.)* No.

LATISHA: You promise? Because if you do . . .

YVONNE: *(To Latisha.)* I promise you. *(Pause.)* I promise you.

PAT: *(Reading from copy.)* "Sadeeka killed Tim Dunn."

LATISHA: All those arrests and stuff. It's crazy. I can't sleep. I can't eat. I'm sick of it. I'm sick of this life.

JEFF: I'm calling my lawyer.

YVONNE: I know this is serious Jeff.

PAT: Hello, Neil? Are you there?

YVONNE: I know this could mean trouble.

NEIL: Yeah, I'm here.

JEFF: A lot of trouble.

PAT: Well?

YVONNE: But, you know, I'm not afraid.

NEIL: *(To Pat.)* Damn.

YVONNE: *(To Jeff.)* Because I got the story, Jeff.

NEIL: *(To Pat.)* Damn, damn, damn.

YVONNE: I got the story.

END OF ACT I

ACT II

SCENE ONE
Lights up on Jessica watching TV.

YVONNE: *(At a press conference.)* As a member of the human race, I feel for Ms. Dunn. I can't imagine her loss, but as a reporter I did my duty and those duties and responsibilities are protected by the First Amendment. Let the police investigate. It is their obligation to do so, but I won't reveal my sources under any circumstances.

TALKING HEAD 1: Well, I mean, as a black woman doesn't Miss Robinson have a responsibility to . . .

TALKING HEAD 2: Are you saying that black reporters should follow a different set of rules?

TALKING HEAD 1: Because the First Amendment doesn't have one set of rights for white reporters and one . . .

(Jessica switches channels. There is the sound of protesters chanting.)

ACTIVIST 1: We are here to protest police brutality.

ACTIVIST 2: These sweeps ain't right.

ACTIVIST 3: My daughter can't do anything. She can't go to the store. She can't even go to school without being questioned by some cop.

ACTIVIST 1: I ain't seen so many cops here since Rodney King.

ACTIVIST 2: And this situation here ain't no Rodney King.

(Jessica switches channels quickly. After each sentence she switches the channel. Each sentence is spoken by a different voice.)

VOICES: The First Amendment says . . . Tonight on News 12, girl gangs, where they live, how they live, and how you can protect yourself.

YVONNE: As a member of the human race, I feel for Ms. Dunn.

VOICES: Reporters aren't police officers . . . Nobody cares when black people get killed . . .

YVONNE: I can't imagine her loss.

VOICES: Tonight on News 9, Teach America teachers speak out about the violence they face daily . . .

YVONNE: But as a reporter, I did my duty.

(Jessica throws remote at screen then lights up on Detective.)

DETECTIVE: How are you feeling? *(Pause.)* How is everything with . . . ? *(Points to Jessica's stomach. Indicating baby.)* My fourth grandchild was born just yesterday. Ten pounds, two ounces. A boy. *(Pause.)* You have to try and take care of yourself now. Especially now. I know it must be hard to . . .

JESSICA: It's a girl.

DETECTIVE: Oh, really? That's wonderful. I . . .

JESSICA: No, not that. The person who killed my husband was a girl.

DETECTIVE: Are you changing your statement?

JESSICA: It was a girl dressed like a boy. That's what the article said.

DETECTIVE: Yes, but . . . Are you changing your statement?

JESSICA: Do I have to? *(The detective doesn't answer. Continuing.)* I want to change my statement. It was a girl. *(Pause.)* It was a girl.

DETECTIVE: Are you sure?

JESSICA: What difference does that make? *(Pause.)* Now, I hear they're wondering if maybe it was a student of Tim's seeking revenge or something. Did you hear that?

DETECTIVE: Yes.

JESSICA: But you know black kids don't really do that, do they? Black kids don't go into the cafeteria and shoot up everybody or stalk teachers and shoot them. Isn't that true? If one of Tim's black students was angry with him, the black student would have shot Tim right there in the moment. Isn't that right? *(Pause.)* Isn't that right? *(Detective doesn't answer. Continuing.)* Then we wouldn't be here. The black student would have been arrested and we wouldn't be here. *(Pause.)* A couple of months ago some people were even saying I had something to do with it. Like it was all some elaborate scheme I thought up. *(Pause.)* I don't know if it was a girl dressed like a guy or a guy dressed like a girl dressed like a guy. I only know the killer was black. *(Pause.)* The killer was black.

SCENE TWO

Lights up on Yvonne and Jeff reading letters.

YVONNE: Listen to this. *(Reading from letter.)* "Sellouts like you deserve to be lynched." *(To Jeff.)* A black person advocating lynching. How about that?

JEFF: How can you tell they're black?

YVONNE: The handwriting. Ghetto-like.

JEFF: Yvonne.

YVONNE: I'm just kidding.

JEFF: That's real funny, especially now.

YVONNE: Nobody's here but us. *(Pause.)* Did you read Pat's column?
(Lights up on Pat.)

PAT: "Inner-City Blues," by Pat Johnson *(Pause.)* A few months ago I wrote an editorial about life lessons I had to teach my son. I sat him down and told him what it means to be a black man in America. I told him to keep his hands in the open when walking into a store. I told him to always say yes sir and no sir when addressing a police officer. I told him to expect the worst. *(Pause.)* I never imagined that one day I would have to tell my daughter the same thing.

YVONNE: She went after me again.

JEFF: I don't think it was about you. You know Pat's really angry about me taking that story. She sends like fifty memos a day about it.

(Jeff hands Yvonne memo.)

YVONNE: You knew she would be. *(Yvonne reads memo.)* "Regarding Confessions of a Girl Gang Member by Yvonne Robinson. Mr. Morgan's actions were not only a disrespectful violation of trust, they were a violation of newspaper policy. Miss Robinson is a rookie reporter still under probation. Since when is a rookie reporter allowed to break so many rules with so little consequence?"

JEFF: I really put myself out there for you.

YVONNE: I know you did. Pat would have destroyed that story. *(Pause.)* Anyway, like I was saying, the lawyer says if the police haven't done anything yet they probably won't do anything at all and, besides all that, I have First Amendment guarantees. She was really optimistic. *(Pause.)* I tried to tell Latisha that.

JEFF: You spoke to Latisha?

YVONNE: At home, about an hour ago. *(Noticing Jeff's expression.)* What's wrong?

JEFF: *(Looking at letters.)* Nothing. *(Pause.)* This one is short and sweet.

YVONNE: What does it say?

JEFF: "You're lying. I know you are."

SCENE THREE

Lights up on Pat and Yvonne at Pat's desk.

PAT: Congratulations.

YVONNE: Uh-huh. Thank you. *(Handing her papers.)* These are my transfer papers.

PAT: So, you're on your way huh?

YVONNE: They need your signature.

(Lights up on Neil and Jeff.)

NEIL: *(To Pat.)* She could have let the intern handle that.

PAT: *(To Neil.)* I know. *(To Yvonne.)* I'd like to speak with you a minute.

YVONNE: *(Shoving papers at Pat.)* I'd really like to get over to Metro. Please send the papers over when you're done. *(Yvonne begins to walk away.)*

PAT: They're promoting you on one story, but your work here has been . . .

YVONNE: Fine.

PAT: Sloppy.

YVONNE: It was fine.

PAT: You don't really believe that. *(Pause.)* The things you say and the way you say them matters because words matter. When I was going through hell integrating this paper that was the only thing that kept me going, knowing the power of words to effect change. You had an opportunity to do some great things at Outlook . . .

YVONNE: If you hadn't given me such a hard time . . .

PAT: If you liked me then you would have done your job? What kind of journalist do you want to be? *(Pause.)* You have to decide that. You can do a lot of good in Metro or you can do a lot of harm, but either way, every move you make reflects on us.

YVONNE: Us. Us who? You and Neil?

PAT: Us. Black people.

YVONNE: Sign here and here. *(To Jeff.)* I think she knew they were coming. *(Two police enter.)*

POLICE: Yvonne Robinson?

PAT: *(To Neil.)* I had no idea.

POLICE: You're under arrest for obstruction of justice.

SCENE FOUR

Jeff and Yvonne in a car. Jeff is driving.

REPORTER: *(Voice-over on radio.)* In a precedent-setting motion, Judge Andrew Parker gave Metro reporter Yvonne Robinson forty-eight hours to reveal her source. If she fails to do so, Miss Robinson will be taken back into custody and incarcerated for an indefinite period of time.

YVONNE: No, left at that corner, left at that corner.

JEFF: Yvonne, just think OK? Think. We have been driving around here for four hours.

YVONNE: It was dark Jeff. Very dark and I was scared.

JEFF: Yvonne, you have two days.

YVONNE: We stopped around here somewhere. It was around here.

JEFF: Just two days.

YVONNE: I'm looking! What do you think anyway? Latisha will just be hanging on the street corner pitching quarters?! *(Jeff turns a corner.)* Where are you going?

JEFF: Home. Fuck this.

YVONNE: No, no wait. Jeff.

JEFF: I just don't understand.

YVONNE: Understand what? I told you it was dark. Latisha got into the car and told me to drive.

JEFF: Did you check your notes?

YVONNE: I couldn't take notes while I was driving.

JEFF: What about after?

YVONNE: After what?

JEFF: After you stopped. *(Pause.)* Just . . . just show me where you went.

YVONNE: I'm trying.

JEFF: OK . . . OK . . . You met her at the community center.

YVONNE: Yes.

JEFF: Latisha got in your car and told you to drive.

YVONNE: Yes.

JEFF: You drove for something like fifteen minutes then . . .

YVONNE: Went into an apartment.

JEFF: Who's apartment?

YVONNE: I told you already, Jeff. I don't know. Look around you. Do you see any street signs?

JEFF: You didn't think to ask where you were?

YVONNE: Latisha just started talking. I didn't want to interrupt her flow by asking her where we were at. *(Pause.)* It was run-down.

JEFF: Run-down? Really? In this neighborhood? How'd you get back then?

YVONNE: What?

JEFF: How'd you get back from wherever you were?

YVONNE: I don't know. I went toward something that looked like a ramp that led me back to civilization.

JEFF: Something that looked like a ramp. *(Pause.)* Aren't you scared?

YVONNE: Yes.

JEFF: I can't tell.

YVONNE: What do you want me to do? Cry?

JEFF: Why not? I have.

YVONNE: My father always said: Never let your enemies see you cry.

JEFF: I'm not your enemy. *(Pause.)* You cried that night.

YVONNE: What night?

JEFF: The night you saw Latisha. You fell into my arms crying.

YVONNE: Yeah.

JEFF: First time. Ever.

YVONNE: I wish it could be the last.

JEFF: I don't.

YVONNE: Why? Is the sex better when I cry?

JEFF: Goddamn it, Yvonne!

YVONNE: OK . . . OK . . . I'm sorry. I'm sorry. *(Pause.)* I should have gone straight to the National desk. I have the qualifications. If I were . . .

JEFF: What?

YVONNE: You know.

JEFF: Then say it.

YVONNE: No.

JEFF: Yvonne, do you have something you want to tell me?

YVONNE: Something like?

JEFF: I don't know . . . Anything. *(Pause.)* You know no matter what you tell me . . . *(Yvonne turns her head suddenly. She sees something out the car window. Continuing.)* What?

YVONNE: Nothing. I thought I saw . . . *(Pause.)* For a second . . . Let's go around the corner again.

JEFF: Two days, Yvonne. Two days.

SCENE FIVE

Lights up on a black girl getting arrested by two cops. Yvonne watches arrest.

GIRL: Hey! Hey! I didn't do nothing. I didn't do nothing. Ask that reporter. Ain't she said who did it?

COP: No.

GIRL: Well, ask her.

COP: They will. Day after tomorrow.

GIRL: Day after . . . ?! Ask her now.

COP: Come on.

GIRL: Ask her now. I ain't do nothing. I ain't do nothing. I ain't do nothing.

SCENE SIX

Neil and Pat enter on either side. During the following Neil and Pat only speak to each other and Yvonne and Jeff only speak to each other.

YVONNE: One day left. Twenty-four hours. Will you miss me when they take me to the big house?

PAT: What'd you find out?

NEIL: A lot.

YVONNE: *(Noticing Jeff.)* What's wrong?

JEFF: Nothing.

YVONNE: Why are you so . . .

PAT: Well, tell me.

YVONNE: . . . sullen? I'm the one going to jail.

PAT: Tell me!

JEFF: I'm not, but . . .

NEIL: Lie number one.

YVONNE: But what?

JEFF: I was thinking about that story.

NEIL: . . . she told on TV a few days ago.

PAT: What story?

YVONNE: What story?

NEIL: You didn't hear?

JEFF: The story about your friend that was killed.

NEIL: At twelve or thirteen, I can't remember which, sister-girl says she learned some harsh realities about race.

YVONNE: What about it?

NEIL: Her best friend was murdered.

YVONNE: I told you that story before.

JEFF: No, you didn't.

PAT: Wait a minute.

JEFF: Not that way.

PAT: Is this the story about some white friend who was killed and she didn't understand about death, let alone race, and she was shocked, just shocked to learn her friend was murdered by a black person and she had to learn forgiveness and grace and blah, blah, blah. She told that story in her interview. After that I was glad to leave.

JEFF: You told me a different story.

NEIL: She told a slightly different story.

JEFF: On TV, you said your friend was black and was killed by a white. You said . . .

NEIL: . . . At that moment she learned that race didn't matter because she knew that . . .

JEFF: . . . if your friend had been killed by a black person it would hurt just as bad.

PAT: Ha!

YVONNE: So?

JEFF: You lied to me.

NEIL: Story never happened.

YVONNE: I didn't.

NEIL: In black or white.

YVONNE: I made the story more interesting.

NEIL: I checked thoroughly. Yvonne has told that story seven or eight times, and each time the race of the victim has changed.

YVONNE: For the TV interviewer.

NEIL: One time the victim was Chinese.

YVONNE: More relevant.

NEIL: But the thing is this.

JEFF: Yvonne . . .

NEIL: I checked that exclusive little boarding school she went to. The one she loved . . .

JEFF: Did it even happen at all?

NEIL: And I came across an award-winning essay written by one of Yvonne's classmates.

YVONNE: What are you asking me?

NEIL: It was a very touching story about a murdered best friend and lessons learned.

JEFF: I'm asking you what I'm asking you.

NEIL: Never happened to Yvonne at all.

JEFF: Did it happen at all?

PAT: If she lied about that then . . .

YVONNE: What do you think Jeff?

NEIL: We should start an office pool. Will sister-girl cave in?

YVONNE: What do you think?

PAT: Or will she get caught?

SCENE SEVEN

Lights up on Pat and Yvonne.

PAT: I need to speak with you a minute.

YVONNE: I'm on my way out.

PAT: Neil ran a background check on you. *(Pause.)* You never attended the Sorbonne. Never went to Harvard. Just U. Mass for two semesters before dropping out due to stress. I can't believe you got past Human Resources. When they hired me they checked everything, including my pee. When you walked into the room I guess they thought they hit the jackpot. You were living, breathing proof that black folks have and can make it to the promised land without bitterness, without blemish.

YVONNE: You want me to break down and cry?

PAT: I want to understand why you hate being black.

YVONNE: I don't hate being black. We have different definitions of the word.

PAT: I've never seen such self-hatred.

YVONNE: Oh, how nice for you. I didn't grow up in middle-class black utopia. Everybody singing songs and supporting each other. I got beat up for the very same things you got rewarded for.

PAT: That's your excuse? Bullies in the playground? Every black reporter is going to catch hell now.

YVONNE: Oh, well.

PAT: You're crazy. I guess you thought I would buy into your Latisha mess and when I didn't you circumvented me in an attempt to make me look weak and foolish, but when I expose you . . .

YVONNE: Complain and cajole, Pat. Maybe you'll get another section. Outlook two. *(Pause.)* I have an appointment at three.

PAT: When you go down, you're not taking me . . . you're not taking Outlook with you.

SCENE EIGHT

Lights up on Yvonne alone, upset. Trying to compose herself.

YVONNE: *(To herself.)* She laughed at me.
    (Lights up on Latisha.)

LATISHA: Listen, I heard you were looking for me, and I have to tell you something. First off, my name is not Latisha, and I'm really, really sorry.

YVONNE: Sorry about what?

LATISHA: I'm not . . . I'm not in a gang. *(Pause.)* And I don't know about any murder.

YVONNE: What? What the fuck are you talking about?

LATISHA: I was just playing with you. I was just playing.

YVONNE: Playing?! Are you kidding me? Playing?!

LATISHA: You know I just . . . I go to boarding school and they are fascinated by a ghetto girl like me. Fascinated. How do you get your hair like that? Have you ever seen anybody murdered? I get so sick of it. So, you know, I just make up shit to pass the time. I tell them I'm in a gang, and my mother is on crack. They think I'm supposed to be like that so I just . . . My mother is a librarian. I barely leave the house when I come home from school. *(Seeing Yvonne's expression.)* Are . . . Are you alright?

YVONNE: Why would you do this to me? Why would you? I told you about my sister, my life. I encouraged you. I helped you.

LATISHA: You helped me? No . . . I . . . See . . . I . . . *(Pause.)* Listen, I'm sorry. I'm . . . *Mi dispiace* (*I am sorry.) (Pause.)* I tell you it's hard keeping it real sometimes. *(Pause.)* I don't know . . . *(Pause.)* When I saw you that day I wondered if it would work on one of us. I mean, I could tell you were different. Not really one of us. Like me kinda. Just the way you . . . I don't know. *(Pause.)* I look around my neighborhood and I wish I could move. Everybody acts so stupid. You know Frantz Fanon says the oppressed are taught to believe the worst about themselves. So I just wanted to see. I spoke Italian and German to you and you still believed I was in a gang. *(Pause.)* Just like the people at school. *(Pause.)* Just like them. *(Pause.)* So, you need to . . .

YVONNE: I'm writing the story you told me. I'm writing about the AOBs.

LATISHA: There are no AOBs. There are no AOBs. I'll call the paper and tell. I'll . . .

YVONNE: You call the paper and I will tell the police that you killed Tim Dunn. You already told people at your school you are in a gang. No one will believe you. You fucking brat. This is my career. I will hurt you. I will.

LATISHA: This is crazy.

YVONNE: You laughed at me. Forget that Frantz Fanon bullshit, only a stupid-ass Oreo like me would fall for such a ridiculous story, right? You think you are the only one who has something to prove. It never ends, honey. It never ends.

LATISHA: I'm telling . . .

YVONNE: You think anyone will take your word over mine? They won't because keeping-it-real, wanna-be-gangster niggers like you make all black folks look guilty of something.

LATISHA: I'll . . . I'll jack you up for real . . . I'll . . . *(Yvonne laughs at her.)* I'll get somebody to . . . to . . . *(Pause.)* Please . . . please . . . I just . . . I was just playing!

YVONNE: You think it's funny all the white kids at school think you're in a gang? You think it's funny to be ignorant and crude? *(Latisha runs away.)* You want to keep keeping it real now? You want to keep — *(Pause to herself.)* — keeping it . . .
(Yvonne realizes she is alone. Phone rings lead us into the next scene.)

SCENE NINE

Lights up Neil, Pat, Jeff, Jessica, and Detective, then the sound of a phone ringing. Jessica and Detective only speak to each other.

JESSICA: *(Answering phone.)* Hello?

NEIL: *(To Pat.)* I've never seen a white man turn so white.

DETECTIVE: *(On phone.)* Jessica Dunn, please.

PAT: *(To Neil.)* What'd you say to him?

JESSICA: This is Jessica.

NEIL: *(To Pat.)* I said . . .

DETECTIVE: This is Detective Williams. I have some good news.

NEIL: *(To Jeff.)* Listen, I need to speak with Yvonne right now. Do you know where she is?

DETECTIVE: Miss Robinson is at the police station.

JESSICA: Excuse me?

DETECTIVE: I said . . .

JEFF: Yvonne is at the police station right now.

NEIL: *(To Jeff.)* Really?

DETECTIVE: Yes.

JESSICA: And?

NEIL: *(To Jeff.)* And what is she saying to the police?

DETECTIVE: *(To Jessica.)* She is going to ID the killer.

JESSICA: *(To Detective.)* Thank you. *(Pause.)* Thank you.
(Lights up on Yvonne speaking with Detective.)

YVONNE: Three weeks ago, about 11 P.M., I received a phone call from Sadeeka. She told me to meet her at the community center in the Northside area. I was alone.

NEIL: Wow. Giving up her source. Was that your suggestion?

JEFF: How can I help you, Neil?

NEIL: How long have you known Yvonne?

JEFF: About as long as you have.

NEIL: Really?

JEFF: Is there something you need something I can . . .

NEIL: It just seems you two are pretty close.

JEFF: What is it, Neil.

NEIL: I'm just saying . . . I was looking for Latisha too you know.

JEFF: Yeah, I know.

NEIL: So, I'm just curious how she suddenly turned up at one in the morning. I mean, were you with Yvonne that night? Did you meet Latisha?

JEFF: OK. Let's just . . . Let's not play this reporter game OK?

NEIL: OK.

JEFF: What is it?

NEIL: Well, I was going to go straight to Human Resources but I guess I'll tell you.

JEFF: Tell me what?

NEIL: I did a background check on Yvonne.

JEFF: What are you talking about?

NEIL: Her entire résumé is a lie. *(To Pat.)* White boy was in total disbelief. You know, rumor has it he and sister-girl are more than just friends. I almost feel sorry for her. I mean, it must be hard walking around pretending to be super-nigger all of the time. Most bourgie Negroes pretend they're ghetto. She ghetto pretending to be bourgie. I was wrong. She's not an uncertain at all.

PAT: Don't you ever go over my head again, Neil. You understand me? Don't you ever do that again.

• • •

YVONNE: Just listen to me Jeff.

JEFF: Is your résumé a lie?

YVONNE: Just listen.

JEFF: Neil told me. *(Pause.)* Neil. Do you know what that felt like to have Neil question me like that? You played me. From the beginning. You just . . . How could you do that to me Yvonne?

YVONNE: I am who I was supposed to be. I was supposed to go on to the Sorbonne. I was supposed to graduate *summa cum laude*. I was supposed to have a master's degree in journalism.

JEFF: You were supposed to?

YVONNE: My father had expectations.

JEFF: So this is all your daddy's fault? You laugh at people who say things like that. Supposed to? Were you supposed to fuck me over too?

NEIL: Don't talk to me like a child.

PAT: Did you tell anybody else?

NEIL: No, what is wrong with you?

PAT: You just don't think, Neil. You don't think. I was going to have someone outside the paper call and inform management. I didn't want Outlook dragged into this mess.

NEIL: Trust-fund baby printed that AOB bullshit not you.

PAT: They'll comb every single Outlook story for one error or typo and blame it on me. Me and Affirmative Action.

. . .

YVONNE: I fell apart.

JEFF: What does that mean? You don't fall apart. You don't even cry . . . You . . .

YVONNE: I did. All the time. For a while. I woke up one day and I couldn't stop crying. When I got better everyone I knew had graduated. Successfully. What they were supposed to be. So, I thought, easier to pretend than to explain. Just easier. *(Pause.)* You don't understand.

JEFF: No, I don't.

YVONNE: I didn't have a trust fund to fall back on. *(Pause.)* I grew up border-line ghetto.

JEFF: So? Did Pat have a trust fund? Did Neil?

YVONNE: I'm not talking about Pat and Neil. I'm talking about me. Four people. Two-room house. Government cheese and food stamps. All I ever wanted to do was get out.

JEFF: You crying poverty? I can't believe it. Poor little black girl Yvonne.

YVONNE: Shut up.

JEFF: Poor little welfare baby, gotta lie to The Man to get ahead.

YVONNE: Shut the fuck up. Poor little trust-fund baby need a black girl on your arm to feel like somebody.

JEFF: I don't need you for anything.

YVONNE: Right. *(Pause.)* You could buy everything, except what I gave you.

JEFF: No, I could buy that too.

. . .

PAT: We have to keep quiet about this.

NEIL: Keep quiet? What good will that do? Trust-fund baby has probably told by now anyway.

PAT: You said they're involved. He wouldn't risk revealing that.

NEIL: So call your friend or whoever was going to call management.

PAT: Then Jeff will know that the call came from us and he'll take Outlook down with him.

NEIL: This is crazy. She ain't OJ. She ain't even Michael. She's Clarence. Keep quiet? I just don't understand. Keep quiet. I won't.

PAT: You won't? You work for Outlook Neil. *(Pause.)* You work for me.

.   .   .

YVONNE: That's accurate. You treated me like a whore. I never met your parents. You never asked to meet mine.

JEFF: Oh, OK. Let's drive over to the hood right now, and you can introduce me to Mr. and Mrs . . . Is Robinson even your real name?

YVONNE: Did you even tell your parents about us?

JEFF: Thank God I didn't.

YVONNE: The way you treated me at the office no one would believe we'd been dating. *(Pause.)* Unless I showed them the letters, notes, and cards you've sent me.

JEFF: Oh, fuck. Are you blackmailing me or something?

YVONNE: No . . . I'm just trying to show you that everybody has secrets. I have secrets. You have secrets. Latisha has secrets.

JEFF: There is no Latisha. There is no you. There is no Latisha. You think that you can still play me? You think that you can threaten me and I'll keep quiet? *(Long pause.)* I won't have to say anything, Yvonne. Pat and Neil will destroy you all by themselves.

.   .   .

NEIL: If we turn Yvonne in we can get to the bottom of this. We can get the community back on track.

PAT: What will the community be like when they take Outlook from us. All the work I . . . we put in, gone. I'm saying they will take it from us. There will be some investigation. Internal. That's first. And then they'll give us some supervisor. It might even be a black person, a black Yvonne, but much worse, 'cause she'll be real. And then slowly but surely Outlook will be just like Metro. Nothing but black pathology and pain.

YVONNE: Maybe they won't.

JEFF: *(Laughing at Yvonne.)* Maybe they won't! You think Pat and Neil are going to link arms with you and march? I don't have to do anything. Say anything. Just step out of the way.

YVONNE: My father always said when trouble comes to our own we . . . black people . . . always, always close ranks.

JEFF: My father always said blacks are like crabs in a barrel. Dragging each other down.

•   •   •

NEIL: So, we'll fight for Outlook. You've done it before.

PAT: You weren't here before. I was. I know. *(Pause.)* Sister-girl wasn't the only one to have a breakdown.

•   •   •

YVONNE: I will fight for my story. An innocent man was murdered and I found his killer. That's worth fighting for.

JEFF: It's over Yvonne. Just . . . please. I'll go with you to the paper if you want. But you have to tell the truth about this. You have to. You made Latisha up didn't you? *(Pause. No answer from Yvonne.)* Didn't you? If you tell . . . *(Pause.)* Jesus, Yvonne what did you say to the police.

•   •   •

NEIL: So we say nothing? Do nothing?

PAT: She will get caught eventually.

NEIL: Eventually. But in the meantime, there will be more arrests. In the meantime, the paper . . . *(Pause.)* Oh, my God.

PAT: What? What's wrong?

NEIL: Oh, my God. Pat . . . I just . . . I just had a thought . . . I mean, What if . . . ?

•   •   •

YVONNE: I told them the truth Jeff. I told them the truth.
   (Lights up on Detective.)

DETECTIVE: We'd like you to take a look at our lineup.
   (Lights up on black girls in a lineup.)

JEFF: The police will check your story.

NEIL: What if she . . . ?

DETECTIVE: *(To Yvonne.)* Do you recognize anyone?

YVONNE: Yes.

JEFF: The cops won't just . . . They wouldn't just . . .

(Jeff realizes what she is saying.)

DETECTIVE: Are you sure?

(Yvonne points to someone in lineup.)

YVONNE: Her.

NEIL: What will we do then?

END OF PLAY